Entity Framework 6 Recipes

Second Edition

Brian Driscoll

Nitin Gupta

Rob Vettor

Zeeshan Hirani

Larry Tenny

Apress®

Entity Framework 6 Recipes, Second Edition

Copyright © 2013 by Brian Driscoll, Nitin Gupta, Rob Vettor, Zeeshan Hirani, and Larry Tenny

ISBN-13 (pbk): 978-1-4302-5788-2

ISBN-13 (electronic): 978-1-4302-5789-9

President and Publisher: Paul Manning
Lead Editor: Gary Schwartz
Technical Reviewer: Sergey Barskiy
Editorial Board: Steve Anglin, Mark Beckner, Ewan Buckingham, Gary Cornell, Louise Corrigan,
     Jonathan Gennick, Jonathan Hassell, Robert Hutchinson, Michelle Lowman, James Markham,
     Matthew Moodie, Jeff Olson, Jeffrey Pepper, Douglas Pundick, Ben Renow-Clarke, Dominic Shakeshaft,
     Gwenan Spearing, Matt Wade, Steve Weiss, Tom Welsh
Coordinating Editor: Mark Powers
Copy Editor: Richard Isomaki
Compositor: SPi Global
Indexer: SPi Global
Artist: SPi Global
Cover Designer: Anna Ishchenko

Distributed to the book trade worldwide by Springer Science+Business Media New York, 233 Spring Street, 6th Floor, New York, NY 10013. Phone 1-800-SPRINGER, fax (201) 348-4505, e-mail orders-ny@springer-sbm.com, or visit www.springeronline.com. Apress Media, LLC is a California LLC and the sole member (owner) is Springer Science + Business Media Finance Inc (SSBM Finance Inc). SSBM Finance Inc is a Delaware corporation.

For information on translations, please e-mail rights@apress.com, or visit www.apress.com.

Apress and friends of ED books may be purchased in bulk for academic, corporate, or promotional use. eBook versions and licenses are also available for most titles. For more information, reference our Special Bulk Sales–eBook Licensing web page at www.apress.com/bulk-sales.

Any source code or other supplementary material referenced by the author in this text is available to readers at www.apress.com/9781430257882. For detailed information about how to locate your book's source code, go to www.apress.com/source-code/.

To Susan, Holden, and Henry who bring me laughter, love, and the occasional banana nut muffin to my work.

—Brian Driscoll

To the "leading light" of my life—Sahibji, and to the most important and lovely part of my life, my wife Nancy and daughter Arushi.

—Nitin Gupta

As you might imagine, a great deal of effort goes into writing a book. Across the many months of late-night sessions, many people provided guidance and inspiration: many thanks to Rowan Miller, Program Manager for Microsoft Entity Framework, and to Sergey Barskiy, our fearless technical reviewer, for their technical expertise and oversight. Much appreciation goes to John Mason and Ben Williams from the Microsoft Developer Consulting Team for their technical guidance. A special thanks goes to the Microsoft Premier leadership team: Jeremy Rule, Kevin Carberry, Niel Sutton, and especially Bill Wenger for their inspiration, leadership, and direction. Finally, and most important, all my love goes to my beautiful wife Laura and our "very cool" twin boys, Jeremy and Nicholas.

—Rob Vettor

Contents at a Glance

Contents

About the Authors

Brian Driscoll has been developing business information systems using both Microsoft and traditional open source technologies since 2002. He specializes in providing consultative solutions to small- and mediumsized businesses in industries ranging from healthcare to market research. Brian earned a Master of Software Engineering degree with a concentration in expert systems from Drexel University in 2011.

Nitin Gupta is a Microsoft-certified technology consultant in .NET, and he is a certified PRINCE2 practitioner. He has extensive experience developing enterprise applications using a broad range of development tools since .NET 1.1. He's also worked on a variety of applications ranging from middleware business components, datadriven services using different ORM technologies, to customer-facing windows and web applications in a number of business domains including e-commerce, banking, digital advertising and marketing, travel, ERP procurement, financial accounting, and insurance. He has led and worked on projects for Allstate Insurance, Citigroup, Janus Capital, and United Healthcare. In his spare time, he enjoys traveling, world history, movies, and documentaries.

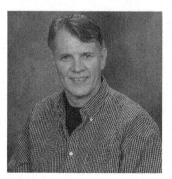

Rob Vettor is a Developer Consultant with Microsoft, helping Microsoft Enterprise customers build high-quality software. Rob's focus is on application architecture along with the Microsoft web and data programmability stack, including ASP.NET MVC, Web API, and the Entity Framework. An INETA Regional Speaker, user group leader, and former three-time C# MVP, Rob is a frequent presenter at regional technical conferences, and he has built systems for a number of corporations including Avanade, Raytheon, American Express, and Jack Henry and Associates. Rob lives in Dallas, TX, with his wife, twin sons, and two dogs. You can contact Rob at robvet@microsoft.com.

Zeeshan Hirani actively uses Entity framework in the development of an e-commerce website for a top-300 e-commerce retailer. He has written several articles and maintains an active and influential Entity framework blog at http://weblogs.asp.net/zeeshanhirani.

Larry Tenny has more than 20 years' experience developing applications using a broad range of development tools, primarily targeting the Microsoft platform. He has extensive .NET development experience. He has a Ph.D. in computer science from Indiana University.

About the Technical Reviewer

Sergey Barskiy is an architect with Tyler Technologies. He is a Microsoft MVP and holds the following certifications: MCPD, MCTS, MCSD for .NET, MCAD for .NET, MCDBA, and MCP. He has been working with Microsoft technologies for over 15 years, and he is a frequent speaker at various regional and national conferences, such as VS Live, DevLink, CodeStock, and Atlanta Code Camp, as well as at local user groups. He is one of the organizers of Atlanta Code Camp and the Atlanta Windows Apps users group. He is also the INETA membership mentor for the state of Georgia.

Preface

Anyone who has been developing on the Microsoft platform for the last several years knows the drill: there's a new database access technology every few years. There was ODBC, then DAO and RDO, OLEDB, ADO, and ADO.NET, LINQ to SQL, and now Entity Framework! Although this progression of technologies has introduced rapid change, it has also been wonderfully refreshing as we have evolved from simple open connectivity, to componentized connectivity, to disconnected access in a managed environment, to frictionless access syntax, and finally to conceptual modeling.

Conceptual modeling is the defining feature of Entity Framework, and it is at the heart of this book. Entity Framework builds upon the previous data access paradigms, and it provides an environment that supports rich, real-world domain-level modeling. We can now think of and program against real-world items, such as orders and customers, and leverage concepts, such as inheritance, to reason about things in our domain and not just rows and columns.

There is no question that Entity Framework is the future of data access for the Microsoft platform. The first release in August 2008, although somewhat deficient, was widely considered a good first step. Now, many releases later, Entity Framework 6 has matured into a full-featured data access technology ready for production use in both greenfield and legacy applications.

The concepts and patterns that you will learn as you work with the recipes in this book will serve you well into the future as Microsoft continues to evolve Entity Framework in the years to come.

Who This Book Is For

This book is for anyone who develops applications for the Microsoft platform. All of us who work in this field need access to data in our applications. We are all interested in more powerful and intuitive ways to reason about and program against the real-world objects in our applications. It makes much more sense for us to architect, design, and build applications in terms of customers, orders, and products rather than rows and columns scattered among tables locked away in a database. Because we can reason about problem space in terms of real-world objects, we have a lot more confidence in our design and in the code that we build. We are also better able to document and explain our applications to others. This makes our code much more maintainable.

Entity Framework is not just for development teams building custom applications. Microsoft is aggressively positioning the modeling concepts in Entity Framework to serve as the conceptual domain for Reporting Services and Integration Services as well as other technologies that process, report on, and transform data. Entity Framework is quickly becoming a core data access foundation for many other Microsoft technologies.

This book contains well over 100 recipes that you can put to work right away. Entity Framework is a large and complex topic. Perhaps it's too big for a monolithic reference book. In this book, however, you will find direct and self-contained answers to just about any problem that you're facing in building your Entity Framework-powered applications. Along the way, you'll learn an enormous amount about Entity Framework.

What's in This Book

We've organized the recipes in this book by topic. Often we've found that a recipe fits into more than one chapter, and sometimes we find that a recipe doesn't fit perfectly into any chapter. We think it's better to include all of the important recipes rather than just the ones that fit, so you might find yourself wondering why a particular recipe is in a certain chapter. Don't worry. If you find the recipe useful, we hope that you can forgive its (mis)placement. At least we got it into the book.

The following is a list of the chapters and a brief synopsis of the recipes that you'll find within them:

Chapter 1: Getting Started with Entity Framework. We explain the motivation behind Entity Framework. We also explain what the framework is and what it does for you.

Chapter 2: Entity Data Modeling Fundamentals. This chapter covers the basics in modeling. Here you'll find out how to get started with modeling and with Entity Framework in general. If you're just getting started, this chapter probably has the recipes you're seeking.

Chapter 3: Querying an Entity Data Model. We'll show you how to query your model using both LINQ to Entities and Entity SQL.

Chapter 4: Using Entity Framework in ASP.NET MVC. Web applications are an important part of the development landscape, and Entity Framework is ideally suited for ASP.NET. In this chapter, we focus on using the EntityDataSource to interact with your model for selects, inserts, updates, and deletes.

Chapter 5: Loading Entities and Navigation Properties. The recipes in this chapter cover just about every possibility for loading entities from the database.

Chapter 6: Beyond the Basics with Modeling and Inheritance. Modeling is a key part of Entity Framework. This is the second of three chapters with recipes specifically about modeling. In this chapter, we included recipes that cover many of the more complicated, yet all-too-common modeling problems that you'll find in real-world applications.

Chapter 7: Working with Object Services. In this chapter, we included recipes that provide practical solutions for the deployment of your models. We also provide recipes for using the Pluralization Service, using the edmgen.exe utility, and working with so-called *identifying relationships*.

Chapter 8: Plain Old CLR Objects. Using code-generated entities is fine in many scenarios, but there comes a time when you need to use your own classes as EntityTypes. The recipes in this chapter cover Plain Old CLR Objects (POCO) in depth. They show you how to use your own classes and reduce code dependence on Entity Framework.

Chapter 9: Using Entity Framework in N-Tier Applications. The recipes in this chapter cover a wide range of topics using Entity Framework across the wire. We cover Entity Framework usage with WCF and ASP.NET Web API services, as well as related topics such as serialization and concurrency.

Chapter 10: Stored Procedures. If you are developing or maintaining a real-world, data-centric application, you most likely work with stored procedures. The recipes in this chapter show you how to consume the data exposed by those stored procedures.

Chapter 11: Functions. The recipes in this chapter show you how to create and use model-defined functions. We also show you how to use functions provided by Entity Framework, as well as functions exposed by the storage layer.

Chapter 12: Customizing Entity Framework Objects. The recipes in this chapter show you how to respond to key events, such as when objects are persisted. We also show you how to customize the way those events are handled.

Chapter 13: Improving Performance. For many applications, getting the best performance possible is an important goal. This chapter shows you several ways to improve the performance of your Entity Framework applications.

Chapter 14: Concurrency. Lots of instances of your application are changing the database. How do you control who wins? The recipes in this chapter show you how to manage concurrency.

About the Recipes

At present, there are three perspectives on model development in Entity Framework. Each of these perspectives is at a different level of maturity in the product and at a different level of use in the community.

The initial perspective supported by Entity Framework is called Database First. Using Database First, a developer starts with an existing database that is used to create an initial conceptual model. This initial model serves as the starting point for further development. As changes occur in the database, the model can be updated from these database changes. Database First was the initial perspective supported in Entity Framework. It is the best-supported approach, and it is widely used to migrate existing applications to Entity Framework.

Another perspective for model development is the Model-First approach. With Model First, the developer starts with a blank design surface and creates a conceptual model. Once the conceptual model is complete, Entity Framework can automatically generate a script to create a complete database for the conceptual model.

Finally, there is the Code-First perspective for model development. In this approach, there is no .edmx file, which encapsulates model and mapping information. Your objects create and use a model dynamically at runtime. This approach is gaining popularity quickly as it enables you to create and maintain your own domain classes, but still hook into Entity Framework features, like query generation, lazy loading, and change tracking.

In this book, we focus on both the Database-First and Code-First perspectives. Both are widely used across the community.

Many, if not most, developers in the Entity Framework community find themselves working with existing applications or developing models that are not readily supported by the other perspectives. We also have to share a dirty little secret: many existing applications don't exactly use the best database designs. Way too often we find ourselves working with databases (of course, created by other, less-talented developers) that are poorly designed. As developers, sometimes working in larger organizations with lots of process control, or with lots of fragile legacy code, we can't change the database enough to truly fix the design. In these cases, we simply have to work with the database design that we have.

Many of the recipes that we selected for this book take on the task of modeling some of these more challenged database designs. We've found hundreds of examples of these databases in the wild, and we've worked with many developers in the Entity Framework community who have struggled to model these databases. We've learned from these experiences, and we've selected a number of recipes that will help you solve these problems.

Stuff You Need to Get Started

Okay, what do you need? First off, you will need Microsoft's latest software development environment. Microsoft Visual Studio 2013 comes complete with full support for Entity Framework 6. If you are using Microsoft Visual Studio 2012, you can easily install Entity Framework 6. Keep in mind that the Visual Studio 2013 Express Edition is freely available. The other versions of Visual Studio fully support Entity Framework.

You'll need a database. Microsoft SQL Server 2012 is the preferred choice, but there are Entity Framework providers for databases from other vendors. Keep in mind that Microsoft SQL Server 2012 Express is freely available. Make sure that you apply the latest service packs and updates. These recipes were built and tested using Microsoft SQL Server 2012. Previous versions of SQL Server or other databases may not play well with a few of the recipes.

Code Examples

This book is all about recipes that solve very specific problems in a way that allows you to apply the solution directly to your code. Feel free to use and adapt any of the code you find here to help build or maintain your applications. Of course, it's not okay to copy large parts of this material and distribute it for fun or profit. If you need to copy large parts of this material, contact our publisher, Apress, to get permission.

If you use our code publicly (in blogs, forums, and so on), we would appreciate, but don't require, some modest attribution, such as author, title, and ISBN.

We've taken a decidedly low-tech approach in the code in each recipe. We've tried not to clutter the code with unnecessary constructs and clever tricks. In the text, we show just the code of interest, but we also show enough to give the proper context. In the download for the code, we have complete solutions for each recipe. The solutions build simple applications that you can modify and run over and over again to play with various changes that suit your needs.

The Database

Of course, there is more to each recipe than just the code. We created a single database for all of the recipes. This makes it much easier to work through the recipes because there is just one database to create in your development environment.

To keep some sanity in the table names and provide at least a little organization, we created a schema for each chapter. The recipes in the chapter use the tables in the corresponding schema. In the text, we often show database diagrams similar to the one in Figure 0-1. This helps clarify the table structure with which we're working. Each table in a diagram is annotated (courtesy of SQL Server Management Studio) with the name of the table and the schema for the table. Because we reuse table names throughout the book (we're just not creative enough not to), this helps to keep straight exactly which tables we're referring to in the database.

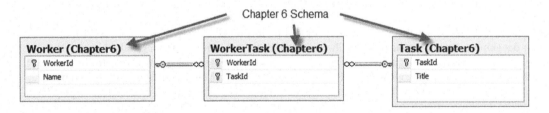

Figure 0-1. Each database diagram in the text has the schema name next to the table name

We've also provided the complete set of database diagrams for each recipe as part of the database. If something isn't clear from just the tables, especially when several tables are involved, it often helps to look at the diagram to sort things out.

Apress Website

Visit the Apress website for this book (http://apress.com/9781430257882) for the complete code download as well as the database with all of the tables and database diagrams used in the book. Please look for the "Source Code" link underneath the cover image.

CHAPTER 1

■ ■ ■

Getting Started with Entity Framework

When working with relational databases, we think in terms of tables with rows and columns. Tables are highly structured and excel at set-based processing. Before the wide adoption of object-oriented programming, we thought about problems "procedurally" and solved them by writing code in a structured, top-down manner, function after function. Both worlds lined up well: Tables, rows, and columns closely matched the structured and procedural patterns in our code. Life was good - for a time ...

Much has evolved on the code side. We now think in terms of objects and domain models. We architect, design, and program against real-world things, like customers and orders. We draw nouns in our problem space on whiteboards. We draw lines between them, denoting relationships and interactions. We build specifications and assign work to development teams in terms of these drawings. In short, we architect, design, and program at a *conceptual level* that is very distant from the logical and physical organization of the database.

While the software development process has dramatically matured and the way in which we reason and solve problems has evolved, the database has not. The data remains locked in the same tables, rows, and columns paradigm, where it has been for many years. Unfortunately, this creates a mismatch (an *impedance mismatch*, as Microsoft fellow Anders Hejlsberg might call it): Object-oriented class hierarchies vs. a highly normalized database structure.

To cope with this gap, software projects often introduce a "database layer" that translates application domain classes into the rows and columns saved in tables. This approach has spawned many commercial and open-source data access frameworks; all attempting to bridge the ever widening gap between evolving development processes and structured data. Interestingly, an entire new field of Object Relational Mapping (ORM) has come out it.

The Entity Framework, coupled with the Language-Integrated Query (LINQ) framework, both from Microsoft, enables us to address the mismatch problem head-on. Using Entity Framework, we model *entity classes* for our application on a design surface or directly in code. Then we model relationships (*associations*) between these entities. In our code, we construct LINQ queries to program against these entities and associations. LINQ allows us to express relational database set concepts directly into our code while working in terms of entity types and associations. All of this helps to streamline our development experience while reducing the overall effort. Instead of coding large numbers of highly redundant ADO.NET data access constructs, we express our data needs in simple LINQ queries. Instead of programming against the schema of a highly normalized database, we code against entity classes. Entity Framework maps entity classes to the underlying database for you.

■ **Note**   We use the term *entity class* or *entity object* to refer to a class that typically represents a domain item in an application. Domain classes represent real-world objects, such as an Employee, Department, or Manager, which your application will represent and track. The end users and stakeholders of your application should be able to look at the domain classes in your application and say, "Yes, that's what our business does." Entity classes define the *schema*, or properties, but not the behavior, of a domain class. In essence, entity classes expose the *state* of an object.

1-1. A Brief Tour of the Entity Framework World

Entity Framework is Microsoft's strategic approach to data access technology for building software applications. Unlike earlier data access technologies, Entity Framework, coupled with Visual Studio, delivers a comprehensive, model-based ecosystem that enables you to develop a wide range of data-oriented applications, including desktop, Internet, cloud, and service-based applications, many of which will be covered in this book.

The History

Entity Framework is not new. The product dates back to Visual Studio 2008 and has come a long way in features and functionality. Figure 1-1 gives the pictorial history.

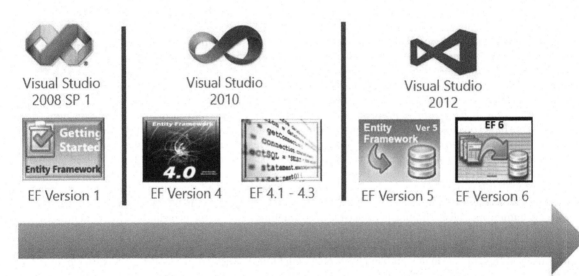

Figure 1-1. *A short history of the Entity Framework*

The first version of Entity Framework was limited, featuring basic ORM support and the ability to implement a single approach known as *Database First*, which we thoroughly demonstrate in this book. Version 4 brought us another approach to using Entity Framework: Model First, along with full Plain Old CLR Object (POCO) support and default lazy loading behavior. Soon after, the Entity Framework team released three smaller, or point releases, 4.1 through 4.3, which represented yet another approach to using Entity Framework: Code First. As shown above, Version 5 of Entity Framework coordinated with the release of the .NET 4.5 framework and Visual Studio 2012, delivering significant performance improvements along with support for enums, table value functions, spatial types, the batch import of stored procedures, and deep support with the ASP.NET MVC framework.

Now we are at Version 6 of the Entity Framework. Version 6 delivers asynchronous support for querying and updates, stored procedure support for updates in Code First, improved performance, and a long list of new features, which we will focus on in this book.

■ **Note** Version 5 of Entity Framework can also be used with Visual Studio 2010. Version 6 of Entity Framework, released with Visual Studio 2013, has tooling/runtime support for Visual Studio 2012 and runtime support for Visual Studio 2010.

To level set, let's take a brief look at some of the key components of the Entity Framework ecosystem. What follows is not by any means a comprehensive description of Entity Framework; that would take hundreds of pages. We'll look at just a few key areas to help get you oriented for the recipes that are at the heart of this book.

The Model

Entity Framework is a technology with a strong focus on modeling. As you model with Entity Framework, you will see many familiar genetic markers from previous technologies and patterns. For example, you will, no doubt, see a resemblance to entity-relationship diagrams and the widely adopted conceptual, logical, and physical design layering approach.

The model that you create in Entity Framework is characterized by a construct called an Entity Data Model (EDM), which enables you to code against strongly typed entity classes, not database schema and objects. (Figure 1-2 shows this model in conceptual form.) The Entity Data Model enables you to customize the mappings between entity classes and database tables to move beyond the classic, one-to-one mapping, or class-to-table mapping.

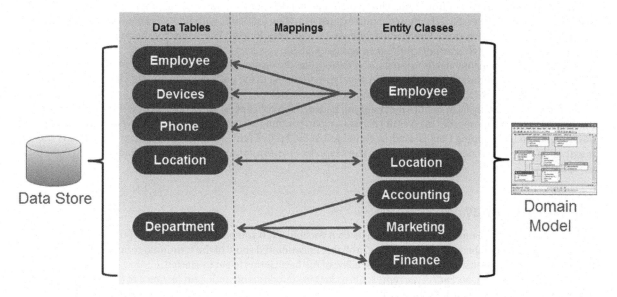

Figure 1-2. *The Entity Data Model*

In Figure 1-2, note how the database tables (on the left) do not directly map to the entity classes, which we code against (on the right). Instead, the mapping capabilities built into the Entity Data Model enable the developer to code against a set of entity classes that more closely resemble the problem domain, as opposed to a highly normalized database, designed for performance, scalability, and maintainability.

For example, note above how the Employees, Devices, and Phone numbers) are physically stored in three different tables, which from a DBA perspective makes perfect sense. But the developer codes against a single Employee entity class that contains a collection of Devices and Phone Numbers. From a developer and project stakeholder perspective, an employee is a single object, which happens to contain phone numbers and devices. The developer is unaware, and does not care, that the DBA has normalized this employee object into three separate database tables. Once configured, the mapping between the single class and three database tables is abstracted away and handled by the Entity Framework.

A reverse situation can be seen for the single Department table, which programmatically maps to three entity classes that represent individual departments. Again, to the developer and project stakeholders, a separate entity object represents each department (Accounting, Marketing, Finance, and so on), but DBA optimizes and collapses these objects into a single database table for data storage purposes.

Of course, as can be seen in the Location table, you can easily map a single entity class to a single database table, which is the *default behavior* for Entity Framework.

The key takeaway here is that developer and project stakeholders work with a representation of domain classes that make sense in the context of the application. The DBA can structure the underlying database tables in order to efficiently tune the database. And you can easily bridge these two worlds with the Entity Framework.

The Layers

The Entity Data Model consists of three separate layers: the conceptual, store, and mapping layers. Each layer is decoupled from the others.

The entity classes are contained in the *conceptual layer* of the Entity Data Model. This is layer in which developers and project stakeholders work. Depending upon how you implement the Entity Framework, the conceptual layer can be modeled with a designer or from code. Once you make that decision, you can reverse- engineer your model from an existing database, leveraging the designer and extensive tooling that ships with Entity Framework or create your model with code and have Entity Framework generate the database for you. The syntax for the conceptual layer is defined in the *Conceptual Schema Definition Language* (CSDL).

Every useful application needs to persist objects to some data store. The *store layer* of the Entity Data Model defines the tables, columns, relationships, and data types that map to the underlying database. The *Store Schema Definition Language* (SSDL) defines the syntax for the store model.

Finally, the mapping layer defines the mapping between the conceptual and store *layer*. Among other things, this layer defines how properties from entity classes map to columns in database tables. This layer is exposed to the developer from the Mapping Details window contained in the Entity Framework designer or data annotations and fluent API if choosing a code-based approach. The *Mapping Specification Language* (MSL) defines the syntax for the mapping layer.

The Terminology

As expected, the Entity Framework comes with its own vocabulary. If you have used any of the popular ORM tools or are familiar with database modeling, you've probably encountered some of the terminology before. Although the entire vocabulary is extensive, we'll provide just a few of the basic terms to get us started.

As discussed earlier, an *EntityType* represents a class in your domain model. An instance of an EntityType is often referred to as an *entity*. If you are using the Entity Framework designer, an EntityType is represented on the design surface as a box with various properties. Figure 1-3 shows two EntityTypes: Employee and Task.

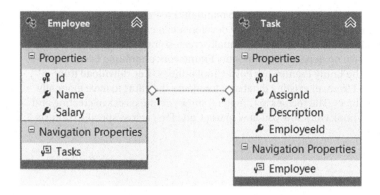

Figure 1-3. *A model with Employee and Task with a one-to-many association between them*

An EntityType usually has one or more *properties*. Just like with a class, a property is a named value with a specific data type. Properties can have simple types like integer, string, and so on; or have ComplexTypes; or be collections. *Navigation properties* refer to other related entities (typically represented by foreign key relationships in a database). The non-navigation properties on an EntityType are usually just called *scalar properties*.

A relationship between two entities is called an *association*. Associations between EntityTypes are shown on the design surface as a line connecting the EntityTypes. The line is annotated to show the *multiplicity* on each end of the association. The association in Figure 1-3 is a one-to-many association between Employee and Task. An Employee can have zero or more tasks. Each Task is associated to exactly one Employee.

Every EntityType has a property or set of properties that denote its *EntityKey*. An EntityKey uniquely *identifies* the entity to Entity Framework and is most often mapped to a primary key from the entity's representation in the underlying database.

Finally, no discussion on Entity Framework would be complete without mentioning the *context object*. The context object for Entity Framework is your gateway into the Entity Framework services. The context object exposes entity objects, manages the database connection, generates parameterized SQL, marshals data to and from the database, caches objects, helps maintain change tracking and *materializes*, or transforms, an untyped result set into a collection of strongly typed objects.

In the beginning, there was the *ObjectContext* object. Now, Entity Framework supports an alternate, more streamlined context object called the *DbContext*. The DbContext greatly simplifies the developer experience when working with Entity Framework. Interestingly, the DbContext is a wrapper, or facade, around the ObjectContext, exposing the underlying ObjectContext functionality in an intuitive, friendly and productive way.

Clearly, the DbContext is the preferred approach for working with Entity Framework as we will demonstrate in great detail in this book.

The Code

Despite a tremendous emphasis on visual design support, the Entity Framework is all about code. The models, EntityTypes, associations, mappings, and so on are ultimately expressed in concrete code that becomes part of your application. This code is either generated by Visual Studio and Entity Framework or created manually by the development team. You can choose quite a bit about the code-generation process or the lack of it by changing various properties on your project or modifying the underlying code-generation templates.

Visual Studio uses a code-generation technology called *Text Template Transformation Toolkit*, simply referred to as *T4 templates*. The Visual Studio tooling uses T4 templates to generate, or *scaffold*, code automatically. The great thing about T4 template support in Visual Studio is that you can edit the templates to tailor the code-generation process to match your exact needs. This is an advanced technique, but it is necessary in some cases. We'll show you how to do this in a few recipes.

Alternatively, you can leverage the more recent *Code-First* approach to manually create the concrete code yourself, gaining direct control over the entire process. With Code First, the developer can create entity classes, mappings and context object, all without the help of a designer. These manually created entity classes, commonly referred to as POCO, or Plain Old CLR Objects, have no dependence on Entity Framework plumbing. Even more interesting, the development team can leverage the Entity Framework Power Tool utilities (free download from Microsoft) to reverse-engineer a Code First model from an existing database, foregoing the effort to have manually create the entity classes, mappings and context object. The recipes in Chapter 8 show you the basics of creating and using POCO. Many of the recipes throughout the book will show you how to use Code First across specific contexts such as in n-Tier applications.

Visual Studio

Of course, the main tool we use when developing applications for the Windows environment is Visual Studio. This Integrated Development Environment has evolved over many years from a simple C++ compiler and editor to a highly integrated, multi-language environment that supports the entire software development lifecycle. Visual Studio and its related tools and services provide for design, development, unit testing, debugging, software configuration management, build management and continuous integration, and much more. Don't be worried if you haven't used all these in your work; few developers have. The point is that Visual Studio is a full-featured toolset. Visual Studio plays a vital role in the development of Entity Framework applications.

Visual Studio provides an integrated design surface for Entity Framework models. Using this design surface and other tools in Visual Studio, you can create models from scratch or create them from an existing database. You also have the option to completely eliminate the designer and manually craft your Entity Types and configuration.

If you have an existing database, which is the case for many of us with existing applications, Visual Studio provides tools for importing your tables and relationships into a model. This fits nicely with the real world because few of us have the luxury of developing brand-new applications. Most of us have to extend, maintain, and evolve our existing code and databases.

Alternately, you can create a model from scratch by starting with an empty design surface and adding new EntityTypes to the surface, creating both associations and inheritance hierarchies for your model. When you are done creating the model, right-click the design surface and select Generate Database from Model.

If your project team is code-centric, you can instead create a set of domain classes, including relationships and a context class and then wire up these classes to hook into the Entity Framework engine and features without having to use a designer.

Once you have created your model, changes often happen. That's the nature of software development. Visual Studio provides tools for updating the model from the database. This will keep the model synchronized with changes in the database. Additionally, the Entity Framework Team also supports a tool called *Code First Migrations*, which can be used to keep your database up-to-date with changes in your model.

1-2. Using Entity Framework

Entity Framework is tightly integrated with Visual Studio. To implement Entity Framework in your application, add a new ADO.NET Entity Data Model in your project. Right-click your project and select Add ➤ New Item. In the dialog box (see Figure 1-4), choose the ADO.NET Entity Data Model template. This template is located under the Data templates. Click Add to launch the Entity Data Model Wizard.

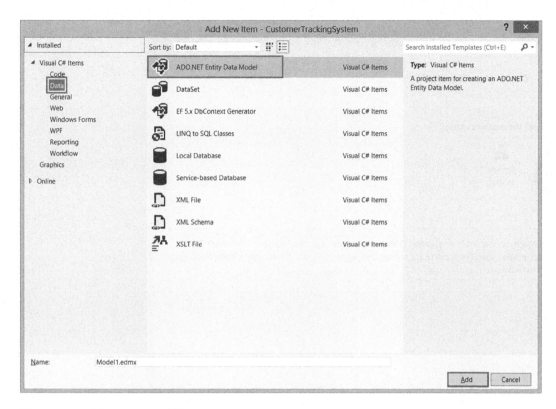

Figure 1-4. *Adding a new model to your project*

There are two options on the first page of the Entity Data Model Wizard: start with an existing database or start with an empty model. (The former option is actually labeled "Generate from database.") This first page is shown in Figure 1-5.

Figure 1-5. *The Entity Data Model Wizard gives you a choice between creating a model from an existing database or starting with an empty model*

Generating a model from an existing database is the Database-First approach. From the tables, views, and stored procedures that you select from the underlying database, the wizard will create a model and entity classes, against which you can write code. The immediate benefit here is that you write code against strongly typed entity classes, which Entity Framework maps to the underlying database tables and columns. If the tables you include are related in the database, these relationships will be modeled as associations. This is one way to create your model if you already have a database for your application. However, if you prefer to use the Code-First approach with an existing database, worry not. The Entity Framework team has created tooling (*The Entity Framework Power Tools*) that reverse-engineers an existing database into domain entity classes, just as if you coded them by hand.

If you're working on a brand-new application, without an existing database, you have options as well. In the Entity Framework designer, you can start with an empty design surface. Right-click the design surface to create new EntityTypes, associations, or inheritances. You can also drag them from the Toolbox onto the design surface. Once your model is complete, just right-click the design surface and select Generate Database from Model. This will generate a script you can use to create the database tables and relationships for the model.

Alternately, you can manually create each of your entity classes in Visual Studio and simply register them in the DbContext object, then hook into the Entity Framework services. Entity Framework will map the classes to the underlying databases and automatically create a model in memory at runtime.

With the Model-First or Database-First approaches, you use the Entity Framework designer to develop your model. The key parts of a model in the designer are shown in Figure 1-6. In this model, a Customer has a one-to-many association with an Order. Each customer may have many orders, but each order is associated with just one customer. The Mapping Details window shows that the Customer EntityType maps to the Customer table in the database. The Mapping Detail window also shows the mapping between the columns in the Customer table and the scalar properties in the Customer EntityType. Keep in mind that you can make the same kind of mapping configurations using the data annotations or fluent API features found in the Code First approach to using Entity Framework.

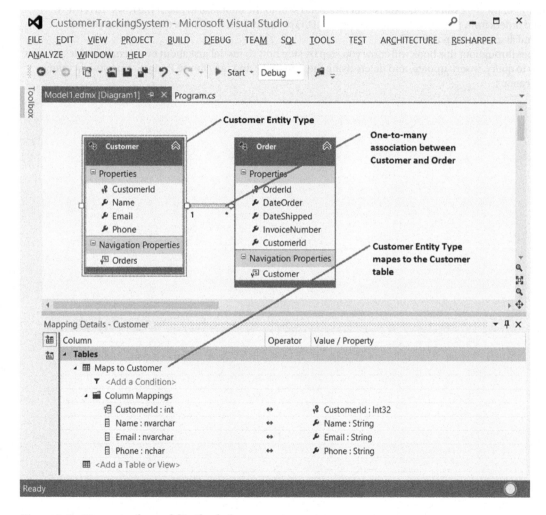

Figure 1-6. *Key parts of a model in the designer*

Of course, there's more to the designer and model than just the few key parts illustrated in Figure 1-6. In the recipes in this book, we'll cover just about every aspect of using the designer to create models. In some cases, we go beyond what can be done with the designer and show you how to create models that require direct editing of the underlying .edmx file. The .edmx file contains the complete model definition, including the conceptual layer, store layer, and mapping layer.

So, whether we implement Entity Framework with the Database-First, Model-First or Code-First approach, we always end up with a model. We gain significant productivity, as we can program against objects in the model (EntityTypes) as you do with other objects in your application. For the model in Figure 1-6, your code uses Customer and Order in much the same way as you use other objects.

If you want to insert a new customer and order into the database, you can create instances of the Customer and Order types, set the properties, add them to the in-memory context that represents the model, and call SaveChanges(). All the necessary SQL code is generated and sent to the database to insert the rows. To retrieve customers and orders from the database, you use either LINQ or Entity SQL to create a query in terms of the EntityTypes and associations in the model.

The recipes throughout this book will show you step by step how to model just about every conceivable database scenario; how to query, insert, update, and delete using these models; and how to use Entity Framework in many kinds of applications.

CHAPTER 2

Entity Data Modeling Fundamentals

More likely than not, you are just beginning to explore Entity Framework, and you are probably asking the question, "Okay, how do I get started?" If this describes you, this chapter is a great place to start. If, on the other hand, you have built some working models and feel comfortable with a few key modeling concepts, such as entity splitting and inheritance, you can skip this chapter.

In this chapter, we will walk you through the basic examples of modeling with Entity Framework. Modeling is the core feature of Entity Framework and what distinguishes Entity Framework from previous Microsoft data access platforms. Once you have built your model, you can write code against the model rather than against the rows and columns in the relational database.

We start off this chapter with an example of how to create a simple conceptual model, and then let Entity Framework create the underlying database. In the remaining examples, we will show you how to create models from existing tables and relationships in your databases.

2-1. Creating a Simple Model

Problem

You have a brand new project, and you want to create a model.

Solution

Let's imagine that you want to create an application to hold the names and phone numbers of people that you know. To keep things simple, let's assume that you need just one entity type: Person.

To create the new model, do the following:

1. Right-click your project, and select Add ➤ New Item.

2. From the templates, select ADO.NET Entity Data Model and click Add. This template is located in Data under Visual C# Items (see Figure 2-1).

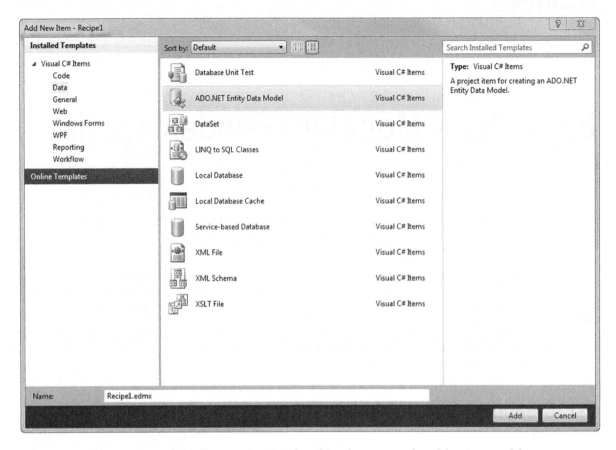

Figure 2-1. *Adding a new* `.emdx` *file that contains XML describing the conceptual model, storage model, and mapping layer*

3. In the first step of the wizard, choose Empty Model and click Finish. The wizard will create a new conceptual model with an empty design surface.

4. Right-click the design surface, and select Add ➤ Entity.

5. Type `Person` in the Entity name field, and select the box to Create a key property. Use `Id` as the Key Property. Make sure that its Property Type is `Int32`. Click OK, and a new Person entity will appear on the design surface (see Figure 2-2).

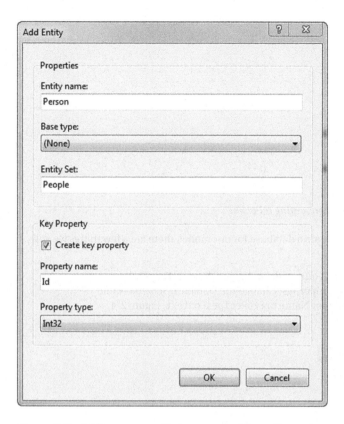

Figure 2-2. *Adding a new entity type representing a Person in our conceptual model*

6. Right-click near the top of the Person entity, and select Add ➤ Scalar Property. A new scalar property will be added to the Person entity.

7. Rename the scalar property FirstName. Add scalar properties for LastName, MiddleName, and PhoneNumber.

8. Right-click the Id property, and select Properties. In the properties view, change the StoreGeneratedPattern property to Identity if it is not already set to Identity. This flags the Id property as a value that will be computed by the store layer (database). The database script we get at the end will flag the Id column as an identity column, and the storage model will know that the database will automatically manage the values in this column.

The completed conceptual model should look like the model in Figure 2-3.

Figure 2-3. Our completed model with an entity type representing a Person

You now have a simple conceptual model. To generate a database for our model, there are a few things we still have to do:

9. We need to change a couple of properties of our model to help with housekeeping. Right-click the design surface, and select properties. Change the Database Schema Name to Chapter2, and change the Entity Container Name to EF6RecipesContext. Figure 2-4 illustrates these changes.

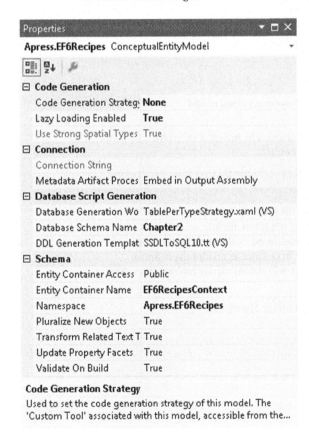

Figure 2-4. Changing the properties of our model

10. Right-click the design surface, and select Generate Database Script from Model. Select an existing database connection or create a new one. In Figure 2-5, we've opted to create a new connection to our local machine and to the database EF6Recipes.

Figure 2-5. *Creating a new database connection that will be used by Entity Framework to create a database script that we can use to create a database from our conceptual model*

11. Click OK to complete the connection properties, and click Next to preview the database script (see Figure 2-6). Once you click Finish, the generated script is added to your project.

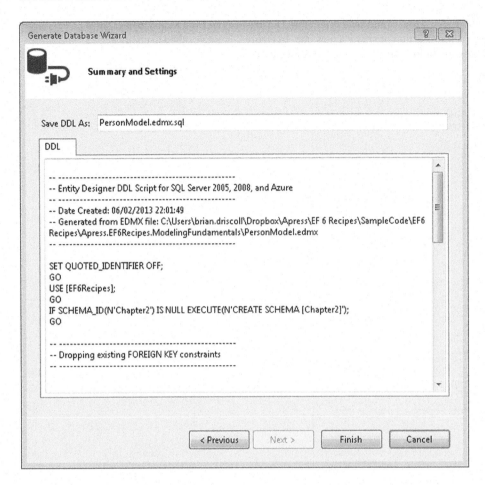

Figure 2-6. Generating the storage model in the .edmx *file and creating the database script*

12. Run the database script in an SSMS query window to create the database and the People table.

How It Works

The Entity Framework Designer is a powerful tool for creating and updating a conceptual model, storage model, and mapping layer. This tool provides support for bidirectional model development. You can either start with a clean design surface and create a model; or start with a database that you already have and import it to create a conceptual model, storage model, and mapping layer. The current version of the Designer supports somewhat limited roundtrip modeling, allowing you to re-create your database from a model and update the model from changes in your database.

The model has a number of properties that affect what goes in the generated storage model and database script. We changed two of these properties. The first was the name of the container. This is the class derived from DbContext. We called this EF6RecipesContext to be consistent with the contexts we use throughout this book.

Additionally, we changed the schema to "Chapter 2." This represents the schema used to generate the storage model as well as the database script.

The code in Listing 2-1 demonstrates one simple way to create and insert instances of our Person entity type. The code also demonstrates iterating through all the Person entities in our database.

Listing 2-1. Inserting into and Retrieving from Our Model

```
using (var context = new EF6RecipesContext())
{
    var person = new Person { FirstName = "Robert", MiddleName="Allen",
                              LastName = "Doe", PhoneNumber = "867-5309" };
    context.People.Add(person);
    person = new Person { FirstName = "John", MiddleName="K.",
                          LastName = "Smith", PhoneNumber = "824-3031" };
    context.People.Add(person);
    person = new Person { FirstName = "Billy", MiddleName="Albert",
                          LastName = "Minor", PhoneNumber = "907-2212" };
    context.People.Add(person);
    person = new Person { FirstName = "Kathy", MiddleName="Anne",
                          LastName = "Ryan", PhoneNumber = "722-0038" };
    context.People.Add(person);

    context.SaveChanges();
}

using (var context = new EF6RecipesContext())
{
    foreach (var person in context.People)
    {
        System.Console.WriteLine("{0} {1} {2}, Phone: {3}",
                                 person.FirstName, person.MiddleName,
                                 person.LastName, person.PhoneNumber);
    }
}
```

The output of the code in Listing 2-1 should look something like the following:

```
John K. Smith, Phone: 824-3031
Robert Allen Doe, Phone: 867-5309
Kathy Anne Ryan, Phone: 722-0038
Billy Albert Minor, Phone: 907-2212
```

Best Practice

When we created a new instance of the database context, we did it within a using() statement:

```
using (var context = new EF6RecipesContext())
{
...
}
```

If you are not familiar with this pattern, it's really pretty simple. Normally, when we get a new instance of an object, we use the new operator and assign the result to some variable. When the variable goes out of scope and the object is no longer referenced by anything else, the garbage collector will do its job at some point and reclaim the memory for the object. That works great for most of the objects that we create in our .NET applications because most objects hold on to resources that can wait around for whenever the garbage collector has a chance to reclaim them. The garbage collector is rather nondeterministic. It reclaims resources pretty much on its own schedule, which we can only partially influence.

Instances of DbContext hold on to system resources such as database connections that we want to release as soon as we're done with them. We don't really want these database connections to stay open waiting for the garbage collector eventually to reclaim them.

There are a few nice features of using() statements. First, when the code execution leaves the using() {} block, the Dispose() method on the context will be called because DbContext implements the IDisposable interface. For DbContext, the Dispose() method closes any active database connections and properly cleans up any other resources that need to be released.

Second, no matter how the code leaves the using(){} block, the Dispose() method is called. Most importantly, this includes return statements and exceptions that may be thrown within the code block. The using(){} block is kind of a guarantee that critical resources will be reclaimed properly.

The best practice here is always to wrap your code in the using(){} block when creating new instances of DbContext. It's one more step to help bulletproof your code.

2-2. Creating a Model from an Existing Database

Problem

You have an existing database with tables, perhaps a few views, and some foreign key constraints, and you want to create a model for this database.

Solution

Let's say that you have database describing poets and their poetry. Your relational database might look something like the diagram in Figure 2-7.

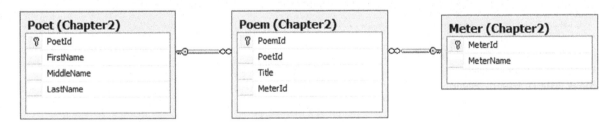

Figure 2-7. *A simple database for poets and their poetry*

From this database diagram, you can see that a poet can be the author of one or more poems, and each poem can be categorized by its meter, which is the basic pattern of a poem's verse. It's not shown in this diagram, but our database also has a view that joins the tables together so that we can more easily enumerate each poet and poem, as well as the poem's meter.

To import the view, tables, and relationships into a model, do the following:

1. Right-click your project, and select Add ➤ New Item.

2. From the Visual C# Items Data templates, select ADO.NET Entity Data Model.

3. Select Generate from database to create the model from our existing tables. Click Next.

4. Either choose an existing connection to your database or create a new connection. If you are creating a new connection, you will need to select your database server, your authentication method (Windows or SQL Server), and the database. Once you have selected these, it's a good idea to click Test Connection to be sure that the connection is ready to go. Once you have tested the connection, click Next.

The next dialog box shows all of the tables, views, and stored procedures in the database. Check the items you want to include in the model. We want to select all of the tables (Meter, Poem, and Poet). We also want to select the view (vwLibrary). For now, leave the two check boxes for pluralizing and including foreign key columns selected. We will discuss them further momentarily. Figure 2-8 shows the things we've selected.

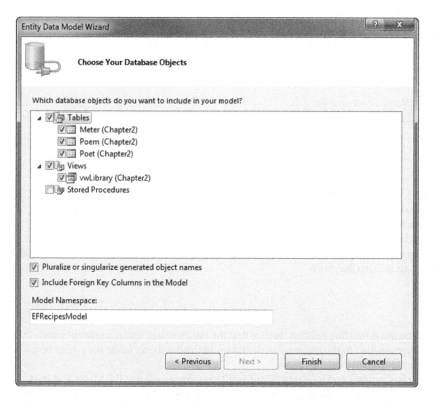

Figure 2-8. Selecting the tables and view to include in our model. Leave the Pluralize or singularize generated object names and Include Foreign Key Columns in the model checked

When you click Finish, the wizard will create a new model with our three tables and the view. The wizard will also read the foreign key constraints from the database and infer a one-to-many relationship between Poet and Poem(s) as well as a one-to-many relationship between Meter and Poem(s).

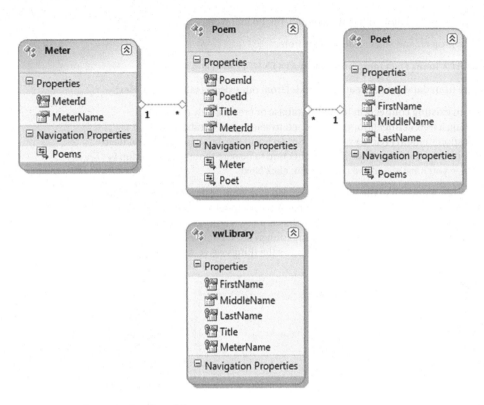

Figure 2-9. *Our completed model*

Figure 2-9 shows the new model created for us by including the Poet, Poem, and Meter tables as well as the vwLibrary view.

You now have a model that you can use in your code. Note that the vwLibrary entity is based on the vwLibrary view in our database. In most databases, views are read-only objects: inserts, deletes, and updates are typically not supported at the database layer. This is also the case with Entity Framework. Entity Framework considers views read only. You can get around this by mapping stored procedures for the create, update, and delete actions for view-based entities. We will show you how to do just that in Chapter 6.

How It Works

Let's look at the model created for us by the importing process. Notice that the entities have scalar properties and navigation properties. The scalar properties map to the columns in the tables of the database, while the navigation properties are derived from the relationships between the tables.

In our database diagram, a poem has a meter and a poet (the author). These correspond to the Meter and Poet navigation properties. If we have an instance of a Poem entity, the Poet navigation property holds an instance of a Poet entity, while the Meter navigation property holds an instance of a Meter entity.

A poet can be the author of any number of poems. The Poems navigation property contains a collection of instances of the Poem entity. This collection can be empty, of course, for those poets that have yet to write any poetry. For the Meter entity, the Poems navigation property is also a collection. For this navigation property, the collection holds instances of Poems that have the given meter. SQL Server does not support relationships defined on views, and our model reflects this with an empty set of navigation properties on the vwLibrary entity.

Notice that the Import Wizard was smart enough to pluralize the navigation properties that contained collections. If you right-click the entities and look at their properties, you will notice that the entity set names for each of the entities are also property pluralized. For example, the entity set name for the Poem entity is Poems. This automatic pluralization happened because we left the Pluralize or singularize generated object names option checked.

The Include Foreign Key Columns in the model option also caused the foreign keys to be included in the model. Although it may seem a little unnecessary to have both foreign keys and navigation properties, we'll see in many of the following recipes that having direct access to the foreign keys can be useful.

The code in Listing 2-2 demonstrates how to create instances of Poet, Poem, and Meter entities in our model and how to save these entities to our database. The code also shows you how to query the model to retrieve the poets and poems from the database.

Listing 2-2. Inserting into and Querying Our Model

```
using (var context = new EF6RecipesContext())
{
    var poet = new Poet { FirstName = "John", LastName = "Milton" };
    var poem = new Poem { Title = "Paradise Lost" };
    var meter = new Meter { MeterName = "Iambic Pentameter" };
    poem.Meter = meter;
    poem.Poet = poet;
    context.Poems.Add(poem);
    poem = new Poem { Title = "Paradise Regained" };
    poem.Meter = meter;
    poem.Poet = poet;
    context.Poems.Add(poem);

    poet = new Poet { FirstName = "Lewis", LastName = "Carroll" };
    poem = new Poem { Title = "The Hunting of the Shark" };
    meter = new Meter { MeterName = "Anapestic Tetrameter" };
    poem.Meter = meter;
    poem.Poet = poet;
    context.Poems.Add(poem);

    poet = new Poet { FirstName = "Lord", LastName = "Byron" };
    poem = new Poem { Title = "Don Juan" };
    poem.Meter = meter;
    poem.Poet = poet;
    context.Poems.Add(poem);

    context.SaveChanges();

}

using (var context = new EF6RecipesContext())
{
    var poets = context.Poets;
    foreach (var poet in poets)
    {
        Console.WriteLine("{0} {1}", poet.FirstName, poet.LastName);
        foreach (var poem in poet.Poems)
        {
            Console.WriteLine("\t{0} ({1})", poem.Title, poem.Meter.MeterName);
        }
    }
}
```

```
// using our vwLibrary view
using (var context = new EF6RecipesContext())
{
    var items = context.vwLibraries;
    foreach (var item in items)
    {
        Console.WriteLine("{0} {1}", item.FirstName, item.LastName);
        Console.WriteLine("\t{0} ({1})", item.Title, item.MeterName);
    }
}
```

In the first block of code in Listing 2-2, we create instances of the Poet, Poem, and Meter entity types for the poet John Milton, his poem "Paradise Lost," and the meter for the poem, which in this case is Iambic Pentameter. Once we have created the instances of the entity types, we set the poem's Meter property to the meter instance and the poem's Poet property to the poet instance. Using the same approach, we build up the other entities relating each poem to its meter and poet. Once we have everything in place, we call SaveChanges() to generate and execute the appropriate SQL statements to insert the rows into the underlying database.

The output from the code in Listing 2-2 is as follows:

```
Lord Byron
        Don Juan (Anapestic Tetrameter)
Lewis Carroll
        The Hunting of the Shark (Anapestic Tetrameter)
John Milton
        Paradise Regained (Iambic Pentameter)
        Paradise Lost (Iambic Pentameter)
Lewis Carroll
        The Hunting of the Shark (Anapestic Tetrameter)
Lord Byron
        Don Juan (Anapestic Tetrameter)
John Milton
        Paradise Regained (Iambic Pentameter)
John Milton
        Paradise Lost (Iambic Pentameter)
```

In the code, we start by creating and initializing instances of the poet, poem, and meter for the first of John Milton's poems. Once we have these in place, we set the poem's Meter navigation property and the poem's Poet navigation property to the instances of poem and meter. Now that we have the poem instance completed, we add it using the Add() method. Entity Framework does all of the remaining work of adding the poem to the Poems collection on the poet instance and adding the poem to the Poems collection on the meter instance. The rest of the setup follows the same pattern. To shorten the code, we reuse variables and instances where we can.

Once we have all of the objects created and all the navigation properties initialized, we have completed the object graph. Entity Framework keeps track of the changes we've made to build the object graph. These changes are tracked in the database context. Our context variable contains an instance of the database context (it's of type DbContext), and it is what we used to build the object graph. To send these changes to the database, we call the SaveChanges() method.

To query our model and, of course, verify that we did indeed save everything to the database, we grab a fresh instance of the object context and query it using LINQ to Entities. We could have reused the same instance of the database context, but then we know it has the object graph and any subsequent queries we run against it won't flow through to the database because the graph is already in memory.

Using LINQ to Entities, we query for all of the poets, and for each poet we print out the poet's name and the details for each of their poems. The code is pretty simple, but it does use a couple of nested for loops.

The last block of code uses the vwLibrary entity. This entity is based on our vwLibrary view. This view joins the tables together to flatten things out a bit and provide a cleaner perspective. When we query for each poet against the vwLibraries entity set, we can get by with just one for loop. The output is a little different because we repeat the poet's name for each poem.

There is one last thing to note in this example. We didn't insert the poets, poems, and meters using the vwLibrary entity because views are always read-only in most database systems. In Entity Framework, we can't insert (or update, or delete) entities that are based on views. Of course, we'll show you exactly how to overcome this little challenge in many of the recipes in this book!

2-3. Modeling a Many-to-Many Relationship with No Payload
Problem

You have a couple of tables in an existing database that are related to each other via a link or junction table. The link table contains just the foreign keys used to link the two tables together into a many-to-many relationship. You want to import these tables to model this many-to-many relationship.

Solution

Let's say that your database tables look something like the database diagram in Figure 2-10.

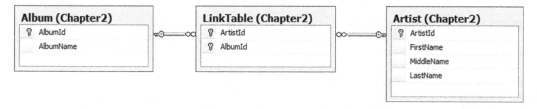

Figure 2-10. *Artists and albums in a many-to-many relationship*

To create a model and import these tables and relationships, do the following:

1. Add a new model to your project by right-clicking your project and selecting Add ➤ New Item. Choose ADO.NET Entity Data Model from the Visual C# Items Data templates.

2. Select Generate from database. Click Next.

3. Use the wizard to select an existing connection to your database, or create a new connection.

4. From the Choose Your Database Object dialog box, select the tables Album, LinkTable, and Artist. Leave the Pluralize and Foreign Key options checked. Click Finish.

The wizard will create the model shown in Figure 2-11.

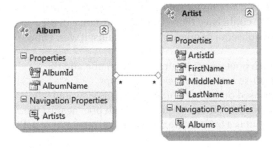

Figure 2-11. *The model with a many-to-many relationship between our tables*

The many-to-many relationship between Album and Artist is represented by a line with the * character on both ends. Because an Album can have many Artists, and an Artist can responsible for many Albums, each of these navigation properties is of type `EntityCollection`.

How It Works

In Figure 2-11, an artist can be related to many albums, whereas an album can be the work of many artists. Notice that the link table from Figure 2-10 is not represented as an entity in our model. Because our link table has no scalar properties (that is, it has no payload), Entity Framework assumes that its sole purpose is to create the association between Album and Artist. If the link table had scalar properties, Entity Framework would have created a very different model, as we will see in the next recipe.

The code in Listing 2-3 demonstrates how to insert new albums and artists into our model and how to query our model for both artists and their albums and albums with their artists.

Listing 2-3. *Inserting and Querying Our Artists and Albums Model Through the Many-to-Many Association*

```
using (var context = new EF6RecipesContext())
{
    // add an artist with two albums
    var artist = new Artist { FirstName = "Alan", LastName = "Jackson" };
    var album1 = new Album { AlbumName = "Drive" };
    var album2 = new Album { AlbumName = "Live at Texas Stadium" };
    artist.Albums.Add(album1);
    artist.Albums.Add(album2);
    context.Artists.Add(artist);

    // add an album for two artists
    var artist1 = new Artist { FirstName = "Tobby", LastName = "Keith" };
    var artist2 = new Artist { FirstName = "Merle", LastName = "Haggard" };
    var album = new Album { AlbumName = "Honkytonk University" };
    artist1.Albums.Add(album);
    artist2.Albums.Add(album);
    context.Albums.Add(album);

    context.SaveChanges();
}
```

```
using (var context = new EF6RecipesContext())
{
    Console.WriteLine("Artists and their albums...");
    var artists = context.Artists;
    foreach (var artist in artists)
    {
        Console.WriteLine("{0} {1}", artist.FirstName, artist.LastName);
        foreach (var album in artist.Albums)
        {
            Console.WriteLine("\t{0}", album.AlbumName);
        }
    }

    Console.WriteLine("\nAlbums and their artists...");
    var albums = context.Albums;
    foreach (var album in albums)
    {
        Console.WriteLine("{0}", album.AlbumName);
        foreach (var artist in album.Artists)
        {
            Console.WriteLine("\t{0} {1}", artist.FirstName, artist.LastName);
        }
    }
}
```

The output from the code in Listing 2-3 looks like the following:

```
Artists and their albums...
Alan Jackson
        Drive
        Live at Texas Stadium
Tobby Keith
        Honkytonk University
Merle Haggard
        Honkytonk University

Albums and their artists...
Drive
        Alan Jackson
Live at Texas Stadium
        Alan Jackson
Honkytonk University
        Tobby Keith
        Merle Haggard
```

After getting an instance of our database context, we create and initialize an instance of an Artist entity type and a couple of instances of the Album entity type. We add the albums to the artist and then add the artist to the Database Context.

Next we create and initialize a couple of instances of the Artist entity type and an instance of the Album entity type. Because the two artists collaborated on the album, we add the album to both artists' Albums navigation property (which is of type EntityCollection). Adding the album to the Database Context causes the artists to get added as well.

25

Now that the completed object graph is part of the database context, the only thing left to do is to use SaveChanges() to save the whole thing to the database.

When we query the database in a brand-new Database Context, we grab the artists and display their albums. Then we grab the albums and print the artists that created the albums.

Notice that we never refer to the underlying LinkTable from Figure 2-10. In fact, this table is not even represented in our model as an entity. The LinkTable is represented in the many-to-many association, which we access via the Artists and Albums navigation properties.

2-4. Modeling a Many-to-Many Relationship with a Payload

Problem

You have a many-to-many relationship in which the link table contains some payload data (any additional columns beyond the foreign keys), and you want to create a model that represents the many-to-many relationship as two one-to-many associations.

Solution

Entity Framework does not support associations with properties, so creating a model like the one in the previous recipe won't work. As we saw in the previous recipe, if the link table in a many-to-many relationship contains just the foreign keys for the relationship, Entity Framework will surface the link table as an association and not as an entity type. If the link table contains additional information, Entity Framework will create a separate entity type to represent the link table. The resulting model will contain two one-to-many associations with an entity type representing the underlying link table.

Suppose we have the tables and relationships shown in Figure 2-12.

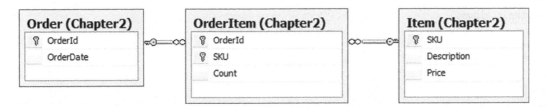

Figure 2-12. *A many-to-many relationship with payload*

An Order can have many Items. An Item can be on many Orders. Additionally, we have a Count property connected to each instance of the Order, Item relationship. This Count property is referred to as a *payload*.

To create a model and import these tables and relationships into the model, do the following:

1. Add a new model to your project by right-clicking your project and selecting Add ➤ New Item. Choose ADO.NET Entity Data Model from the Visual C# Data templates.

2. Select Generate from database. Click Next.

3. Use the wizard to select an existing connection to your database or create a new connection.

4. From the Choose Your Database Object dialog box, select the tables Order, OrderItem, and Item. Leave the Pluralize and Foreign Key options checked. Click Finish.

The wizard will create the model in Figure 2-13.

Figure 2-13. *Two one-to-many associations from a many-to-many relationship with payload*

How It Works

As we saw in the previous recipe, for a many-to-many relationship with no payload, the model is clean and simple to navigate. Because Entity Framework does not support the notion of payloads on associations, it surfaces the link table as an entity with two one-to-many associations to the related entities. In this case, the OrderItem table is represented not as an association, but as an entity type with a one-to-many association to Order and a one-to-many association to Item. In the previous recipe, the payload-free link table did not translate into an entity type in the model. Instead, it became part of the many-to-many association.

The addition of a payload requires an additional hop through the entity representing the link table to retrieve the related items. This is illustrated in code in Listing 2-4.

Listing 2-4. Inserting into and Retrieving from the Model

```
using (var context = new EF6RecipesContext())
{
    var order = new Order { OrderId = 1,
                            OrderDate = new DateTime(2010, 1, 18) };
    var item = new Item { SKU = 1729, Description = "Backpack",
                          Price = 29.97M };
    var oi = new OrderItem { Order = order, Item = item, Count = 1 };
    item = new Item { SKU = 2929, Description = "Water Filter",
                      Price = 13.97M };
    oi = new OrderItem { Order = order, Item = item, Count = 3 };
    item = new Item { SKU = 1847, Description = "Camp Stove",
                      Price = 43.99M };
    oi = new OrderItem { Order = order, Item = item, Count = 1 };
    context.Orders.Add(order);
    context.SaveChanges();
}

using (var context = new EF6RecipesContext())
{    foreach (var order in context.Orders)
    {
        Console.WriteLine("Order # {0}, ordered on {1}",
                          order.OrderId.ToString(),
                          order.OrderDate.ToShortDateString());
```

```
        Console.WriteLine("SKU\tDescription\tQty\tPrice");
        Console.WriteLine("---\t-----------\t---\t-----");
        foreach (var oi in order.OrderItems)
        {
            Console.WriteLine("{0}\t{1}\t{2}\t{3}", oi.Item.SKU,
                              oi.Item.Description, oi.Count.ToString(),
                              oi.Item.Price.ToString("C"));
        }
    }
}
```

The following is the output from the code shown in Listing 2-4.

```
Order # 1, ordered on 1/18/2010
SKU     Description   Qty    Price
----    -----------   ---    ------
1729    Backpack      1      $29.97
1847    Camp Stove    1      $43.99
2929    Water Filter  3      $13.97
```

After we create an instance of our database context, we create and initialize an Order entity as well as the items and order items for the order. We connect the order with the items by initializing the OrderItem entities with the instances of the Order entity and the Item entity. We use the Add() method to add the order to the context.

With the object graph complete and the order added to the context, we update the database with the SaveChanges() method.

To retrieve the entities from the database, we create a fresh instance of the context and iterate through the context.Orders collection. For each order (well, we just have one in this example), we print the order detail and we iterate through the entity collection on the OrderItems navigation property. These instances of the OrderItem entity type give us access to the Count scalar property (the payload) directly, and each item on the order via the Item navigation property. Going through the OrderItems entity to get to the items is the "extra" hop that is the cost of having a payload in the link table (OrderItems, in our example) in a many-to-many relationship.

Best Practice

Unfortunately, a project that starts out with several payload-free many-to-many relationships often ends up with several payload-rich many-to-many relationships. Refactoring a model, especially late in the development cycle, to accommodate payloads in the many-to-many relationships can be tedious. Not only are additional entities introduced, but the queries and navigation patterns through the relationships change as well. Some developers argue that every many-to-many relationship should start off with some payload, typically a synthetic key, so that the inevitable addition of more payload has significantly less impact on the project.

So here's the best practice: If you have a payload-free many-to-many relationship and you think there is some chance that it may change over time to include a payload, start with an extra identity column in the link table. When you import the tables into your model, you will get two one-to-many relationships, which means the code you write and the model you have will be ready for any number of additional payload columns that come along as the project matures. The cost of an additional integer identity column is usually a pretty small price to pay to keep the model more flexible.

2-5. Modeling a Self-Referencing Relationship with a Code-First Approach

Problem

You have a table that references itself, and you want to model this as an entity with a self-referencing association using a Code-First approach.

Solution

Let's say that you have a self-referencing table that's like the one shown in the database diagram in Figure 2-14.

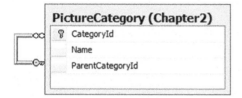

Figure 2-14. *A self-referencing table*

To create a model and import this table and the self-referencing relationship into the model, do the following:

1. Create a new class that inherits from DbContext in your project.

2. Use the code in Listing 2-5 to create the `PictureCategory` POCO entity.

   Listing 2-5. Creating the PictureCategory POCO Entity

```
public class PictureCategory
{
    [Key]
    [DatabaseGenerated(DatabaseGeneratedOption.Identity)]
    public int CategoryId { get; private set; }
    public string Name { get; set; }
    public int? ParentCategoryId { get; private set; }

    [ForeignKey("ParentCategoryId")]
    public PictureCategory ParentCategory { get; set; }

    public List<PictureCategory> Subcategories { get; set; }

    public PictureCategory()
    {
        Subcategories = new List<PictureCategory>();
    }
}
```

3.   Add a DbSet<PictureCategory> auto property to your DbContext subclass.

4.   Override the OnModelCreating method in your DbContext class to configure the
     bidirectional association (ParentCategory and SubCategories), as seen in Listing 2-6.

Listing 2-6.   Overriding OnModelCreating in DbContext Subclass

```
public class EF6RecipesContext : DbContext
{
    public DbSet<PictureCategory> PictureCategories { get; set; }

    public PictureContext() : base("name=EF6CodeFirstRecipesContext")
    {

    }

    protected override void OnModelCreating(DbModelBuilder modelBuilder)
    {
        base.OnModelCreating(modelBuilder);

        modelBuilder.Entity<PictureCategory>()
                    .HasMany(cat => cat.SubCategories)
                    .WithOptional(cat => cat.ParentCategory);
    }
}
```

How It Works

Database relationships are characterized by degree, multiplicity, and direction. *Degree* is the number of entity types
that participate in the relationship. Unary and binary relationships are the most common. Tertiary and n-place
relationships are more theoretical than practical.

   Multiplicity is the number of entity types on each end of the relationship. You have seen the multiplicities 0..1
(zero or 1), 1 (one), and * (many).

   Finally, the *direction* is either one-way or bidirectional.

   The Entity Data Model supports a particular kind of database relationship called an *Association Type*.
An Association Type relationship has either unary or binary degree, multiplicities 0..1, 1, or *, and a direction that
is bidirectional.

   In this example, the degree is unary (just the entity type PictureCategory is involved), the multiplicity is 0..1
and *, and the direction is, of course, bidirectional.

   As is the case in this example, a self-referencing table often denotes a parent-child relationship, with each parent
having many children while each child has just one parent. Because the parent end of the relationship is 0..1 and
not 1, it is possible for a child to have no parent. This is just what you want to leverage in representing the root node;
that is, the one node that has no parent and is the top of the hierarchy.

   Listing 2-7 shows how you can recursively enumerate the picture categories starting with the root node, which,
of course, is the only node that has no parent.

Listing 2-7. *Inserting into Our Model and Recursively Enumerating All of the Instances of the Self-referencing entity*

```
static void RunExample()
{
    using (var context = new EF6RecipesContext())
    {
        var louvre = new PictureCategory { Name = "Louvre" };
        var child = new PictureCategory { Name = "Egyptian Antiquites" };
        louvre.Subcategories.Add(child);
        child = new PictureCategory { Name = "Sculptures" };
        louvre.Subcategories.Add(child);
        child = new PictureCategory { Name = "Paintings" };
        louvre.Subcategories.Add(child);
        var paris = new PictureCategory { Name = "Paris" };
        paris.Subcategories.Add(louvre);
        var vacation = new PictureCategory { Name = "Summer Vacation" };
        vacation.Subcategories.Add(paris);
        context.PictureCategories.Add(paris);
        context.SaveChanges();
    }

    using (var context = new EF6RecipesContext())
    {
     var roots = context.PictureCategories.Where(c => c.ParentCategory == null);
        roots.ForEach(root => Print(root, 0));
    }
}

static void Print(PictureCategory cat, int level)
{
    StringBuilder sb = new StringBuilder();
    Console.WriteLine("{0}{1}", sb.Append(' ', level).ToString(), cat.Name);
    cat.Subcategories.ForEach(child => Print(child, level + 1));
}
```

The output of the code in Listing 2-7 shows our root node: Summer Vacation. The first (and only) child is Paris. Paris has Louvre as a child. Finally, at the Louvre, we categorized our pictures by the various collections we visited.

```
Summer Vacation
 Paris
  Louvre
   Egyptian Antiquities
   Sculptures
   Paintings
```

Clearly, the code is a little involved. We start by creating and initializing the instances of our entity types. We wire them together in the object graph by adding the PictureCategories to our louvre category. Then we add the louvre category to the paris category. Finally, we add the paris category to our summer vacation category. We build the hierarchy from the bottom up.

Once we do a SaveChanges(), the inserts are all done on the database, and it's time to query our tables to see whether we've actually inserted all of the rows correctly.

For the retrieval part, we start by getting the root entity. This is the one that has no parent. In our case, we created a summer vacation entity, but we didn't make it the child of any other entity. This makes our summer vacation entity the root of the hierarchy.

Now, with the root, we call another method we wrote: Print(). The Print() method takes a couple of parameters. The first parameter is an instance of a PictureCategory. The second parameter is a level, or depth, we are at in the hierarchy. With the root category, summer vacation, we're at the top of the hierarchy, so we pass in 0. The method call looks like Print(root, 0).

In the Print() method, we write out the name of the category preceded by a space for each level deep in the hierarchy. One of the Append() methods of the StringBuilder class takes a character and an integer. It creates an instance of StringBuilder with the character appended the number of times specified by the integer parameter. In our call, we send in a space and level, and it returns a string with a space for every level deep that we are in the hierarchy. We use the ToString() method to convert the StringBuilder instance to a string.

Now for the recursive part: We iterate through the children and call the Print() method on each child, making sure to increment the level by one. When we run out of children, we simply return. The result is the output shown previously.

In Recipe 6-5, we show another approach to this problem using a Common Table Expression in a stored procedure on the store side to iterate through the graph and return a single flattened result set.

2-6. Splitting an Entity Among Multiple Tables
Problem

You have two or more tables that share the same primary key, and you want to map a single entity to these two tables.

Solution

Let's illustrate the problem with the two tables shown in Figure 2-15.

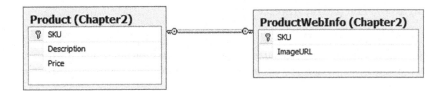

Figure 2-15. *Two tables, Product and ProductWebInfo, with common primary keys*

To create a model with a single entity representing these two tables, do the following:

1. Create a new class in your project that inherits from DbContext.

2. Create a Product POCO entity using the code in Listing 2-8.

Listing 2-8. Creating the Product POCO Entity

```
public class Product
{
    [Key]
    [DatabaseGenerated(DatabaseGeneratedOption.None)]
    public int SKU { get; set; }
    public string Description { get; set; }
    public decimal Price { get; set; }
    public string ImageURL { get; set; }
}
```

3.   Add an auto-property of type DbSet<Product> to your DbContext subclass.

4.   Override the OnModelCreating() method of DbContext with the code in Listing 2-9.

Listing 2-9. Overriding OnModelCreating in the DbContext Subclass

```
public class EF6RecipesContext : DbContext
{
    public DbSet<Product> Products { get; set; }

    public ProductContext() : base("name=EF6CodeFirstRecipesContext")
    {
    }

    protected override void OnModelCreating(DbModelBuilder modelBuilder)
    {
        base.OnModelCreating(modelBuilder);

        modelBuilder.Entity<Product>()
                    .Map(m =>
                        {
                            m.Properties(p => new {p.SKU, p.Description, p.Price});
                            m.ToTable("Product", "Chapter2");
                        })
                    .Map(m =>
                        {
                            m.Properties(p => new {p.SKU, p.ImageURL});
                            m.ToTable("ProductWebInfo", "Chapter2");
                        });
    }
}
```

How It Works

It seems all too common in legacy systems to find "extra" information for each row in one table tucked away in another table. Often this happens over time as a database evolves, and no one is willing to break existing code by adding columns to some critical table. The answer is to "graft on" a new table to hold the additional columns.

By merging two or more tables into a single entity or, as it is usually perceived, splitting a single entity across two or more tables, we can treat all of the parts as one logical entity. This process is often referred to as *vertical splitting*.

The downside of vertical splitting is that retrieving each instance of our entity now requires an additional join for each additional table that makes up the entity type. This extra join is shown in Listing 2-10.

Listing 2-10. Additional Join Required by Vertical Splitting

```
SELECT
[Extent1].[SKU] AS [SKU],
[Extent2].[Description] AS [Description],
[Extent2].[Price] AS [Price],
[Extent1].[ImageURL] AS [ImageURL]
FROM  [dbo].[ProductWebInfo] AS [Extent1]
INNER JOIN [dbo].[Product] AS [Extent2] ON [Extent1].[SKU] = [Extent2].[SKU]
```

Nothing special is required to insert into or retrieve from the Product entity. Listing 2-11 demonstrates working with the vertically split Product entity type.

Listing 2-11. Inserting into and Retrieving from Our Model with the Product Entity Type

```
using (var context = new EF6RecipesContext())
{
    var product = new Product { SKU = 147,
                                Description = "Expandable Hydration Pack",
                                Price = 19.97M, ImageURL = "/pack147.jpg" };
    context.Products.Add(product);
    product = new Product { SKU = 178,
                                Description = "Rugged Ranger Duffel Bag",
                                Price = 39.97M, ImageURL = "/pack178.jpg" };
    context.Products.Add(product);
    product = new Product { SKU = 186,
                                Description = "Range Field Pack",
                                Price = 98.97M, ImageURL = "/noimage.jp" };
    context.Products.Add(product);
    product = new Product { SKU = 202,
                                Description = "Small Deployment Back Pack",
                                Price = 29.97M, ImageURL = "/pack202.jpg" };
    context.Products.Add(product);

    context.SaveChanges();
}

using (var context = new EF6RecipesContext())
{
    foreach (var p in context.Products)
    {
        Console.WriteLine("{0} {1} {2} {3}", p.SKU, p.Description,
                        p.Price.ToString("C"), p.ImageURL);
    }
}
```

The code in Listing 2-7 produces the following results:

```
147 Expandable Hydration Pack $19.97 /pack147.jpg
178 Rugged Ranger Duffel Bag $39.97 /pack178.jpg
186 Range Field Pack $98.97 /noimage.jpg
202 Small Deployment Back Pack $29.97 /pack202.jpg
```

2-7. Splitting a Table Among Multiple Entities

Problem

You have a table with some frequently used fields and a few large, but rarely needed fields. For performance reasons, you want to avoid needlessly loading these expensive fields on every query. You want to split the table across two or more entities.

Solution

Let's say that you have a table like the one shown in Figure 2-16, which holds information about photographs as well as the bits for both the thumbnail and full-resolution image of the photograph.

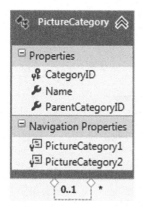

Figure 2-16. *A Photograph table with a field holding the binary large object (blob) representing the data for the image*

To create an entity type that contains the reasonably low-cost and frequently used columns, as well as an entity type containing the high-cost but rarely used HighResolutionBits column, do the following:

1. Create a new class in your project that inherits from DbContext.

2. Create a Photograph POCO entity class using the code in Listing 2-12.

Listing 2-12. Creating the Photograph POCO Entity

```
public class Photograph
{
    [Key]
    [DatabaseGenerated(DatabaseGeneratedOption.Identity)]
    public int PhotoId { get; set; }
    public string Title { get; set; }
    public byte[] ThumbnailBits { get; set; }

    [ForeignKey("PhotoId")]
    public virtual PhotographFullImage PhotographFullImage { get; set; }
}
```

3. Create a PhotographFullImage POCO entity class using the code in Listing 2-13.

Listing 2-13. Creating the PhotographFullImage POCO Entity

```
public class PhotographFullImage
{
    [Key]
    public int PhotoId { get; set; }
    public byte[] HighResolutionBits { get; set; }

    [ForeignKey("PhotoId")]
    public virtual Photograph Photograph { get; set; }
}
```

4. Add an auto-property of type DbSet<Photograph> to your DbContext subclass.

5. Add another auto-property type of DbSet<PhotographFullImage> to your DbContext subclass.

6. Override the OnModelCreating() method of the DbContext class, as shown in Listing 2-14.

Listing 2-14. Overriding the OnModelCreating Method of DbContext

```
protected override void OnModelCreating(DbModelBuilder modelBuilder)
{
    base.OnModelCreating(modelBuilder);

            modelBuilder.Entity<Photograph>()
                .HasRequired(p => p.PhotographFullImage)
                .WithRequiredPrincipal(p => p.Photograph);

    modelBuilder.Entity<Photograph>().ToTable("Photograph", "Chapter2");
    modelBuilder.Entity<PhotographFullImage>().ToTable("Photograph", "Chapter2");
}
```

How It Works

Entity Framework does not directly support the notion of lazy loading of individual entity properties. To get the effect of lazy loading expensive properties, we exploit Entity Framework's support for lazy loading of associated entities. We created a new entity type to hold the expensive full image property and created a one-to-one association between our Photograph entity type and the new PhotographFullImage entity type. We added a referential constraint on the conceptual layer that, much like a database referential constraint, tells Entity Framework that a PhotographFullImage can't exist without a Photograph.

Due to the referential constraint, there are a couple of things to note about our model. If we have a newly created PhotographFullImage, an instance of Photograph must exist in the object context or the data source prior to calling SaveChanges(). Also, if we delete a photograph, the associated PhotographFullImage is also deleted. This is just like cascading deletes in database referential constraints.

The code in Listing 2-15 demonstrates inserting and retrieving from our model.

Listing 2-15. Inserting into and Lazy Loading Expensive Fields

```
byte[] thumbBits = new byte[100];
byte[] fullBits = new byte[2000];
using (var context = new EF6RecipesContext())
{
    var photo = new Photograph { Title = "My Dog",
                                 ThumbnailBits = thumbBits };
    var fullImage = new PhotographFullImage { HighResolutionBits = fullBits };
    photo.PhotographFullImage = fullImage;
    context.Photographs.Add(photo);
    context.SaveChanges();
}

using (var context = new EF6RecipesContext())
{
    foreach (var photo in context.Photographs)
    {
        Console.WriteLine("Photo: {0}, ThumbnailSize {1} bytes",
                          photo.Title, photo.ThumbnailBits.Length);

        // explicitly load the "expensive" entity,
PhotographFullImagecontext.Entry(photo).Reference(p => p.PhotographFullImage).Load();
        Console.WriteLine("Full Image Size: {0} bytes",
                photo.PhotographFullImage.HighResolutionBits.Length);
    }
}
```

The output from Listing 2-15 is as follows:

```
Photo: My Dog, Thumbnail Size: 100 bytes
Full Image Size: 2000 bytes
```

The code in Listing 2-15 creates and initializes instances of the Photograph and PhotographFullImage entities, adds them to the object context, and calls SaveChanges().

On the query side, we retrieve each of the photographs from the database, print some information about the photograph, and then explicitly load the associated `PhotographFullImage` entity. Notice that we did not change the default context option to turn off lazy loading. This puts the burden on us to load related entities explicitly. This is just what we want. We could have chosen not to load the associated instances of `PhotographFullImage`, and if we were iterating through hundreds or thousands of photographs, this would have saved us an awful lot of cycles and bandwidth.

2-8. Modeling Table per Type Inheritance

Problem

You have some tables that contain additional information about a common table, and you want to model this using table per type inheritance.

Solution

Suppose that you have two tables that are closely related to a common table, as shown in Figure 2-17. The Business table is on the 1 side of a 1:0..1 relationship with the eCommerce and the Retail tables. The key feature here is that the eCommerce and Retail tables extend information about a business represented in the Business table.

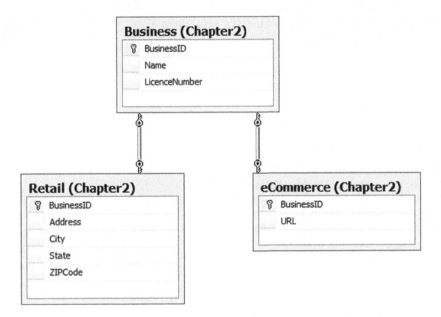

Figure 2-17. *Closely related tables ripe for inheritance*

The tables Retail and eCommerce are related to the Business table, which holds a few properties that we would naturally associate with any business. To model table per type inheritance such that entities Retail and eCommerce inherit from the Business base entity type, perform the following steps:

1. Create a new class in your project that inherits from DbContext.

2. Create a `Business` POCO entity class using the code in Listing 2-16.

Listing 2-16. Creating the Business POCO Entity Class

```
[Table("Business", Schema = "Chapter2")]
public class Business
{
    [Key]
    [DatabaseGenerated(DatabaseGeneratedOption.Identity)]
    public int BusinessId { get; protected set; }
    public string Name { get; set; }
    public string LicenseNumber { get; set; }
}
```

3. Create an eCommerce POCO entity class that inherits from the Business class using the code in Listing 2-17.

Listing 2-17. Creating the eCommerce POCO Entity Class

```
[Table("eCommerce", Schema = "Chapter2")]
public class eCommerce : Business
{
    public string URL { get; set; }
}
```

4. Create a Retail POCO entity class that inherits from the Business class using the code in Listing 2-18.

Listing 2-18. Creating the Retail POCO Entity Class

```
[Table("Retail", Schema = "Chapter2")]
public class Retail : Business
{
    public string Address { get; set; }
    public string City { get; set; }
    public string State { get; set; }
    public string ZIPCode { get; set; }
}
```

5. Add an auto-property of type DbSet<Business> to your DbContext subclass.

How It Works

Both the Retail and the eCommerce tables are on the 0..1 side of a 1:0..1 relationship with the Business table. This means that we could have a business with no additional information or a business with additional Retail or eCommerce information. In object-oriented programming terms, we have a base type, Business, with two derived types, Retail and eCommerce.

Because of the 1:0..1 relationship, we cannot have a row in the Retail or eCommerce tables without a corresponding row in the Business table. In object-oriented terms, an instance of a derived type has the properties of the base type. This concept of a derived type extending the properties of a base type is a key feature of inheritance. In table per type (often abbreviated TPT) inheritance, each of the derived types is represented in separate tables.

Listing 2-19 demonstrates inserting and retrieving from our model.

Listing 2-19. Inserting and Retrieving Entities in TPT Inheritance

```
using (var context = new EF6RecipesContext())
{
    var business = new Business { Name = "Corner Dry Cleaning",
                                  LicenseNumber = "100x1" };
    context.Businesses.Add(business);
    var retail = new Retail { Name = "Shop and Save", LicenseNumber = "200C",
                              Address = "101 Main", City = "Anytown",
                              State = "TX", ZIPCode = "76106" };
    context.Businesses.Add(retail);
    var web = new eCommerce { Name = "BuyNow.com", LicenseNumber = "300AB",
                              URL = "www.buynow.com" };
    context.Businesses.Add(web);
    context.SaveChanges();
}

using (var context = new EF6RecipesContext())
{
    Console.WriteLine("\n--- All Businesses ---");
    foreach (var b in context.Businesses)
    {
        Console.WriteLine("{0} (#{1})", b.Name, b.LicenseNumber);
    }

    Console.WriteLine("\n--- Retail Businesses ---");
    foreach (var r in context.Businesses.OfType<Retail>())
    {
        Console.WriteLine("{0} (#{1})", r.Name, r.LicenseNumber);
        Console.WriteLine("{0}", r.Address);
        Console.WriteLine("{0}, {1} {2}", r.City, r.State, r.ZIPCode);
    }

    Console.WriteLine("\n--- eCommerce Businesses ---");
    foreach (var e in context.Businesses.OfType<eCommerce>())
    {
        Console.WriteLine("{0} (#{1})", e.Name, e.LicenseNumber);
        Console.WriteLine("Online address is: {0}", e.URL);
    }
}
```

The code in Listing 2-19 creates and initializes instances of the Business entity type and the two derived types. To add these to the Database Context, we use the Add() method exposed on the Business entity set in the context.

On the query side, to access all of the businesses, we iterate through the Businesses entity set. For the derived types, we use the OfType<>() method specifying the derived type to filter the Business entity set.

The output of Listing 2-19 looks like the following:

```
--- All Businesses ---
Corner Dry Cleaning (#100X1)
Shop and Save (#200C)
BuyNow.com (#300AB)

--- Retail Businesses ---
Shop and Save (#200C)
101 Main
Anytown, TX 76106

---- eCommerce Businesses ---
BuyNow.com (#300AB)
Online address is: www.buynow.com
```

Table per type is one of three inheritance models supported by Entity Framework. The other two are Table per Hierarchy (discussed in this chapter) and Table per Concrete Type (see Chapter 15).

Table per type inheritance provides a lot of database flexibility because we can easily add tables as new derived types find their way into our model as an application develops. However, each derived type involves additional joins that can reduce performance. In real-world applications, we have seen significant performance problems with TPT when many derived types are modeled.

Table per hierarchy, as you will see in Recipe 2-10, stores the entire hierarchy in a single table. This eliminates the joins of TPT and thereby provides better performance, but at the cost of some flexibility.

Table per concrete type is supported by the Entity Framework runtime, but not by the designer. Table per Concrete Type has some important applications, as we will see in Chapter 15.

2-9. Using Conditions to Filter an ObjectSet
Problem

You want to create a permanent filter on an entity type so that it maps to a subset of the rows in a table.

Solution

Let's say that you have a table holding account information, as shown in the database diagram in Figure 2-18. The table has a DeletedOn nullable column that holds the date and time the account was deleted. If the account is still active, the DeletedOn column is null. We want our Account entity to represent only active accounts; that is, an account without a DeletedOn value.

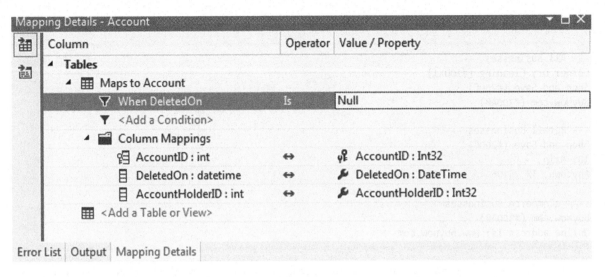

Figure 2-18. Account table with DeletedOn DateTime column

To model this table so that only active accounts are used to populate the Account entity type, do the following:

1. Add a new model to your project by right-clicking your project and selecting Add ➤ New Item. Choose ADO.NET Entity Data Model from the Visual C# Data templates.

2. Select Generate from database. Click Next.

3. Use the wizard to select an existing connection to your database, or create a new connection.

4. From the Choose Your Database Object dialog box, select the Account table. Leave the Pluralize and Foreign Key options checked. Click Finish.

5. Click the Account entity to view the Mapping Details window. If the Mapping Details window is not visible, show it by selecting View ➤ Other Windows ➤ Entity Data Model Mapping Details. Click Add a Condition, and select the DeletedOn column. In the Operator column, select Is, and in the Value/Property column, select Null. This creates a mapping condition when the DeletedOn column is Is Null (see Figure 2-19).

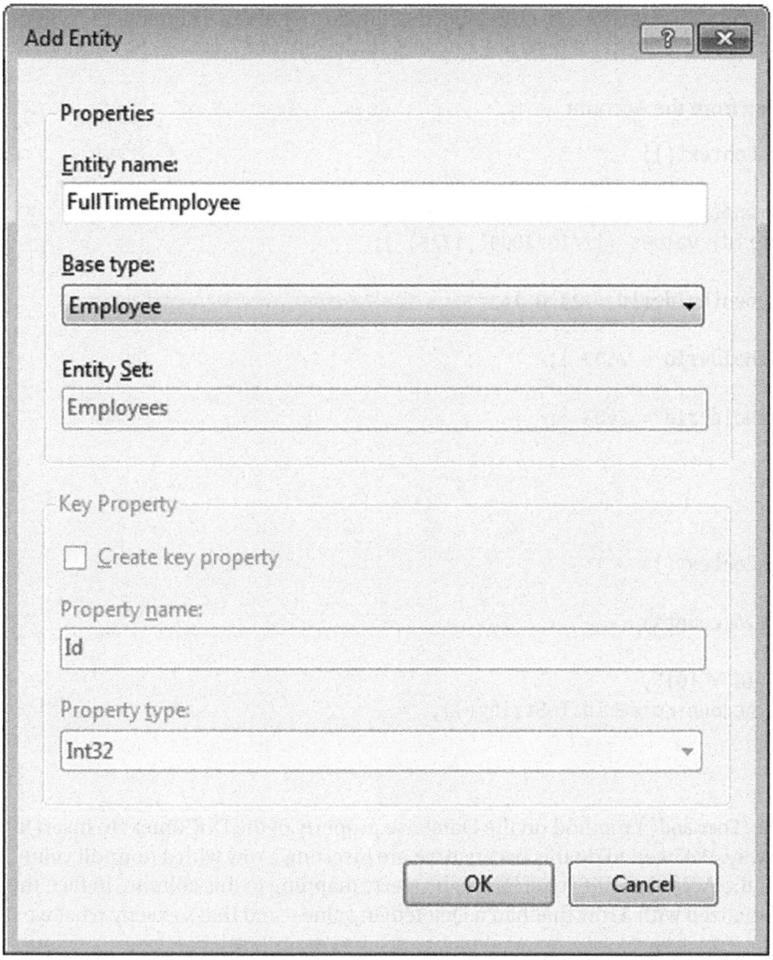

Figure 2-19. *Creating the conditional mapping for the Account entity to the Account table*

6. Right-click the DeletedOn property and select Delete. Because we're using the DeletedOn column in a conditional mapping, we can't map it to a property. Its value would always be null anyway in our model.

How It Works

Conditional mappings are often used when you want to apply a permanent filter on an entity. Conditional mappings are also key to implementing Table per Hierarchy Inheritance. You can apply conditions using the following:

```
<value> Is Null
<value> Is Not Null
<integer> = <value>
<string> = <value>
```

In this example, we applied an Is Null condition on the Account entity that filters out rows that contain a DeletedOn date/time. The code in Listing 2-20 demonstrates inserting into and retrieving rows from the Account table.

Listing 2-20. Inserting into and Retrieving from the Account

```
using (var context = new EF6RecipesContext())
{
    context.Database.ExecuteSqlCommand(@"insert into chapter2.account
            (DeletedOn,AccountHolderId) values ('2/10/2009',1728)");

    var account = new Account { AccountHolderId = 2320 };
    context.Accounts.Add(account);
    account = new Account { AccountHolderId = 2502 };
    context.Accounts.Add(account);
    account = new Account { AccountHolderId = 2603 };
    context.Accounts.Add(account);
    context.SaveChanges();
}

using (var context = new EF6RecipesContext())
{
    foreach (var account in context.Accounts)
    {
        Console.WriteLine("Account Id = {0}",
                          account.AccountHolderId.ToString());
    }
}
```

In Listing 2-20, we use the ExecuteSqlCommand() method on the Database property of the DbContext to insert a row into the database the old-fashioned way. We need to do this because we are inserting a row with a nonnull value for the DeletedOn column. In our model, the Account entity type has no property mapping to this column; in fact, the Account entity type would never be materialized with a row that had a DeletedOn value—and that's exactly what we want to test.

The rest of the first part of the code creates and initializes three additional instances of the Account entity type. These are saved to the database with the SaveChanges() method.

When we query the database, we should get only the three instances of the Account entity type that we added with the SaveChanges() method. The row that we added using the ExecuteSqlCommand() method should not be visible. The following output confirms it:

```
Account Id = 2320
Account Id = 2502
Account Id = 2603
```

2-10. Modeling Table per Hierarchy Inheritance

Problem

You have a table with a type or discriminator column that you use to determine what the data in a row represents in your application. You want to model this with table per hierarchy inheritance.

Solution

Let's say that your table looks like the one shown in Figure 2-20. This Employee table contains rows for both hourly employees and salaried employees. The EmployeeType column is used to discriminate between the two types of rows. When EmployeeType is 1, the row represents a salaried or full-time employee. When the EmployeeType is 2, the row represents an hourly employee.

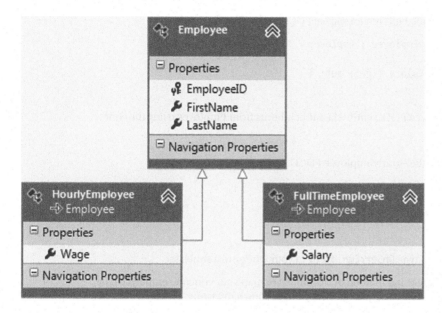

Figure 2-20. *An Employee table containing both hourly and full-time employees*

To create a model using table per hierarchy inheritance based on the Employee table, do the following:

1. Create a new class in your project that inherits from DbContext.

2. Create an abstract Employee POCO entity class using the code in Listing 2-21.

Listing 2-21. Creating the Abstract Employee POCO Entity Class

```
[Table("Employee", Schema="Chapter2")]
public abstract class Employee
{
    [Key]
    [DatabaseGenerated(DatabaseGeneratedOption.Identity)]
    public int EmployeeId { get; protected set; }
    public string FirstName { get; set; }
    public string LastName { get; set; }
}
```

3. Create a `FullTimeEmployee` POCO entity class that inherits from Employee using the code in Listing 2-22.

Listing 2-22. Creating the FullTimeEmployee POCO Entity Class

```
public class FullTimeEmployee : Employee
{
    public decimal? Salary { get; set; }
}
```

4. Create an `HourlyEmployee` POCO entity class that inherits from Employee using the code in Listing 2-23.

Listing 2-23. Creating the HourlyEmployee POCO Entity Class

```
public class HourlyEmployee : Employee
{
    public decimal? Wage { get; set; }
}
```

5. Add an auto-property of type `DbSet<Employee>` to your DbContext subclass.

6. Override the `OnModelCreating` method of DbContext to map your concrete employee type classes to the EmployeeType discriminator column, as shown in Listing 2-24.

Listing 2-24. Overriding the OnModelCreating Method of DbContext

```
protected override void OnModelCreating(DbModelBuilder modelBuilder)
{
    base.OnModelCreating(modelBuilder);

    modelBuilder.Entity<Employee>()
                .Map<FullTimeEmployee>(m => m.Requires("EmployeeType").HasValue(1))
                .Map<HourlyEmployee>(m => m.Requires("EmployeeType").HasValue(2));
}
```

▪ **Note** Nonshared properties (for example, Salary and Wage) must have nullable types.

How It Works

In table per hierarchy inheritance, often abbreviated TPH, a single table is used to represent the entire inheritance hierarchy. Unlike table per type inheritance, the TPH rows for the derived types as well as the base type are intermingled in the same table. The rows are distinguished by a discriminator column. In our example, the discriminator column is EmployeeType.

In TPH, mapping conditions, which are set in entity configuration, are used to indicate the values of the discriminator column that cause the table to be mapped to the different derived types. We marked the base type as abstract. By marking it as abstract, we didn't have to provide a condition for the mapping because an abstract entity can't be created. We will never have an instance of an Employee entity. We did not implement an EmployeeType property in the Employee entity. A column used in a condition is not, in general, mapped to a property.

The code in Listing 2-25 demonstrates inserting into and retrieving from our model.

Listing 2-25. *Inserting into and Retrieving from Our TPH Model*

```
using (var context = new EF6RecipesContext())
{
    var fte = new FullTimeEmployee { FirstName = "Jane", LastName = "Doe",
                                     Salary = 71500M};
    context.Employees.Add(fte);
    fte = new FullTimeEmployee { FirstName = "John", LastName = "Smith",
                                 Salary = 62500M };
    context.Employees.Add(fte);
    var hourly = new HourlyEmployee { FirstName = "Tom", LastName = "Jones",
                                      Wage = 8.75M };
    context.Employees.Add(hourly);
    context.SaveChanges();
}

using (var context = new EF6RecipesContext())
{
    Console.WriteLine("--- All Employees ---");
    foreach (var emp in context.Employees)
    {
        bool fullTime = emp is HourlyEmployee ? false : true;
        Console.WriteLine("{0} {1} ({2})", emp.FirstName, emp.LastName,
                          fullTime ? "Full Time" : "Hourly");
    }

    Console.WriteLine("--- Full Time ---");
    foreach (var fte in context.Employees.OfType<FullTimeEmployee>())
    {
        Console.WriteLine("{0} {1}", fte.FirstName, fte.LastName);
    }

    Console.WriteLine("--- Hourly ---");
    foreach (var hourly in context.Employees.OfType<HourlyEmployee>())
    {
        Console.WriteLine("{0} {1}", hourly.FirstName, hourly.LastName);
    }
}
```

Following is the output of the code in Listing 2-25:

```
--- All Employees ---
Jane Doe (Full Time)
John Smith (Full Time)
Tom Jones (Hourly)
--- Full Time ---
Jane Doe
John Smith
--- Hourly ---
Tom Jones
```

The code in Listing 2-25 creates, initializes, and adds two full-time employees and an hourly employee. On the query side, we retrieve all of the employees and use the `is` operator to determine what type of employee we have. We indicate the employee type when we print out the employee's name.

In separate code blocks, we retrieve the full-time employees and the hourly employees using the `OfType<>()` method.

Best Practice

There is some debate over when to use abstract base entities in TPH inheritance and when to create a condition on the base entity. The difficulty with a concrete base entity is that it can be very cumbersome to query for all of the instances in the hierarchy. The best practice is that if your application never needs instances of the base entity is to make it abstract.

If your application needs instances of the base entity, consider introducing a new derived entity to cover the condition for the concrete base entity. For example, we might create a new derived class, such as UnclassifiedEmployee. Once we have this new derived entity, we can safely make our base entity abstract. This provides us with a simple way to query for condition formally covered by the base entity with a condition.

There are some rules to keep in mind when using TPH. First, the conditions used must be mutually exclusive. That is, you cannot have a row that can conditionally map to two or more types.

Second, the conditions used must account for every row in the table. You cannot have a row in the table that has a discriminator value that does not map the row to exactly one type. This rule can be particularly troubling if you are working with a legacy database in which other applications are creating rows for which you have no appropriate condition mappings. What will happen in these cases? The rows that do not map to your base or derived types will simply not be accessible in your model.

The discriminator column cannot be mapped to an entity property unless it is used in an `is not null` condition At first, this last rule might seem overly restrictive. You might ask, "How can I insert a row representing a derived type if I can't set the discriminator value?" The answer is rather elegant. You simply create an instance of the derived type and add it to the context in the same way that you would any other entity instance. Object Services takes care of creating the appropriate insert statements to create a row with the correct discriminator value.

2-11. Modeling Is-a and Has-a Relationships Between Two Entities

Problem

You have two tables that participate in both Is-a and Has-a relationships, and you want to model them as two entities with the corresponding Is-a and Has-a relationships.

Solution

Let's say that you have two tables that describe scenic parks and their related locations. In your database, you represent these with a Location table and a Park table. For the purposes of your application, a park is simply a type of location. Additionally, a park can have a governing office with a mailing address, which is also represented in the Location table. A park, then, is both a derived type of Location and can have a location that corresponds to the park's governing office. It is entirely possible that the office is not located on the grounds of the park. Perhaps several parks share an office in a nearby town. Figure 2-21 shows a database diagram with the Park and Location tables.

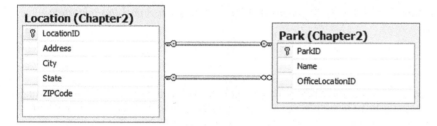

Figure 2-21. *Location and Park in both a Has-a and Is-a relationship*

Follow these steps to model both of these relationships:

1. Add a new model to your project by right-clicking your project and selecting Add ➤ New Item. Choose ADO.NET Entity Data Model from the Visual C# Data templates.

2. Select Generate from database. Click Next.

3. Use the wizard to select an existing connection to your database or create a new connection.

4. From the Choose Your Database Object dialog box, select the Location and Park tables. Leave the Pluralize and Foreign Key options checked. Click Finish.

5. Delete the one-to-zero or one association created by the Entity Data Model Wizard.

6. Right-click the Location entity, and select Add ➤ Inheritance. Select the Park entity as the derived entity and the Location entity as the base entity.

7. Delete the ParkId property from the Park entity type.

8. Click the Park entity to view the Mapping Details window. If the Mapping Details window is not visible, show it by selecting View ➤ Other Windows ➤ Entity Data Model Mapping Details. Map the ParkId column to the LocationId property.

9. Change the name of the Location1 navigation property in the Park entity type to Office. This represents the office location for the park.

The completed model is shown in Figure 2-22.

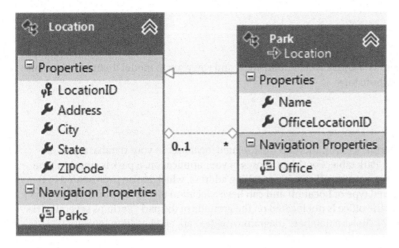

Figure 2-22. *The completed model with Park deriving from Location. A Park is-a location. A park has-a location for its office*

How It Works

Entities can have more than one association with other entities. In this example, we created an Is-a relationship using table per type inheritance with Location as the base entity type and Park as the derived entity type. We also created a Has-a relationship with a one-to-many association between the Location and Park entity types.

In Listing 2-26, we demonstrate creating a new Park entity that also results in creating a Location because of the Is-a relationship. We attach an office Location to the Park, which results in a second row in the Location table.

Listing 2-26. Creating and Retrieving Park and Location Entities

```
using (var context = new EF6RecipesContext())
{
    var park = new Park { Name = "11th Street Park",
                        Address = "801 11th Street", City = "Aledo",
                        State = "TX", ZIPCode = "76106" };
    var loc = new Location { Address = "501 Main", City = "Weatherford",
                        State = "TX", ZIPCode = "76201" };
    park.Office = loc;
    context.Locations.Add(park);
    park = new Park { Name = "Overland Park", Address = "101 High Drive",
                    City = "Springtown", State = "TX", ZIPCode = "76081" };
    loc = new Location { Address = "8705 Range Lane", City = "Springtown",
                    State = "TX", ZIPCode = "76081" };
    park.Office = loc;
    context.Locations.Add(park);
    context.SaveChanges();
}
```

```
using (var context = new EF6RecipesContext())
{
    context.ContextOptions.LazyLoadingEnabled = true;
    Console.WriteLine("-- All Locations -- ");
    foreach (var l in context.Locations)
    {
        Console.WriteLine("{0}, {1}, {2} {3}", l.Address, l.City,
                            l.State, l.ZIPCode);
    }

    Console.WriteLine("--- Parks ---");
    foreach (var p in context.Locations.OfType<Park>())
    {
        Console.WriteLine("{0} is at {1} in {2}", p.Name, p.Address, p.City);
        Console.WriteLine("\tOffice: {0}, {1}, {2} {3}", p.Office.Address,
                            p.Office.City, p.Office.State, p.Office.ZIPCode);
    }
}
```

The output of the code in Listing 2-26 is as follows:

```
-- All Locations --
501 Main, Weatherford, TX 76201
801 11th Street, Aledo, TX 76106
8705 Range Lane, Springtown, TX 76081
101 High Drive, Springtown, TX 76081
--- Parks ---
11th Street Park is at 801 11th Street in Aledo
        Office: 501 Main, Weatherford, TX 76201
Overland Park is at 101 High Drive in Springtown
        Office: 8705 Range Lane, Springtown, TX 76081
```

2-12. Creating, Modifying, and Mapping Complex Types

Problem

You want to create a complex type, set it as a property on an entity, and map the property to some columns on a table.

Solution

Let's say that you have the table shown in Figure 2-23. You want to create a Name complex type for the FirstName and LastName columns. You also want to create an Address complex type for the AddressLine1, AddressLine2, City, State, and ZIPCode columns. You want to use these complex types for properties in your model, as shown in Figure 2-24.

Figure 2-23. *The Agent table with the name and address of the agent*

Figure 2-24. *The completed model with the name and address components refactored into complex types*

Follow these steps to create the model with the Name and Address complex types:

1. Add a new model to your project by right-clicking your project and selecting Add ➤ New Item. Choose ADO.NET Entity Data Model from the Visual C# Data templates.

2. Select Generate from database. Click Next.

3. Use the wizard to select an existing connection to your database or create a new connection.

4. From the Choose Your Database Object dialog box, select the Agent table. Leave the Pluralize and Foreign Key options checked. Click Finish.

5. Select the FirstName and LastName properties, then right-click and select Refactor Into Complex Type.

6. In the Model Browser, rename the new complex type from ComplexType1 to Name. This changes the name of the type. On the Agent, rename the ComplexTypeProperty to Name. This changes the name of the property.

7. We'll create the next complex type from scratch so that you can see an alternative approach. Right-click on the design surface, and select Add ➤ Complex Type.

8. In the Model Browser, rename the new complex type from ComplexType1 to Address.

9. Select the AddressLine1, AddressLine2, City, State, and ZIPCode properties in the Agent. Right-click and select Cut. Paste these properties onto the Address complex type in the Model Browser.

10. Right-click the Agent, and select Add ➤ Complex Property. Rename the property Address.

11. Right-click on the new Address property and select Properties. Change its type to Address. This changes the new property's type to the new Address complex type.

12. View the Mapping Details window for the Agent. Map the columns from the Agent table to the properties on the two complex types we've created. The mappings are shown in Figure 2-25.

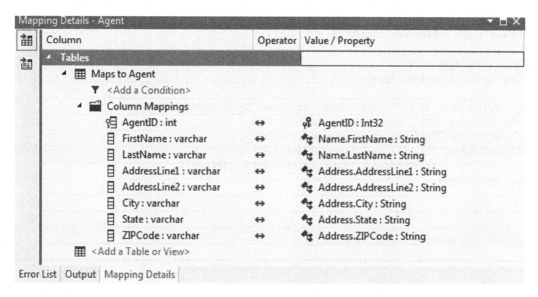

Figure 2-25. *Mapping the fields of the complex types to the columns in the Agent table*

How It Works

Complex types allow you to group several properties into a single type for a property on an entity. A complex type can contain scalar properties or other complex types, but they cannot have navigation properties or entity collections. A complex type cannot be an entity key. Complex types are not tracked on their own in an object context.

A property whose type is a complex type cannot be null. When you work with entities with complex type properties, you have to be mindful of this rule. Occasionally, when the value of a complex type property is unimportant for a particular operation, you may need to create a dummy value for the property so that it has some nonnull value.

When you modify any field in complex type property, the property is marked as changed by Entity Framework, and an update statement will be generated that will update all of the fields of the complex type property.

In Listing 2-27, we demonstrate this using the model by inserting a few agents and displaying them.

Listing 2-27. Inserting Agents and Selecting from Our Model

```
using (var context = new EF6RecipesContext())
{
    var name1 = new Name { FirstName = "Robin", LastName = "Rosen" };
    var name2 = new Name { FirstName = "Alex", LastName = "St. James" };
    var address1 = new Address { AddressLine1 = "510 N. Grant",
                                 AddressLine2 = "Apt. 8",
                                 City = "Raytown", State = "MO",
                                 ZIPCode = "64133" };
    var address2 = new Address { AddressLine1 = "222 Baker St.",
                                 AddressLine2 = "Apt.22B",
                                 City = "Raytown", State = "MO",
                                 ZIPCode = "64133" };
```

```
    context.Agents.Add(new Agent { Name = name1, Address = address1 });
    context.Agents.Add(new Agent {Name = name2, Address = address2});
    context.SaveChanges();
}

using (var context = new EF6RecipesContext())
{
    Console.WriteLine("Agents");
    foreach (var agent in context.Agents)
    {
        Console.WriteLine("{0} {1}", agent.Name.FirstName, agent.Name.LastName);
        Console.WriteLine("{0}", agent.Address.AddressLine1);
        Console.WriteLine("{0}", agent.Address.AddressLine2);
        Console.WriteLine("{0}, {1} {2}", agent.Address.City,
                            agent.Address.State, agent.Address.ZIPCode);
        Console.WriteLine();
    }
}
```

The output of the code in Listing 2-27 is as follows:

```
Agents
Robin Rosen
510 N. Grant
Apt. 8
Raytown, MO 64133

Alex St. James
222 Baker St.
Apt.22B
Raytown, MO 64133
```

CHAPTER 3

■ ■ ■

Querying an Entity Data Model

In the previous chapter, we showed you many ways to model some fairly common database scenarios. The recipes in this chapter will show you how to query your model. Generally speaking, you can query your model three different ways, using:

1. LINQ to Entities

2. Entity SQL

3. Native SQL

We'll demonstrate all three approaches in this chapter and, at the same time, cover a wide range of common, and not so common, scenarios that will help you understand the basics of querying models with Entity Framework. We'll also explore some of the new capabilities for querying data available with Entity Framework 6.

3-1. Querying Asynchronously

You have a long-running Entity Framework querying operation. You do not want to *block* the application running on the main thread while the query executes. Instead, you'd like the user to be able to perform other operations until data is returned. Equally important, you will want to query the model leveraging the Microsoft LINQ-to-Entities framework, which is the preferred approach for querying an entity data model.

Solution

Let's say that you have a model like the one shown in Figure 3-1.

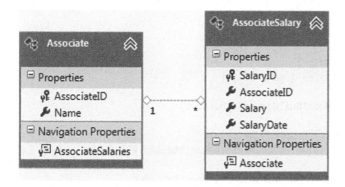

Figure 3-1. *A model with an Associate entity type representing an associate; and an AssociateSalary entity type representing the salary history for the associate*

In this simple model, we have entities that represent associates and their salary history.

To start, this example leverages the Code-First approach for Entity Framework. In Listing 3-1, we create the entity classes.

Listing 3-1. Associate and AssociateSalary Entity Types

```
public class Associate
{
    public Associate()
    {
        AssociateSalaries = new HashSet<AssociateSalary>();
    }

    public int AssociateId { get; set; }
    public string Name { get; set; }
    public virtual ICollection<AssociateSalary> AssociateSalaries { get; set; }
}

public class AssociateSalary
{
    public int SalaryId { get; set; }
    public int AssociateId { get; set; }
    public decimal Salary { get; set; }
    public DateTime SalaryDate { get; set; }
    public virtual Associate Associate { get; set; }
}
```

Next, in Listing 3-2, we create the DbContext object required for our Code-First approach. Note in the OnModelCreating method how we explicitly map the SalaryId property as the primary key for the AssociateSalary. When using Code First, if a property has the name Id or <table name>Id, Entity Framework assumes that it is the primary key for the table. Otherwise, you must explicitly specify the key, as we have done here.

Listing 3-2. The DbContext Object

```
public class EFRecipesEntities : DbContext
{
    public EFRecipesEntities()
        : base("ConnectionString")
    {
    }

    public DbSet<Associate> Associates { get; set; }
    public DbSet<AssociateSalary> AssociateSalaries { get; set; }

    protected override void OnModelCreating(DbModelBuilder modelBuilder)
    {
        modelBuilder.Entity<Associate>().ToTable("Chapter3.Associate");
        modelBuilder.Entity<AssociateSalary>().ToTable("Chapter3.AssociateSalary");

        // Explicilty assign key as primary key in AssociateSalary does not meet
        // Entity Framework default mapping conventions.
```

```
        modelBuilder.Entity<AssociateSalary>().HasKey(x => x.SalaryId);
        base.OnModelCreating(modelBuilder);
    }
}
```

Listing 3-3 demonstrates how we can leverage the new Entity Framework Async methods to implement asynchronous processing for the queries that remove, load, and fetch data.

Listing 3-3. Asynchronously Processing Entity Framework Queries

```
private static void Main()
{
    var asyncTask = EF6AsyncDemo();

    foreach (var c in BusyChars())
    {
        if (asyncTask.IsCompleted)
        {
            break;
        }
        Console.Write(c);
        Console.CursorLeft = 0;
        Thread.Sleep(100);
    }
    Console.WriteLine("\nPress <enter> to continue...");
    Console.ReadLine();
}

private static IEnumerable<char> BusyChars()
{
    while (true)
    {
        yield return '\\';
        yield return '|';
        yield return '/';
        yield return '-';
    }
}

private static async Task EF6AsyncDemo()
{
    await Cleanup();
    await LoadData();
    await RunForEachAsyncExample();
    await RunToListAsyncExampe();
    await RunSingleOrDefaultAsyncExampe();
}
```

```csharp
private static async Task Cleanup()
{
    using (var context = new EFRecipesEntities())
    {
        // delete previous test data
        // execute raw sql statement asynchronoulsy
        Console.WriteLine("Cleaning Up Previous Test Data");
        Console.WriteLine("=========\n");

        await context.Database.ExecuteSqlCommandAsync("delete from chapter3.AssociateSalary");
        await context.Database.ExecuteSqlCommandAsync("delete from chapter3.Associate");
        await Task.Delay(5000);
    }
}

private static async Task LoadData()
{
    using (var context = new EFRecipesEntities())
    {
        // add new test data
        Console.WriteLine("Adding Test Data");
        Console.WriteLine("=========\n");

        var assoc1 = new Associate { Name = "Janis Roberts" };
        var assoc2 = new Associate { Name = "Kevin Hodges" };
        var assoc3 = new Associate { Name = "Bill Jordan" };
        var salary1 = new AssociateSalary
        {
            Salary = 39500M,
            SalaryDate = DateTime.Parse("8/4/09")
        };
        var salary2 = new AssociateSalary
        {
            Salary = 41900M,
            SalaryDate = DateTime.Parse("2/5/10")
        };
        var salary3 = new AssociateSalary
        {
            Salary = 33500M,
            SalaryDate = DateTime.Parse("10/08/09")
        };
        assoc1.AssociateSalaries.Add(salary1);
        assoc2.AssociateSalaries.Add(salary2);
        assoc3.AssociateSalaries.Add(salary3);
        context.Associates.Add(assoc1);
        context.Associates.Add(assoc2);
        context.Associates.Add(assoc3);

        // update datastore asynchronoulsy
        await context.SaveChangesAsync();
        await Task.Delay(5000);
    }
}
```

```
private static async Task RunForEachAsyncExample()
{
    using (var context = new EFRecipesEntities())
    {
        Console.WriteLine("Async ForEach Call");
        Console.WriteLine("=========");

        // leverage ForEachAsync
        await context.Associates.Include(x => x.AssociateSalaries).ForEachAsync(x =>
        {
            Console.WriteLine("Here are the salaries for Associate {0}:", x.Name);

            foreach (var salary in x.AssociateSalaries)
            {
                Console.WriteLine("\t{0}", salary.Salary);
            }
        });
        await Task.Delay(5000);
    }
}

private static async Task RunToListAsyncExampe()
{
    using (var context = new EFRecipesEntities())
    {
        Console.WriteLine("\n\nAsync ToList Call");
        Console.WriteLine("=========");

        // leverage ToListAsync
        var associates = await context.Associates.Include(x => x.AssociateSalaries).OrderBy(x =>
x.Name).ToListAsync();

        foreach (var associate in associates)
        {
            Console.WriteLine("Here are the salaries for Associate {0}:", associate.Name);
            foreach (var salaryInfo in associate.AssociateSalaries)
            {
                Console.WriteLine("\t{0}", salaryInfo.Salary);
            }
        }
        await Task.Delay(5000);
    }
}

private static async Task RunSingleOrDefaultAsyncExampe()
{
    using (var context = new EFRecipesEntities())
    {
        Console.WriteLine("\n\nAsync SingleOrDefault Call");
        Console.WriteLine("=========");
```

```
        var associate = await context.Associates.
            Include(x => x.AssociateSalaries).
                OrderBy(x => x.Name).
                    FirstOrDefaultAsync(y => y.Name == "Kevin Hodges");

        Console.WriteLine("Here are the salaries for Associate {0}:", associate.Name);
        foreach (var salaryInfo in associate.AssociateSalaries)
        {
            Console.WriteLine("\t{0}", salaryInfo.Salary);
        }
        await Task.Delay(5000);
    }
}
```

Listing 3-3 outputs the following result:

```
Cleaning Up Previous Test Data
=========
Adding Test Data
=========
Async ForEach Call
=========
Here are the salaries for Associate Janis Roberts:
        39500.00
Here are the salaries for Associate Kevin Hodges:
        41900.00
Here are the salaries for Associate Bill Jordan:
        33500.00
Async ToList Call
=========
Here are the salaries for Associate Bill Jordan:
        33500.00
Here are the salaries for Associate Janis Roberts:
        39500.00
Here are the salaries for Associate Kevin Hodges:
        41900.00
Async SingleOrDefault Call
=========
Here are the salaries for Associate Kevin Hodges:
        41900.00
```

How It Works

In this example, we demonstrate two key concepts of Entity Framework usage: Querying the model using the LINQ extensions for Entity Framework and the new asynchronous capabilities implemented in Entity Framework 6.

For the vast majority of your query operations, you want to use LINQ. Doing so will give you *IntelliSense*, compile-time checking, and a great strongly typed experience. If you have a use case that requires the construction of a dynamic query at runtime, you may consider using Entity SQL, which enables you to concatenate strings for various parts of the query expression. You will find Entity SQL examples contained in the recipes in this chapter.

We start by clearing out any previous test data in the underlying data store. Notice how we wrap the Cleanup() operation inside an async method. We then generate native SQL statements using the new ExecuteSqlCommandAsync() method. Note how we leverage the async/await patterns found in the 4.5 version of the .NET framework. This pattern enables asynchronous operations without explicitly instantiating a background thread; additionally, it frees up the current CLR thread while it is waiting for the database operation to complete.

Next we load test data for both Associate and Associate Salaries. To execute the call asynchronously, as before, we wrap the LoadData() operation inside an async method and insert new test data into the underlying data store by calling the newly added SaveChangesAsync() method.

Next, we present three different queries that go against the model. Each leverages the LINQ extensions for Entity Framework. Each is contained within an async method, leveraging the await/async pattern. In the RunForEachAsyncExample() method, we make use of the ForEachAsync() extension method, as there is no async equivalent of a foreach statement. Leveraging this async method, along with the Include() method, we are able to query and enumerate these objects asynchronously.

In the subsequent RunToListAsyncExample() and RunSingelOrDefaultAsyncExample() queries, we leverage the new asynchronous methods for ToList() and SingleOrDefault().

Entity Framework now asynchronously exposes a large number of its operational methods. The naming convention appends the suffix Async to the existing API name, making it relatively simple to implement asynchronous processing when adding or fetching data from the underlying data store.

3-2. Updating with Native SQL Statements
Problem

You want to execute a native SQL statement against the Entity Framework to update the underlying data store.

Solution

Let's say that you have a Payment database table like the one shown in Figure 3-2, and you have created a model such as the one in Figure 3-3, which is from the Entity Framework designer tool.

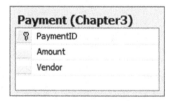

Figure 3-2. *A Payment table that contains information about a payment made by a vendor*

Figure 3-3. *A model with a Payment entity*

To execute one or more SQL statements directly against the underlying Payment table, use the ExecuteSqlCommand() method available from the Database property from DbContext.class. Although we could query the Payment entity in our model, the ExecuteSqlCommand enables us to query the underlying database table directly, forgoing some Entity Framework features such as change tracking. We simply need a model object that inherently contains a context object against which we execute ad hoc SQL commands.

Follow the pattern in Listing 3-4 to execute one or more SQL statements.

Listing 3-4. Executing an Insert Statement

```
// delete previous test data
using (var context = new EFRecipesEntities())
{
    context.Database.ExecuteSqlCommand("delete from chapter3.payment");
}
// insert two rows of data
using (var context = new EFRecipesEntities())
{
    // note how using the following syntax with parameter place holders of @p0 and @p1
    // automatically create the ADO.NET SqlParameters object for you
    var sql = @"insert into Chapter3.Payment(Amount, Vendor) values (@p0, @p1)";
    var rowCount = context.Database.ExecuteSqlCommand(sql, 99.97M, "Ace Plumbing");
    rowCount += context.Database.ExecuteSqlCommand(sql, 43.83M, "Joe's Trash Service");
    Console.WriteLine("{0} rows inserted", rowCount);
}

// retrieve and materialize data using (var context = new EFRecipesEntities())
{
    Console.WriteLine("Payments");
    Console.WriteLine("========");
    foreach (var payment in context.Payments)
    {
        Console.WriteLine("Paid {0} to {1}", payment.Amount.ToString(),
                          payment.Vendor);
    }
}
```

Following is the output of the code in Listing 3-4:

```
2 rows inserted
Payments
========
Paid $99.97 to Ace Plumbing
Paid $43.83 to Joe's Trash Service
```

How It Works

In Listing 3-4, we start by removing any previous test data. Notice how we use the ExecuteSqlCommand method from the Database object from the DbContext object to execute this operation. Note how we feed a native SQL Delete statement directly into the method.

Then we create a string containing a SQL Insert statement. This statement contains two parameters: @Amount and @Vendor. These are placeholders that will be replaced by values when the statement is executed.

Next we create two DbParameter parameter objects, which bind the placeholder names to specific values. For the first insert, we bind the value 99.97 to the Amount placeholder along with "Ace Plumbing" to the Vendor placeholder. We then create another vendor record. Notice how both vendors are assigned to an array of type DbParameter. To execute the SQL statement, we pass both the string containing the SQL statement and the array of DbParameter objects to the ExecuteSqlCommand() method. ExecuteSqlCommand() returns the count of rows affected by the statement. In our case, one row is inserted each time we call ExecuteSqlCommand().

If you don't have any parameters for a SQL statement, there is an overload of the ExecuteSqlCommand() method with a single parameters that expects only a SQL statement.

- The pattern in Listing 3-4 is similar to how we would query data leveraging the Microsoft ADO. NET framework with the SqlClient object. The difference is that we don't need to construct a connection string and explicitly open a connection. The underlying Entity Framework context object automatically performs this work. Note that there are two versions of the context object in Entity Framework: The DbContext object in Entity Framework versions 5, 6, and the 4.x Code-First approach.

- The ObjectContext in earlier versions of Entity Framework.

Keep in mind as well that the DbContext is simply a wrapper, or "Façade," which wraps the legacy ObjectContext, making the context object significantly more intuitive and easy to use. All functionality from the underlying ObjectContext is still available.

The way we express the command text and the parameters is also different. With the ADO.NET ExecuteNonQuery() method, the command text and parameters are set on the underlying Command object. Here, these are passed into the ExecuteSqlCommand() method as simple arguments.

Of course, the observant reader will notice here (and this is important) that we're really not querying the model. In fact, as we mentioned, you don't need to have the Payment entity shown in Figure 3-3. The ExecuteSqlCommand() method simply uses the object's DbContext for its connection to the underlying data store.

Best Practice

To parameterize or not to parameterize, that is the question ... Okay, Shakespeare aside, should you use parameters for SQL statements or just create the SQL statement strings dynamically? The best practice is to use parameters whenever possible. Here are some reasons why:

- Parameterized SQL statements help prevent SQL Injection attacks. If you construct a complete SQL statement as a string by dynamically appending together strings that you get from a user interface, such as an ASP.NET TextBox control, you may end up inadvertently exposing yourself to injected SQL statements that can significantly damage your database and reveal sensitive information. When you use parameterized SQL statements, the parameters are handled in a way that prevents this.

- Parameterized SQL statements, as we have shown in this recipe, allow you to reuse parts of the statement. This reuse can make your code more simple and easier to read.

- Following the re-use idea, most enterprise-class databases like Oracle Database, IBM DB2, and even Microsoft SQL Server in some circumstances, can take advantage of parameterized queries by reusing the parsed version of the query even if the parameters have changed. This boosts performance and lowers the processing overhead for SQL statement re-use.

- Parameterized SQL statements make your code more maintainable and configurable. For example, the statements could come from a configuration file. This would allow you to make some changes to the application without changing the code.

3-3. Fetching Objects with Native SQL Statements

Problem

You want to execute a native SQL statement and fetch objects from your database.

Solution

Let's say that you have a model with a Student entity type, as shown in Figure 3-4.

Figure 3-4. *A model with a Student entity type*

You want to execute a native SQL statement that returns a collection of instances of the Student entity type. As you saw in the previous recipe, the ExecuteSqlCommand() method is similar to ADO.NET SQLCommand's ExecuteNonQuery() method. It executes a given SQL statement and returns the number of rows affected. To have Entity Framework materialize this untyped data into strongly-typed entity objects, we can use the SqlQuery() method.

To start, this example leverages the Code-First approach for Entity Framework. In Listing 3-5, we create the Student entity class.

Listing 3-5. Student Entity Class

```
public class Student
{
    public int StudentId { get; set; }
    public string Degree { get; set; }
    public string FirstName { get; set; }
    public string LastName { get; set; }
}
```

Next, in Listing 3-6, we create the DbContext object required for our Code-First approach.

Listing 3-6. The DbContext Object

```
public class EFRecipesEntities : DbContext
{
    public EFRecipesEntities()
        : base("ConnectionString") {}

    public DbSet<Student> Students { get; set; }
```

```
    protected override void OnModelCreating(DbModelBuilder modelBuilder)
    {
        modelBuilder.Entity<Student>().ToTable("Chapter3.Student");
    }
}
```

To execute a SQL statement and get back a collection of instances of the Student entity type, follow the pattern in Listing 3-7.

Listing 3-7. Using ExecuteStoreQuery() to Execute a SQL statement and Get Back Objects

```
using (var context = new EFRecipesEntities())
{
    // delete previous test data
    context.Database.ExecuteSqlCommand("delete from chapter3.student");

    // insert student data
    context.Students.Add (new Student
    {
        FirstName = "Robert",

        LastName = "Smith",
        Degree = "Masters"
    });

    context.Students.Add (new Student
    {
        FirstName = "Julia",
        LastName = "Kerns", Degree = "Masters"
    });

    context.Students.Add (new Student
    {
        FirstName = "Nancy",

        LastName = "Stiles", Degree = "Doctorate"
    });

    context.SaveChanges();}

using (var context = new EFRecipesEntities())
{
    string sql = "select * from Chapter3.Student where Degree = @Major";
    var parameters = new DbParameter[] {
        new SqlParameter {ParameterName = "Major", Value = "Masters"}};
    var students = context.Students.SqlQuery(sql, parameters);
    Console.WriteLine("Students...");
    foreach (var student in students)
    {
        Console.WriteLine("{0} {1} is working on a {2} degree",
                    student.FirstName, student.LastName, student.Degree);
    }
}
```

Following is the output of the code in Listing 3-7:

```
Students...
Robert Smith is working on a Masters degree
Julia Kerns is working on a Masters degree
```

How It Works

In Listing 3-7, we add three Students to the DbContext and save them to the database using SaveChanges().

To retrieve the Students who are working on a master's degree, we use the SqlQuery() method with a parameterized SQL statement and a parameter set to "Masters." We iterate through the returned collection of Students and print each of them. Note that the associated context object implements change tracking for these values.

Here we use * in place of explicitly naming each column in the select statement. This works because the columns in the underlying table match the properties in the Student entity type. Entity Framework will match the returned values to the appropriate properties. This works fine in most cases, but if fewer columns returned from your query, Entity Framework will throw an exception during the materialization of the object. A much better approach and best practice is to enumerate the columns explicitly (that is, specify each column name) in your SQL statement.

If your SQL statement returns more columns than required to materialize the entity (that is, more column values than properties in the underlying entity object), Entity Framework will happily ignore the additional columns. If you think about this for a moment, you'll realize that this isn't a desirable behavior. Again, consider explicitly enumerating the expected columns in your SQL statement to ensure they match your entity type.

There are some restrictions around the SqlQuery() method. If you are using Table per Hierarchy inheritance and your SQL statement returns rows that could map to different derived types, Entity Framework will not be able to use the discriminator column to map the rows to the correct derived types. You will likely get a runtime exception because some rows don't contain the values required for the type being materialized.

Interestingly, you can use SqlQuery() to materialize objects that are not entities at all. For example, we could create a StudentName class that contains just first and last names of a student. If our SQL statement returned just these two strings, we could use SqlQuery<StudentName>() along with our SQL statement to fetch a collection of instances of StudentName.

We've been careful to use the phrase SQL statement rather than select statement because the SqlQuery() method works with any SQL statement that returns a row set. This includes, of course, Select statements, but it can also include statements that execute stored procedures.

3-4. Querying a Model with Entity SQL

Problem

You want to execute an Entity SQL statement that queries your underlying entity data model and returns strongly-typed objects.

Solution

Let's say that you have a model like the one shown in Figure 3-5, which contains a single Customer entity type. The Customer entity type has a Name and an Email property. You want to query this model using Entity SQL.

Figure 3-5. *A model with a Customer entity*

To query the model using Entity SQL (eSQL), a dialect of SQL implemented by Entity Framework, follow the pattern in Listing 3-8. Keep in mind that when querying the underlying data store, you should favor LINQ-to-Entity queries over eSQL, due to feature-rich and strong-typing experience that LINQ provides. Entity SQL gives you the flexibility to construct database queries dynamically against the entity data model.

Listing 3-8. Executing an Entity SQL Statement Using Both Object Services and EntityClient

```
using (var context = new EFRecipesEntities())
{
// delete previous test data
context.Database.ExecuteSqlCommand("delete from chapter3.customer");          // add new
 test data
var cus1 = new Customer { Name = "Robert Stevens",
                                Email = "rstevens@mymail.com" };
    var cus2 = new Customer { Name = "Julia Kerns",
                                Email = "julia.kerns@abc.com" };
    var cus3 = new Customer { Name = "Nancy Whitrock",
                                Email = "nrock@myworld.com" };
    context.Customers.Add(cus1);
    context.Customers.Add(cus2);
    context.Customers.Add(cus3);
    context.SaveChanges();
}

// using object services from ObjectContext object
using (var context = new EFRecipesEntities())
{
    Console.WriteLine("Querying Customers with eSQL Leveraging Object Services...");
    String esql = "select value c from Customers as c";
// cast the DbContext to the underlying ObjectContext, as DbContext does not
    // provide direct support for EntitySQL queries

    var customers = ((IObjectContextAdapter)context).ObjectContext.CreateQuery<Customer>(esql);
     Foreach (var customer in customers)
    {
        Console.WriteLine ("{0}'s email is: {1}",
                        customer.Name, customer.Email);
    }
}
```

```
Console.WriteLine();

// using EntityClient
using (var conn = new EntityConnection("name=EFRecipesEntities"))
{
    Console.WriteLine("Querying Customers with eSQL Leveraging Entity Client...");
    var cmd = conn.CreateCommand();
    conn.Open();
    cmd.CommandText = "select value c from EFRecipesEntities.Customers as c";
    using (var reader = cmd.ExecuteReader(CommandBehavior.SequentialAccess))
    {
        while (reader.Read())
        {
            Console.WriteLine("{0}'s email is: {1}",
                            reader.GetString(1), reader.GetString(2));
        }
    }
}
```

Following is the output from the code in Listing 3-8:

```
Querying Customers with eSQL Leveraging Object Services...
Robert Stevens's email is: rstevens@mymail.com
Julia Kerns's email is: julia.kerns@abc.com
Nancy Whitrock's email is: nrock@myworld.com
Customers Customers with eSQL Leveraging Entity Client...
Robert Stevens's email is: rstevens@mymail.com
Julia Kerns's email is: julia.kerns@abc.com
Nancy Whitrock's email is: nrock@myworld.com
```

How It Works

In Listing 3-8, we start by removing previous test data from the database. Then we create three customers, add them to the context object, and call SaveChanges() to insert them into the database.

With customers in the database, we demonstrate two different approaches to retrieving them using Entity SQL. In the first approach, we use the CreateQuery() method exposed by the legacy object context to create an ObjectQuery object. Note how we cast the DbContext to an ObjectContextAdapter type to get to its underlying ObjectContext type (keep in mind the newer DbContext *wraps* the older ObjectContext to improve the developer experience). We do so as the DbContext does not provide direct support for eSQL queries. Note as well how we assign the Customer class type to the generic placeholder value for CreateQuery() and pass in the eSQL query as a parameter. As we iterate over the customers collection, the query is executed against the database and the resulting collection is printed to the console. Because each element in the collection is an instance of our Customer entity type, we can use the properties of the Customer entity type to gain strongly typed usage.

In the second approach, we use the EntityClient libraries in a pattern that is very similar to how we would use SqlClient or any of the other client providers in ADO.NET. We start by creating a connection to the database. With the connection in hand, we create a command object and open the connection. Next we initialize the command object with the text of the Entity SQL statement we want to execute. We execute the command using ExecuteReader() and obtain an EntityDataReader, which is a type of the familiar DbDataReader. We iterate over the resulting collection using the Read () method.

Note that the Entity SQL statement in listing 3-8 uses the `value` keyword. This keyword is useful when we need to fetch the entire entity. If our Entity SQL statement projected a specific subset of columns (that is, we use some of the columns and/or create columns using Entity SQL expressions), we can dispense with the `value` keyword. When working with a context object, this means working with a `DbDataRecord` directly as demonstrated in Listing 3-9.

Listing 3-9. Projecting with Both Object Services and EntityClient

```
// using object services without the VALUE keyword
using (var context = new EFRecipesEntities())
{
    Console.WriteLine("Customers...");
    string esql = "select c.Name, c.Email from Customers as c";
    var records = context.CreateQuery<DbDataRecord>(esql);
    foreach (var record in records)
    {
        var name = record[0] as string;
        var email = record[1] as string;
        Console.WriteLine("{0}'s email is: {1}", name, email);
    }
}

Console.WriteLine();

// using EntityClient without the VALUE keyword
using (var conn = new EntityConnection("name=EFRecipesEntities"))
{
    Console.WriteLine("Customers...");
    var cmd = conn.CreateCommand();
    conn.Open();
    cmd.CommandText = @"select c.Name, C.Email from
                        EFRecipesEntities.Customers as c";
    using (var reader = cmd.ExecuteReader(CommandBehavior.SequentialAccess))
    {
        while (reader.Read())
        {
            Console.WriteLine("{0}'s email is: {1}",
                        reader.GetString(0), reader.GetString(1));
        }
    }
}
```

When you form a projection in Entity SQL, the results are returned in a `DbDataRecord` object that contains one element for each column in the projection. With the `value` keyword, the single object resulting from the query is returned in the first element of the `DbDataRecord`.

3-5. Finding a Master That Has Detail in a Master-Detail Relationship

Problem

You have two entities in a one-to-many association (aka Master-Detail), and you want to find all the master entities that have at least one associated detail entity.

Solution

Imagine that you have a model for blog posts and the comments associated with each post. Some posts have lots of comments. Some posts have few or no comments. The model might look something like the one shown in Figure 3-6.

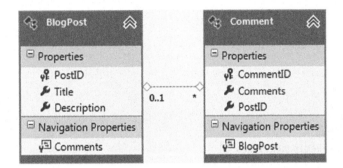

Figure 3-6. *A model for blog posts and the associated comments*

You want to find all of the blog posts that have at least one comment. To do this using either LINQ to Entities or Entity SQL, follow the pattern in Listing 3-10.

Listing 3-10. Finding the Masters That Have Detail Using Both LINQ and Entity SQL

```
using (var context = new EFRecipesEntities())
{
    // delete previous test data
    context.Database.ExecuteSqlCommand("delete from chapter3.blogpost");
    context.Database.ExecuteSqlCommand("delete from chapter3.comment");

    // add new test data
    var post1 = new BlogPost { Title = "The Joy of LINQ",
            Description = "101 things you always wanted to know about LINQ" };
    var post2 = new BlogPost { Title = "LINQ as Dinner Conversation",
            Description = "What wine goes with a Lambda expression?" };
    var post3 = new BlogPost {Title = "LINQ and our Children",
            Description = "Why we need to teach LINQ in High School"};
    var comment1 = new Comment {
        Comments = "Great post, I wish more people would talk about LINQ" };
    var comment2 = new Comment {
        Comments = "You're right, we should teach LINQ in high school!" };
    post1.Comments.Add(comment1);
    post3.Comments.Add(comment2);
```

```csharp
    context.BlogPosts.Add(post1);
    context.BlogPosts.Add(post2);
    context.BlogPosts.Add(post3);
    context.SaveChanges();
}

using (var context = new EFRecipesEntities())
{
    Console.WriteLine("Blog Posts with comments...(LINQ)");
    var posts = from post in context.BlogPosts
                where post.Comments.Any()
                select post;
    foreach (var post in posts)
    {
        Console.WriteLine("Blog Post: {0}", post.Title);
        foreach (var comment in post.Comments)
        {
            Console.WriteLine("\t{0}", comment.Comments);
        }
    }
}

Console.WriteLine();

using (var context = new EFRecipesEntities())
{
    Console.WriteLine("Blog Posts with comments...(ESQL)");
    var esql = "select value p from BlogPosts as p where exists(p.Comments)";
    var posts = ((IObjectContextAdapter)context).ObjectContext.CreateQuery<BlogPost>(esql);
    foreach (var post in posts)
    {
        Console.WriteLine("Blog Post: {0}", post.Title);
        foreach (var comment in post.Comments)
        {
            Console.WriteLine("\t{0}", comment.Comments);
        }
    }
}
```

Following is the output of the code in Listing 3-10:

```
Blog Posts with comments...(LINQ)
Blog Post: The Joy of LINQ
        Great post, I wish more people would talk about LINQ
Blog Post: LINQ and our Children
        You're right, we should teach LINQ in high school!
Blog Posts with comments...(ESQL)
Blog Post: The Joy of LINQ
        Great post, I wish more people would talk about LINQ
Blog Post: LINQ and our Children
        You're right, we should teach LINQ in high school!
```

How It Works

We start off the code in Listing 3-10 by deleting prior test data and inserting new blog posts and comments into the database. We left one of the blog posts without any comments to make sure our query performs correctly.

In the LINQ query, we leverage the LINQ Extension Method Any() in the where clause to determine whether there are comments for a given post. The query finds all of the posts for which the Any() method returns true. In this usage, we iterate through each blog post with Any() returning true if there are comments for the specific post. Moreover, that's just what we want: all of the posts for which there is at least one comment.

For the Entity SQL approach, we use the SQL exists() operator, again in a where clause, to determine whether the given post has at least one comment.

Of course there are other ways to get the same result. For example, we could use the Count() method in the LINQ query's where clause and test to see if the count is greater than 0. For the Entity SQL approach, we could use count(select value 1 from p.Comments) > 0 in the where clause. Either one of these approaches would work. However, the code in Listing 3-10 seems a bit cleaner and, from a performance perspective, the semantics behind Any() and exists() don't require the enumeration of the entire collection on the server (meaning that, after finding the first comment for a blog entry, the process moves onto to the next blog entry), whereas count() does require a full enumeration on the server (meaning that, each comment will be enumerated, despite the fact that one was already found).

3-6. Setting Default Values in a Query
Problem

You have a use case for which you must assign a default value to a property when the query returns a null value. In our recipe, we'll assign a value of '0' to the Years Worked property when a null value for it is returned from the database.

Solution

Let's say that you have a model like the one shown in Figure 3-7. You want to query the model for employees. In the database, the table representing employees contains a nullable YearsWorked column. This is the column mapped to the YearsWorked property in the Employee entity. You want the rows that contain a null value for the YearsWorked to default to the value 0.

Figure 3-7. *A model with an Employee entity type containing an EmployeeId property, a Name property, and a YearsWorked property*

To start, this example leverages the Code-First approach for Entity Framework. In Listing 3-11, we create the Student entity class.

Listing 3-11. Employee Entity Class

```
public class Employee
{
    public int EmployeeId { get; set; }
    public string Name { get; set; }
    public int? YearsWorked { get; set; }
}
```

Next, in Listing 3-12, we create the DbContext object required for our Code-First approach.

Listing 3-12. The DbContext Object

```
public class EFRecipesEntities : DbContext
{
    public EFRecipesEntities()
        : base("ConnectionString") {}

    public DbSet<Employee> Employees { get; set; }

    protected override void OnModelCreating(DbModelBuilder modelBuilder)
    {
        modelBuilder.Entity<Employee>().ToTable("Chapter3.Employee");
        base.OnModelCreating(modelBuilder);
    }
}
```

Since we are implementing the Code-First approach for Entity Framework, we can *programmatically* assign default values via a query as shown in Listing 3-13. Note that the pattern in Listing 3-13 doesn't actually materialize (return from the database) instances of the Employee entity type with the default value. Instead, it projects, that is, places the results of the query into a collection of an anonymous type whose YearsWorked property is programmatically set to the value of 0 whenever the underlying value is null. Thus the underlying value in the column remains NULL, but we project a value of zero as a default value in our Entity Framework result. Keep in mind that an anonymous type, as shown in Listing 3-13, is a class that gets created on the fly at runtime based on the properties that we include within the curly braces that immediately precede the new keyword.

Listing 3-13. Using Both LINQ and Entity SQL to Fill in Default Values for Nulls

```
using (var context = new EFRecipesEntities())
{
    // delete previous test data
    context.Database.ExecuteSqlCommand("delete from chapter3.employee");
    // add new test data
    context.Employees.Add(new Employee { Name = "Robin Rosen",
                                         YearsWorked = 3 });
    context.Employees.Add(new Employee { Name = "John Hancock" });
    context.SaveChanges();
}

using (var context = new EFRecipesEntities())
{
    Console.WriteLine("Employees (using LINQ)");
    var employees = from e in context.Employees
                    select new {Name = e.Name, YearsWorked = e.YearsWorked ?? 0};
```

```
        foreach(var employee in employees)
        {
            Console.WriteLine("{0}, years worked: {1}",employee.Name,
                              employee.YearsWorked);
        }
    }
}

using (var context = new EFRecipesEntities())
{
    Console.WriteLine("Employees (using ESQL w/named constructor)");
    string esql = @"select value Recipe3_6.Employee(e.EmployeeId,
                        e.Name,
                        case when e.YearsWorked is null then 0
                            else e.YearsWorked end)
                    from Employees as e";
    var employees = context.Database.SqlQuery<Employee>(esql);
    foreach(var employee in employees)
    {
        Console.WriteLine("{0}, years worked: {1}",employee.Name,
                          employee.YearsWorked.ToString());
    }
}
```

Following is the output of the code in Listing 3-13:

```
Employees (using LINQ)
Robin Rosen, years worked: 3
John Hancock, years worked: 0
Employees (using ESQL w/named constructor)
Robin Rosen, years worked: 3
John Hancock, years worked: 0
```

How It Works

Here, our approach is to use either LINQ or eSQL to project the results into a collection of an anonymous type. The query sets the YearsWorked to 0 when the underlying value is null.

For the LINQ approach, we use the C# null-coalescing operator ?? to assign the value of 0 when the underlying value is null. We project the results into a collection of an anonymous type.

For Entity SQL, we use a case statement to assign the value of 0 to YearsWorked when the underlying value is null. Here, we demonstrate how to use Entity SQL to materialize instances of the Employee entity type without setting the Default Value property for the entity. To do this, we use the named constructor for the entity type. This constructor assigns the values from the parameters to the properties in the same order as the properties are defined in the entity. In our case, the properties for the Employee entity are defined in the following order: EmployeeId, Name, and YearsWorked. The parameters to the constructor, as do our arguments in the eSQL query, follow this same order. Unfortunately, there is no corresponding name constructor syntax for LINQ to Entities.

3-7. Returning Multiple Result Sets from a Stored Procedure

Problem

You have a stored procedure that returns multiple result sets, and you want to materialize entities from each result set.

Solution

Suppose that you have a model like the one shown in Figure 3-8 and a stored procedure like the one shown in Listing 3-14, which returns both jobs and bids.

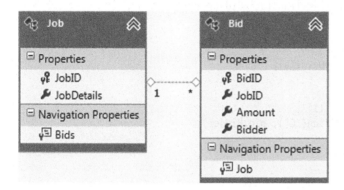

Figure 3-8. *A model representing jobs and bids for the jobs*

Listing 3-14. A Stored Procedure That Returns Multiple Result Sets

```
create procedure Chapter3.GetBidDetails
as
begin
  select * from Chapter3.Job
  select * from Chapter3.Bid
end
```

In our model, for each job we have zero or more bids. Our stored procedure returns all of the jobs and all of the bids. We want to execute the stored procedure and materialize all of the jobs and all of the bids from the two result sets. To do this, follow the pattern in Listing 3-15.

Listing 3-15. Materializing Jobs and Bids from the Two Result Sets Returned by Our Stored Procedure

```
using (var context = new EFRecipesEntities())
{
    var job1 = new Job { JobDetails = "Re-surface Parking Log" };
    var job2 = new Job { JobDetails = "Build Driveway" };
    job1.Bids.Add(new Bid { Amount = 948M, Bidder = "ABC Paving" });
    job1.Bids.Add(new Bid { Amount = 1028M, Bidder = "TopCoat Paving" });
    job2.Bids.Add(new Bid { Amount = 502M, Bidder = "Ace Concrete" });
    context.Jobs.AddObject(job1);
    context.Jobs.AddObject(job2);
    context.SaveChanges();
}
```

```
using (var context = new EFRecipesEntities())
{
    var conn = context.Database.Connection;
    var cmd = conn.CreateCommand();
    cmd.CommandType = System.Data.CommandType.StoredProcedure;
    cmd.CommandText = "Chapter3.GetBidDetails";
    conn.Open();
    var reader = cmd.ExecuteReader(CommandBehavior.CloseConnection);
    var jobs = ((IObjectContextAdapter)context).ObjectContext.Translate<Job>(reader, "Jobs",
                                MergeOption.AppendOnly).ToList();
    reader.NextResult();
    ((IObjectContextAdapter)context).ObjectContext.Translate<Bid>(reader, "Bids",
MergeOption.AppendOnly).ToList();
    foreach (var job in jobs)
    {
        Console.WriteLine("\nJob: {0}", job.JobDetails);
        foreach (var bid in job.Bids)
        {
            Console.WriteLine("\tBid: {0} from {1}",
                            bid.Amount.ToString("C"), bid.Bidder);
        }
    }
}
```

Following is the output of the code in Listing 3-15:

```
Job: Re-surface Parking Log
        Bid: $948.00 from ABC Paving
        Bid: $1,028.00 from TopCoat Paving

Job: Build Driveway
        Bid: $502.00 from Ace Concrete
```

How It Works

We start out by adding a couple of jobs and a few bids for the jobs. After adding them to the context, we use
SaveChanges() to save them to the database.

Entity Framework 5.0 has improved capabilities for working with multiple results sets returned from a stored
procedure. However, to leverage this functionality, you'll have to use the legacy ObjectContext object, as the more
recent DbContext object does not directly support multiple result sets. To solve the problem, we read the stored
procedure data using the familiar SqlClient pattern. This pattern involves creating a SqlConnection, SqlCommand
setting the command text to the name of the stored procedure and calling ExecuteReader() to get a data reader.

With a reader in hand, we use the Translate() method from the ObjectContext to materialize instances of the
Job entity from the reader. This method takes a reader; the entity set name, and a merge option. The entity set name
is required because an entity can live in multiple entity sets. Entity Framework needs to know which to use.

The merge option parameter is a little more interesting. Using MergeOption.AppendOnly causes the new instances
to be added to the object context and tracked. We use this option because we want to use Entity Framework's entity
span to *fix up* the associations automatically between jobs and bids. For this to happen, we simply add to the context
all of the jobs and all of the bids. Entity Framework will automatically associate the bids to the right jobs. This saves us
a great deal of tedious code.

A simpler version of the `Translate()` method does not require a `MergeOption`. This version materializes objects that are disconnected from the object context. This is subtly different from objects that are not tracked in that the objects are created completely outside of the object context. If you were to use this simpler `Translate()` to read the jobs, you would not be able later to materialize new bids into the object context because Entity Framework would not have any reference to the associated jobs. Those jobs are completely disconnected from the object context. Additionally, you cannot change the properties of the instances and expect Entity Framework to be able to save those changes.

We used `ToList()` to force the evaluation of each query. This is required because the `Translate()` method returns an `ObjectResult<T>`. It does not actually cause the results to be read from the reader. We need to force the results to be read from the reader before we can use `NextResult()` to advance to the next result set. In practice, you would most likely construct your code to continue to loop through each result set with `NextResult()` that the stored procedure might return.

Although we didn't run into it in this example, it is important to note that `Translate()` bypasses the mapping layer of the model. If you try to map an inheritance hierarchy or use an entity that has complex type properties, `Translate()` will fail. `Translate()` requires that the `DbDataReader` have columns that match each property on the entity. This matching is done using simple name matching. If a column name can't be matched to a property, `Translate()` will fail.

3-8. Comparing Against a List of Values
Problem

You want to query entities in which a specific property value matches a value contained in a given list.

Solution

Suppose that you have a model like the one shown in Figure 3-9.

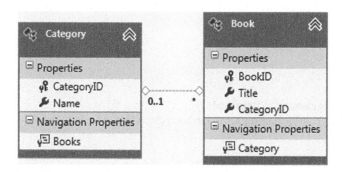

Figure 3-9. A model for books and their categories

You want to find all of the books in a given list of categories. To do this using LINQ or Entity SQL, follow the pattern in Listing 3-16.

Listing 3-16. Finding Books in a List of Categories Using Both LINQ and Entity SQL

```
using (var context = new EFRecipesEntities())
{
    // delete previous test data
    context.Database.ExecuteSqlCommand("delete from chapter3.category");
    context.Database.ExecuteSqlCommand("delete from chapter3.book");
    // add new test data
    var cat1 = new Category { Name = "Programming" };
    var cat2 = new Category { Name = "Databases" };
    var cat3 = new Category {Name = "Operating Systems"};
    context.Books.Add(new Book { Title = "F# In Practice", Category = cat1 });
    context.Books.Add(new Book { Title = "The Joy of SQL", Category = cat2 });
    context.Books.Add(new Book { Title = "Windows 7: The Untold Story",
                                    Category = cat3 });
    context.SaveChanges();
}

using (var context = new EFRecipesEntities())
{
    Console.WriteLine("Books (using LINQ)");
    var cats = new List<string> { "Programming", "Databases" };
    var books = from b in context.Books
                where cats.Contains(b.Category.Name)
                select b;
    foreach (var book in books)
    {
        Console.WriteLine("'{0}' is in category: {1}", book.Title,
                            book.Category.Name);
    }
}

using (var context = new EFRecipesEntities())
{
    Console.WriteLine("Books (using ESQL)");
    var esql = @"select value b from Books as b
                where b.Category.Name in {'Programming','Databases'}";
    var books = ((IObjectContextAdapter)context).ObjectContext.CreateQuery<Book>(esql);
    foreach (var book in books)
    {
        Console.WriteLine("'{0}' is in category: {1}", book.Title,
                            book.Category.Name);
    }
}
```

Following is the output of the code in Listing 3-16:

```
Books (using LINQ)
'F# In Practice' is in category: Programming
'The Joy of SQL' is in category: Databases
Books (using ESQL)
'F# In Practice' is in category: Programming
'The Joy of SQL' is in category: Databases
```

How It Works

For the LINQ query, we build a simple list of category names and include the list in the query along with the LINQ Contains query operator. The observant reader will note that we start with the cats collection and determine if it contains any category names. Entity Framework translates the Contains clause to a SQL statement with an in clause, as shown in Listing 3-17.

Listing 3-17. The SQL Statement Created for the LINQ Expression from Listing 3-16

```
SELECT
[Extent1].[BookId] AS [BookId],
[Extent1].[Title] AS [Title],
[Extent1].[CategoryId] AS [CategoryId]
FROM  [chapter3].[Books] AS [Extent1]
LEFT OUTER JOIN [chapter3].[Category] AS [Extent2] ON [Extent1].[CategoryId] = [Extent2].[CategoryId]
WHERE [Extent2].[Name] IN (N'Programming',N'Databases')
```

It is interesting to note that the generated SQL statement in Listing 3-17 does not use parameters for the items in the in clause. This is different from the generated code we would see with LINQ to SQL, where the items in the list would be parameterized. With this code, we don't run the risk of exceeding the parameters limit that is imposed by SQL Server.

If we are interested in finding all of the books in a given list of categories that are not yet categorized, we simply include null in the category list. The generated code is shown in Listing 3-18.

Listing 3-18. The SQL Statement Created for a LINQ Expression Like the One in Listing 3-16, but with a Null in the List of Categories

```
SELECT
[Extent1].[BookId] AS [BookId],
[Extent1].[Title] AS [Title],
[Extent1].[CategoryId] AS [CategoryId]
FROM  [chapter3].[Books] AS [Extent1]
LEFT OUTER JOIN [chapter3].[Category] AS [Extent2] ON [Extent1].[CategoryId] = [Extent2].[CategoryId]
WHERE [Extent2].[Name] IN (N'Programming',N'Databases')

    OR [Extent2].[Name] IS NULL
```

For parity, we also include an Entity SQL version of the query, in which we explicitly include a SQL IN clause.

3-9. Filtering Related Entities

Problem

You want to want to retrieve some, but not all, related entities.

Solution

Let's say that you have a model like the one shown in Figure 3-10.

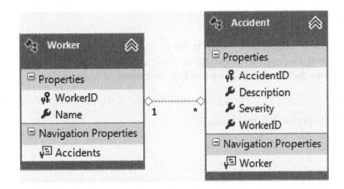

Figure 3-10. *A model for a Worker and their Accidents*

In this model, we have a Worker who has experienced zero or more accidents. Each accident is classified by its severity. We want to retrieve all workers, but we are interested only in serious accidents. These are accidents with a severity greater than 2.

To start, this example leverages the Code-First approach for Entity Framework. In Listing 3-19, we create entity classes for Worker and Accidents.

Listing 3-19. Worker Entity Class

```
public class Worker
{
    public Worker()
    {
        Accidents = new HashSet<Accident>();
    }

    public int WorkerId { get; set; }
    public string Name { get; set; }

    public virtual ICollection<Accident> Accidents { get; set; }
}

public class Accident
{
    public int AccidentId { get; set; }
    public string Description { get; set; }
```

```
    public int? Severity { get; set; }
    public int WorkerId { get; set; }

    public virtual Worker Worker { get; set; }
}
```

Next, in Listing 3-20, we create the DbContext object required for our Code-First approach.

Listing 3-20. The DbContext Object

```
public class EFRecipesEntities : DbContext
{
    public EFRecipesEntities()
        : base("ConnectionString") {}

    public DbSet<Accident> Accidents { get; set; }
    public DbSet<Worker> Workers { get; set; }

    protected override void OnModelCreating(DbModelBuilder modelBuilder)
    {
        modelBuilder.Entity<Accident>().ToTable("Chapter3.Accident");
        modelBuilder.Entity<Worker>().ToTable("Chapter3.Worker");
        base.OnModelCreating(modelBuilder);
    }
}
```

To retrieve all of the workers, but limit the accidents retrieved to just the serious ones, follow the pattern in Listing 3-21.

Listing 3-21. Retrieving Serious Accidents Using Anonymous Types and Using CreateSourceQuery()

```
using (var context = new EFRecipesEntities())
{
    // delete previous test data
    context.Database.ExecuteSqlCommand("delete from chapter3.accident");
    context.Database.ExecuteSqlCommand("delete from chapter3.worker");
    // add new test data
    var worker1 = new Worker { Name = "John Kearney" };
    var worker2 = new Worker { Name = "Nancy Roberts" };
    var worker3 = new Worker { Name = "Karla Gibbons" };
    context.Accidents.Add(new Accident {
                Description = "Cuts and contusions",
                Severity = 3, Worker = worker1 });
    context.Accidents.Add(new Accident {
                Description = "Broken foot",
                Severity = 4, Worker = worker1});
    context.Accidents.Add(new Accident {
                Description = "Fall, no injuries",
                Severity = 1, Worker = worker2});
    context.Accidents.Add(new Accident {
                Description = "Minor burn",
                Severity = 3, Worker = worker2});
```

```
        context.Accidents.Add(new Accident {
                    Description = "Back strain",
                    Severity = 2, Worker = worker3});
        context.SaveChanges();
}

using (var context = new EFRecipesEntities())
{
    // explicitly disable lazy loading
    context.Configuration.LazyLoadingEnabled = false;
    var query = from w in context.Workers
                select new
                {
                    Worker = w,
                    Accidents = w.Accidents.Where(a => a.Severity > 2)
                };
    query.ToList();
    var workers = query.Select(r => r.Worker);
    Console.WriteLine("Workers with serious accidents...");
    foreach (var worker in workers)
    {
        Console.WriteLine("{0} had the following accidents", worker.Name);
        if (worker.Accidents.Count == 0)
            Console.WriteLine("\t--None--");
        foreach (var accident in worker.Accidents)
        {
            Console.WriteLine("\t{0}, severity: {1}",
                    accident.Description, accident.Severity.ToString());
        }
    }
}
```

Following is the output of the code in Listing 3-21:

```
Workers with serious accidents...
John Kearney had the following accidents
        Cuts and contusions, severity: 3
        Broken foot, severity: 4
Nancy Roberts had the following accidents
        Minor burn, severity: 3
Karla Gibbons had the following accidents
        --None--
```

How It Works

As you will see in Chapter 5, when we want to eagerly load a related collection, we often use the Include() method with a query path. (The Include() method returns the parent entity along with all of the child entities in a single query.) However, the Include() method does not allow filtering on the related child entities. In this recipe, we show a slight variation that allows you to load and filter related child entities.

In the block of code, we create a few workers and assign them accidents of varying levels of severity. Granted, it's a little creepy to assign accidents to people, but it's all in the name of getting some data with which you can work.

In the subsequent query, we select from all of the workers and project the results into an anonymous type. The type includes the worker and the collection of accidents. For the accidents, notice how we filter the collection to get just the serious accidents.

The very next line is important. Here we force the evaluation of the query by calling the ToList() method. (Keep in mind that LINQ queries typically default to deferred loading, meaning that the query is not actually executed until necessary. The ToList() method forces this very execution.) Enumerating this query brings all of the workers and all of the serious accidents into the DbContext. The anonymous type didn't attach the accidents to the workers, but by bringing them into the Context, Entity Framework will fix up the navigation properties, attaching each collection of serious accidents to the appropriate worker. This process, commonly known as *Entity Span*, is a powerful yet subtle side effect that happens behind the scenes to fix up relationships between entities as they are materialized into the Entity Framework Context object.

We've turned off lazy loading so that only the accidents in our filter are loaded. (We'll discuss lazy loading further Chapter 5.) With lazy loading on, all of the accidents would get loaded when we referenced each worker's accidents. That would defeat the purpose of the filter.

Once we have the collection, we iterate through it, printing out each worker and their serious accidents. If a worker didn't have any serious accidents, we print none to indicate their stellar safety record.

3-10. Applying a Left-Outer Join
Problem

You want to combine the properties of two entities using a left-outer join.

Solution

Suppose that you have a model like the one shown in Figure 3-11.

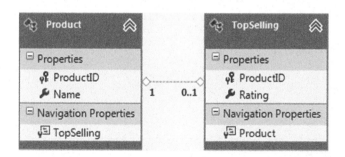

Figure 3-11. *Our model with a Product entity type and its related TopSelling entity type*

The top-selling products have a related TopSelling entity. Of course, not all products are top sellers, and that's why the relationship is one to zero or one. When a product is a top seller, the related TopSeller entity also contains the customer rating for the product. You want to find and present all of the products and their related TopSeller entities even if, in some cases, the product is not a top seller. In the case where a product does not have a related TopSelling entity, we simply set to the rating to "0". In database terms, this is called a *left-outer join*.

The code in Listing 3-22 demonstrates three slightly different approaches to this problem.

Listing 3-22. Doing a Left-Outer Join Between Entities

```
using (var context = new EFRecipesEntities())
{
    // delete previous test data
    context.Database.ExecuteSqlCommand("delete from chapter3.topselling");
    context.Database.ExecuteSqlCommand("delete from chapter3.product");
    // add new test data
    // note that p1 has no associated TopSelling entity as do the other products
    var p1 = new Product { Name = "Trailrunner Backpack" };
    var p2 = new Product { Name = "Green River Tent",
                             TopSelling = new TopSelling { Rating = 3 } };
    var p3 = new Product { Name = "Prairie Home Dutch Oven",
                             TopSelling = new TopSelling { Rating = 4 } };
    var p4 = new Product { Name = "QuickFire Fire Starter",
                             TopSelling = new TopSelling { Rating = 2 } };
    context.Products.Add(p1);
    context.Products.Add(p2);
    context.Products.Add(p3);
    context.Products.Add(p4);
    context.SaveChanges();
}

using (var context = new EFRecipesEntities())
{
    var products = from p in context.Products
                   orderby p.TopSelling.Rating descending
                   select p;
    Console.WriteLine("All products, including those without ratings");
    foreach (var product in products)
    {
        Console.WriteLine("\t{0} [rating: {1}]", product.Name,
            product.TopSelling == null ? "0"
                : product.TopSelling.Rating.ToString());
    }
}

using (var context = new EFRecipesEntities())
{
    var products = from p in context.Products
                   join t in context.TopSellings on
                       // note how we project the results together into another
                       // sequence, entitled 'g' and apply the DefaultIfEmpty method
                       p.ProductID equals t.ProductID into g
                   from tps in g.DefaultIfEmpty()
                   orderby tps.Rating descending
                   select new
                   {
                       Name = p.Name,
                       Rating = tps.Rating == null ? 0 : tps.Rating
                   };
```

```
        Console.WriteLine("\nAll products, including those without ratings
                                                                  ");
        foreach (var product in products)
        {
            if (product.Rating != 0)
                Console.WriteLine("\t{0} [rating: {1}]", product.Name,
                    product.Rating.ToString());
        }
}

using (var context = new EFRecipesEntities())
{
    var esql = @"select value p from products as p
                    order by case when p.TopSelling is null then 0
                                        else p.TopSelling.Rating end desc";
    var products =((IObjectContextAdapter)context).ObjectContext.CreateQuery<Product>(esql);
    Console.WriteLine("\nAll products, including those without ratings
                                      ");
    foreach (var product in products)
    {
        Console.WriteLine("\t{0} [rating: {1}]", product.Name,
            product.TopSelling == null ? "0"
                : product.TopSelling.Rating.ToString());

    }
}
```

Following is the output of the code in Listing 3-22:

```
Top selling products sorted by rating
        Prairie Home Dutch Oven [rating: 4]
        Green River Tent [rating: 3]
        QuickFire Fire Starter [rating: 2]
                Trailrunner Backpack [rating: 0]Top selling products sorted by rating
        Prairie Home Dutch Oven [rating: 4]
        Green River Tent [rating: 3]
        QuickFire Fire Starter [rating: 2]
                Trailrunner Backpack [rating: 0]Top selling products sorted by rating
        Prairie Home Dutch Oven [rating: 4]
        Green River Tent [rating: 3]
        QuickFire Fire Starter [rating: 2]
                Trailrunner Backpack [rating: 0]
```

How It Works

In Listing 3-22, we show three slightly different approaches to this problem. The first approach is the simplest, as Entity Framework handles the join automatically for related entities based on a navigation property that was created between the two entities when the model was created. The entities are in a one-to-zero or one association, which means that Entity Framework will automatically generate a SQL query that includes a left-outer join between the two entities. When the product entities are materialized, any associated top sellers are also materialized. The TopSeller navigation property is either set to the associated TopSeller entity or to null if no TopSeller exists. If a TopSeller entity does not exist for a given Product (that is, it has not been rated as a top seller), we simply assign a value of "0" for the Product Rating.

In some cases, you might not have a relationship (for instance, a navigation property) between the entities that you want to join. In these cases, you can *explicitly join* the entities, projecting the results into an anonymous type. We need to project into an anonymous type because the unrelated entities won't have navigation properties, so we wouldn't otherwise be able to reference the related entity.

The code in the second query block illustrates this approach. Here we join the entities on the ProductId key and put the result into a new sequence entitled "g". Then, from g we apply the DefaultIfEmpty() method to fill in nulls when g is empty. Sure enough, when the SQL is generated, it includes a left-outer join between the two entities. We include an orderby clause to order the results by the rating. Finally, we project the results into an anonymous type.

In the third approach, we show you how to do the left-outer join more explicitly using Entity SQL, embedding an Entity SQL Case statement within the query.

3-11. Ordering by Derived Types
Problem

You are using Table per Hierarchy inheritance, and you want to sort results by the derived type.

Solution

Let's suppose that you have a model like the one shown in Figure 3-12.

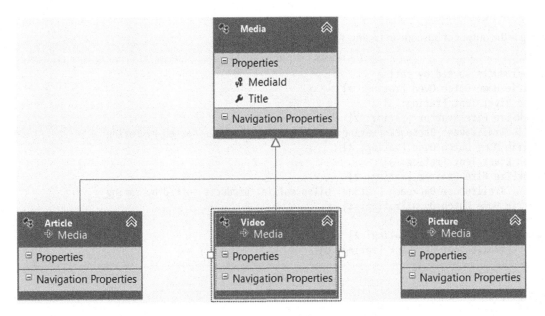

Figure 3-12. *A model using Table per Hierarchy inheritance with three derived types*

This model uses Table per Hierarchy inheritance (TPH), which is a feature of Entity Framework. TPH creates an inheritance structure where a parent and given number of related child classes all derive from a single database table.

In this example, the Media entity has a property entitled MediaType, which is used as a *discriminator property* for our TPH construct. The value of MediaType determines which derived type (Article, Picture, or Video) is represented by a row from the database. The discriminator column has a value of 1 for an Article type, 2 for a Video type, and 3 for the Picture type. Because the property is used only to determine the derived type, it is not shown as part of the Media entity.

To start, this example leverages the Code-First approach for Entity Framework. In Listing 3-23, we create the entity classes. To keep the example simple, we'll create empty child objects, as we only want to demonstrate how to order a query based on a derived type.

Listing 3-23. Parent and Child Entity Types

```
public class Media
{
    public int MediaId { get; set; }
    public string Title { get; set; }
}

public class Article : Media
{
}

public class Picture : Media
{
}
public class Video : Media
{
}
```

Next, in Listing 3-24, we create the DbContext object, which is your gateway into Entity Framework functionality when leveraging the Code-First approach. Note how in the OnModelCreating method, we explicitly map the discriminator column, MediaType, to the child entities using a FluentAPI coding approach (that is, chaining together extension methods to create an operation).

Listing 3-24. The DbContext Object

```
public class EFRecipesEntities : DbContext
{
    public EFRecipesEntities()
        : base("ConnectionString")
    {
    }

    public DbSet<Media> Media { get; set; }

    protected override void OnModelCreating(DbModelBuilder modelBuilder)
    {
        modelBuilder.Entity<Media>().ToTable("Chapter3.Media");
```

```
        // Map child entities to the 'Discriminator' column, MediaType, from parent table,
        // which will determine the type of medium
        modelBuilder.Entity<Media>().Map<Article>(x => x.Requires("MediaType").HasValue(1));
        modelBuilder.Entity<Media>().Map<Picture>(x => x.Requires("MediaType").HasValue(2));
        modelBuilder.Entity<Media>().Map<Video>(x => x.Requires("MediaType").HasValue(3));

        base.OnModelCreating(modelBuilder);
    }
}
```

With the Code-First artifacts created, we'll query the model for all of the media and sort the results by the derived types: Article, Video, and Picture. To do this, follow the pattern in Listing 3-25.

Listing 3-25. Sorting Table per Hierarchy Inheritance by Type

```
using (var context = new EFRecipesEntities())
{
    context.Media.Add(new Article {
                Title = "Woodworkers' Favorite Tools" });
    context.Media.Add(new Article {
                Title = "Building a Cigar Chair" });
    context.Media.Add(new Video {
                Title = "Upholstering the Cigar Chair" });
    context.Media.Add(new Video {
                Title = "Applying Finish to the Cigar Chair" });
    context.Media.Add(new Picture {
                Title = "Photos of My Cigar Chair" });
    context.Media.Add(new Video {
                Title = "Tour of My Woodworking Shop" });
    context.SaveChanges();
}

using (var context = new EFRecipesEntities())
{
    var allMedia = from m in context.Media
                let mediatype = m is Article ? 1 :
                                    m is Video ? 2 : 3
                orderby mediatype
                select m;
    Console.WriteLine("All Media sorted by type...");
    foreach (var media in allMedia)
    {
        Console.WriteLine("Title: {0} [{1}]", media.Title, media.GetType().Name);
    }
}
```

Following is the output of the code in Listing 3-25:

```
All Media sorted by type...
Title: Woodworkers' Favorite Tools [Article]
Title: Building a Cigar Chair [Article]
Title: Upholstering the Cigar Chair [Video]
Title: Applying Finish to the Cigar Chair [Video]
Title: Tour of My Woodworking Shop [Video]
Title: Photos of My Cigar Chair [Picture]
```

How It Works

When we use Table per Hierarchy inheritance, we leverage a column in the table to distinguish which derived type represents any given row. This column, often referred to as the discriminator column, can't be mapped to a property of the base entity. Because we don't have a property with the discriminator value, we need to create a variable to hold comparable discriminator values so that we can do the sort. To do this, we use a LINQ let clause, which creates a the mediatype variable. We use a conditional statement to assign an integer to this variable based on the type of the media. For Articles, we assign the value 1. For Videos, we assign the value 2. We assign a value of 3 to anything else, which will always be of type Picture because no other derived types remain.

3-12. Paging and Filtering

Problem

You want to create a query with a filter and paging.

Solution

Let's say that you have a Customer entity type in a model, as shown in Figure 3-13.

Figure 3-13. *A model with a Customer entity type*

You have an application that displays customers based on a filter. Your company has many customers (perhaps millions!), and to keep the user experience as responsive as possible, you want to show only a limited number of customers on each page. To create a query that both filters the customers and returns a manageable set for each results page in your application, follow the pattern in Listing 3-26.

Listing 3-26. *Filtering and Paging a Query*

```
using (var context = new EFRecipesEntities())
{
    // delete previous test data
    context.Database.ExecuteSqlCommand("delete from chapter3.customer");
    // add new test data
    context.Customers.Add(new Customer { Name = "Roberts, Jill",
                                Email = "jroberts@abc.com" });
    context.Customers.Add(new Customer { Name = "Robertson, Alice",
                                Email = "arob@gmail.com" });
    context.Customers.Add(new Customer { Name = "Rogers, Steven",
                                Email = "srogers@termite.com" });
    context.Customers.Add(new Customer { Name = "Roe, Allen",
                                Email = "allenr@umc.com" });
    context.Customers.Add(new Customer { Name = "Jones, Chris",
                                Email = "cjones@ibp.com" });
    context.SaveChanges();
}

using (var context = new EFRecipesEntities())
{
    string match = "Ro";
    int pageIndex = 0;
    int pageSize = 3;

    var customers = context.Customers.Where(c => c.Name.StartsWith(match))
                        .OrderBy(c => c.Name)
                        .Skip(pageIndex * pageSize)
                        .Take(pageSize);
    Console.WriteLine("Customers Ro*");
    foreach (var customer in customers)
    {
        Console.WriteLine("{0} [email: {1}]", customer.Name, customer.Email);
    }
}
using (var context = new EFRecipesEntities())
{
    string match = "Ro%";
    int pageIndex = 0;
    int pageSize = 3;

    var esql = @"select value c from Customers as c
                where c.Name like @Name
                order by c.Name
                skip @Skip limit @Limit";
    Console.WriteLine("\nCustomers Ro*");
```

```
    var customers =
        ((IObjectContextAdapter)context).ObjectContext.CreateQuery<Customer>(esql, new[]
                        {
                            new ObjectParameter("Name",match),
                            new ObjectParameter("Skip",pageIndex * pageSize),
                            new ObjectParameter("Limit",pageSize)
                        });
    foreach (var customer in customers)
    {
        Console.WriteLine("{0} [email: {1}]", customer.Name, customer.Email);
    }
}
```

Following is the output from the code in Listing 3-26:

```
Customers Ro*
Roberts, Jill [email: jroberts@abc.com]
Robertson, Alice [email: arob@gmail.com]
Roe, Allen [email: allenr@umc.com]

Customers Ro*
Roberts, Jill [email: jroberts@abc.com]
Robertson, Alice [email: arob@gmail.com]
Roe, Allen [email: allenr@umc.com]
```

How It Works

In Listing 3-26, we show two different approaches to the problem. In the first approach, we use LINQ-To-Entities extension methods to construct a LINQ query. We use the Where() method to filter the results to customers whose last name starts with Ro. Because we are using the StartsWith() extension method inside the lambda expression, we don't need to use a SQL wildcard expression such as "Ro%".

After filtering, we use the OrderBy() method to order the results. Ordered results are required by the Skip() method. We use the Skip() method to move over pageIndex number of pages, each of size pageSize. We limit the results with the Take() method. We only need to take one page of results.

Note that in this code block, we create the entire query using LINQ extension methods and not the SQL query-like expressions that we have seen in examples up to now. Both the Skip() and Take() methods are only exposed by extension methods, not query syntax.

For the second approach, we construct a complete, parameterized Entity SQL expression. This is perhaps the most familiar way to solve the problem, but it exposes some of the inherent mismatch risks between a query language expressed using strings and executable code expressed, in this case, in C#.

3-13. Grouping by Date
Problem

You have an entity type with a DateTime property, and you want to group instances of this type based on just the date portion of the property.

Solution

Let's say that you have a Registration entity type in your model, and the Registration type has a DateTime property. Your model might look like the one shown in Figure 3-14.

Figure 3-14. *A model with a single Registration entity type. The entity type's RegistrationDate property is a DateTime*

To start, this example leverages the Code-First approach for Entity Framework. In Listing 3-27, we create the entity classes.

Listing 3-27. Registration Entity Type

```
public class Registration
{
    public int RegistrationId { get; set; }
    public string StudentName { get; set; }
    public DateTime? RegistrationDate { get; set; }
}
```

Next, in Listing 3-28, we create the DbContext object, which is your gateway into Entity Framework functionality when leveraging the Code-First approach.

Listing 3-28. The DbContext Object

```
public class EFRecipesEntities : DbContext
{
    public EFRecipesEntities()
        : base("ConnectionString") {}

    public DbSet<Registration> Registrations { get; set; }

    protected override void OnModelCreating(DbModelBuilder modelBuilder)
    {
        modelBuilder.Entity<Registration>().ToTable("Chapter3.Registration");
        base.OnModelCreating(modelBuilder);
    }
}
```

We want to group all of the registrations by just the date portion of the RegistrationDate property. You might be tempted in LINQ to group by RegistrationDate.Date. Although this will compile, you will receive a runtime error complaining that Date can't be translated into SQL. To group by just the date portion of the RegistrationDate, follow the pattern in Listing 3-29.

Listing 3-29. Grouping by the Date Portion of a DateTime Property

```
using (var context = new EFRecipesEntities())
{
    context.Registrations.Add(new Registration {
            StudentName = "Jill Rogers",
            RegistrationDate = DateTime.Parse("12/03/2009 9:30 pm") });
    context.Registrations.Add(new Registration {
            StudentName = "Steven Combs",
            RegistrationDate = DateTime.Parse("12/03/2009 10:45 am") });
    context.Registrations.Add(new Registration {
            StudentName = "Robin Rosen",
            RegistrationDate = DateTime.Parse("12/04/2009 11:18 am") });
    context.Registrations.Add(new Registration {
            StudentName = "Allen Smith",
            RegistrationDate = DateTime.Parse("12/04/2009 3:31 pm") });
    context.SaveChanges();
}

using (var context = new EFRecipesEntities())
{
    var groups = from r in context.Registrations
    // leverage built-in TruncateTime function to extract date portion
                 group r by DbFunctions.TruncateTime(r.RegistrationDate)
                    into g
                    select g;
    foreach (var element in groups)
    {
        Console.WriteLine("Registrations for {0}",
                ((DateTime)element.Key).ToShortDateString());
        foreach (var registration in element)
        {
            Console.WriteLine("\t{0}", registration.StudentName);
        }
    }
}
```

Following is the output of the code in Listing 3-29:

```
Registrations for 12/3/2009
        Jill Rogers
        Steven Combs
Registrations for 12/4/2009
        Robin Rosen
        Allen Smith
```

How It Works

The key to grouping the registrations by the date portion of the RegistrationDate property is to use the `Truncate()` function. This built-in Entity Framework function, contained in the `DbFunctions` class, extracts just the date portion of the DateTime value. The built-in `DbFunctions` contain a wide array of formatting, aggregation, string manipulation, date-time, and mathematical services, and they are found in the `System.Data.Entity` namespace. The legacy class, `EntityFunctions`, used prior to Entity Framework 6, will still work with Entity Framework 6, but will give you a compiler warning suggesting you move to the `DbFunctions` class. We'll have a lot more to say about functions in Chapter 11.

3-14. Flattening Query Results
Problem

You have two entity types in a one-to-many association, and you want, in one query, to obtain a flattened projection of all of the entities in the association. By flattened, we are referring to denormalizing, or compressing, an object graph with parent/child relationships into a result represented by a single class.

Solution

Let's say that you have a couple of entity types in a one-to-many association. Perhaps your model looks something like the one shown in Figure 3-15.

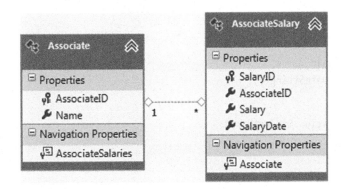

Figure 3-15. *A model with an Associate entity type representing an associate, and an AssociateSalary entity type representing the salary history for the associate*

You want to get all of the associates and all of their salary history in one query. There may be some new hires that are in the system, but they don't yet have a salary set. You want your query results to include these associates as well.

To query the model and get the results you want, follow the pattern in Listing 3-30.

Listing 3-30. Flattening Out the Results Using Both LINQ and Entity SQL

```
using (var context = new EFRecipesEntities())
{
    // delete previous test data
    context.Database.ExecuteSqlCommand("delete from chapter3.associatesalary");
    context.Database.ExecuteSqlCommand("delete from chapter3.associate");
    // add new test data
```

```
    var assoc1 = new Associate { Name = "Janis Roberts" };
    var assoc2 = new Associate { Name = "Kevin Hodges" };
    var assoc3 = new Associate { Name = "Bill Jordan" };
    var salary1 = new AssociateSalary { Salary = 39500M,
                        SalaryDate = DateTime.Parse("8/4/09") };
    var salary2 = new AssociateSalary { Salary = 41900M,
                        SalaryDate = DateTime.Parse("2/5/10") };
    var salary3 = new AssociateSalary { Salary = 33500M,
                        SalaryDate = DateTime.Parse("10/08/09") };
    assoc2.AssociateSalaries.Add(salary1);
    assoc2.AssociateSalaries.Add(salary2);
    assoc3.AssociateSalaries.Add(salary3);
    context.Associates.Add(assoc1);
    context.Associates.Add(assoc2);
    context.Associates.Add(assoc3);
    context.SaveChanges();
}

using (var context = new EFRecipesEntities())
{
    Console.WriteLine("Using LINQ...");
    var allHistory = from a in context.Associates
                     from ah in a.AssociateSalaries.DefaultIfEmpty()
                     orderby a.Name
                     select new
                     {
                         Name = a.Name,
                         Salary = (decimal ?) ah.Salary,
                         Date = (DateTime ?) ah.SalaryDate
                     };
    Console.WriteLine("Associate Salary History");
    foreach (var history in allHistory)
    {
        if (history.Salary.HasValue)
            Console.WriteLine("{0} Salary on {1} was {2}", history.Name,
                            history.Date.Value.ToShortDateString(),
                            history.Salary.Value.ToString("C"));
        else
            Console.WriteLine("{0} --", history.Name);
    }
}

using (var context = new EFRecipesEntities())
{
    Console.WriteLine("\nUsing Entity SQL...");
    var esql = @"select a.Name, h.Salary, h.SalaryDate
                from Associates as a outer apply
                    a.AssociateSalaries as h order by a.Name";
    var allHistory =
        ((IObjectContextAdapter)context).ObjectContext.CreateQuery<DbDataRecord>(esql);
Console.WriteLine("Associate Salary History");
foreach (var history in allHistory)
```

```
    {
        if (history["Salary"] != DBNull.Value)
            Console.WriteLine("{0} Salary on {1:d} was {2:c}", history["Name"],
                                history["SalaryDate"], history["Salary"]);
        else
            Console.WriteLine("{0} --",history["Name"]);
    }
}
```

The trick here is that we want to "flatten" out hierarchical data, such as an associate with multiple salary inputs. Following is the output of the code in Listing 3-30:

```
Using LINQ...
Associate Salary History
Bill Jordan Salary on 10/8/2009 was $33,500.00
Janis Roberts --
Kevin Hodges Salary on 8/4/2009 was $39,500.00
Kevin Hodges Salary on 2/5/2010 was $41,900.00
Using Entity SQL...
Bill Jordan Salary on 10/8/2009 was $33,500.00
Janis Roberts --
Kevin Hodges Salary on 8/4/2009 was $39,500.00
Kevin Hodges Salary on 2/5/2010 was $41,900.00
```

How It Works

To flatten the query results, we followed the strategy in Recipe 3-10 and used a nested from clause and the DefaultIfEmpty() method to get a left-outer join between the tables. The DefaultIfEmpty() method ensured that we have rows from the left side (the Associate entities), even if there are no corresponding rows on the right side (AssociateSalary entities). We project the results into an anonymous type, being careful to capture null values for the salary and salary date when there are no corresponding AssociateSalary entities.

For the Entity SQL solution, we use the outer apply operator to create unique pairings between each Associate entity and AssociateSalary entity. Both the cross and outer apply operators are available in SQL Server.

3-15. Grouping by Multiple Properties
Problem

You want to group the results of a query by multiple properties so as to group by multiple columns when the query executes against the database.

Solution

Let's say that you have a model with an Event entity type like the one shown in Figure 3-16. Event has a name, city, and state. You want to group events by state and then by city.

Figure 3-16. *A model with an Event entity type that has properties for the event's name, state, and city*

To start, this example leverages the Code-First approach for Entity Framework. In Listing 3-31, we create the entity classes.

Listing 3-31. Event Entity Type

```
public class Event
{
    public int EventId { get; set; }
    public string Name { get; set; }
    public string State { get; set; }
    public string City { get; set; }
}
```

Next, in Listing 3-32, we create the DbContext object, which is your gateway into Entity Framework functionality when leveraging the Code-First approach.

Listing 3-32. The DbContext Object

```
public class EFRecipesEntities : DbContext
{
    public EFRecipesEntities()
        : base("ConnectionString") {}

    public DbSet<Event> Events { get; set; }

    protected override void OnModelCreating(DbModelBuilder modelBuilder)
    {
        modelBuilder.Entity<Event>().ToTable("Chapter3.Event");
        base.OnModelCreating(modelBuilder);
    }
}
```

To get all of the events grouped by state and then city, follow the pattern in Listing 3-33.

Listing 3-33. Grouping by Multiple Properties

```
using (var context = new EFRecipesEntities())
{
    // delete previous test data
    context.Database.ExecuteSqlCommand("delete from chapter3.event");
    // add new test data
    context.Events.Add(new Event { Name = "TechFest 2010",
                                    State = "TX", City = "Dallas" });
    context.Events.Add(new Event { Name = "Little Blue River Festival",
                                    State = "MO", City = "Raytown" });
    context.Events.Add(new Event { Name = "Fourth of July Fireworks",
                                    State = "MO", City = "Raytown" });
    context.Events.Add(new Event { Name = "BBQ Ribs Championship",
                                    State = "TX", City = "Dallas" });
    context.Events.Add(new Event { Name = "Thunder on the Ohio",
                                    State = "KY", City = "Louisville" });
    context.SaveChanges();
}

using (var context = new EFRecipesEntities())
{
    Console.WriteLine("Using LINQ");
    var results = from e in context.Events
                  // create annonymous type to encapsulate composite
                  // sort key of State and City
                  group e by new { e.State, e.City } into g
                  select new
                      {
                          State = g.Key.State,
                          City = g.Key.City,
                          Events = g                          };
    Console.WriteLine("Events by State and City...");
    foreach (var item in results)
    {
        Console.WriteLine("{0}, {1}", item.City, item.State);
        foreach (var ev in item.Events)
        {
            Console.WriteLine("\t{0}", ev.Name);
        }
    }
}

using (var context = new EFRecipesEntities())
{
    Console.WriteLine("\nUsing Entity SQL");
    var esql = @"select e.State, e.City, GroupPartition(e) as Events
                from Events as e
                group by e.State, e.City";
```

```
    var records =
        ((IObjectContextAdapter)context).ObjectContext.CreateQuery<DbDataRecord>(esql);
    Console.WriteLine("Events by State and City...");
    foreach (var rec in records)
    {
        Console.WriteLine("{0}, {1}", rec["City"], rec["State"]);
        var events = (List<Event>)rec["Events"];
        foreach (var ev in events)
        {
            Console.WriteLine("\t{0}", ev.Name);
        }
    }
}
```

Following is the output of the code in Listing 3-33:

```
Using LINQ
Events by State and City...
Louisville, KY
        Thunder on the Ohio
Raytown, MO
        Little Blue River Festival
        Fourth of July Fireworks
Dallas, TX
        TechFest 2010
        BBQ Ribs Championship

Using Entity SQL
Events by State and City...
Louisville, KY
        Thunder on the Ohio
Raytown, MO
        Little Blue River Festival
        Fourth of July Fireworks
Dallas, TX
        TechFest 2010
        BBQ Ribs Championship
```

How It Works

In Listing 3-33, we show two different approaches to the problem. The first approach uses LINQ and the group by operator to group the results by state and city. When using the group by operator for multiple properties, we create an anonymous type to initially group the data. We use an into clause to send the groups to g, which is a second sequence created to hold the results of the query.

We project the results from g into a second anonymous type getting the State from the group key's State field (from the first anonymous type) and the City from the group key's City field. For the events, we simply select all of the members of the group.

For the Entity SQL approach, we can only project columns used in the group by clause, a constant value, or a computed value from using an aggregate function. In our case, we project the state, city, and the collection of events for each grouping.

3-16. Using Bitwise Operators in a Filter

Problem

You want to use bitwise operators to filter a query.

Solution

Let's say that you have an entity type with an integer property that you want to use as a set of bit flags. You'll use some of the bits in this property to represent the presence or absence of some particular attribute for the entity. For example, suppose you have an entity type for patrons of a local art gallery. Some patrons contribute money. Some volunteer during gallery hours. A few patrons serve on the board of directors. A few patrons support the art gallery in more than one way. A model with this entity type is shown in Figure 3-17.

Figure 3-17. *A Patron entity type with a SponsorType property that we use as a collection of bit flags indicating the sponsorship type for the patron*

We want to query for patrons and filter on the type of sponsorship provided by the patron. To do this, follow the pattern in Listing 3-34.

Listing 3-34. Using Bitwise Operators in a Query

```
static void Main()
{
    RunExample();
}

[Flags]
public enum SponsorTypes
{
    None = 0,
    ContributesMoney = 1,
    Volunteers = 2,
    IsABoardMember = 4
};
```

```
static void RunExample()
{
    using (var context = new EFRecipesEntities())
    {
        // delete previous test data
        context.Database.ExecuteSqlCommand("delete from chapter3.patron");
        // add new test data
        context.Patrons.Add(new Patron { Name = "Jill Roberts",
                    SponsorType = (int)SponsorTypes.ContributesMoney });
        context.Patrons.Add(new Patron { Name = "Ryan Keyes",
                    // note the useage of the bitwise OR operator: '|'
                    SponsorType = (int)(SponsorTypes.ContributesMoney |
                                        SponsorTypes.IsABoardMember)});
        context.Patrons.Add(new Patron {Name = "Karen Rosen",
                    SponsorType = (int)SponsorTypes.Volunteers});
        context.Patrons.Add(new Patron {Name = "Steven King",
                    SponsorType = (int)(SponsorTypes.ContributesMoney |
                                        SponsorTypes.Volunteers)});
        context.SaveChanges();
    }

    using (var context = new EFRecipesEntities())
    {
        Console.WriteLine("Using LINQ...");
        var sponsors = from p in context.Patrons
                        // note the useage of the bitwise AND operator: '&'
                        where (p.SponsorType &
                                (int)SponsorTypes.ContributesMoney) != 0
                        select p;
        Console.WriteLine("Patrons who contribute money");
        foreach (var sponsor in sponsors)
        {
            Console.WriteLine("\t{0}", sponsor.Name);
        }
    }

    using (var context = new EFRecipesEntities())
    {
        Console.WriteLine("\nUsing Entity SQL...");
        var esql = @"select value p from Patrons as p
                    where BitWiseAnd(p.SponsorType, @type) <> 0";
        var sponsors = ((IObjectContextAdapter)context).ObjectContext.CreateQuery<Patron>(esql,
            new ObjectParameter("type", (int)SponsorTypes.ContributesMoney));
        Console.WriteLine("Patrons who contribute money");
        foreach (var sponsor in sponsors)
        {
            Console.WriteLine("\t{0}", sponsor.Name);
        }
    }
}
```

Following is the output of the code in Listing 3-34:

```
Using LINQ...
Patrons who contribute money
        Jill Roberts
        Ryan Keyes
        Steven King

Using Entity SQL...
Patrons who contribute money
        Jill Roberts
        Ryan Keyes
        Steven King
```

How It Works

In our model, the Patron entity type packs multiple bit flags into a single integer property. A patron can sponsor the gallery in a number of ways. Each type of sponsorship is represented as a different bit in the SponsorType property. We represent each of the ways a sponsor can contribute in the SponsorTypes enum. We are careful to assign integers in power of 2 increments for each sponsor type. This means that each will have exactly one unique bit in the bits of the SponsorType property.

When we insert patrons, we assign the sponsorship type to the SponsorType property. For patrons that contribute in more than one way, we simply use the bitwise OR (|) operator to build the bit pattern representing all of the ways the patron contributes to the gallery.

For the LINQ query, we use the bitwise AND (&) operator to extract the bit for the ContributesMoney flag from the SponsorType property value. If the result is nonzero, then the patron has the ContributesMoney flag set. If we needed to find patrons that contribute in more than one way, we would OR all of the SponsorTypes we're interested in together before we used the AND operator to extract one or more set bits.

The second solution demonstrates the same approach using Entity SQL. Here we use the BitWiseAnd() function to extract the set bit. Entity SQL supports a full complement of bitwise functions.

3-17. Joining on Multiple Columns
Problem

You want to join two entity types on multiple properties.

Solution

Let's say that you have a model like the one shown in Figure 3-18. The Account entity type is in a one-to-many association with the Order type. Each account may have many orders, while each order is associated with exactly one account. You want to find all of the orders that are being shipped to the same city and state as the account.

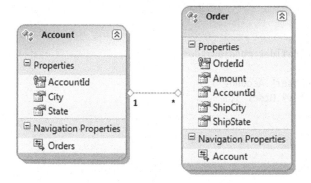

Figure 3-18. *A model with an Account entity type and its associated Order entity type*

To start, this example leverages the Code-First approach for Entity Framework. In Listing 3-35, we create the entity classes.

Listing 3-35. Account and Order Entity Types

```
public class Account
{
    public Account()
    {
        Orders = new HashSet<Order>();
    }
    public int AccountId { get; set; }
    public string City { get; set; }
    public string State { get; set; }
    public virtual ICollection<Order> Orders { get; set; }
}

public class Order
{
    public int OrderId { get; set; }
    public Decimal Amount { get; set; }
    public int AccountId { get; set; }
    public string ShipCity { get; set; }
    public string ShipState { get; set; }
    public virtual Account Account { get; set; }
}
```

Next, in Listing 3-36, we create the DbContext object, which is your gateway into Entity Framework functionality when leveraging the Code-First approach.

Listing 3-36. The DbContext Object

```
public class EFRecipesEntities : DbContext
{
    public EFRecipesEntities()
        : base("ConnectionString") {}
```

```
    public DbSet<Order> Orders { get; set; }
    public DbSet<Account> Accounts { get; set; }

    protected override void OnModelCreating(DbModelBuilder modelBuilder)
    {
        modelBuilder.Entity<Account>().ToTable("Chapter3.Account");
        modelBuilder.Entity<Order>().ToTable("Chapter3.Order");

        base.OnModelCreating(modelBuilder);
    }
}
```

To find the orders, follow the pattern in Listing 3-37.

Listing 3-37. Using a Join on Multiple Properties to Find All of the Orders Being Shipped to the Account's City and State

```
using (var context = new EFRecipesEntities())
{
    var a1 = new Account { City = "Raytown", State = "MO" };
    a1.CustomerOrders.Add(new CustomerOrder { Amount = 223.09M, ShipCity = "Raytown",
                          ShipState = "MO" });
    a1. CustomerOrders.Add(new CustomerOrder { Amount = 189.32M, ShipCity = "Olathe",
                          ShipState = "KS" });

    var a2 = new Account { City = "Kansas City", State = "MO" };
    a2. CustomerOrders.Add(new CustomerOrder { Amount = 99.29M, ShipCity = "Kansas City",
                          ShipState = "MO" });

    var a3 = new Account { City = "North Kansas City", State = "MO"};
    a3. CustomerOrders.Add(new CustomerOrder { Amount = 102.29M, ShipCity = "Overland Park",
                          ShipState = "KS" });
    context.Accounts.Add(a1);
    context.Accounts.Add(a2);
    context.Accounts.Add(a3);
    context.SaveChanges();
}

using (var context = new EFRecipesEntities())
{
    var orders = from o in context.CustomerOrders
                 join a in context.Accounts on
                   new {Id = o.AccountID, City = o.ShipCity, State = o.ShipState }
                 equals
                   new {Id = a.AccountID, City = a.City, State = a.State }
                 select o;

    Console.WriteLine("Orders shipped to the account's city, state...");
    foreach (var order in orders)
    {
        Console.WriteLine("\tOrder {0} for {1}", order.AccountID.ToString(),
                          order.Amount.ToString());
    }
}
```

Following is the output of the code in Listing 3-37:

```
Orders shipped to the account's city, state...
       Order 31 for $223.09
       Order 32 for $99.29
```

How It Works

To solve this problem, you could find all the accounts and then go through each Orders collection and find the orders that are in the same city and state as the account. For a small number of accounts, this may be a reasonable solution. But in general, it is best to push this sort of processing into the store layer where it can be handled much more efficiently.

Out-of-the-gate, both Account and Order are joined by the AccountId property. However, in this solution, we form an explicit join by creating an anonymous type on each side of the equals clause for each of the entities. The anonymous construct is required when we join entities on more than one property. We need to make sure that both anonymous types are the same. They must have the same properties in the same order. Here, we are explicitly creating an inner-join relationship between the two tables on the database, meaning that orders to other cities and states would not be included due to the join condition.

CHAPTER 4

■ ■ ■

Using Entity Framework in ASP.NET MVC

ASP.NET is a free Web framework that supports three different technologies to create websites and Web applications; that is, Web Pages, Web Forms, and MVC. Although MVC is a very popular and well-established concept designed to be used as a pattern in software development, MVC in ASP.NET framework is fairly new technology. The latest version of ASP.NET MVC 4 was released in 2012. Since the release of the initial version in 2008, it has become a popular means for ASP.NET Web Forms development. Therefore, this chapter shows you recipes made only with ASP.NET MVC 4 and Entity Framework. Two other forms of ASP.NET technology—ASP.NET Web Forms and ASP.NET Web Pages—are not covered in this chapter.

The recipes in this chapter cover everything from building an insert, update, delete, and list page to implementing search functionality.

Each of the recipes in this chapter is shown using an ASP.NET MVC 4 Web application project in Visual Studio 2012. We've tried to keep things simple by not including all of the extra code that comes with the default project template.

4.1. Building CRUD Operations in an ASP.NET MVC Page

The create, read, update, and delete (CRUD) operations are fundamental to almost every software application. We are going to implement these operations in this section using ASP.NET MVC.

Problem

You want to build an ASP.NET MVC page that allows inserting, updating, deleting, and reading from your model.

Solution

Let's say you have a Web application that manages the list of software apps for a mobile device. You have a model like the one shown in Figure 4-1.

Figure 4-1. *A model with a Category entity that contains an application's category name and description*

The model contains a Category entity. You want to create a few simple ASP.NET MVC pages to show the list of all of the app categories. You also want to allow the user to create a new app category, update an existing app category, and delete an app category. Although there are number of ways to do this, we will do it in a very simple way to build your understanding of the integration of Entity Framework with ASP.NET MVC. To create an MVC application, you will need three parts: a model, a controller, and a view. We have used the file MyStore.mdf as our database for this recipe. We are also using the Razor engine for all of the views. There is only one model but with multiple views, depending on the actions or operations required. In this case, we will have four views: one each for Create, Update, Delete, and List.

First we will create an ASP.NET MVC 4 Web Application using the project template Internet Application, as demonstrated in Figure 4-2 and Figure 4-3.

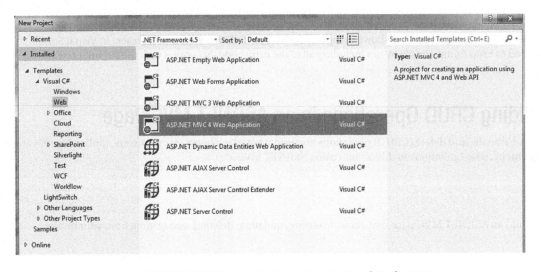

Figure 4-2. *Selecting an ASP.NET MVC Web Application project in Visual Studio 2012*

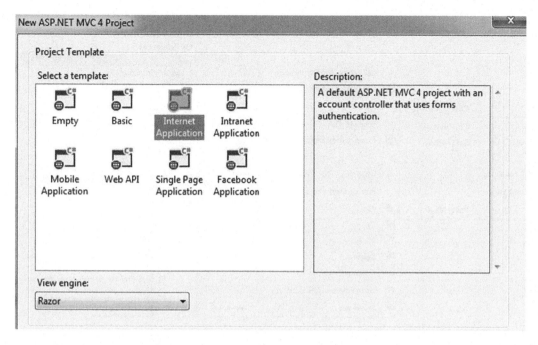

Figure 4-3. Selecting a project template for an ASP.NET MVC application

A new project is created in Visual Studio IDE with number of default files and folders.

Now we have to set up the database for this application. We will use a MyStore.mdf file database within our project to make everything simple and clear.

An MDF file-based database can easily be created within the Visual Studio development environment. This MDF file-based database can then be attached to a SQL Server Express instance and used as a normal, full-fledged database. The difference here is that it is attached through a connection string and not as a permanently attached database onto a SQL Server instance.

Right click on the App_Data folder to add a new .mdf file. This file can be added in two ways: either click on New Item in the Add context menu, as shown in Figure 4-4, or click on SQL Server Database entry, as shown in Figure 4-5.

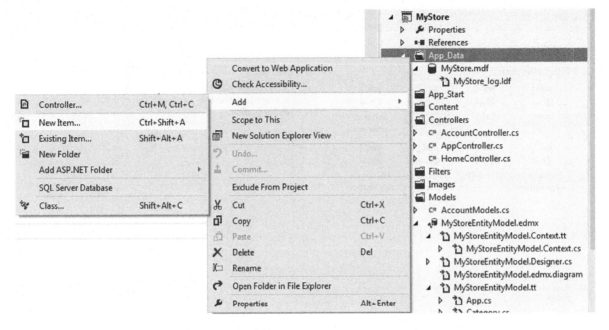

Figure 4-4. *Adding a new item in the App_Data folder*

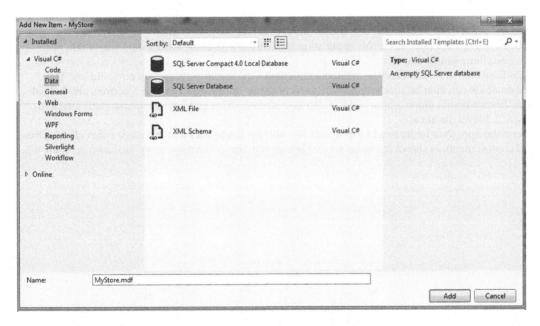

Figure 4-5. *Selecting a SQL Server Database file as a new item to add*

After creating the three tables as .mdf files, as shown in Figure 4-6, we generated a new model using Entity Framework.

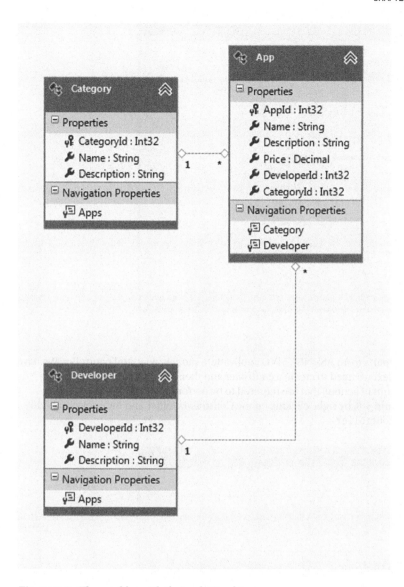

Figure 4-6. *Three tables with their relationships*

The model is generated by adding an ADO.NET Entity Data Model into Models folder of your project, as shown in Figure 4-7.

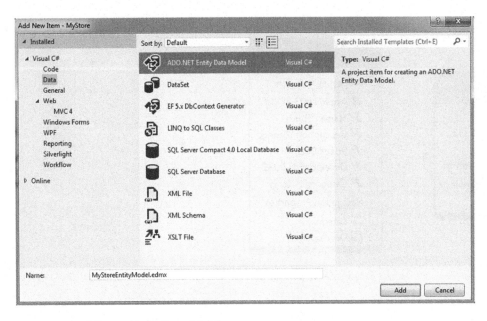

Figure 4-7. *Adding an Entity Data Model*

As we have discussed, there are three parts to an ASP.NET MVC application: model, view, and controller. We have now completed the model creation part. Next we need to create a controller and then finally create the views. The number of views is dependent on the amount of actions that are required to be performed through the controller.

Add a new controller, as shown in Figure 4-8, by right-clicking on the Controllers folder and then selecting Add Controller. Name the controller CategoryController.

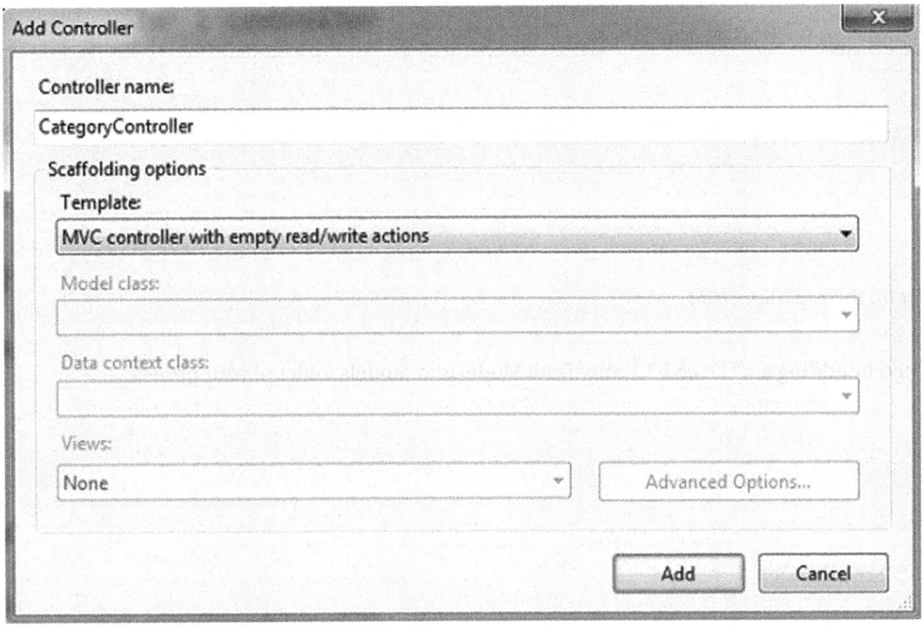

Figure 4-8. *Adding a controller*

As you know, we selected the template of empty read/write actions while adding `CategoryController`. It will create all of the dummy action methods in the controller code. The DbContext code for this recipe is shown in Listing 4-1.

Listing 4-1. Inherited DbContext Class to Perform Operations in the Database Using Entity Framework

```
namespace MyStore.Models
{
    using System;
    using System.Data.Entity;
    using System.Data.Entity.Infrastructure;

    public partial class MyStoreEntities : DbContext
    {
        public MyStoreEntities()
            : base("name=MyStoreEntities")
        {
        }

        protected override void OnModelCreating(DbModelBuilder modelBuilder)
        {
            throw new UnintentionalCodeFirstException();
        }

        public DbSet<App> Apps { get; set; }
        public DbSet<Category> Categories { get; set; }
        public DbSet<Developer> Developers { get; set; }
    }
}
```

We have to change the code, as shown in Listing 4-2, in these action methods to perform insert, delete, edit, and view on models using DbContext class.

Listing 4-2. Controller Code for Category Model

```
using System;
using System.Collections.Generic;
using System.Linq;
using System.Web;
using System.Web.Mvc;
using MyStore.Models;
namespace MyStore.Controllers
{
    public class CategoryController : Controller
    {
        // GET: /Category/
```

```
public ActionResult Index()
{
    using (var db = new MyStoreEntities())
        {
            return View(db.Categories.ToList());
        }
}

//
// GET: /Category/Details/5

public ActionResult Details(int id)
{
    using (var db = new MyStoreEntities())
        {
            return View(db.Categories.Find(id));
        }
}

//
// GET: /Category/Create

public ActionResult Create()
{
    return View();
}

//
// POST: /Category/Create

[HttpPost]
public ActionResult Create(Category categoryValue)
{
    try
        {
            using (var db = new MyStoreEntities())
                {
                    db.Categories.Add(categoryValue);
                    db.SaveChanges();
                }
                    return RedirectToAction("Index");
        }
    catch
        {
            return View();
        }
}
```

```
// GET: /Category/Edit/5
public ActionResult Edit(int id)
{
    using (var db = new MyStoreEntities())
        {
            return View(db.Categories.Find(id));
        }
}

// POST: /Category/Edit/5
[HttpPost]
public ActionResult Edit(int id, Category categoryValue)
{
    try
        {
            using (var db = new MyStoreEntities())
                {
                    db.Entry(categoryValue).State = System.Data.EntityState.Modified;
                    db.SaveChanges();
                    return RedirectToAction("Index");
                }
        }
    catch
        {
            return View();
        }
}

//
// GET: /Category/Delete/5

public ActionResult Delete(int id)
{
    using (var db = new MyStoreEntities())
        {
            return View(db.Categories.Find(id));
        }
}

//
// POST: /Category/Delete/5

[HttpPost]
public ActionResult Delete(int id, Category categoryValue)
{
    try
        {
            using (var db = new MyStoreEntities())
```

```
                    {
                        db.Entry(categoryValue).State = System.Data.EntityState.Deleted;
                        db.SaveChanges();
                        return RedirectToAction("Index");
                    }
                }
            catch
                {
                    return View();
                }
            }
        }
    }
}
```

Create five views for all of the actions as Create, Delete, Details, Edit, and Index in CategoryController. You can add a view, as shown in Figure 4-9, by right-clicking on any operation in the controller and selecting AddView. A new view will be added into the Views ➤ Category folder, as shown in Figure 4-9.

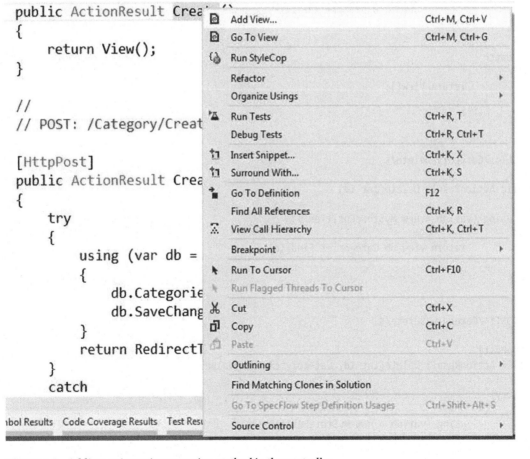

Figure 4-9. *Adding a view using an action method in the controller*

In the Add View dialog box shown in Figure 4-10, select View Engine as Razor (CSHTML), and then click the checkbox to create a strongly-typed view, and finally select the Model class as Category (MyStore.Models).

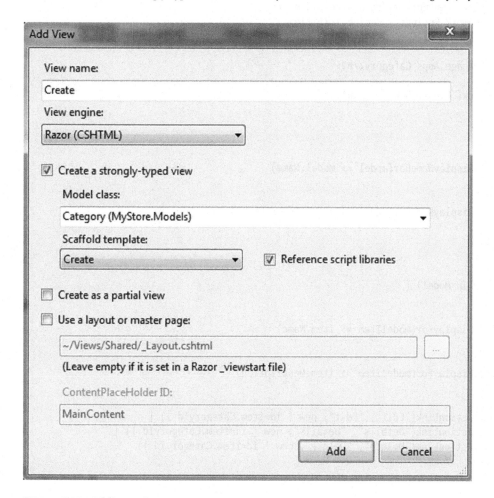

Figure 4-10. *Adding a view*

The index view in Listing 4-3 displays a page that lists the app categories, along with buttons for inserting new categories as well as editing and deleting current categories. The create view page in Listing 4-4 is used to insert a new application category.

Listing 4-3. The Code of Index View

```
@model IEnumerable<MyStore.Models.Category>

@{
    Layout = null;
}

<!DOCTYPE html>
```

```
<html>
<head>
    <meta name="viewport" content="width=device-width" />
    <title>Entity Framework Recipes - Recipe 1</title>
</head>
<body>
                    <h2>Manage Apps Category</h2>
        <p>
            @Html.ActionLink("Create New", "Create")
        </p>
        <table>
            <tr>
                <th>
                    @Html.DisplayNameFor(model => model.Name)
                </th>
                <th>
                    @Html.DisplayNameFor(model => model.Description)
                </th>
                <th></th>
            </tr>

    @foreach (var item in Model) {
        <tr>
            <td>
                @Html.DisplayFor(modelItem => item.Name)
            </td>
            <td>
                @Html.DisplayFor(modelItem => item.Description)
            </td>
            <td>
                @Html.ActionLink("Edit", "Edit", new { id=item.CategoryId }) |
                @Html.ActionLink("Details", "Details", new { id=item.CategoryId }) |
                @Html.ActionLink("Delete", "Delete", new { id=item.CategoryId })
            </td>
        </tr>
    }

    </table>
</body>
</html>
```

Listing 4-4. The Code of Create View

```
@model MyStore.Models.Category

@{
    Layout = null;
}

<!DOCTYPE html>
```

```
<html>
<head>
    <meta name="viewport" content="width=device-width" />
    <title>Entity Framework Recipes - Recipe 1</title>
</head>
<body>
                <h2>Manage Apps Category</h2>

    @using (Html.BeginForm()) {
        @Html.AntiForgeryToken()
        @Html.ValidationSummary(true)

        <fieldset>
            <legend>Category</legend>

            <div class="editor-label">
                @Html.LabelFor(model => model.Name)
            </div>
            <div class="editor-field">
                @Html.EditorFor(model => model.Name)
                @Html.ValidationMessageFor(model => model.Name)
            </div>

            <div class="editor-label">
                @Html.LabelFor(model => model.Description)
            </div>
            <div class="editor-field">
                @Html.EditorFor(model => model.Description)
                @Html.ValidationMessageFor(model => model.Description)
            </div>

            <p>
                <input type="submit" value="Create" />
            </p>
        </fieldset>
    }

    <div>
        @Html.ActionLink("Back to List", "Index")
    </div>
    <script src="~/Scripts/jquery-1.8.2.min.js"></script>
    <script src="~/Scripts/jquery.validate.min.js"></script>
    <script src="~/Scripts/jquery.validate.unobtrusive.min.js"></script>
</body>
</html>
```

The code of the index view in Listing 4-3 displays a page that lists the app categories, along with the buttons for inserting new categories as well as those for editing and deleting current categories. This index page is shown in Figure 4-11.

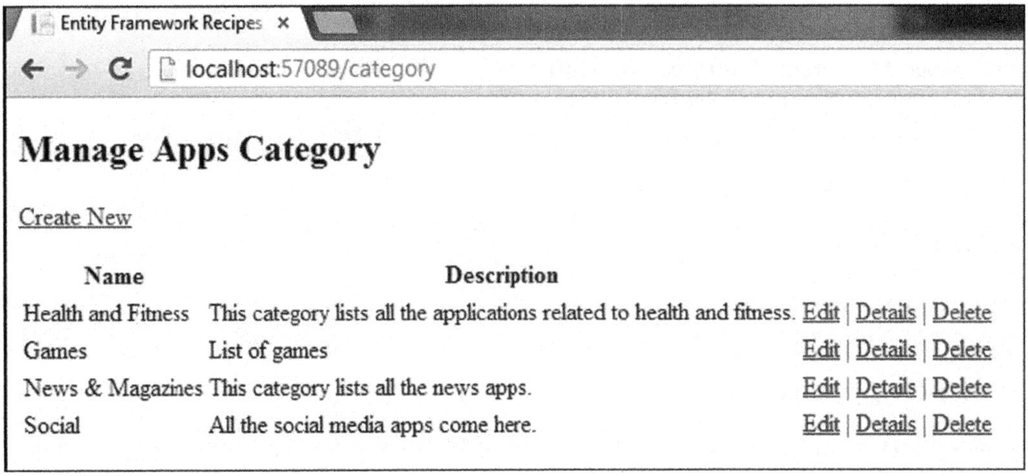

Figure 4-11. *The listing of the app categories*

The text boxes shown in Figure 4-12 allow the user to enter the category information. Clicking the Create button causes the new record to be added to the database.

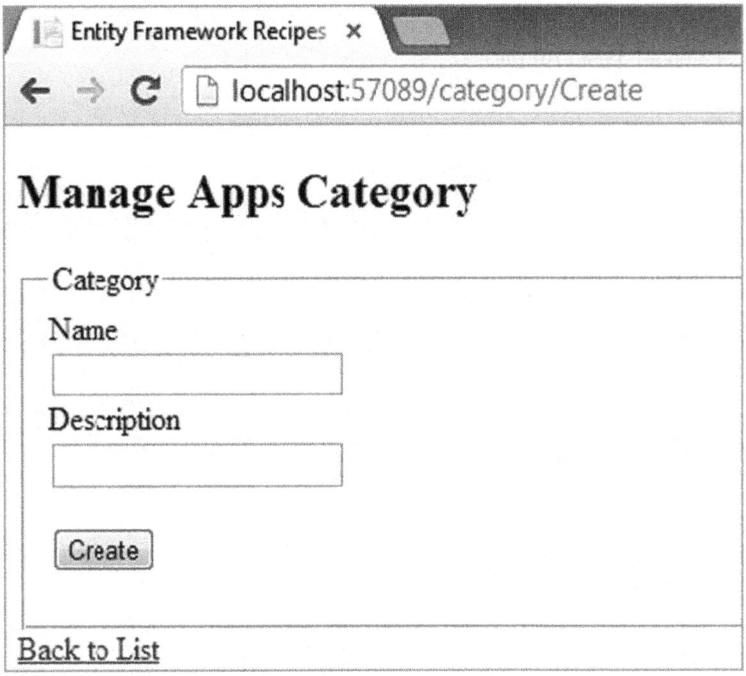

Figure 4-12. *Inserting a new app category*

Clicking the Edit button on a category shows the view that allows editing of an existing app category as shown in Figure 4-13.

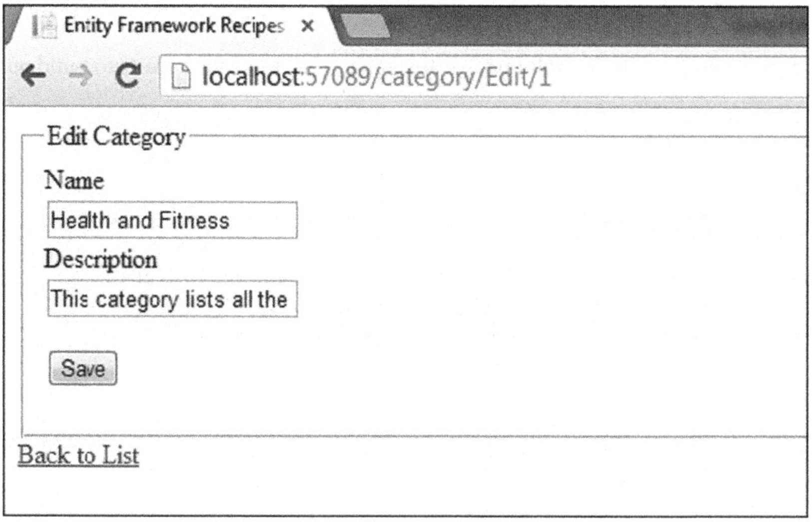

Figure 4-13. *Editing an app category*

How It Works

The entire code base is divided into three parts:

1. Model with DbContext class (Listing 4-1)

2. Controller code (Listing 4-2)

3. View code (Listing 4-3 and Listing 4-4)

The controller is the largest piece of the code, and it is the heart of the functionality of all the operations. The views are created on the basis of action methods in the Controller. All of the code that is used to fetch, create, update, and delete is addressed in the action methods. Whenever a view is accessed through a URL or another view, the corresponding action method of that operation is called upon in the controller to perform that action. We selected the scaffolding option while creating new views, which automatically generates the HTML code of edit, create, and list using the Razor view engine, depending upon the scaffolding option selected.

4-2. Building a Search Query

Searching data is a very basic functionality that most of the applications have. It is very dynamic in nature, as users can use any criteria, if provided, to search, or none. So we discuss below in detail the basic implementation of search functionality.

Problem

You want to build a search page in ASP.NET MVC 4 using Entity Framework.

Solution

Let's say you have a model like the one in Figure 4-14. In the solution, we are going to use three basic parts to build our search page:

1. A table to structure the query parameters.

2. A WebGrid to present the results in Razor view.

3. A Controller to incorporate the logic for the view.

In the database, you have a Customer table, which stores the Name, City and State information of all the customers. The data model (schema) of the Customer table is shown in Figure 4-14.

Figure 4-14. *A model with a Customer entity*

After having the Customer view model created, we need to write the view using Razor. In this view, we are using WebGrid control to show the Customer records as mentioned in Listing 4-5.

Listing 4-5. Using WebGrid in MVC Razor View

```
@model EntityFrameworkRecipe2.ViewModels.CustomerVM

@{
    Layout = null;
}

@{
    ViewBag.Title = "Customer";
    WebGrid grid = new WebGrid(canPage:false,canSort:false);
                grid.Bind(Model.Customers,
                autoSortAndPage: false
    );
}

@using (Html.BeginForm())
{
<table>
    <tr>
        <td>
            Name
        </td>
```

```
            <td>
                @Html.TextBoxFor(model => model.Name)
            </td>
        </tr>
        <tr>
            <td>
                City
            </td>
            <td>
                @Html.TextBoxFor(model => model.City)
            </td>
        </tr>
        <tr>
            <td>
                State
            </td>
            <td>
                @Html.TextBoxFor(model => model.State)
            </td>
        </tr>
        <tr>
            <td colspan="2">
                <input type="submit" id="search" title="Search" value="Search" />
            </td>
        </tr>
    </table>
    <div id="searchResults">
        <!-- placeHolder for search results -->
            @grid.GetHtml(
            fillEmptyRows: true,
            alternatingRowStyle: "alternate-row",
            headerStyle: "grid-header",
            footerStyle: "grid-footer",
            columns: new [] {
            grid.Column("Name"),
            grid.Column("City"),
            grid.Column("State")
            })
    </div>
}
```

Once this view is written, we are going to write the Controller with both Get and Post actions of Search function, in which we are going to provide the implementation to fetch the Customer data from database and populate into the view model. This implementation is shown in Listing 4-6.

Listing 4-6. The Controller Code That Builds the Data to Test Our Search Page

```
public class CustomerController : Controller
    {
        public ActionResult Search()
            {
                using (var db = new CustomerEntities())
                    {
                        var customer = db.Customers.ToList();
                        var data = new CustomerVM()
                            {
                                Customers = customer
                            };
                        return View(data);
                    }
            }
    [HttpPost]
        public ActionResult Search(CustomerVM customerVmValue)
            {
                using (var db = new CustomerEntities())
                    {
                        var customerSearchResults = from customerRec in db.Customers
                        where ((customerVmValue.Name == null) || (customerRec.Name ==
customerVmValue.Name.Trim()))
                            && ((customerVmValue.City == null) || (customerRec.City ==
customerVmValue.City.Trim()))
                            && ((customerVmValue.State == null) || (customerRec.State ==
customerVmValue.State.Trim()))
                        select new
                            {

                                Id = customerRec.CustomerId,
                                Name = customerRec.Name,
                                City = customerRec.City,
                                State = customerRec.State
                            };
                        List<Customer> lstCustomer = new  List<Customer>();
                            foreach (var record in customerSearchResults)
                                {
                                    Customer customerValue = new Customer();
                                    customerValue.Id = record.Id;
                                    customerValue.Name = record.Name;
                                    customerValue.City = record.City;
                                    customerValue.State = record.State;
                                    lstCustomer.Add(customerValue);
                                }
                                customerVmValue.Customers = lstCustomer;
                                return View(customerVmValue);
                    }
            }
    }
```

In your browser, the page should appear similar to the one shown in Figure 4-15.

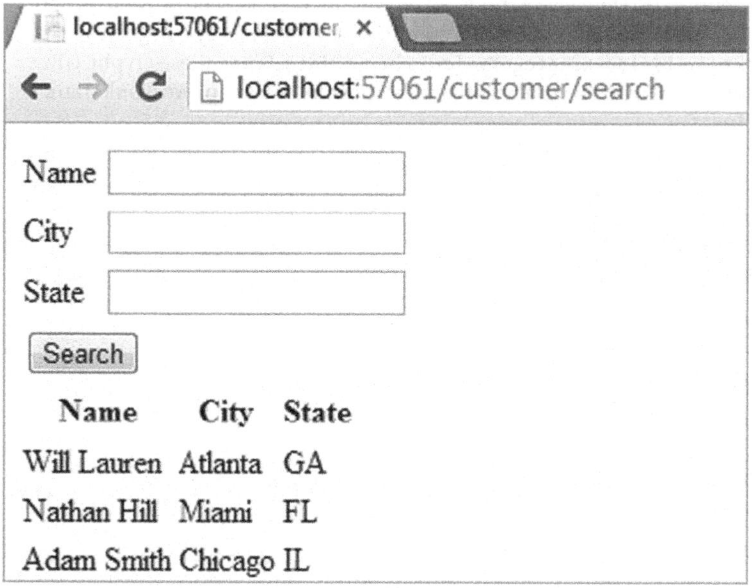

Figure 4-15. *The rendered view shown in a browser*

How It Works

In the first section of the page (see Listing 4-5), we format the query fields using a table. There's nothing fancy here—the idea is to provide some structure to capture the three query fields: Name, City, and State. These values, or the lack of them, will be used in the Controller's Search action method after the Search button is clicked. Thus these parameters will form the filter for the query.

Next we use an HTML helper to show the result set using WebGrid control. The data source will be the view model. Take note here that we have created two models: one to fetch the data from the database and one to be used as a model for the view that will capture the query parameters from the page and also show the customer records. Actually, the first model will be created at the moment we generate the entity data model for Customer table.

We are using Linq-to-entities to query the Customer entity data model. The where clause and parameter variables define the filter of our query. In the view, we map the parameters of the search query to the Name, City, and State HTML helper text boxes. We map the Name property of the model to the Name text box, and so on.

We use a WebGrid to display the results. The WebGrid is bound with the Customer model list, which is a model that is capturing only the search results.

The controller code, shown in Listing 4-6, is used fetch the results from database and fill the view the first time view is rendered and also when the Search button is clicked. We have used an .mdf file local database and filled the records in Customer table.

4-3. Filtering with ASP.NET's URL Routing
Problem

You want to simplify the URLs on your site using a MapRoute. You also want to leverage these routes to filter the result sets in the Razor view engine.

Solution

Suppose your model looks like the one in Figure 4-16. Here we've modeled our products, represented by the Product entity, together with their categories. In a typical eCommerce website, we would show products by category. We want to avoid exposing query strings like /Products/Index?Category=Tents in our URLs. While these cryptic URLs simplify programming a little, they don't help much when it comes to search engine optimization. We would rather have URLs that look more like /Products/Tents.

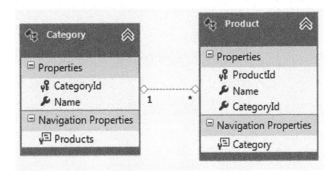

Figure 4-16. *A model for products and their categories*

We can get this more *Search Engine Optimization*-friendly URL structure by using routing. Routes are typically created in the Application_Start() event handler in Global.asax. The code in Listing 4-7 illustrates adding a route for the Product controller.

Listing 4-7. Adding the Route in Global.asax

```
protected void Application_Start()
{
    RouteTable.Routes.MapRoute("Product", "{controller}/{name}", new { controller = "Product",
action = "Index" });
    RouteConfig.RegisterRoutes(RouteTable.Routes);
}
```

In the Index view as shown in the Listing 4-8, we use the category name bound to the name parameter in the Index method of Product controller, as illustrated in Listing 4-7. We use the controller code in Listing 4-9 to fetch the value of the category name parameter and produce the results through View. Figure 4-17 and Figure 4-18 show the rendered pages for categories Tents and Cooking Equipment.

Listing 4-8. The Index View Code That Displays the Products Filtered by Category

```
@model IEnumerable<EntityFrameworkRecipe3.ViewModels.ProductVM>

@{
    Layout = null;
}

<!DOCTYPE html>
```

```
<html>
<head>
    <meta name="viewport" content="width=device-width" />
    <title>Index</title>
</head>
<body>
    <table>
        <tr>
            <th>
                @Html.DisplayNameFor(model => model.Name)
            </th>
            <th>
                @Html.DisplayNameFor(model => model.CategoryName)
            </th>
            <th></th>
        </tr>

    @foreach (var item in Model) {
        <tr>
            <td>
                @Html.DisplayFor(modelItem => item.Name)
            </td>
            <td>
                @Html.DisplayFor(modelItem => item.CategoryName)
            </td>
        </tr>
    }

    </table>
</body>
</html>
```

Listing 4-9. The Controller Code That Populates the Model with the Product Data Filtered by Category Name

```
public class ProductController : Controller
    {
        //
        // GET: /Product/

        public ActionResult Index(string name)
        {
            using (var db = new ProductEntities())
                {
                    var query = from productRec in db.Products
                    join categoryRec in db.Categories
                    on productRec.CategoryId
                    equals categoryRec.CategoryId
                    where categoryRec.Name == name
                    select new
```

```
                              {
                                  Name = productRec.Name,
                                  CategoryName = categoryRec.Name
                              };
                              List<ProductVM> lstProduct = new List<ProductVM>();
                              foreach(var record in query)
                                  {
                                      ProductVM productValue = new ProductVM();
                                      productValue.Name = record.Name;
                                      productValue.CategoryName = record.CategoryName;
                                      lstProduct.Add(productValue);
                                  }
                              return View(lstProduct);
                      }
                  }

          }
```

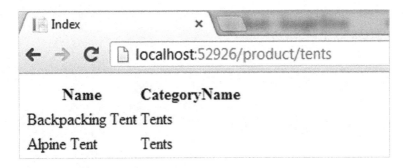

Figure 4-17. *Using the route /Product/Tents, the result set is filtered to the Tents category*

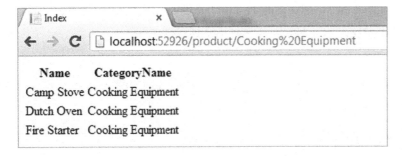

Figure 4-18. *Using the route /Product/Cooking Equipment, the result set is filtered to the Cooking Equipment category*

How It Works

In the `Application_Start()` event handler in `Global.asax`, we mapped the route `/Product/{name}` to the `/Product/Index?name=category`. The route key, `category`, is bound to the actual category string in the URL. In the Product controller, we used the name route key in a MapRoute to filter the result set to filter those products in the given category.

CHAPTER 5

■ ■ ■

Loading Entities and Navigation Properties

Entity Framework provides a rich modeling environment that enables the developer to work visually with entity classes that map to database tables, views, stored procedures, and relationships. The recipes in this chapter show you how to control the loading of related entities in your query operations.

The default behavior for Entity Framework is to load only the entities directly needed by your application. In general, this is exactly what you want. If Entity Framework aggressively loaded all of the entities related through one or more associations, you would likely end up loading more entities than you needed. This would increase the memory footprint of your application as well as impact performance.

In Entity Framework, you can control when the loading of related entities occurs and optimize the number of database queries executed. Carefully managing if and when related entities are loaded can increase application performance and provide you more control over your data.

In this chapter, we illustrate the various options available for loading related data along with an explanation about the benefits and drawbacks of each. Specifically, we discuss the default behavior of *lazy loading* and what it really means. Then we'll look at a number of recipes illustrating the various options you have to load some or all of the related entities in a single query. This type of loading, called *eager loading*, is used both to reduce the number of round trips to the database and, more precisely, to control which related entities are loaded.

Sometimes you need to defer loading of certain related entities because they may be expensive to load or are not used very often. For these cases, we'll cover yet another approach to loading related entities, entitled *explicit loading*, and demonstrate a number of scenarios using the Load() method to control precisely when to load one or more related entities.

Finally, we'll take a brief look at some of the asynchronous operations that are now available.

5-1. Lazy Loading Related Entities
Problem

You want to load an entity and then load related entities, only if and when they are needed by your application.

Solution

Let's say that you have a model like the one shown in Figure 5-1.

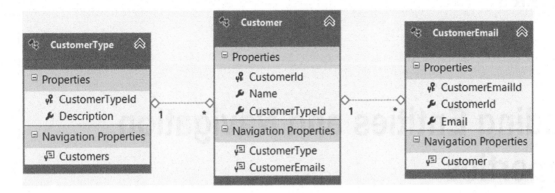

Figure 5-1. *A model with a Customer and its related information*

In this model, we have a Customer entity with a single CustomerType and many CustomerEmail addresses. The association with CustomerType is one-to-many with CustomerType on the *one* side of the association. This is an *entity reference*.

The association with CustomerEmail is also one-to-many but with CustomerEmail on the *many* side of the association. This is an *entity collection*.

When we put all three entity classes together, we arrive at a construct called an *object graph*. An object graph is a set of individual, but related entities, which together form a *logical whole unit*. Specifically, an object graph is a view of a given entity and its related entities at a specific point in time. For example, during an operation in our application, a customer with an Id of 5 may contain the name "John Smith," have a customer type of "preferred," and a collection of 10 customer emails.

Listing 5-1 demonstrates the lazy loading behavior of Entity Framework, which is the default behavior for loading related entity objects.

Listing 5-1. Lazy Loading of Instances of Customertype and Customeremail Along with Instances of Customer

```
using (var context = new EFRecipesEntities())
{
    var customers = context.Customers;

    Console.WriteLine("Customers");
    Console.WriteLine("=========");

    // Only information from the Customer entity is requested
    foreach (var customer in customers)
    {
        Console.WriteLine("Customer name is {0}", customer.Name);
    }

    // Now, application is requesting information from the related entities, CustomerType
    // and CustomerEmail, resulting in Entity Framework generating separate queries to each
    // entity object in order to obtain the requested information.
    foreach (var customer in customers)
    {
        Console.WriteLine("{0} is a {1}, email address(es)", customer.Name,
                            customer.CustomerType.Description);
        foreach (var email in customer.CustomerEmails)
```

```
        {
            Console.WriteLine("\t{0}", email.Email);
        }
    }
}

// Extra credit:
// If you enable SQL Profiler, the following query will not requery the database
// for related data. Instead, it will return the in-memory data from the prior query.
foreach (var customer in customers)
{
    Console.WriteLine("{0} is a {1}, email address(es)", customer.Name,
                        customer.CustomerType.Description);
    foreach (var email in customer.CustomerEmails)
    {
        Console.WriteLine("\t{0}", email.Email);
    }
}
}
```

The output of the code in Listing 5-1 is the following:

```
Customers
=========
Customer name is Joan Smith
Customer name is Bill Meyers
Joan Smith is a Web Customer, email address(es)
        jsmith@gmail.com
        joan@smith.com
Bill Meyers is a Retail Customer, email address(es)
        bmeyers@gmail.com
Joan Smith is a Web Customer, email address(es)
        jsmith@gmail.com
        joan@smith.com
Bill Meyers is a Retail Customer, email address(es)
        bmeyers@gmail.com
```

How It Works

By default, Entity Framework loads only entities that you specifically request. This is known as *lazy loading*, and it is an important principle to keep in mind. The alternative, loading the parent and every associated entity, known as *eager loading*, may load a much larger object graph into memory than you need, not to mention the added overhead of retrieving, marshaling, and materializing a larger amount of data.

In this example, we start by issuing a query against the Customer entity to load all customers. Interestingly, the query itself is not executed immediately, but rather when we first enumerate the Customer entity in the first foreach construct. This behavior follows the principle of deferred loading upon which LINQ is built.

In the first foreach construct, we only request data elements from the underlying Customer table and not any data from the CustomerType or CustomerEmail table. In this case, Entity Framework only queries the Customer table and not the related CustomerType or CustomerEmail tables.

Then, in the second foreach construct, we explicitly reference the Description property from the CustomerType entity and the Email property from the CustomerEmail entity. Directly accessing these properties results in Entity Framework generating a query to each related table for the requested data. It's important to understand that Entity Framework generates a separate query the first time either of the related tables are accessed. Once a query has been invoked for a property from a related entity, Entity Framework will mark the property as loaded and will retrieve the data from memory as opposed to requerying the underlying table over and over again. In this example, four separate queries are generated for child data:

- A select statement against CustomerType and CustomerEmail for Joan Smith

- A select statement against CustomerType and CustomerEmail for Bill Meyers

This separate query for each child table works well when a user is browsing your application and requests different data elements depending on his or her needs at the moment. It can improve application response time, since data is retrieved as needed with a series of small queries, as opposed to loading a large amount of data up front, potentially causing a delay in rendering the view to the user.

This approach, however, is not so efficient when you know, up front, that you will require a large set of data from related tables. In those cases, a query with eager loading may be a better option as it can retrieve all of the data (from both the parent and related tables) in a single query.

The last code block, entitled 'Extra Credit,' demonstrates that once child properties are loaded, Entity Framework will retrieve their values from in-memory and not requery the database. Turn on the SQL Server Profiler Tool, run the example and note how the 'Extra Credit' code block does not generate SQL Select statements when child properties are referenced.

■ **Note** SQL Server Profiler is a great tool for inspecting the actual query statements generated by SQL Server. It is free and included with SQL Server Developer Edition and better: `http://technet.microsoft.com/en-us/library/ms181091.aspx`

5-2. Eager Loading Related Entities
Problem

You want to load an entity along with some related entities in a single trip to the database.

Solution

Let's say that you have a model like the one shown in Figure 5-2.

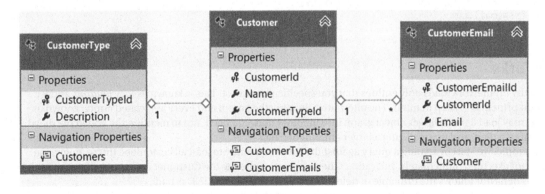

Figure 5-2. *A model with a Customer and its related information*

Similar to Recipe 5-1, in this model we have a Customer entity with a single CustomerType and many CustomerEmail addresses. The association with CustomerType is one-to-many with CustomerType on the *one* side of the association. This is an *entity reference.*

To fetch the parent customer entity objects and all of the related CustomerEmail entities and CustomerType entity objects at once, we use the Include( ) method syntax, as shown in Listing 5-2.

Listing 5-2. Eager Loading of Instances of Customertype and Customeremail Along with Instances of Customer

```
using (var context = new EFRecipesEntities())
{
    var web = new CustomerType { Description = "Web Customer",
                                 CustomerTypeId = 1 };
    var retail = new CustomerType { Description = "Retail Customer",
                                    CustomerTypeId = 2 };
    var customer = new Customer { Name = "Joan Smith", CustomerType = web };
    customer.CustomerEmails.Add(new CustomerEmail
                                    { Email = "jsmith@gmail.com" });
    customer.CustomerEmails.Add(new CustomerEmail { Email = "joan@smith.com" });
    context.Customers.Add(customer);
    customer = new Customer { Name = "Bill Meyers", CustomerType = retail };
    customer.CustomerEmails.Add(new CustomerEmail
                                    { Email = "bmeyers@gmail.com" });
    context.Customers.Add(customer);
    context.SaveChanges();
}

using (var context = new EFRecipesEntities())
{
    // Include() method with a string-based query path to the
    // corresponding navigation properties
    var customers = context.Customers
            .Include("CustomerType")
            .Include("CustomerEmails");

    Console.WriteLine("Customers");
    Console.WriteLine("=========");
    foreach (var customer in customers)
    {
        Console.WriteLine("{0} is a {1}, email address(es)", customer.Name,
                            customer.CustomerType.Description);
        foreach (var email in customer.CustomerEmails)
        {
            Console.WriteLine("\t{0}", email.Email);
        }
    }
}

using (var context = new EFRecipesEntities())
{
    // Include() method with a strongly typed query path to the
    // corresponding navigation properties
    var customerTypes = context.CustomerTypes
            .Include(x => x.Customers)
            .Select(y =>y.CustomerEmails));
```

```
Console.WriteLine("\nCustomers by Type");
Console.WriteLine("==================");
foreach (var customerType in customerTypes)
{
    Console.WriteLine("Customer type: {0}", customerType.Description);
    foreach (var customer in customerType.Customers)
    {
        Console.WriteLine("{0}", customer.Name);
        foreach (var email in customer.CustomerEmails)
        {
            Console.WriteLine("\t{0}", email.Email);
        }
    }
}
}
```

The output of the code in Listing 5-2 is the following:

```
Customers
=========
Joan Smith is a Web Customer, email address(es)
        jsmith@gmail.com
        joan@smith.com
Bill Meyers is a Retail Customer, email address(es)
        bmeyers@gmail.com

Customers by Type
=================
Customer type: Web Customer
Joan Smith
        jsmith@gmail.com
        joan@smith.com
Customer type: Retail Customer
Bill Meyers
        bmeyers@gmail.com
```

How It Works

By default, Entity Framework loads only entities that you specifically request. This is known as *lazy loading* and can be quite efficient in the use case where a user is browsing your application and may navigate to different views based upon his or her needs.

An alternative, loading the parent and related entities (keep in mind that our object graph is a set of parent/child entities based on relationships, similar to parent/child database tables with foreign key relationships) at once, is known as *eager loading*. This approach can be efficient when you know, up front, that you will require a large set of related data, as it can retrieve all data (both from the parent and related entities) in a single query.

In Listing 5-2, to fetch the object graph all at once, we use the Include() method twice. In the first use, we start the object graph with Customer and include an entity reference to the CustomerType entity. This is on the *one* side of the one-to-many association. Then, in the subsequent Include() method (contained in the same line of code, chained together), we get the *many* side of the one-to-many association, bringing along all of the instances of the

CustomerEmail entity for the customer. By chaining together the Include() method twice in a fluent API manner, we fetch referenced entities from both of the Customer's navigation properties. Note that in this example we use string representations of the navigation properties, separated by the "." character, to identify the related entity objects. The string representation is referred as the *query path* of the related objects.

In the following foreach construct, we perform the exact same operation, but using strongly typed query paths. Note here how we use lambda expressions to identify each of the related entities. The strongly typed usage provides us with both IntelliSense, compile-time safety and refactoring support.

Note that the SQL query that is generated in Listing 5-3 is generated from usage of the Include() method. Entity Framework automatically removes data that is duplicated by the query, as shown in Figure 5-3, before the result is materialized and sent back to the application.

Listing 5-3. The SQL Query Resulting from Our Use of the Include() Method

```sql
SELECT
[Project1].[CustomerId] AS [CustomerId],
[Project1].[Name] AS [Name],
[Project1].[CustomerTypeId] AS [CustomerTypeId],
[Project1].[CustomerTypeId1] AS [CustomerTypeId1],
[Project1].[Description] AS [Description],
[Project1].[C1] AS [C1],
[Project1].[CustomerEmailId] AS [CustomerEmailId],
[Project1].[CustomerId1] AS [CustomerId1],
[Project1].[Email] AS [Email]
FROM ( SELECT
                [Extent1].[CustomerId] AS [CustomerId],
                [Extent1].[Name] AS [Name],
                [Extent1].[CustomerTypeId] AS [CustomerTypeId],
                [Extent2].[CustomerTypeId] AS [CustomerTypeId1],
                [Extent2].[Description] AS [Description],
                [Extent3].[CustomerEmailId] AS [CustomerEmailId],
                [Extent3].[CustomerId] AS [CustomerId1],
                [Extent3].[Email] AS [Email],
                CASE WHEN ([Extent3].[CustomerEmailId] IS NULL) THEN CAST(NULL AS int) ELSE 1 END AS [C1]
                FROM    [Chapter5].[Customer] AS [Extent1]
                INNER JOIN [Chapter5].[CustomerType] AS [Extent2] ON
[Extent1].[CustomerTypeId] = [Extent2].[CustomerTypeId]
                LEFT OUTER JOIN [Chapter5].[CustomerEmail] AS [Extent3] ON
[Extent1].[CustomerId] = [Extent3].[CustomerId]
) AS [Project1]
ORDER BY [Project1].[CustomerId] ASC, [Project1].[CustomerTypeId1] ASC, [Project1].[C1] ASC
```

	CustomerId	Name	CustomerTypeId	CustomerTypeId1	Description	C1	CustomerEmailId	CustomerId1	Email
1	34	Joan Smith	1	1	Web Customer	1	51	34	jsmith@gmail.com
2	34	Joan Smith	1	1	Web Customer	1	52	34	joan@smith.com
3	35	Bill Meyers	2	2	Retail Customer	1	53	35	bmeyers@gmail.com

Figure 5-3. *Redundant data resulting from the Include() method*

5-3. Finding Single Entities Quickly

Problem

You want to load a single entity, but you do not want to make another trip to the database if the entity is already loaded in the context. Additionally, you want to implement the Code-First approach for Entity Framework 6 to manage data access.

Solution

Let's say that you have a model like the one shown in Figure 5-4.

Figure 5-4. *A simple model that represents Club entity objects*

In this model, we have a Club entity that we can query to obtain information about various clubs.

Start by adding a console application project to Visual Studio entitled Recipe3. Be certain to reference the Entity Framework 6 libraries. Leveraging the NuGet Package Manager does this best. Right-click on Reference, and select Manage NuGet Packages. From the Online tab, locate and install the Entity Framework 6 package. Doing so will download, install, and configure the Entity Framework 6 libraries in your project.

To create the club entity, create a class entitled Club and copy the properties into it from Listing 5-4.

Listing 5-4. Club Entity Class

```
public class Club
{
    public int ClubId { get; set; }
    public string Name { get; set; }
    public string City { get; set; }
}
```

Next create a class entitled Recipe3Context and add the code from Listing 5-5 to it, ensuring the class derives from the Entity Framework DbContext class.

Listing 5-5. Context Class

```
public class Recipe3Context : DbContext
{
    public Recipe3Context()
        : base("Recipe3ConnectionString")
```

```
{
    // Disable Entity Framework Model Compatibility
    Database.SetInitializer<Recipe3Context>(null);
}

public DbSet<Club> Clubs { get; set; }

protected override void OnModelCreating(DbModelBuilder modelBuilder)
{
    modelBuilder.Entity<Club>().ToTable("Chapter5.Club");
}
}
```

Next add an App.Config class to the project, and add the code from Listing 5-6 to it under the ConnectionStrings section.

Listing 5-6. Connection String

```
<connectionStrings>
  <add name="Recipe3ConnectionString"
      connectionString="Data Source=.;
      Initial Catalog=EFRecipes;
      Integrated Security=True;
      MultipleActiveResultSets=True"
      providerName="System.Data.SqlClient" />
</connectionStrings>
```

If we are searching for an entity by a key value, a common operation, we can leverage the Find() method first to search the in-memory context object for a requested entity before attempting to fetch it from the database. Keep in mind that the default behavior of Entity Framework is to query the database each time you issue an operation to retrieve data, even if that data has already been loaded into memory in the context object.

The Find() method is a member of the DbSet class, which we use to register each entity class in the underlying DbContext object. The pattern is demonstrated in Listing 5-7.

Listing 5-7. Leveraging the Find() Method in Entity Framework to Avoid Fetching Data That Has Already Been Loaded into the Context

```
using (var context = new Recipe3Context())
{
    var starCity = new Club {Name = "Star City Chess Club", City = "New York"};
    var desertSun = new Club {Name = "Desert Sun Chess Club", City = "Phoenix"};
    var palmTree = new Club {Name = "Palm Tree Chess Club", City = "San Diego"};

    context.Clubs.Add(starCity);
    context.Clubs.Add(desertSun);
    context.Clubs.Add(palmTree);
    context.SaveChanges();

    // SaveChanges() returns newly created Id value for each club
    starCityId = starCity.ClubId;
    desertSunId = desertSun.ClubId;
    palmTreeId = palmTree.ClubId;
}
```

```
using (var context = new Recipe3Context())
{
    var starCity = context.Clubs.SingleOrDefault(x => x.ClubId == starCityId);
    starCity = context.Clubs.SingleOrDefault(x => x.ClubId == starCityId);
    starCity = context.Clubs.Find(starCityId);
    var desertSun = context.Clubs.Find(desertSunId);
    var palmTree = context.Clubs.AsNoTracking().SingleOrDefault(x => x.ClubId == palmTreeId);
    palmTree = context.Clubs.Find(palmTreeId);
    var lonesomePintId = -999;
    context.Clubs.Add(new Club {City = "Portland", Name = "Lonesome Pine", ClubId = lonesomePintId,});
    var lonesomePine = context.Clubs.Find(lonesomePintId);
    var nonexistentClub = context.Clubs.Find(10001);
}
```

How It Works

When querying against the context object, a round trip will always be made to the database to retrieve requested data, even if that data has already been loaded into the context object in memory. When the query completes, entity objects that do not exist in the context are added and then tracked. By default, if the entity object is already present in the context, it is not overwritten with more recent database values.

However, the DbSet object, which wraps each of our entity objects, exposes a Find() method. Specifically, Find() expects an argument that represents the primary key of the desired object. Find() is very efficient, as it will first search the underlying context for the target object. If the object is not found, it then automatically queries the underlying data store. If still not found, Find() simply returns NULL to the caller. Additionally, Find() will return entities that have been added to the context (think, having a state of "Added"), but not yet saved to the underlying database. Fortunately, the Find() method is available with any of three modeling approaches: Database First, Model First, or Code First.

In this example, we start by adding three new clubs to the Club entity collection. Note how we are able to reference the newly created Id for each Club entity immediately after the call to SaveChanges(). The context will return the Id for the new object immediately after the SaveChanges() operation completes.

We next query the Clubs entity from the DbContext object to return the StarCity Club entity. Note how we leverage the SingleOrDefault() LINQ extension method, which returns exactly one object, or NULL, if the object does not exist in the underlying data store. SingleOrDefault() will throw an exception if more than one object with the search criteria is found. SingleOfDefault() is an excellent approach to querying entities by a primary key property. If you should desire the first object when many exist, consider the FirstOrDefault() method.

If you were to run SQL Profiler tool (available in SQL Server Developer Edition or better, not in SQL Express) to examine the underlying database activity, you would see that the SQL query shown in Figure 5-5 was generated.

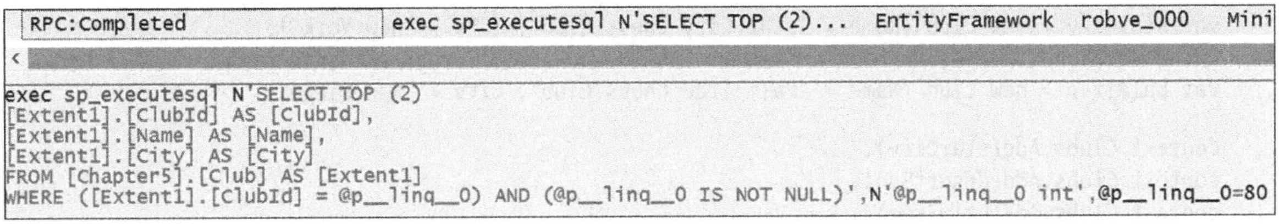

```
RPC:Completed                        exec sp_executesql N'SELECT TOP (2)...  EntityFramework  robve_000    Mini
<
exec sp_executesql N'SELECT TOP (2)
[Extent1].[ClubId] AS [ClubId],
[Extent1].[Name] AS [Name],
[Extent1].[City] AS [City]
FROM [Chapter5].[Club] AS [Extent1]
WHERE ([Extent1].[ClubId] = @p__linq__0) AND (@p__linq__0 IS NOT NULL)',N'@p__linq__0 int',@p__linq__0=80
```

Figure 5-5. *SQL query returning the Star City Club*

Note in Figure 5-5 how querying Clubs in the context object always results in a SQL query generated against the underlying data store. Here we retrieve the Club with the Id of 80, materialize the data into a Club entity object, and store it in the context. Interestingly, note how the SingleOrDefault() LINQ extension method always generates a Select Top 2 SQL query. Interestingly, the Select Top 2 SQL query ensures that only one row is returned. If more than one row is returned, Entity Framework will throw an exception as the SingleOrDefault() method guarantees a single result.

The next line of code re-queries the database for the exact same Star City Club. Note that, even though this entity object already exists in the context, the default behavior of the DbContext is to re-query the database for the record. In profiler, we see the exact same SQL query generated. What's more, since the Star City entity is already loaded in the context, the DbContext does not overwrite the current values with updated values from the database, as shown in Figure 5-6.

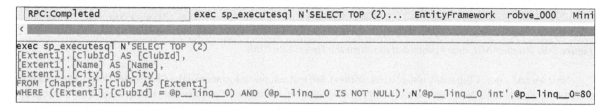

```
RPC:Completed                          exec sp_executesql N'SELECT TOP (2)...   EntityFramework   robve_000   Mini
<
exec sp_executesql N'SELECT TOP (2)
[Extent1].[ClubId] AS [ClubId],
[Extent1].[Name] AS [Name],
[Extent1].[City] AS [City]
FROM [Chapter5].[Club] AS [Extent1]
WHERE ([Extent1].[ClubId] = @p__linq__0) AND (@p__linq__0 IS NOT NULL)',N'@p__linq__0 int',@p__linq__0=80
```

Figure 5-6. *SQL query returning the Star City Club*

In the next line of code we once again search for the Star City Club. This time, however, we leverage the Find() method that is exposed by the DbSet Class. Since the Club entity is a DbSet class, we simply call the Find() method on it and pass in the primary key of the entity as an argument to Find(), which in this case is the value of 80.

Find() first searches the context object in memory for Star City, finds the object, and returns a reference to it. The key point is that Find() only queries the database if it cannot find the requested object in the context object. Note in Figure 5-7 how a SQL query was not generated.

```
EventClass                          TextData                          ApplicationName
```

Figure 5-7. *The Find() method locates the object in the context, and it never generates a query to the database*

Next we again use the Find() method to retrieve the entity for the Desert Sun Club. This Find() does not locate the target entity in the context object, and it next queries the underlying data store to return the information. Note in Figure 5-8 the SQL query that is generated to retrieve the data.

```
RPC:Completed                          exec sp_executesql N'SELECT TOP (2)...   EntityFramework   robve_000   Mini
<
exec sp_executesql N'SELECT TOP (2)
[Extent1].[ClubId] AS [ClubId],
[Extent1].[Name] AS [Name],
[Extent1].[City] AS [City]
FROM [Chapter5].[Club] AS [Extent1]
WHERE [Extent1].[ClubId] = @p0',N'@p0 int',@p0=84
```

Figure 5-8. *SQL query generated to return the Desert Sun Club*

In the next query, we retrieve entity information for the Palm Tree Club, but pay particular attention to the LINQ query. Note the AsNoTracking() clause that has been appended to Clubs. The NoTracking option disables object state tracking for the specific entity. With NoTracking, Entity Framework will not track changes to the Palm Tree object, nor will it load it into the underlying context object.

When we issue a subsequent request to obtain the Palm Tree club entity object, Find() generates a SQL query to retrieve the entity from the data store, as shown in Figure 5-9. The round trip to the database is necessary as we instructed Entity Framework not to track the object in the context object with the AsNoTracking() clause. Keep in mind that Find() requires the entity object to be tracked in the context in order to avoid a call to the database.

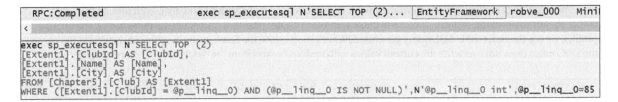

```
RPC:Completed                    exec sp_executesql N'SELECT TOP (2)...  EntityFramework  robve_000    Mini
<
exec sp_executesql N'SELECT TOP (2)
[Extent1].[ClubId] AS [ClubId],
[Extent1].[Name] AS [Name],
[Extent1].[City] AS [City]
FROM [Chapter5].[Club] AS [Extent1]
WHERE (([Extent1].[ClubId] = @p__linq__0) AND (@p__linq__0 IS NOT NULL)',N'@p__linq__0 int',@p__linq__0=85
```

Figure 5-9. Another SQL query generated to return the Desert Sun Club

Next we add a new Club entity object to the context. We instantiate an instance of the Club entity class and populate it with the necessary data. We assign it a temporary Id of –999. Keep in mind that we have not yet requested a SaveChanges() operation to commit this new club, the Lonesome Pine Club, to the data store. Interestingly, when we issue a Find() operation and pass in the argument –999, Entity Framework returns the newly created Lonesome Pine Club entity from the context object. You can see in Figure 5-10 that the Find() call generated no database activity. Take note: Find() will return a newly added entity instance from the underlying context object that has not yet been saved to the data store.

EventClass	TextData	ApplicationName

Figure 5-10. The Find() method locates the newly created, but not yet saved object in the context and returns it without generating a query to the database

Finally, we issue a Find() query passing in an argument value that does not exist in the data store. Here we pass an Id value of 10001. In Figure 5-11, we see that Find() issues a SQL query to the database attempting to return a record with an Id of 10001. Similar to the SingleOrDefault() LINQ extension method, Find() returns NULL to calling method when it does not find the record.

```
RPC:Completed                    exec sp_executesql N'SELECT TOP (2)...  EntityFramework  robve_000    Mini
<
exec sp_executesql N'SELECT TOP (2)
[Extent1].[ClubId] AS [ClubId],
[Extent1].[Name] AS [Name],
[Extent1].[City] AS [City]
FROM [Chapter5].[Club] AS [Extent1]
WHERE [Extent1].[ClubId] = @p0',N'@p0 int',@p0=10001
```

Figure 5-11. The Find() method generates a SQL query and returns NULL if the record is not found in the database

5-4. Querying In-Memory Entities

Problem

You want to work with entity objects from your model, but do not want to make a round trip to the database if the desired entity is already loaded in the in-memory context object. Additionally, you want to implement the Code-First approach for Entity Framework 6 to manage data access.

Solution

Let's say that you have a model like the one shown in Figure 5-12.

Figure 5-12. *A simple model that represents Club entity objects*

Start by adding a console application project to Visual Studio entitled Recipe4. Be certain to reference the Entity Framework 6 libraries. Leveraging the NuGet Package Manager does this best. Right-click on Reference, and select Manage NuGet Packages. From the Online tab, locate and install the Entity Framework 6 package. Doing so will download, install, and configure the Entity Framework 6 libraries in your project.

To create the club entity, create a class entitled Club and copy the information into it from Listing 5-8.

Listing 5-8. Club Entity Class

```
public class Club
{
    public int ClubId { get; set; }
    public string Name { get; set; }
    public string City { get; set; }
}
```

Next create a class entitled Recipe4Context, and add the code from Listing 5-9 to it, ensuring the class derives from the Entity Framework DbContext class.

Listing 5-9. Context Class

```
public class Recipe4Context : DbContext
{
    public Recipe4Context()
        : base("Recipe4ConnectionString")
    {
        // disable Entity Framework Model Compatibility
        Database.SetInitializer<Recipe4Context>(null);
    }

    public DbSet<Club> Clubs { get; set; }

    protected override void OnModelCreating(DbModelBuilder modelBuilder)
    {
        modelBuilder.Entity<Club>().ToTable("Chapter5.Club");
    }
}
```

Next add an App.Config classd to the project, and add the code from Listing 5-10 to it under the ConnectionStrings section.

Listing 5-10. Connection String

```
<connectionStrings>
  <add name="Recipe4ConnectionString"
      connectionString="Data Source=.;
      Initial Catalog=EFRecipes;
      Integrated Security=True;
      MultipleActiveResultSets=True"
      providerName="System.Data.SqlClient" />
</connectionStrings>
```

In this model, we have a Club entity from which we can query information about various clubs. We can reduce round trips to the database by directly querying the Local property of the underlying DbSet, which we use to wrap the Club entity. The Local property exposes an observable collection of in-memory entity objects, which stays in sync with the underlying context. Usage of the Local collection is demonstrated in Listing 5-11.

Listing 5-11. Common Usage of the Local Property for a DbSet Object

```
using (var context = new Recipe4Context())
{
    Console.WriteLine("\nLocal Collection Behavior");
    Console.WriteLine("=================");

    Console.WriteLine("\nNumber of Clubs Contained in Local Collection: {0}",
context.Clubs.Local.Count);
    Console.WriteLine("=================");

    Console.WriteLine("\nClubs Retrieved from Context Object");
    Console.WriteLine("=================");
    foreach (var club in context.Clubs.Take(2))
    {
        Console.WriteLine("{0} is located in {1}", club.Name, club.City);
    }

    Console.WriteLine("\nClubs Contained in Context Local Collection");
    Console.WriteLine("=================");
    foreach (var club in context.Clubs.Local)
    {
        Console.WriteLine("{0} is located in {1}", club.Name, club.City);
    }

    context.Clubs.Find(desertSunId);

    Console.WriteLine("\nClubs Retrieved from Context Object - Revisted");
    Console.WriteLine("=================");
```

```
    foreach (var club in context.Clubs)
    {
        Console.WriteLine("{0} is located in {1}", club.Name, club.City);
    }

    Console.WriteLine("\nClubs Contained in Context Local Collection - Revisted");
    Console.WriteLine("==================");
    foreach (var club in context.Clubs.Local)
    {
        Console.WriteLine("{0} is located in {1}", club.Name, club.City);
    }

    // Get reference to local observable collection
    var localClubs = context.Clubs.Local;

    // Add new Club
    var lonesomePintId = -999;
    localClubs.Add(new Club
    {
        City = "Portland",
        Name = "Lonesome Pine",
        ClubId = lonesomePintId
    });

    // Remove Desert Sun club
    localClubs.Remove(context.Clubs.Find(desertSunId));

    Console.WriteLine("\nClubs Contained in Context Object - After Adding and Deleting");
    Console.WriteLine("==================");
    foreach (var club in context.Clubs)
    {
        Console.WriteLine("{0} is located in {1} with a Entity State of {2}",
            club.Name, club.City, context.Entry(club).State);
    }

    Console.WriteLine("\nClubs Contained in Context Local Collection - After Adding and Deleting");
    Console.WriteLine("==================");
    foreach (var club in localClubs)
    {
        Console.WriteLine("{0} is located in {1} with a Entity State of {2}",
        club.Name, club.City, context.Entry(club).State);
    }

    Console.WriteLine("\nPress <enter> to continue...");
    Console.ReadLine();
}
```

The code in Listing 5-11 produces the following output:

```
Local Collection Behavior
==================

Number of Clubs Contained in Local Collection: 0
==================

Clubs Retrieved from Context Object
==================
Star City Chess Club is located in New York
Desert Sun Chess Club is located in Phoenix

Clubs Contained in Context Local Collection
==================
Star City Chess Club is located in New York
Desert Sun Chess Club is located in Phoenix

Clubs Retrieved from Context Object - Revisted
==================
Star City Chess Club is located in New York
Desert Sun Chess Club is located in Phoenix
Palm Tree Chess Club is located in San Diego

Clubs Contained in Context Local Collection - Revisted
==================
Star City Chess Club is located in New York
Desert Sun Chess Club is located in Phoenix
Palm Tree Chess Club is located in San Diego

Clubs Contained in Context Object - After Adding and Deleting
==================
Star City Chess Club is located in New York with a Entity State of Unchanged
Desert Sun Chess Club is located in Phoenix with a Entity State of Deleted
Palm Tree Chess Club is located in San Diego with a Entity State of Unchanged

Clubs Contained in Context Local Collection - After Adding and Deleting
==================
Star City Chess Club is located in New York with a Entity State of Unchanged
Palm Tree Chess Club is located in San Diego with a Entity State of Unchanged
Lonesome Pine is located in Portland with a Entity State of Added
```

How It Works

This example works with Club entity objects. We begin by requesting a count of Club entity objects from the observable collection that is exposed by the Local property from the Club entity object. Note in Figure 5-13 that no SQL query is generated, as a query against the Local Property never generates a SQL query to the data store.

EventClass	TextData	ApplicationName
Trace Start		

Figure 5-13. *Accessing the Local collection never generates a SQL query*

Right now, the result is zero, as we have not yet executed a query for Clubs against the context object. Keep in mind that the Local collection is automatically kept in sync with the underlying context object.

Next we query the context object for the first two Club entities in the data store and loop through them, rendering the name and location of each, as shown in Figure 5-14.

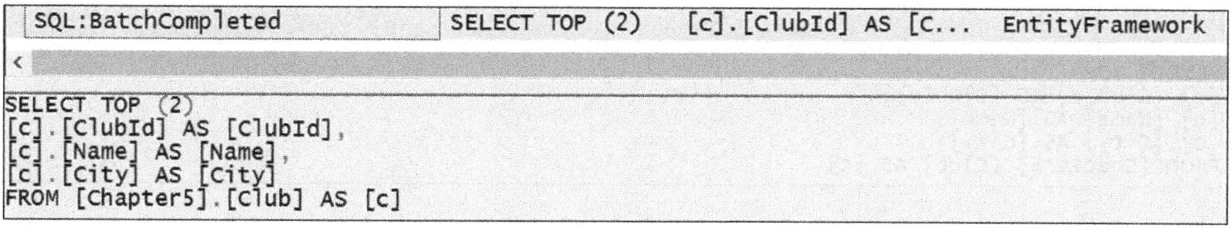

SQL:BatchCompleted	SELECT TOP (2) [c].[ClubId] AS [C...	EntityFramework
<		

```
SELECT TOP (2)
[c].[ClubId] AS [ClubId],
[c].[Name] AS [Name],
[c].[City] AS [City]
FROM [Chapter5].[Club] AS [c]
```

Figure 5-14. *Querying the context object always generates a SQL query*

Immediately after, we loop through the corresponding Local collection for Clubs and get the same result. Remember that the results are identical, as the Local collection automatically synchronizes with the DbContext. When new entities are fetched into the context, the Local collection is automatically updated with those entities. However, note in Figure 5-15 that no SQL query was generated when accessing the Local collection.

EventClass	TextData	ApplicationName
Trace Start		

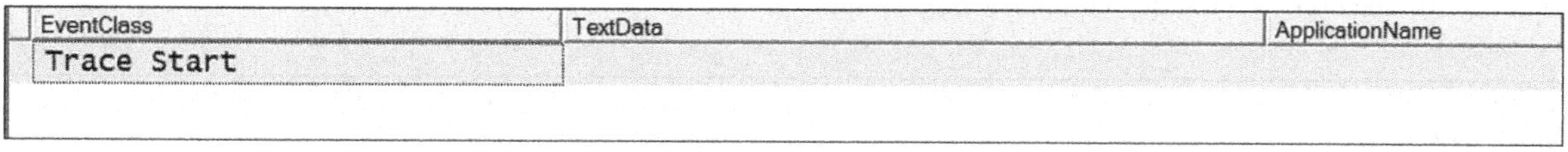

Figure 5-15. *Accessing the Local collection never generates a SQL query*

To demonstrate further the Local Property default behavior, we fetch a third Club entity by querying from the underlying context object. Once again, as we loop through both the context and Local collection, we get the same result. Note in Figure 5-16 that querying the context object always generates a SQL statement and that querying the Local collection does not, as shown in Figure 5-17.

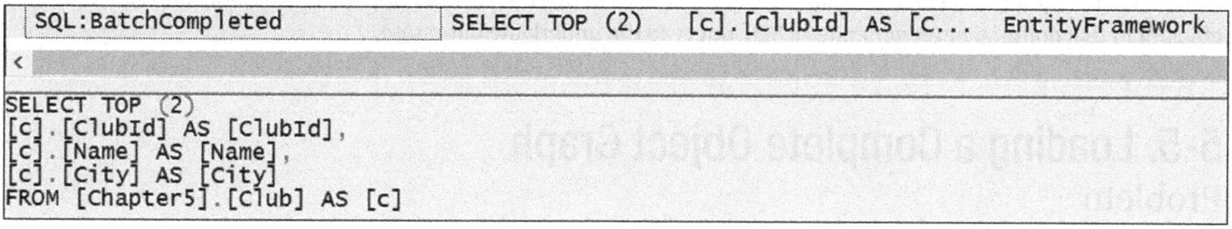

SQL:BatchCompleted	SELECT TOP (2) [c].[ClubId] AS [C...	EntityFramework
<		

```
SELECT TOP (2)
[c].[ClubId] AS [ClubId],
[c].[Name] AS [Name],
[c].[City] AS [City]
FROM [Chapter5].[Club] AS [c]
```

Figure 5-16. *Querying the context object always generates a SQL query*

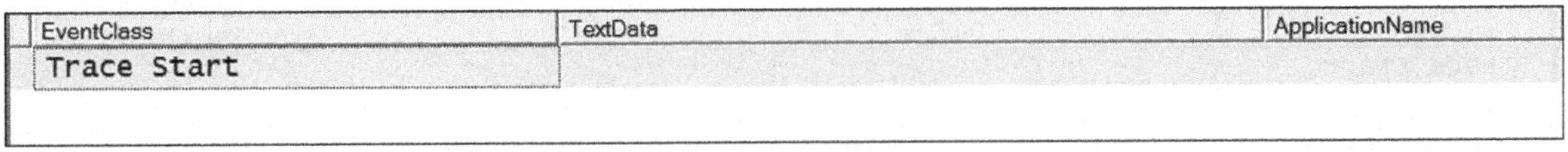

EventClass	TextData	ApplicationName
Trace Start		

Figure 5-17. *Accessing the Local collection never generates a SQL query*

Next we add a new Club entity entitled the Lonesome Pine Club to the Local collection and, at the same time, remove the Desert Sun Club from the Local collection. We then iterate through the context object for Clubs, which as expected, generates a SQL query against the underlying data store, as shown in Figure 5-18.

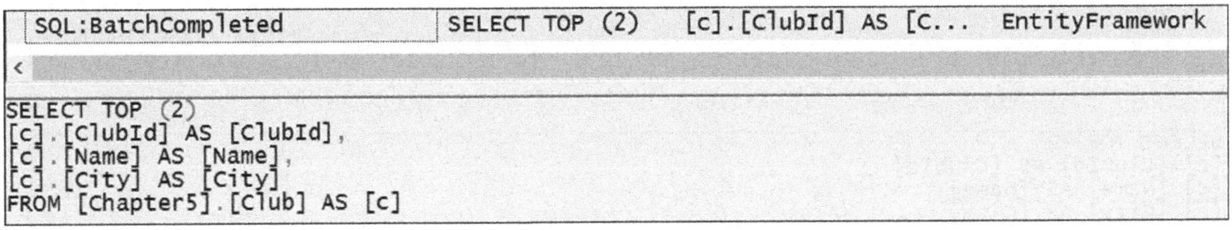

SQL:BatchCompleted	SELECT TOP (2) [c].[ClubId] AS [C... EntityFramework

```
SELECT TOP (2)
[c].[ClubId] AS [ClubId],
[c].[Name] AS [Name],
[c].[City] AS [City]
FROM [Chapter5].[Club] AS [c]
```

Figure 5-18. *Querying the context object always generates a SQL query*

Interestingly, in the context, we see that the Desert Sun Club has been marked for deletion, but we do not see the newly added Lonesome Pine Club. Keep in mind that Lonesome Pine has been added to the Context object, but we have not yet called the SaveChanges() operation to update the underlying data store.

However, when we iterate through the Local collection for Clubs, we do not generate a query to the underlying data store, as shown in Figure 5-19. Instead, we see the newly added Lonesome Pine Club, but we no longer see the Desert Sun Club that is marked for deletion. The default behavior of the Local collection is to hide any entities that are marked for deletion, as these objects are no longer valid.

EventClass	TextData	ApplicationName
Trace Start		

Figure 5-19. *Accessing the Local collection never generates a SQL query*

The bottom line: Accessing the Local collection *never* causes a query to be sent to the database; accessing the context object *always* causes a query to be sent to the database.

To summarize, each entity set exposes a property called Local, which is an observable collection that mirrors the contents of the underlying context object. As demonstrated in this recipe, querying the Local Collection can be very efficient in that doing so never generates a SQL query to the underlying data store.

5-5. Loading a Complete Object Graph

Problem

You have a model with several related entities, and you want to load the complete object graph of all the instances of each entity in a single query. Normally, when a specific view requires a set of related entities in order to render, you'll prefer this approach as opposed to the lazy loading approach that fetches related data with a number of smaller queries.

Solution

Suppose you have a conceptual model like the one in Figure 5-20. Each course has several sections. Each section is taught by an instructor and has several students.

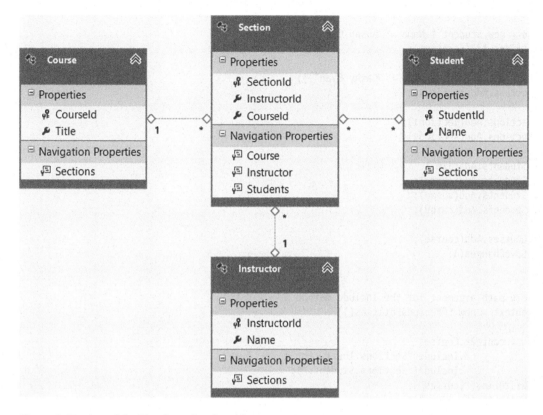

Figure 5-20. *A model with a few related entities*

To retrieve all of the courses, sections, instructors, and students represented in the database in a single query, use the Include() method with a query path parameter, as shown in Listing 5-12.

Listing 5-12. Retrieving an Entire Object Graph in a Single Query

```
using (var context = new EFRecipesEntities())
{
    var course = new Course { Title = "Biology 101" };
    var fred = new Instructor { Name = "Fred Jones" };
    var julia = new Instructor { Name = "Julia Canfield" };

    var section1 = new Section { Course = course, Instructor = fred };
    var section2 = new Section { Course = course, Instructor = julia };
```

```
        var jim = new Student { Name = "Jim Roberts" };
        jim.Sections.Add(section1);

        var jerry = new Student { Name = "Jerry Jones" };
        jerry.Sections.Add(section2);

        var susan = new Student { Name = "Susan O'Reilly" };
        susan.Sections.Add(section1);

        var cathy = new Student { Name = "Cathy Ryan" };
        cathy.Sections.Add(section2);

        course.Sections.Add(section1);
        course.Sections.Add(section2);

        context.Students.Add(jim);
        context.Students.Add(jerry);
        context.Students.Add(susan);
        context.Students.Add(cathy);

        context.Courses.Add(course);
        context.SaveChanges();
    }

    // String query path argument for the Include method
    using (var context = new EFRecipesEntities())
    {
        var graph = context.Courses
                            .Include("Sections.Instructor")
                            .Include("Sections.Students");
        Console.WriteLine("Courses");
        Console.WriteLine("=======");

        foreach (var course in graph)
        {
            Console.WriteLine("{0}", course.Title);
            foreach (var section in course.Sections)
            {
                Console.WriteLine("\tSection: {0}, Instrutor: {1}", section.SectionId,
    section.Instructor.Name);
                Console.WriteLine("\tStudents:");
                foreach (var student in section.Students)
                {
                    Console.WriteLine("\t\t{0}", student.Name);
                }
                Console.WriteLine("\n");
            }
        }
    }
}
```

```
// Strongly typed query path argument for the Include method
using (var context = new EFRecipesEntities())
{
    var graph = context.Courses
                    .Include(x => x.Sections.Select(y => y.Instructor))
                    .Include(x => x.Sections.Select(z => z.Students));

    Console.WriteLine("Courses");
    Console.WriteLine("=======");

    var result = graph.ToList();

    foreach (var course in graph)
    {
        Console.WriteLine("{0}", course.Title);
        foreach (var section in course.Sections)
        {
            Console.WriteLine("\tSection: {0}, Instrutor: {1}", section.SectionId,
section.Instructor.Name);
            Console.WriteLine("\tStudents:");
                foreach (var student in section.Students)
                {
                    Console.WriteLine("\t\t{0}", student.Name);
                }
                Console.WriteLine("\n");
        }
    }

    Console.WriteLine("Press <enter> to continue...");
    Console.ReadLine();
}
```

The code in Listing 5-12 produces the following output:

```
Courses
Courses
=======
Biology 101
        Section: 19, Instructor: Fred Jones
        Students:
                Jim Roberts
                Susan O'Reilly

        Section: 20, Instructor: Julia Canfield
        Students:
                Jerry Jones
                Cathy Ryan
```

How It Works

A query path is a string or strongly typed argument that is passed to the `Include()` method. A query path represents the entire path of the object graph that you want to load with the `Include()` method. The `Include()` method extends the query to include the entities referenced along the query path.

In Listing 5-12, we start by demonstrating the `Include()` method with string-based query parameters. `Include()` is invoked first with a query path parameter that includes the part of the graph extending through Section to Instructor. This modifies the query to include all of the Sections and their Instructors. Then, chained to the first `Include()` method is another `Include()` method that includes a path extending through Section to Student. This modifies the query to include Sections and their Students. The result is a materialization of the complete object graph including all Course entities along with entities on each end of the associations in the model.

In the second part of Listing 5-12, we demonstrate the usage of the `Include()` method with strongly typed query path parameters. Notice how both `Include()` methods here combine one parameter, Sections, with the associated Instructor and Student entity objects by using a `Select()` method.

■ **Note**   The overloaded `Include()` method that accepts strongly-typed parameters is an extension method that is exposed from the `System.Data.Entity` namespace. You will need to add a using directive to your class that references this namespace in order to use the overloaded version of this method.

You can construct query paths from navigation properties to any depth. This gives you a great deal of flexibility in partial or complete object graph loading. Entity Framework attempts to optimize the final query generation by pruning off overlapping or duplicate query paths.

The syntax and semantics of the `Include()` method are deceptively simple. Don't let the simplicity fool you into thinking that there is no performance price to be paid when using the `Include()` method. Eager loading with several `Include()` method invocations can rapidly increase the complexity of the query sent to the database and dramatically increase the amount of data returned from the database. The complex queries generated can lead to poor performance plan generation, and the large amount of returned data can cause Entity Framework to spend an inordinate amount of time removing duplicate data. You would be wise to profile all queries generated from usage of the `Include()` method to ensure that you are not causing potential performance problems for your application.

5-6. Loading Navigation Properties on Derived Types

Problem

You have a model with one or more derived types that are in a Has-a relationship (wherein one object is a part of another object) with one or more other entities. You want to eagerly load all of the related entities in one round trip to the database.

Solution

Suppose that you have a model like the one in Figure 5-21.

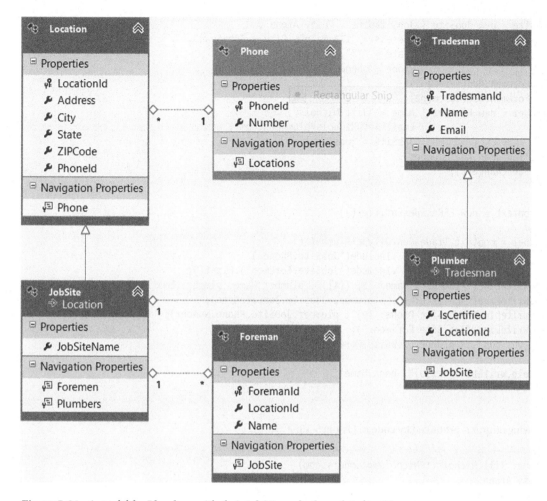

Figure 5-21. *A model for Plumbers with their JobSite and other related entities*

In this model, the Plumber entity extends the Tradesman entity. A Plumber has a JobSite that is represented by a one-to-many association. The JobSite type extends the Location entity. Location has a Phone, which is represented by a one-to-many association. Finally, a JobSite can have zero or more Foremen. A one-to-many association also represents this.

Suppose that you want to retrieve a plumber, the job site she works on, the job site's phone number, and all of the foremen at the job site. You want to retrieve all of this in one round trip to the database.

The code in Listing 5-13 illustrates one way to use the Include() method to eagerly load the related entities in one query.

Listing 5-13. Retrieving Related Entities in One Round Rrip to the Database Using Eager Loading with the Include() Method

```
using (var context = new EFRecipesEntities())
{
    var foreman1 = new Foreman { Name = "Carl Ramsey" };
    var foreman2 = new Foreman { Name = "Nancy Ortega" };
    var phone = new Phone { Number = "817 867-5309" };
```

```
        var jobsite = new JobSite { JobSiteName = "City Arena",
                                    Address = "123 Main", City = "Anytown",
                                    State = "TX", ZIPCode = "76082",
                                    Phone = phone };
        jobsite.Foremen.Add(foreman1);
        jobsite.Foremen.Add(foreman2);
        var plumber = new Plumber { Name = "Jill Nichols",
                                    Email = "JNichols@plumbers.com",
                                    JobSite = jobsite };
        context.Tradesmen.Add(plumber);
        context.SaveChanges();
}

using (var context = new EFRecipesEntities())
{
    var plumber = context.Tradesmen.OfType<Plumber>()
                              .Include("JobSite.Phone")
                              .Include("JobSite.Foremen").First();
    Console.WriteLine("Plumber's Name: {0} ({1})", plumber.Name, plumber.Email);
    Console.WriteLine("Job Site: {0}", plumber.JobSite.JobSiteName);
    Console.WriteLine("Job Site Phone: {0}", plumber.JobSite.Phone.Number);
    Console.WriteLine("Job Site Foremen:");
    foreach (var boss in plumber.JobSite.Foremen)
    {
        Console.WriteLine("\t{0}", boss.Name);
    }
}
```

The following output is produced by code in Listing 5-13:

```
Plumber's Name: Jill Nichols (JNichols@plumbers.com)
Job Site: City Arena
Job Site Phone: 817 867-5309
Job Site Foremen:
        Carl Ramsey
        Nancy Ortega
```

How It Works

Our query starts by selecting instances of the derived type Plumber. To fetch them, we use the OfType<Plumber>() method. The OfType<>() method selects instances of the given subtype from the entity set.

From Plumber, we want to load the related JobSite and the Phone for the JobSite. Notice that the JobSite entity does not have a Phone navigation property, but JobSite derives from Location, which does have a Phone navigation property. Because Phone is a property of the base entity, it's also available on the derived entity. That's the beauty of inheritance. This makes the query path simply: JobSite.Phone.

Then we again use the Include() method with a query path that references the Foreman entities from the JobSite entity. Here we have a one-to-many association, JobSite and Foreman. Notice that the wizard pluralized the navigation property (from Foreman to Foremen).

Finally, we use the First() method to select just the first Plumber instance. Doing so returns a type of Plumber, as opposed to a collection of Plumber objects.

The resulting query is somewhat complex; involving several joins and sub-selects. The alternative, leveraging the default lazy loading behavior of Entity Framework, would require several round trips to the database and could result in a performance hit, especially if we retrieved many Plumbers.

5-7. Using Include() with Other LINQ Query Operators
Problem

You have a LINQ query that uses operators such as group by, join, and where; and you want to use the Include() method to eagerly load additional entities. Additionally, you want to implement the Code-First approach for Entity Framework 6 to manage data access.

Solution

Let's say that you have a model like the one shown in Figure 5-22.

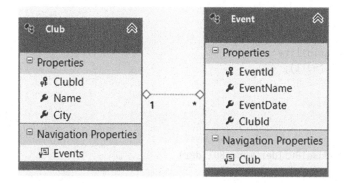

Figure 5-22. *A simple model with a one-to-many association between Club and Event*

Start by adding a console application project to Visual Studio entitled Recipe7. Be certain to reference the Entity Framework 6 libraries. Leveraging the NuGet Package Manager does this best. Right-click on Reference, and select Manage NuGet Packages. From the Online tab, locate and install the Entity Framework 6 package. Doing so will download, install, and configure the Entity Framework 6 libraries in your project.

To create our entity objects, create a class entitled Club and Event and add the code from Listing 5-14.

Listing 5-14. Club Entity Class

```
public class Club
{
    public Club()
    {
        Events = new HashSet<Event>();
    }

    public int ClubId { get; set; }
    public string Name { get; set; }
    public string City { get; set; }

    public virtual ICollection<Event> Events { get; set; }
}
```

```
public class Event
{
    public int EventId { get; set; }
    public string EventName { get; set; }
    public DateTime EventDate { get; set; }
    public int ClubId { get; set; }

    public virtual Club Club { get; set; }
}
```

Next create a class entitled Recipe7Context, and add the code from Listing 5-15 to it, ensuring the class derives from the Entity Framework DbContext class.

Listing 5-15. Context Class

```
public class Recipe7Context : DbContext
{
    public Recipe7Context()
        : base("Recipe7ConnectionString")
    {
        // Disable Entity Framework Model Compatibility
        Database.SetInitializer<Recipe7Context>(null);
    }

    public DbSet<Club> Clubs { get; set; }
    public DbSet<Event> Events { get; set; }

    protected override void OnModelCreating(DbModelBuilder modelBuilder)
    {
        modelBuilder.Entity<Club>().ToTable("Chapter5.Club");
        modelBuilder.Entity<Event>().ToTable("Chapter5.Event");
    }
}
```

Next add an App.Config class to the project, and add the code from Listing 5-16 to it under the ConnectionStrings section.

Listing 5-16. Connection String

```
<connectionStrings>
  <add name="Recipe7ConnectionString"
      connectionString="Data Source=.;
      Initial Catalog=EFRecipes;
      Integrated Security=True;
      MultipleActiveResultSets=True"
      providerName="System.Data.SqlClient" />
</connectionStrings>
```

To use the Include() method in combination with a group by clause, the Include() method must be placed after filtering and grouping operations for the parent entity. The code in Listing 5-17 demonstrates this approach.

Listing 5-17. *The Correct Placement of the Include Method When Applying Filtering and Grouping Expressions on the Parent Entity*

```
using (var context = new Recipes7Context())
{
    var club = new Club {Name = "Star City Chess Club", City = "New York"};
    club.Events.Add(new Event
    {
        EventName = "Mid Cities Tournament",
        EventDate = DateTime.Parse("1/09/2010"), Club = club
    });
    club.Events.Add(new Event
    {
        EventName = "State Finals Tournament",
        EventDate = DateTime.Parse("2/12/2010"), Club = club
    });
    club.Events.Add(new Event
    {
        EventName = "Winter Classic",
        EventDate = DateTime.Parse("12/18/2009"), Club = club
    });

    context.Clubs.Add(club);
    context.SaveChanges();
}

using (var context = new Recipes7Context())
{
    var events = from ev in context.Events
                     where ev.Club.City == "New York"
                     group ev by ev.Club
                         into g
                         select g.FirstOrDefault(e1 => e1.EventDate == g.Min(evt => evt.EventDate));

    var eventWithClub = events.Include("Club").First();

    Console.WriteLine("The next New York club event is:");
    Console.WriteLine("\tEvent: {0}", eventWithClub.EventName);
    Console.WriteLine("\tDate: {0}", eventWithClub.EventDate.ToShortDateString());
    Console.WriteLine("\tClub: {0}", eventWithClub.Club.Name);
}
```

The output of the code in Listing 5-17 is the following:

```
The next New York club event is:
        Event: Winter Classic
        Date: 12/18/2009
        Club: Star City Chess Club
```

How It Works

We start by creating a Club and three Events. In the query, we grab all of the events at clubs in New York, group them by club, and find the first one in date order. Note how the FirstOrDefault() LINQ extension method is cleverly embedded in the Select, or projection, operation. However, the events variable holds just the expression. It hasn't executed anything on the database yet.

Next we leverage the Include() method to eagerly load information from the related Club entity object using the variable, events, from the first LINQ query as the input for the second LINQ query. This is an example of composing LINQ queries—breaking a more complex LINQ query into a series of smaller queries, where the variable of the preceding query is in the source of the query.

Note how we use the First() method to select just the first Event instance. Doing so returns a type of Event, as opposed to a collection of Event objects. Entity Framework 6 contains a new static class entitled IQueryableExtensions, which exposes an Include() method prototype that accepts either a string-based or strongly typed query path parameter. The IQueryableExtensions class replaces the DbExtensions class from EF 4 and EF 5.

Many developers find the Include() method somewhat confusing. In some cases, IntelliSense will not show it as available (because of the type of the expression). At other times, it will be silently ignored at runtime. Surprisingly, the compiler rarely complains unless it cannot determine the resulting type. The problems usually show up at runtime when they can be a more difficult fix. Here are some simple rules to follow when using Include():

1. The Include() method is an extension method on type IQueryable<T>.

2. Include() applies only to the final query results. When Include() is applied to a subquery, join, or nested from clause, it is ignored when the command tree is generated. Under the hood, Entity Framework translates your LINQ-to-Entities query into a construct called a *command tree*, which is then handed to the database provider to construct a SQL query for the target database.

3. Include() can be applied only to results that are entities. If the expression projects results that are not entities, Include() will be ignored.

4. The query cannot change the type of the results between the Include() and the outermost operation. A group by clause, for example, changes the type of the results.

5. The query path used in the Include() expression must start at a navigation property on the type returned from the outermost operation. The query path cannot start at an arbitrary point.

Let's see how these rules apply to the code in Listing 5-17. The query groups the events by the sponsoring club. The group by operator changes the result type from Event to a grouping result. Here Rule 4 says that we need to invoke the Include() method after the group by clause has changed the type. We do this by invoking Include() at the very end. If we applied the Include() method earlier as in from ev in context.Events.Include(), the Include() method would have been *silently dropped* from the command tree and never applied.

5-8. Deferred Loading of Related Entities

Problem

You have an instance of an entity, and you want to defer the loading of two or more related entities in a single query. Especially important here is how we use the Load() method to avoid requerying the same entity twice. Additionally, you want to implement the Code-First approach for Entity Framework 6 to manage data access.

Solution

Suppose that you have a model like the one in Figure 5-23.

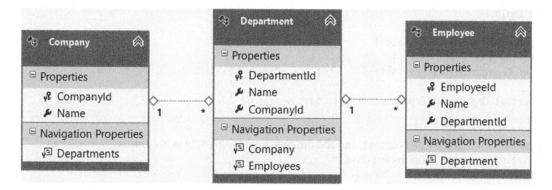

Figure 5-23. *A a model with an employee, her department, and the department's company*

Start by adding a console application project to Visual Studio entitled Recipe8. Be certain to reference the Entity Framework 6 libraries. Leveraging the NuGet Package Manager does this best. Right-click on Reference, and select Manage NuGet Packages. From the Online tab, locate and install the Entity Framework 6 package. Doing so will download, install, and configure the Entity Framework 6 libraries in your project.

Next we create three entity objects: Company, Department, and Employee, and copy the code from Listing 5-18 into three classes.

Listing 5-18. Entity Classes

```
public class Company
{
    public Company()
    {
        Departments = new HashSet<Department>();
    }

    public int CompanyId { get; set; }
    public string Name { get; set; }

    public virtual ICollection<Department> Departments { get; set; }
}

public class Department
{
    public Department()
    {
        Employees = new HashSet<Employee>();
    }

    public int DepartmentId { get; set; }
    public string Name { get; set; }
    public int CompanyId { get; set; }

    public virtual Company Company { get; set; }
    public virtual ICollection<Employee> Employees { get; set; }
}
```

```
public class Employee
{
    public int EmployeeId { get; set; }
    public string Name { get; set; }
    public int DepartmentId { get; set; }

    public virtual Department Department { get; set; }
}
```

Next create a class entitled Recipe8Context, and add the code from Listing 5-19 to it, ensuring that the class derives from the Entity Framework DbContext class.

Listing 5-19. Context Class

```
public class Recipe8Context : DbContext
{
    public Recipe8Context()
        : base("Recipe8ConnectionString")
    {
        // Disable Entity Framework Model Compatibility
        Database.SetInitializer<Recipe8Context>(null);
    }

    protected override void OnModelCreating(DbModelBuilder modelBuilder)
    {
        modelBuilder.Entity<Company>().ToTable("Chapter5.Company");
        modelBuilder.Entity<Employee>().ToTable("Chapter5.Employee");
        modelBuilder.Entity<Department>().ToTable("Chapter5.Department");
    }

    public DbSet<Company> Companies { get; set; }
    public DbSet<Department> Departments { get; set; }
    public DbSet<Employee> Employees { get; set; }
}
```

Next add an App.Config class to the project, and add the code from Listing 5-20 to it under the ConnectionStrings section.

Listing 5-20. Connection String

```
<connectionStrings>
  <add name="Recipe8ConnectionString"
      connectionString="Data Source=.;
      Initial Catalog=EFRecipes;
      Integrated Security=True;
      MultipleActiveResultSets=True"
      providerName="System.Data.SqlClient" />
</connectionStrings>
```

In the model shown in Figure 5-23, an Employee is associated with exactly one Department. Each Department is associated with exactly one Company.

Given an instance of an Employee, you want to load both her department and the department's company. What makes this problem somewhat unique is that we already have an instance of Employee, and we want to avoid going back to the database to get another copy of the Employee just so that we can use the Include() method to obtain the related instances of Company and Department. Perhaps in your real-world problem, Employee is a very expensive entity to retrieve and materialize.

We could use the Load() method twice to load the related Department instance and then again to load the related Company instance. However, this would generate two round trips to the database. To load the related instances using just one query, we can either requery the Employee entity set using the Include() method with a query path including the Department and the Company, or combine the Reference() and Query() methods exposed by the Entry Class. The code in Listing 5-21 shows both approaches.

Listing 5-21. Inserting into the Model and Retrieving the Related Entities Using Two Slightly Different Approaches

```
using (var context = new EFRecipesEntities())
{
    var company = new Company { Name = "Acme Products" };
    var acc = new Department { Name = "Accounting", Company = company };
    var ship = new Department { Name = "Shipping", Company = company };
    var emp1 = new Employee { Name = "Jill Carpenter", Department = acc };
    var emp2 = new Employee { Name = "Steven Hill", Department = ship };
    context.Employees.Add(emp1);
    context.Employees.Add(emp2);
    context.SaveChanges();
}


// First approach
using (var context = new EFRecipesEntities())
{
    // Assume we already have an employee
    var jill = context.Employees.First(o => o.Name == "Jill Carpenter");

    // Get Jill's Department and Company, but we also reload Employees
    var results = context.Employees
                    .Include("Department.Company")
                    .First(o => o.EmployeeId == jill.EmployeeId);

    Console.WriteLine("{0} works in {1} for {2}",
                        jill.Name, jill.Department.Name, jill.Department.Company.Name);
}

// More efficient approach, does not retrieve Employee again
using (var context = new EFRecipesEntities())
{
    // Assume we already have an employee
    var jill = context.Employees.Where(o => o.Name == "Jill Carpenter").First();
```

```
// Leverage the Entry, Query, and Include methods to retrieve Department and Company data
// without requerying the Employee table
context.Entry(jill).Reference(x => x.Department).Query().Include(y => y.Company).Load();

Console.WriteLine("{0} works in {1} for {2}",
                            jill.Name, jill.Department.Name, jill.Department.Company.Name);
}
```

The following is the output of the code in Listing 5-21:

```
Jill Carpenter works in Accounting for Acme Products
Jill Carpenter works in Accounting for Acme Products
```

How It Works

If we didn't already have an instance of the Employee entity, we could simply use the Include() method with a query path Department.Company. This is essentially the approach we take in earlier queries. The disadvantage of this approach is that it retrieves all of the columns for the Employee entity. In many cases, this might be an expensive operation. Because we already have this object in the context, it seems wasteful to gather these columns again from the database and transmit them across the wire.

In the second query, we use the Entry() method exposed by the DbContext object to access the Employee object and perform operations against it. We then chain the Reference() and Query() methods from the DbReferenceEntity class to return a query to load the related Department object from the underlying data store. Additionally, we chain the Include() method to pull in the related Company information. As desired, this query retrieves both Department and Company data without needlessly requerying the data store for Employees data, which has already been loaded into the context.

5-9. Filtering and Ordering Related Entities

Problem

You have an instance of an entity and you want to load a related collection of entities applying both a filter and an ordering.

Solution

Suppose that you have a model like the one shown in Figure 5-24.

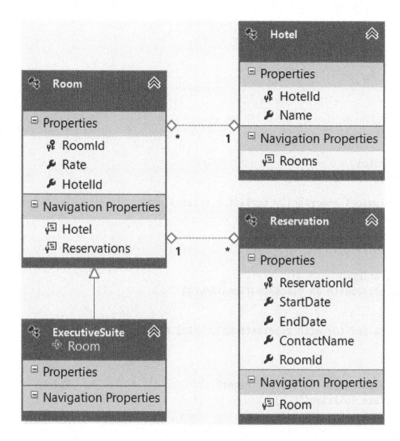

Figure 5-24. *A model for a hotel reservation system*

Let's assume we have an instance of a Hotel entity. To retrieve the executive suite rooms for the hotel, see which have reservations, and order them by room rate, use the pattern shown in Listing 5-22.

Listing 5-22. Filtering and Ordering an Entity Collection Using Explicit Loading Along with the Entry() and Query() Methods

```
using (var context = new EFRecipesEntities())
{
    var hotel = new Hotel { Name = "Grand Seasons Hotel" };
    var r101 = new Room { Rate = 79.95M, Hotel = hotel };
    var es201 = new ExecutiveSuite { Rate = 179.95M, Hotel = hotel };
    var es301 = new ExecutiveSuite { Rate = 299.95M, Hotel = hotel };

    var res1 = new Reservation { StartDate = DateTime.Parse("3/12/2010"),
                EndDate = DateTime.Parse("3/14/2010"), ContactName = "Roberta Jones", Room = es301 };
    var res2 = new Reservation { StartDate = DateTime.Parse("1/18/2010"),
                EndDate = DateTime.Parse("1/28/2010"), ContactName = "Bill Meyers", Room = es301 };
    var res3 = new Reservation { StartDate = DateTime.Parse("2/5/2010"),
                EndDate = DateTime.Parse("2/6/2010"), ContactName = "Robin Rosen", Room = r101 };

    es301.Reservations.Add(res1);
    es301.Reservations.Add(res2);
    r101.Reservations.Add(res3);
```

```
        hotel.Rooms.Add(r101);
        hotel.Rooms.Add(es201);
        hotel.Rooms.Add(es301);

        context.Hotels.Add(hotel);
        context.SaveChanges();
}

using (var context = new EFRecipesEntities())
{
        // Assume we have an instance of hotel
        var hotel = context.Hotels.First();

        // Explicit loading with Load() provides opportunity to filter related data
        // obtained from the Include() method
        context.Entry(hotel)
                    .Collection(x => x.Rooms)
                    .Query()
                    .Include(y => y.Reservations)
                    .Where(y => y is ExecutiveSuite && y.Reservations.Any())
                    .Load();

        Console.WriteLine("Executive Suites for {0} with reservations", hotel.Name);

        foreach (var room in hotel.Rooms)
        {
            Console.WriteLine("\nExecutive Suite {0} is {1} per night",
            room.RoomId.ToString(), room.Rate.ToString("C"));
            Console.WriteLine("Current reservations are:");
            foreach (var res in room.Reservations.OrderBy(r => r.StartDate))
            {
                Console.WriteLine("\t{0} thru {1} ({2})", res.StartDate.ToShortDateString(),
                res.EndDate.ToShortDateString(), res.ContactName);
            }
        }
    }
}
```

The following is the output of the code shown in Listing 5-22:

```
Executive Suites for Grand Seasons Hotel with reservations

Executive Suite 65 is $299.95 per night
Current reservations are:
        1/18/2010 thru 1/28/2010 (Bill Meyers)
        3/12/2010 thru 3/14/2010 (Roberta Jones)

Executive Suite 64 is $79.95 per night
Current reservations are:
        2/5/2010 thru 2/6/2010 (Robin Rosen)

Executive Suite 66 is $179.95 per night
```

How It Works

The code in Listing 5-22 uses explicit loading to retrieve a collection of related entity objects and perform filtering and ordering on them.

Along with lazy and eager loading, *explicit loading* is the third option for loading related data. When explicitly loading data, you are in full control. You issue commands that retrieve the data. You control if, when, and where related data is brought into the context object.

To implement explicit loading, you start with the Entry() method that is exposed by the DbContext object. Entry() accepts an argument that represents the parent entity that you wish to query. Entry() provides a wealth of information about the entity, including access to the related entity objects via the Collection() and Reference() methods.

In the example above, we start with the parent entity, Hotel, and then query related Room entities by chaining the Collection() method and passing in the navigation property, Rooms, as a parameter. The associated Query() method from the DbCollectionEntry class generates a query to load the room objects from the underlying data store.

Finally, we eagerly load the related reservations for each room by querying the Reservations navigation property as a parameter to the Include() method, applying where clause filters to retrieve only the collection of rooms of type ExecutiveSuite that have at least one reservation. We then order the collection by room rate using an OrderBy clause.

Normally, the Include() method returns all related objects for a parent with no opportunity to filter or manipulate the result set. The exception to this rule is when implementing explicit loading. As demonstrated here, we are able to filter and sort the results from related Reservation entities.

Keep in mind that we can only apply filters against related data from an Include() method using this pattern. This feature is not available when implementing lazy loading or eager loading.

5-10. Executing Aggregate Operations on Related Entities

Problem

You want to apply an aggregate operator on a related entity collection without loading the entire collection. Additionally, you want to implement the Code-First approach for Entity Framework 6 to manage data access.

Solution

Suppose that you have a model like the one shown in Figure 5-25.

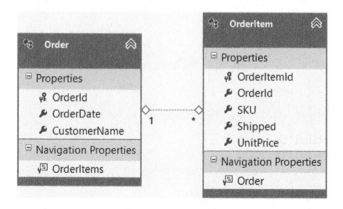

Figure 5-25. *Orders and their associated order items*

Start by adding a console application project to Visual Studio entitled `Recipe10`. Be certain to reference the Entity Framework 6 libraries. Leveraging the NuGet Package Manager does this best. Right-click on Reference, and select Manage NuGet Packages. From the Online tab, locate and install the Entity Framework 6 package. Doing so will download, install, and configure the Entity Framework 6 libraries in your project.

Next we create three entity objects. Create two classes: `Order` and `OrderItem`, and copy the code from Listing 5-23 into the classes.

Listing 5-23. Entity Classes

```
public class Order
{
    public Order()
    {
        OrderItems = new HashSet<OrderItem>();
    }

    public int OrderId { get; set; }
    public System.DateTime OrderDate { get; set; }
    public string CustomerName { get; set; }

    public virtual ICollection<OrderItem> OrderItems { get; set; }
}

public class OrderItem
{
    public int OrderItemId { get; set; }
    public int OrderId { get; set; }
    public int SKU { get; set; }
    public int Shipped { get; set; }
    public decimal UnitPrice { get; set; }

    public virtual Order Order { get; set; }
}
```

Next create a class entitled `Recipe10Context` and add the code from Listing 5-24 to it, ensuring the class derives from the Entity Framework DbContext class.

Listing 5-24. Context Class

```
public class Recipe10Context : DbContext
{
    public Recipe10Context()
        : base("Recipe10ConnectionString")
    {
        // Disable Entity Framework Model Compatibility
        Database.SetInitializer<Recipe10Context>(null);
    }

    protected override void OnModelCreating(DbModelBuilder modelBuilder)
    {
        modelBuilder.Entity<Order>().ToTable("Chapter5.Order");
        modelBuilder.Entity<OrderItem>().ToTable("Chapter5.OrderItem");
    }
```

```
    public DbSet<Order> Orders { get; set; }
    public DbSet<OrderItem> OrderItems { get; set; }
}
```

Next, add an App.Config class to the project and add the code from Listing 5-25 to it under the ConnectionStrings section.

Listing 5-25. Connection String

```
<connectionStrings>
  <add name="Recipe10ConnectionString"
       connectionString="Data Source=.;
       Initial Catalog=EFRecipes;
       Integrated Security=True;
       MultipleActiveResultSets=True"
       providerName="System.Data.SqlClient" />
</connectionStrings>
```

In Figure 5-25, we have a simple model composed of an order and the products (collection of OrderItems) shipped for the order. One way to get the total amount for the order is to use the Load() method to load the entire collection of order items and then iterate through this collection, calculating the sum of the amount for each order item.

Another way to get the same result is to push the iteration to the database, letting it compute the total amount. The advantage to this second approach is that we avoid the potentially costly overhead of materializing each order item for the sole purpose of summing the total order amount. To implement this second approach, follow the pattern shown in Listing 5-26.

Listing 5-26. Applying an Aggregate Operator on Related Entities Without Loading Them

```
using (var context = new EFRecipesEntities())
{
    var order = new Order { CustomerName = "Jenny Craig", OrderDate = DateTime.Parse("3/12/2010") };

    var item1 = new OrderItem { Order = order, Shipped = 3, SKU = 2827, UnitPrice = 12.95M };
    var item2 = new OrderItem { Order = order, Shipped = 1, SKU = 1918, UnitPrice = 19.95M };
    var item3 = new OrderItem { Order = order, Shipped = 3, SKU = 392, UnitPrice = 8.95M };

    order.OrderItems.Add(item1);
    order.OrderItems.Add(item2);
    order.OrderItems.Add(item3);

    context.Orders.Add(order);
    context.SaveChanges();
}

using (var context = new EFRecipesEntities())
{
    // Assume we have an instance of Order
    var order = context.Orders.First();
```

```
    // Get the total order amount
    var amt = context.Entry(order)
                    .Collection(x => x.OrderItems)
                    .Query()
                    .Sum(y => y.Shipped * y.UnitPrice);

    Console.WriteLine("Order Number: {0}", order.OrderId);
    Console.WriteLine("Order Date: {0}", order.OrderDate.ToShortDateString());
    Console.WriteLine("Order Total: {0}", amt.ToString("C"));
}
```

The following is the output of the code in Listing 5-26:

```
Order Number: 6
Order Date: 3/12/2010
Order Total: $85.65
```

How It Works

In Listing 5-26, we implement explicit loading and start with the Entry() method that is exposed by the DbContext object. Entry() accepts an argument of Order, which represents the parent entity that we wish to query. Entry() provides a wealth of information about the Order, including access to related entity objects via the Collection() and Reference() methods.

In the example above, we query related Order Items entities by chaining the Collection() method and passing in the navigation property, OrderItems, as a parameter. The associated Query() method from the DbCollectionEntry class generates a query to load the Order Item objects from the underlying data store.

Finally, we apply the Sum() LINQ extension method, passing in a lambda expression that calculates the item total. The resulting sum over the collection is the order total. This entire expression is converted to the appropriate store layer commands and executed in the storage layer, saving the cost of materializing each order item.

This simple example demonstrates the flexibility of combining explicit loading with the Entry() and Query() method to modify the query used to retrieve the underlying associated entity collection (OrderItems). In this case, we leveraged the query, summing the amounts for OrderItems that are related to the first order without actually loading the collection.

5-11. Testing Whether an Entity Reference or Entity Collection Is Loaded

Problem

You want to test whether the related entity or entity collection is loaded in the context. Additionally, you want to implement the Code-First approach for Entity Framework 6 to manage data access.

Solution

Suppose that you have a model like the one shown in Figure 5-26.

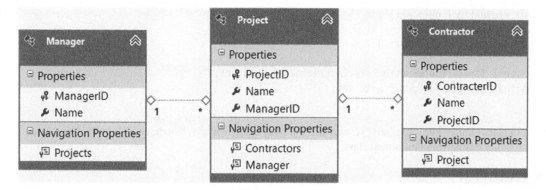

Figure 5-26. *A model for projects, managers, and contractors*

Start by adding a console application project to Visual Studio entitled Recipe11. Be certain to reference the Entity Framework 6 libraries. Leveraging the NuGet Package Manager does this best. Right-click on Reference, and select Manage NuGet Packages. From the Online tab, locate and install the Entity Framework 6 package. Doing so will download, install, and configure the Entity Framework 6 libraries in your project.

Next we create three entity objects: Contractor, Manager, and Project. Then copy the code from Listing 5-27 into the classes.

Listing 5-27. Entity Classes

```
public class Contractor
{
    public int ContracterID { get; set; }
    public string Name { get; set; }
    public int ProjectID { get; set; }

    public virtual Project Project { get; set; }
}

public class Manager
{
    public Manager()
    {
        Projects = new HashSet<Project>();
    }

    public int ManagerID { get; set; }
    public string Name { get; set; }

    public virtual ICollection<Project> Projects { get; set; }
}

public class Project
{
    public Project()
    {
        Contractors = new HashSet<Contractor>();
    }
```

```
    public int ProjectID { get; set; }
    public string Name { get; set; }
    public int ManagerID { get; set; }

    public virtual ICollection<Contractor> Contractors { get; set; }
    public virtual Manager Manager { get; set; }
}
```

Next create a class entitled Recipe11Context, and add the code from Listing 5-28 to it, ensuring the class derives from the Entity Framework DbContext class.

Listing 5-28. Context Class

```
public class Recipe11Context : DbContext
{
    public Recipe11Context()
        : base("Recipe11ConnectionString")
    {
        // Disable Entity Framework Model Compatibility
        Database.SetInitializer<Recipe11Context>(null);
    }

    public DbSet<Contractor> Contractors { get; set; }
    public DbSet<Manager> Managers { get; set; }
    public DbSet<Project> Projects { get; set; }

    protected override void OnModelCreating(DbModelBuilder modelBuilder)
    {
        modelBuilder.Entity<Contractor>().ToTable("Chapter5.Contractor");
        modelBuilder.Entity<Manager>().ToTable("Chapter5.Manager");
        modelBuilder.Entity<Project>().ToTable("Chapter5.Project");

        // Explilcitly map key for Contractor entity
        modelBuilder.Entity<Contractor>().HasKey(x => x.ContracterID);
    }
}
```

Next add an App.Config class to the project, and add the code from Listing 5-29c to it under the ConnectionStrings section.

Listing 5-29. Connection String

```
<connectionStrings>
  <add name="Recipe11ConnectionString"
       connectionString="Data Source=.;
       Initial Catalog=EFRecipes;
       Integrated Security=True;
       MultipleActiveResultSets=True"
       providerName="System.Data.SqlClient" />
</connectionStrings>
```

Entity Framework exposes the IsLoaded property that it sets to true when it is 100% certain that all data from the specified entity or entity collection is loaded and available in the context. The model in Figure 5-26 represents projects, the managers for the projects, and the contractors that work on the projects. To test whether a related entity is loaded into the context object, follow the pattern shown in Listing 5-30.

Listing 5-30. Using IsLoaded to Determine Whether an Entity or Entity Collection Is in the Context

```
using (var context = new EFRecipesEntities())
{
    var man1 = new Manager { Name = "Jill Stevens" };
    var proj = new Project { Name = "City Riverfront Park", Manager = man1 };
    var con1 = new Contractor { Name = "Robert Alvert", Project = proj };
    var con2 = new Contractor { Name = "Alan Jones", Project = proj };
    var con3 = new Contractor { Name = "Nancy Roberts", Project = proj };
    context.Projects.Add(proj);
    context.SaveChanges();
}

using (var context = new EFRecipesEntities())
{
    var project = context.Projects.Include("Manager").First();

    if (context.Entry(project).Reference(x => x.Manager).IsLoaded)
        Console.WriteLine("Manager entity is loaded.");
    else
        Console.WriteLine("Manager entity is NOT loaded.");

    if (context.Entry(project).Collection(x => x.Contractors).IsLoaded)
        Console.WriteLine("Contractors are loaded.");
    else
        Console.WriteLine("Contractors are NOT loaded.");

    Console.WriteLine("Calling project.Contractors.Load()...");
    context.Entry(project).Collection(x => x.Contractors).Load();

    if (context.Entry(project).Collection(x => x.Contractors).IsLoaded)
        Console.WriteLine("Contractors are now loaded.");
    else
        Console.WriteLine("Contractors failed to load.");
}
```

The following is the output from the code in Listing 5-30:

```
Manager entity is loaded.
Contractors are NOT loaded.
Calling project.Contractors.Load()...
Contractors are now loaded.
```

How It Works

We start by using the Include() method to eagerly load the Project entity together with its related Manager for the first Project from the data store.

After the query, we check whether the manager instance is loaded by obtaining a reference to the related Manager entity using the Reference() method and checking the value of the IsLoaded property. Because this is an entity reference (reference to a single parent entity), the IsLoaded property is available on the Reference property of the DbEntityEntry type that is returned for calling the Entry() method. As we loaded both Projects and Manager, the IsLoaded property returns true.

Next we check whether the Contractor entity collection is loaded. It is not loaded because we didn't eagerly load it with the Include() method, nor did we load it directly (yet) with the Load() method. Once we fetch it with the Load() method, the IsLoaded property for it is set to true.

When lazy loading is enabled on the context object, which is the default behavior, the IsLoaded property is set to true when the entity or entity collection is referenced. Lazy loading causes Entity Framework to load the entity or entity collection automatically when referenced. Explicit loading is similar to lazy loading, but is not automatic. Instead, the developer must explicitly load the related entity with the Load() method, giving the developer complete control over if and when related entities are loaded.

The exact meaning of IsLoaded can be a little more confusing than it seems it should be. IsLoaded is set by the results of a query by calling the Load() method, or implicitly by the span of relationship keys. When you query for an entity, there is an implicit query for the key of the related entity. If the result of this implicit query is a null key value, then IsLoaded is set to true, indicating that there is no related entity in the database. This is the same value for IsLoaded that we would expect if we did an explicit load on the relationship and found no related entity.

5-12. Loading Related Entities Explicitly

Problem

You want to load related entities directly, without relying on the default lazy loading behavior of Entity Framework.

Solution

Let's say that you have a model like the one in Figure 5-27.

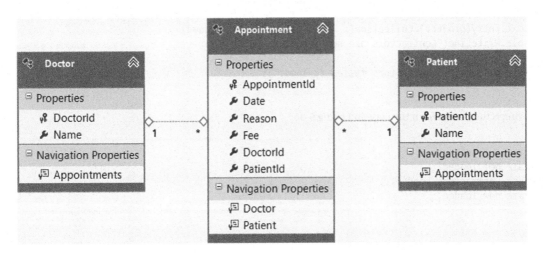

Figure 5-27. *A model for doctors, their patients, and appointments*

The model depicted in Figure 5-27 represents doctors, their patients, and appointments. To explicitly load related entities, follow the pattern in Listing 5-31.

Listing 5-31. Using the Load() Method

```
using (var context = new EFRecipesEntities())
{
    // disable lazy loading feature as we are explicitly loading
    // child entities
    context.Configuration.LazyLoadingEnabled = false;

    var doctorJoan = context.Doctors.First(o => o.Name == "Joan Meyers");

    if (!context.Entry(doctorJoan).Collection(x => x.Appointments).IsLoaded)
    {
        context.Entry(doctorJoan).Collection(x => x.Appointments).Load();
        Console.WriteLine("Dr. {0}'s appointments were explicitly loaded.",
                                    doctorJoan.Name);
    }

    Console.WriteLine("Dr. {0} has {1} appointment(s).",
                                    doctorJoan.Name,
                                    doctorJoan.Appointments.Count());

    foreach (var appointment in context.Appointments)
    {
        if (!context.Entry(appointment).Reference(x => x.Doctor).IsLoaded)
        {
            context.Entry(appointment).Reference(x => x.Doctor).Load();
            Console.WriteLine("Dr. {0} was explicitly loaded.",
                                        appointment.Doctor.Name);
        }
        else
            Console.WriteLine("Dr. {0} was already loaded.",
                                        appointment.Doctor.Name);
    }

    Console.WriteLine("There are {0} appointments for Dr. {1}",
                                    doctorJoan.Appointments.Count(),
                                    doctorJoan.Name);

    doctorJoan.Appointments.Clear();

    Console.WriteLine("Collection clear()'ed");
    Console.WriteLine("There are now {0} appointments for Dr. {1}",
                                    doctorJoan.Appointments.Count(),
                                    doctorJoan.Name);

    context.Entry(doctorJoan).Collection(x => x.Appointments).Load();
    Console.WriteLine("Collection loaded()'ed");
    Console.WriteLine("There are now {0} appointments for Dr. {1}",
                                    doctorJoan.Appointments.Count().ToString(),
                                    doctorJoan.Name);
```

```
    // Currently, there isn't an easy way to refresh entities with the DbContext API.
    // Instead, drop down into the ObjectContext and perform the following actions
    var objectContext = ((IObjectContextAdapter)context).ObjectContext;
    var objectSet = objectContext.CreateObjectSet<Appointment>();
    objectSet.MergeOption = MergeOption.OverwriteChanges;
    objectSet.Load();

    Console.WriteLine("Collection loaded()'ed with MergeOption.OverwriteChanges");
    Console.WriteLine("There are now {0} appointments for Dr. {1}",
                                    doctorJoan.Appointments.Count(),
                                    doctorJoan.Name);
}

// Demonstrating loading part of the collection then Load()'ing the rest
using (var context = new EFRecipesEntities())
{
    // disable lazy loading feature as we are explicitly loading
    // child entities
    context.Configuration.LazyLoadingEnabled = false;

    // Load the first doctor and attach just the first appointment
    var doctorJoan = context.Doctors.First(o => o.Name == "Joan Meyers");

    context.Entry(doctorJoan).Collection(x => x.Appointments).Query().Take(1).Load();

    Console.WriteLine("Dr. {0} has {1} appointments loaded.",
                        doctorJoan.Name,
                        doctorJoan.Appointments.Count());

    // When we need all of the remaining appointments, simply Load() them
    context.Entry(doctorJoan).Collection(x => x.Appointments).Load();
    Console.WriteLine("Dr. {0} has {1} appointments loaded.",
                        doctorJoan.Name,
                        doctorJoan.Appointments.Count());
}
```

The output of the code in Listing 5-31 is the following:

```
Dr. Joan Meyers's appointments were explicitly loaded
Dr. Joan Meyers has 2 appointment(s)
Dr. Joan Meyers was already loaded
Dr. Steven Mills was lazy loaded
Dr. Joan Meyers was already loaded
There are 2 appointments for Dr. Joan Meyers
Collection clear()'ed
There are now 0 appointments for Dr. Joan Meyers
Collection loaded()'ed
There are now 0 appointments for Dr. Joan Meyers
Collection loaded()'ed with MergeOption.OverwriteChanges
There are now 2 appointments for Dr. Joan Meyers
Dr. Joan Meyers has 2 appointments loaded
Dr. Joan Meyers has 2 appointments loaded
```

How It Works

After inserting some sample data into our database, we explicitly disable the lazy loading feature of Entity Framework, as we want to explicitly control the loading of related child entities. We can disable lazy loading in one of two ways:

- Set the LazyLoadingEnabled property from the `Context.Configuration` object to `false`. This approach disables lazy loading for all entities assigned to the context.

- Remove the virtual access modifier from each navigation property in each entity class. This approach disables lazy loading per entity class, giving you explicit control of lazy loading.

The first bit of code retrieves an instance of the Doctor entity. If you are using the explicit loading approach, it would be a good practice to use the IsLoaded property to check whether the entity or entity collection is already loaded. In the code, we check whether the doctor's appointments are loaded. If not, we use the `Load()` method to load them.

In the `foreach` loop, we iterate through the appointments, checking if the associated doctor is loaded. Notice in the output that one doctor was already loaded while the other one was not. This is because our first query retrieved this doctor. During the retrieval process for the appointments, Entity Framework connected the loaded instance of the doctor with her appointments. This process is informally referred to as *relationship fixup*. Relationship fixup will not fix up all associations. In particular, it will not tie in entities across a many-to-many association.

In the last bit of code, we print the number of appointments we have for the doctor. Then we clear the collection from the context using the `Clear()` method. The `Clear()` method removes the relationship between the Doctor and appointments entity objects.. Interestingly, it does not remove the instances from memory;they are still in the context—they are just no longer connected to this instance of the Doctor entity.

Somewhat surprisingly, after we call `Load()` to reload the appointments, we see from the output that no appointments are in our collection! What happened? It turns out that the `Load()` method is overloaded to take a parameter that controls how the loaded entities are merged into the context. The default behavior for the `Load()` method is `MergeOption.AppendOnly`, which simply appends instances that are not already in the context. In our case, none of the appointments was actually removed from the context. Our use of the `Clear()` method simply removed them from the entity collection, not the context. When we called `Load()` with the default `MergeOption.AppendOnly`, no new instances were found, so nothing was added to the entity collection. Other merge options include `NoTracking`, `OverwriteChanges`, and `PreserveChanges`. When we use the `OverwriteChanges` option, the appointments appear in the Doctor's Appointments.

Note in our code how we drop down into the underlying ObjectContext object in order to gain access to the MergeOption behaviors exposed by Entity Framework. The MergeOption type is not directly available in the DbContext. You'll recall that when using Entity Framework, there are two context objects available for use. The preferred context object for Entity Framework 6 is the DbContext object, which provides an intuitive and easy-to-use facade around the legacy Object Context object. The older Object Context object is still available through an explicit cast against the DbContext object, as demonstrated in our recipe.

Along with `AppendOnly`, the MergeOption type exposes three other options:

- The `NoTracking` option turns off object state tracking for the loaded instances. With `NoTracking`, Entity Framework will not track changes to the object and will not be aware that the object is loaded into the context. The `NoTracking` option can be used on a navigation property of an object only if the object was loaded with the `NoTracking` option. `NoTracking` has one additional side effect. If we had loaded an instance of the Doctor entity with `NoTracking`, loading the appointments with the `Load()` method would also occur with `NoTracking`, regardless of the default `AppendOnly` option.

- The `OverwriteChanges` option will update the values in the current instance with that from the database. Entity Framework will continue to use the same instance of the entity object. This option is particularly useful if you need to discard changes made in the context and refresh them from the database. This would be helpful, for example, in implementing an undo operation in an application.

- The PreserveChanges option is, essentially, the opposite of the OverwriteChanges option. It will update the values of any entities that have database changes, but no in-memory changes. An entity that has been modified in memory will not be refreshed. To be precise, the current value of an entity modified in memory will not be changed, but the original value will be updated if it has changed on the database.

There are some restrictions on when you can use Load(). Load() cannot be called on an entity that is in the Added, Deleted, or Detached state.

The Load() method can be helpful in improving performance by restricting how much of a collection is loaded at any one time. For example, suppose our doctors had lots of appointments, but in many cases we needed to work with just a few of them. In the rare case that we need the entire collection, we can simply call Load() to append the remaining appointment instances to the context. This is demonstrated in the code snippet in Listing 5-32.

Listing 5-32. Code Snippet Demonstrating Partial Loading of an Entity Collection

```
// Demonstrating loading part of the collection then Load()'ing the rest
using (var context = new EFRecipesEntities())
{
    // Load the first doctor and attach just the first appointment
    var doctorJoan = context.Doctors.First(o => o.Name == "Joan Meyers");

    context.Entry(doctorJoan).Collection(x => x.Appointments).Query().Take(1).Load();
    // note that IsLoaded returns false here since all related data has not been loaded into the context
    var appointmentsLoaded = context.Entry(doctorJoan).Collection(x => x.Appointments).IsLoaded;

    Console.WriteLine("Dr. {0} has {1} appointments loaded.",
                        doctorJoan.Name,
                        doctorJoan.Appointments.Count());

    // When we need all of the remaining appointments, simply Load() them
    context.Entry(doctorJoan).Collection(x => x.Appointments).Load();
    Console.WriteLine("Dr. {0} has {1} appointments loaded.",
                        doctorJoan.Name,
                        doctorJoan.Appointments.Count());
    }
```

The output of the code snippet in Listing 5-12b is the following:

```
Dr. Joan Meyers has 1 appointments loaded.
Dr. Joan Meyers has 2 appointments loaded.
```

5-13. Filtering an Eagerly Loaded Entity Collection
Problem

You want to filter an eagerly loaded collection. Additionally, you want to implement the Code-First approach for Entity Framework 6 to manage data access.

Solution

Entity Framework does not directly support filtering with the Include() method, but we can accomplish the same thing by creating an anonymous type that includes the entity along with the filtered collection of related entities.

Let's assume that you have a model like the one in Figure 5-28.

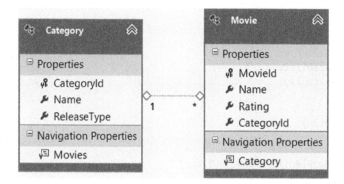

Figure 5-28. *A model for movies and their categories*

Start by adding a console application project to Visual Studio entitled Recipe13. Be certain to reference the Entity Framework 6 libraries. Leveraging the NuGet Package Manager does this best. Right-click on Reference, and select Manage NuGet Packages. From the Online tab, locate and install the Entity Framework 6 package. Doing so will download, install, and configure the Entity Framework 6 libraries in your project.

Next we create three entity objects. Create two classes: Category and Movie, and copy the code from Listing 5-33 into the classes.

Listing 5-33. Entity Classes

```
public class Category
{
    public Category()
    {
        Movies = new HashSet<Movie>();
    }

    public int CategoryId { get; set; }
    public string Name { get; set; }
    public string ReleaseType { get; set; }

    public virtual ICollection<Movie> Movies { get; set; }
}

public class Movie
{
    public int MovieId { get; set; }
    public string Name { get; set; }
    public string Rating { get; set; }
    public int CategoryId { get; set; }

    public virtual Category Category { get; set; }
}
```

Next create a class entitled Recipe13Context and add the code from Listing 5-34 to it, ensuring the class derives from the Entity Framework DbContext class.

Listing 5-34. Context Class

```
public class Recipe13Context : DbContext
{
    public Recipe13Context()
        : base("Recipe13ConnectionString")
    {
        // Disable Entity Framework Model Compatibility
        Database.SetInitializer<Recipe13Context>(null);
    }

    public DbSet<Category> Categories { get; set; }
    public DbSet<Movie> Movies { get; set; }

    protected override void OnModelCreating(DbModelBuilder modelBuilder)
    {
        modelBuilder.Entity<Category>().ToTable("Chapter5.Category");
        modelBuilder.Entity<Movie>().ToTable("Chapter5.Movie");
    }
}
```

Next add an App.Config class to the project, and add the code from Listing 5-35 to it under the ConnectionStrings section.

Listing 5-35. Connection String

```
<connectionStrings>
  <add name="Recipe13ConnectionString"
       connectionString="Data Source=.;
       Initial Catalog=EFRecipes;
       Integrated Security=True;
       MultipleActiveResultSets=True"
       providerName="System.Data.SqlClient" />
</connectionStrings>
```

To eagerly load and filter both the categories and their associated movies, follow the pattern in Listing 5-36.

Listing 5-36. Filtering an Eagerly Loaded Entity Collection

```
using (var context = new EFRecipesEntities())
{
    var cat1 = new Category { Name = "Science Fiction", ReleaseType = "DVD" };
    var cat2 = new Category { Name = "Thriller", ReleaseType = "Blu-Ray" };
    new Movie { Name = "Return to the Moon", Category = cat1, Rating = "PG-13" };
    new Movie { Name = "Street Smarts", Category = cat2, Rating = "PG-13" };
    new Movie { Name = "Alien Revenge", Category = cat1, Rating = "R" };
    new Movie { Name = "Saturday Nights", Category = cat1, Rating = "PG-13" };
    context.Categories.AddObject(cat1);
    context.Categories.AddObject(cat2);
    context.SaveChanges();
}
```

```
using (var context = new EFRecipesEntities())
{
    // filter on ReleaseType and Rating
    // create collection of anonymous types
    var cats = from c in context.Categories
               where c.ReleaseType == "DVD"
               select new
               {
                   category = c,
                   movies = c.Movies.Where(m => m.Rating == "PG-13")
               };

    Console.WriteLine("PG-13 Movies Released on DVD");
    Console.WriteLine("============================");
    foreach (var cat in cats)
    {
        Category category = cat.category;
        Console.WriteLine("Category: {0}", category.Name);
        foreach (var movie in cat.movies)
        {
            Console.WriteLine("\tMovie: {0}", movie.Name);
        }
    }
}
```

The code in Listing 5-36 produces the following output:

```
PG-13 Movies Released on DVD
============================
Category: Science Fiction
        Movie: Return to the Moon
        Movie: Saturday Nights
```

How It Works

We start off in Listing 5-36 by creating and initializing the categories and movies. To keep things short, we've created only a couple of categories and four movies.

In the query, we create a collection of anonymous types with the category instance and the filtered collection of movies in the category. The query also filters the category collection, retrieving only categories whose movies are released on DVD. In this example, just one category was released on DVD. Here we rely on relationship span to attach the movies to the categories.

This approach of leveraging an anonymous type helps gets around the limitation in eager loading that prevents us from filtering an eagerly loaded collection. Note that when explicitly loading, we do have the ability to filter an eagerly loaded collection, as demonstrated in some of the earlier recipes in this chapter. Keep in mind that anonymous types only have scope in the method in which they are created—we cannot return anonymous types from a method. If our goal were to return the entity set for further processing in the application, then we would want to create an explicit type into which we could load the data and then return from a method. In our example, that explicit type would be a simple class with two properties: Category and a collection of Movies.

5-14. Modifying Foreign Key Associations

Problem

You want to modify a foreign key association.

Solution

Entity Framework provides a couple of ways to modify a foreign key association. You can add the associated entity to a navigation property collection or assign it to a navigation property. You can also set the foreign key value with the associated entity's key value.

Suppose that you have a model like the one shown in Figure 5-29.

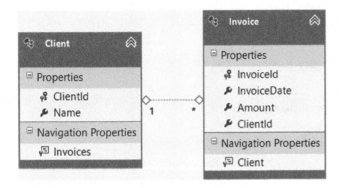

Figure 5-29. *A model for clients and invoices*

To modify the foreign key association between client entities and invoice entities in two different ways, do the following:

1. Right-click your project, and select Add New ➤ ADO.NET Entity Data Model. Import the Client and Invoice tables. Be certain that the Include *foreign key columns in the model* check box is checked, which is the default behavior, as shown in Figure 5-30. Doing so will import foreign key associations from the database that are not many-to-many relationships.

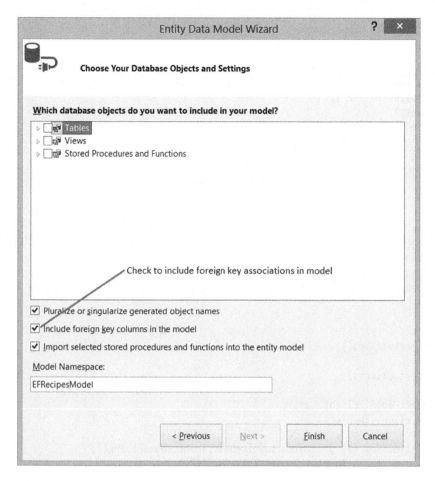

Figure 5-30. *Checking the Include foreign key columns in the model check box will create foreign key associations for database relationships that are not many-to-many*

2. Use the code in Listing 5-37 to demonstrate the ways in which a foreign key association can be modified.

Listing 5-37. *Demonstrating the Ways in Which a Foreign Key Association Can Be Modified*

```
using (var context = new EFRecipesEntities())
{
    var client1 = new Client { Name = "Karen Standfield", ClientId = 1 };

    var invoice1 = new Invoice { InvoiceDate = DateTime.Parse("4/1/10"), Amount = 29.95M };
    var invoice2 = new Invoice { InvoiceDate = DateTime.Parse("4/2/10"), Amount = 49.95M };
    var invoice3 = new Invoice { InvoiceDate = DateTime.Parse("4/3/10"), Amount = 102.95M };
    var invoice4 = new Invoice { InvoiceDate = DateTime.Parse("4/4/10"), Amount = 45.99M };

    // add the invoice to the client's collection
    client1.Invoices.Add(invoice1);
```

```
    // assign the foreign key directly
    invoice2.ClientId = 1;

    // Attach() an existing row using a "fake" entity
    context.Database.ExecuteSqlCommand("insert into chapter5.client values (2, 'Phil Marlowe')");
    var client2 = new Client { ClientId = 2 };
    context.Clients.Attach(client2);

    invoice3.Client = client2;

    // using the ClientReference

    invoice4.Client = client1;

    // save the changes
    context.Clients.Add(client1);
    context.Invoices.Add(invoice2);
    context.Invoices.Add(invoice3);
    context.Invoices.Add(invoice4);
    context.SaveChanges();
}

using (var context = new EFRecipesEntities())
{
    foreach (var client in context.Clients)
    {
        Console.WriteLine("Client: {0}", client.Name);
        foreach (var invoice in client.Invoices)
        {
            Console.WriteLine("\t{0} for {1}", invoice.InvoiceDate.ToShortDateString(),
                                        invoice.Amount.ToString("C"));
        }
    }
}
```

The following is the output of the code in Listing 5-37:

```
Client: Karen Standfield
        4/1/2010 for $29.95
        4/4/2010 for $45.99
        4/2/2010 for $49.95
Client: Phil Marlowe
        4/3/2010 for $102.95
```

How It Works

Entity Framework supports independent associations and foreign key associations. For an independent association, the association between the entities is tracked separately from the entities, and the only way to change the association is through object references.

With foreign key associations, you can change the association by changing object references or by directly changing the foreign key property value. Foreign key associations are not used for many-to-many relationships.

■ **Note**   Keep in mind that Foreign Key Associations are simpler, easier, the default approach and recommended by the Entity Framework team. Unless you have a concrete business reason to use an Independent Association, always consider using a Foreign Key Association.

Table 5-1 illustrates the main differences between foreign key associations and independent associations.

Table 5-1. *The Differences Between Foreign Key Associations and Independent Associations*

Foreign Key Association	Independent Association
Can be set using foreign key and navigation properties	Can only be set using a navigation property
Is mapped as a property and does not require a separate mapping	Is tracked independently from the entity, which means that changing the association does not change the state of the entity
Data binding scenarios are easier because they can bind to a property value.	Data binding is complicated because you have to create a property manually, which reads the foreign key value from the entity key, or traverse the navigation property to load the related key.
Finding the old value for a foreign key is easier because it is a property of an entity.	Accessing an old relationship is complicated because relationships are tracked separately.
To delete an entity that uses a foreign key association, you only need the entity key.	To delete an entity that uses an independent association, you need the entity key and the original values for all reference keys.
N-Tier scenarios are easier because you don't have to send the related end's entity key along with the entity.	The client must send the related end's entity key value along with the entity when the entity is attached. Entity Framework will create a stub entry, and the update statement includes the related end's entity key.
Three representations of the same association are kept in sync: the foreign key, the reference, and the collection navigation property on the other side. Entity Framework handles this with the default code generation.	Two representations are kept in sync: the reference and the navigation property
When you load a related entity, Entity Framework uses the foreign key value currently assigned on the entity, not the foreign key value in the database.	When you load a related entity, the foreign key value is read from the database and, based on this value, the related entity is loaded.

CHAPTER 6

Beyond the Basics with Modeling and Inheritance

By now you have a solid understanding of basic modeling techniques in Entity Framework. In this chapter, you will find recipes that will help you address many common, and often complex, modeling problems. The recipes in this chapter specifically address problems that you are likely to face in modeling existing, real-world databases.

We start this chapter by working with many-to-many relationships. This type of relationship is very common in many modeling scenarios in both existing databases and new projects. Next we'll look at self-referencing relationships and explore various strategies for retrieving nested object graphs. We round out this chapter with several recipes involving more advanced modeling of inheritance and entity conditions.

6-1. Retrieving the Link Table in a Many-to-Many Association
Problem

You want to retrieve the keys in the link table that connect two entities in a many-to-many association.

Solution

Let's say that you have a model with a many-to-many association between Event and Organizer entities, as is shown in Figure 6-1.

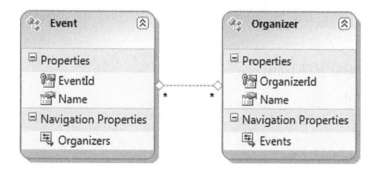

Figure 6-1. *Many-to-many association between Event and Organizer entities*

As we illustrated in several recipes in Chapter 2, a many-to-many relationship is represented in a database using an intermediate table called a *link table*. The link table holds the foreign keys on each side of the relationship (see Figure 6-2). When a link table with no additional columns and the related tables are imported into Entity Framework, the Entity Data Model Wizard creates a many-to-many association between the related tables. The link table is not represented as an entity; however, it is used internally for the many-to-many association.

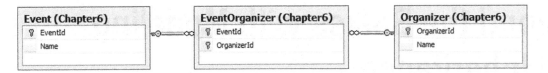

Figure 6-2. *A database diagram showing the EventOrganizer link table holding the foreign keys to the related Event and Organizer tables*

To retrieve the entity keys EventId and OrganizerId, we can use either a nested `from` clause or the `SelectMany()` method. Listing 6-1 shows both approaches.

Listing 6-1. Retrieving a Link Table Using Both a Nested `from` Clause and the `SelectMany()` Method

```
using (var context = new EF6RecipesContext())
{
    var org = new Organizer { Name = "Community Charity" };
    var evt = new Event { Name = "Fundraiser" };
    org.Events.Add(evt);
    context.Organizers.Add(org);
    org = new Organizer { Name = "Boy Scouts" };
    evt = new Event { Name = "Eagle Scout Dinner" };
    org.Events.Add(evt);
    context.Organizers.Add(org);
    context.SaveChanges();
}

using (var context = new EF6RecipesContext())
{
    var evsorg1 = from ev in context.Events
                  from organizer in ev.Organizers
                  select new { ev.EventId, organizer.OrganizerId };
    Console.WriteLine("Using nested from clauses...");
    foreach (var pair in evsorg1)
    {
        Console.WriteLine("EventId {0}, OrganizerId {1}",
                          pair.EventId,
                          pair.OrganizerId);
    }

    var evsorg2 = context.Events
                         .SelectMany(e => e.Organizers,
                            (ev, org) => new { ev.EventId, org.OrganizerId });
    Console.WriteLine("\nUsing SelectMany()");
```

```
    foreach (var pair in evsorg2)
    {
        Console.WriteLine("EventId {0}, OrganizerId {1}",
                          pair.EventId, pair.OrganizerId);
    }
}
```

The output of the code in Listing 6-1 should be similar to the following:

```
Using nested from clauses...
EventId 31, OrganizerId 87
EventId 32, OrganizerId 88

Using SelectMany()
EventId 31, OrganizerId 87
EventId 32, OrganizerId 88
```

How It Works

A link table is a common way of representing a many-to-many relationship between two tables in a database. Because it serves no purpose other than defining the relationship between two tables, Entity Framework represents a link table as a many-to-many association, not as a separate entity.

The many-to-many association between Event and Organizer allows easy navigation from an Event entity to the associated organizers and from an Organizer entity to all of the associated events. However, you may want to retrieve just the keys in the link table. You may want to do this because the keys are themselves meaningful or you want to use these keys for operations on these or other entities. The problem here is that the link table is not represented as an entity, so querying it directly is not an option. In Listing 6-1, we show a couple of ways to get just the underlying keys without materializing the entities on each side of the association.

The first approach in Listing 6-1 uses nested from clauses to retrieve the organizers for each event. Using the Organizers' navigation property on the instances of the Event entity leverages the underlying link table to enumerate all of the organizers for each of the events. We reshape the results to the pairs of corresponding keys for the entities. Finally, we iterate through the results, printing the pair of keys to the console.

In the second approach, we use the SelectMany() method to project the organizers for each event into the pairs of keys for the events and organizers. As with the nested from clauses, this approach uses the underlying link table through the Organizers' navigation property. We iterate through the results in the same way as with the first approach.

6-2. Exposing a Link Table as an Entity

Problem

You want to expose a link table as an entity instead of a many-to-many association.

Solution

Let's say that your database has a many-to-many relationship between workers and tasks, and it looks something like the one in the database diagram shown in Figure 6-3.

Figure 6-3. *A many-to-many relationship between workers and tasks*

The WorkerTask link table contains nothing more than the foreign keys supporting the many-to-many relationship.

To convert the association to an entity representing the WorkerTask link table, follow these steps.

1. Create a WorkerTask POCO entity class, as shown in Listing 6-2.

2. Replace the Tasks property of the Worker POCO entity with a WorkerTasks property of type ICollection<WorkerTask>.

3. Replace the Workers property of the Task POCO entity with a WorkerTasks property of type ICollection<WorkerTask>.

4. Add an auto-property of type DbSet<WorkerTask> to your DbContext subclass.

The final model should look like the one shown in Listing 6-2.

Listing 6-2. *The Final Data Model Including WorkerTask*

```
[Table("Worker", Schema="Chapter6")]
public class Worker
{
    [Key]
    [DatabaseGenerated(DatabaseGeneratedOption.Identity)]
    public int WorkerId { get; set; }
    public string Name { get; set; }

    [ForeignKey("WorkerId")]
    public virtual ICollection<WorkerTask> WorkerTasks { get; set; }
}

[Table("Task", Schema = "Chapter6")]
public class Task
{
    [Key]
    [DatabaseGenerated(DatabaseGeneratedOption.Identity)]
    public int TaskId { get; set; }
    public string Title { get; set; }

    [ForeignKey("TaskId")]
    public virtual ICollection<WorkerTask> WorkerTasks { get; set; }
}
```

```
[Table("WorkerTask", Schema = "Chapter6")]
public class WorkerTask
{
    [Key]
    [Column(Order = 1)]
    public int WorkerId { get; set; }

    [Key]
    [Column(Order = 2)]
    public int TaskId { get; set; }

    [ForeignKey("WorkerId")]
    public virtual Worker Worker { get; set; }

    [ForeignKey("TaskId")]
    public virtual Task Task { get; set; }
}
```

How It Works

During the application development lifecycle, developers often find the need to add payload to the many-to-many associations that started life payload-free. In this recipe, we show how to surface the many-to-many association as a separate entity so that additional scalar properties (for example, payload) can be added.

Many developers choose to assume that all many-to-many relationships will ultimately hold a payload, and they create a synthetic key for the link table rather than the traditional composite key formed by combining the foreign keys.

The downside of our new model is that we do not have a simple way to navigate the many-to-many association. We have two one-to-many associations that require an additional hop through the linking entity. The code in Listing 6-3 demonstrates this additional bit of work on both the insert side and the query side.

Listing 6-3. Inserting into and Retrieving Task and Worker Entities

```
using (var context = new EF6RecipesContext())
{
    var worker = new Worker { Name = "Jim" };
    var task = new Task { Title = "Fold Envelopes" };
    var workertask = new WorkerTask { Task = task, Worker = worker };
    context.WorkerTasks.Add(workertask);
    task = new Task { Title = "Mail Letters" };
    workertask = new WorkerTask { Task = task, Worker = worker };
    context.WorkerTasks.Add(workertask);
    worker = new Worker { Name = "Sara" };
    task = new Task { Title = "Buy Envelopes" };
    workertask = new WorkerTask { Task = task, Worker = worker };
    context.WorkerTasks.Add(workertask);
    context.SaveChanges();
}

using (var context = new EF6RecipesContext())
{
    Console.WriteLine("Workers and Their Tasks");
    Console.WriteLine("=======================");
```

```
    foreach (var worker in context.Workers)
    {
        Console.WriteLine("\n{0}'s tasks:", worker.Name);
        foreach (var wt in worker.WorkerTasks)
        {
            Console.WriteLine("\t{0}", wt.Task.Title);
        }
    }
}
```

The code in Listing 6-3 produces the following output:

```
Workers and Their Tasks
========================

Jim's tasks:
        Fold Envelopes
        Mail Letters

Sara's tasks:
        Buy Envelopes
```

6-3. Modeling a Many-to-Many, Self-Referencing Relationship

Problem

You have a table with a many-to-many relationship with itself, and you want to model this table and relationship.

Solution

Let's say that you have a table that has relationship to itself using a link table, as shown in Figure 6-4.

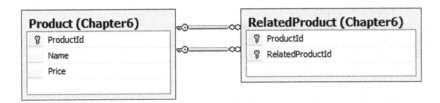

Figure 6-4. *A table with a many-to-many relationship to itself*

To create a model, do the following:

1. Create a new class in your project that inherits from DbContext.

2. Add a Product POCO entity class to your project using the code in Listing 6-4.

Listing 6-4. Creating the Product POCO Entity Class

```
[Table("Product", Schema = "Chapter6")]
public class Product
{
    public Product()
    {
        RelatedProducts = new HashSet<Product>();
        OtherRelatedProducts = new HashSet<Product>();
    }

    [Key]
    [DatabaseGenerated(DatabaseGeneratedOption.Identity)]
    public int ProductId { get; set; }
    public string Name { get; set; }
    public decimal Price { get; set; }

    // Products related to this product
    public virtual ICollection<Product> RelatedProducts { get; set; }

    // Products to which this product is related
    public virtual ICollection<Product> OtherRelatedProducts { get; set; }
}
```

3. Add an auto-property of type DbSet<Product> to your DbContext subclass.

4. Override the OnModelCreating method of DbContext in your subclass to create the many-to-many self-referencing relationship mapping, as shown in Listing 6-5.

Listing 6-5. Overriding OnModelCreating in the DbContext Subclass to Create the Many-to-Many Self-Referencing Mapping

```
protected override void OnModelCreating(DbModelBuilder modelBuilder)
{
    base.OnModelCreating(modelBuilder);

    modelBuilder.Entity<Product>()
                .HasMany(p => p.RelatedProducts)
                .WithMany(p => p.OtherRelatedProducts)
                .Map(m =>
                        {
                            m.MapLeftKey("ProductId");
                            m.MapRightKey("RelatedProductId");
                            m.ToTable("RelatedProduct", "Chapter6");
                        });
}
```

How It Works

As you can see, the Entity Framework supports a many-to-many self-referencing association with little effort. We created two navigation properties in our Product class, RelatedProducts and OtherRelatedProducts, and mapped those properties to the underlying database schema in our DbContext subclass.

The code in Listing 6-6 inserts a few related products and retrieves the related products. To retrieve all of the related products for a given product, we need to traverse both the RelatedProducts navigation property and the OtherRelatedProducts navigation property.

Tent is related to Ground Cover through the RelatedProducts navigation property because we added Ground Cover to Tent's RelatedProducts collection. Pole is related to Tent through Tent's OtherRelatedProducts collection because we added Tent to Pole's RelatedProducts collection. The associations go both ways. In one direction, it's a related product. In the other direction, it's an OtherRelatedProduct.

Listing 6-6. Retrieving the Related Products

```
using (var context = new EF6RecipesContext())
{
    var product1 = new Product { Name = "Pole", Price = 12.97M };
    var product2 = new Product { Name = "Tent", Price = 199.95M };
    var product3 = new Product { Name = "Ground Cover", Price = 29.95M };
    product2.RelatedProducts.Add(product3);
    product1.RelatedProducts.Add(product2);
    context.Products.Add(product1);
    context.SaveChanges();
}

using (var context = new EF6RecipesContext())
{
    var product2 = context.Products.First(p => p.Name == "Tent");
    Console.WriteLine("Product: {0} ... {1}", product2.Name,
                        product2.Price.ToString("C"));
    Console.WriteLine("Related Products");
    foreach (var prod in product2.RelatedProducts)
    {
        Console.WriteLine("\t{0} ... {1}", prod.Name, prod.Price.ToString("C"));
    }
    foreach (var prod in product2.OtherRelatedProducts)
    {
        Console.WriteLine("\t{0} ... {1}", prod.Name, prod.Price.ToString("C"));
    }
}
```

The output of Listing 6-6 is as follows:

```
Product: Tent ... $199.95
Related Products
        Ground Cover ... $29.95
        Pole ... $12.97
```

The code in Listing 6-6 retrieves only the first level of related products. A *transitive relationship* is one that spans multiple levels, like a hierarchy. If we assume that the "related products" relationship is transitive, we might want to form the transitive closure. The transitive closure would be all of the related products regardless of how many hops away they may be. In an eCommerce application, product specialists could create the first level of related products. Additional levels could be derived by computing the transitive closure. The end result would allow the application to show the familiar "…you may also be interested in …" message that we often see during the checkout process.

In Listing 6-7, we use a recursive method to form the transitive closure. In traversing both the RelatedProducts and OtherRelatedProducts associations, we need to be careful not to get stuck in a cycle. If product A is related to B, and product B is related to product A, our application would get trapped in the recursion. To detect cycles, we use a Dictionary<> to help prune off paths that we have already traversed.

Listing 6-7. Forming the Transitive Closure of the "Related Products" Relationship

```
static void RunExample2()
{
    using (var context = new EF6RecipesContext())
    {
        var product1 = new Product { Name = "Pole", Price = 12.97M };
        var product2 = new Product { Name = "Tent", Price = 199.95M };
        var product3 = new Product { Name = "Ground Cover", Price = 29.95M };
        product2.RelatedProducts.Add(product3);
        product1.RelatedProducts.Add(product2);
        context.Products.Add(product1);
        context.SaveChanges();
    }

    using (var context = new EF6RecipesContext())
    {
        var product1 = context.Products.First(p => p.Name == "Pole");
        Dictionary<int, Product> t = new Dictionary<int, Product>();
        GetRelated(context, product1, t);
        Console.WriteLine("Products related to {0}", product1.Name);
        foreach (var key in t.Keys)
        {
            Console.WriteLine("\t{0}", t[key].Name);
        }
    }
}

static void GetRelated(DbContext context, Product p, Dictionary<int, Product> t)
{
    context.Entry(p).Collection(ep => ep.RelatedProducts).Load();
    foreach (var relatedProduct in p.RelatedProducts)
    {
        if (!t.ContainsKey(relatedProduct.ProductId))
        {
            t.Add(relatedProduct.ProductId, relatedProduct);
            GetRelated(context, relatedProduct, t);
        }
    }
    context.Entry(p).Collection(ep => ep.OtherRelatedProducts).Load();
    foreach (var otherRelated in p.OtherRelatedProducts)
    {
        if (!t.ContainsKey(otherRelated.ProductId))
        {
            t.Add(otherRelated.ProductId, otherRelated);
            GetRelated(context, otherRelated, t);
        }
    }
}
```

In Listing 6-7, we use the Load() method (see the recipes in Chapter 5) to ensure that the collections of related products are loaded. Unfortunately, this means that we will end up with many additional round trips to the database. We might be tempted to load all of the rows from the Product table up front and hope that relationship span would fix up the associations. However, relationship span will not fix up entity collections, only entity references. Because our associations are many-to-many (entity collections), we cannot rely on relationship span to help out and we have to resort to using the Load() method.

Following is the output of the code in Listing 6-7. From the first block of code that inserts the relationships, we can see that a Pole is related to a Tent, and a Tent is related to Ground Cover. The transitive closure for the products related to a Pole includes a Tent, Ground Cover, and Pole. Pole is included because it is on the other side of the relationship with Tent, which is a related product.

```
Products related to Pole
        Tent
        Ground Cover
        Pole
```

6-4. Modeling a Self-Referencing Relationship Using Table per Hierarchy Inheritance

Problem

You have a table that references itself. The table represents several different but related kinds of objects in your database. You want to model this table using Table per Hierarchy inheritance.

Solution

Suppose that you have a table like the one shown in Figure 6-5, which describes some things about people. People often have a hero, perhaps the individual who inspired them the most. We can represent a person's hero with a reference to another row in the Person table.

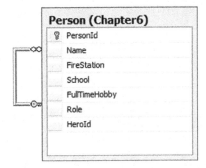

Figure 6-5. *Person table containing people with different roles*

Each person has some role in life. Some people are firefighters. Some people are teachers. Some people are retired. Of course, there could be many other roles. Information about people can be specific to their roles. A firefighter is stationed at a firehouse. A teacher teaches at a school. A retired person often has a hobby.

For our example, the possible roles are firefighter (f), teacher (t), or retired (r). A single character in the role column indicates the role for a person.

To create a model, do the following:

1. Create a new class in your project that inherits from DbContext

2. Add an abstract Person POCO entity class using the code found in Listing 6-8.

Listing 6-8. Creating the Abstract Person POCO Entity Class

```
[Table("Person", Schema = "Chapter6")]
public abstract class Person
{
    [Key]
    [DatabaseGenerated(DatabaseGeneratedOption.Identity)]
    public int PersonId { get; protected set; }
    public string Name { get; set; }

    public virtual Person Hero { get; set; }
    public virtual ICollection<Person> Fans { get; set; }
}
```

3. Add an auto-property of type DbSet<Person> to your DbContext subclass.

4. Add concrete POCO entity classes for Firefighter, Teacher, and Retired entities using the code found in Listing 6-9.

Listing 6-9. Creating Concrete POCO Entities for Firefighter, Teacher, and Retired

```
public class Firefighter : Person
{
    public string FireStation { get; set; }
}

public class Teacher : Person
{
    public string School { get; set; }
}

public class Retired : Person
{
    public string FullTimeHobby { get; set; }
}
```

5. Override the OnModelCreating method of DbContext in your subclass to configure the HeroId foreign key as well as the type hierarchy, as shown in Listing 6-10.

Listing 6-10. Overriding OnModelCreating in the DbContext Subclass

```
protected override void OnModelCreating(DbModelBuilder modelBuilder)
{
    base.OnModelCreating(modelBuilder);

    modelBuilder.Entity<Person>()
```

```
                    .HasMany(p => p.Fans)
                    .WithOptional(p => p.Hero)
                    .Map(m => m.MapKey("HeroId"));

        modelBuilder.Entity<Person>()
                    .Map<Firefighter>(m => m.Requires("Role").HasValue("f"))
                    .Map<Teacher>(m => m.Requires("Role").HasValue("t"))
                    .Map<Retired>(m => m.Requires("Role").HasValue("r"));
    }
```

How It Works

The code in Listing 6-11 demonstrates inserting and retrieving Person entities from our model. We create a single instance of each of the derived types and wire in a few hero relationships. We have a teacher who is the hero of a firefighter and a retired person who is the hero of the teacher. When we set the firefighter as the hero of the retired person, we introduce just enough of a cycle so that Entity Framework generates a runtime error (a DbUpdateException) because it cannot determine the appropriate order for inserting the rows into the table. In the code, we get around this problem by calling the SaveChanges() method before wiring in any of the hero relationships. Once the rows are committed to the database, and the store-generated keys are brought back into the object graph, we are free to update the graph with the relationships. Of course, these changes must be saved with a final call to SaveChanges().

Listing 6-11. Inserting into and Retrieving from Our Model

```
using (var context = new EF6RecipesContext())
{
    var teacher = new Teacher { Name = "Susan Smith",
                                School = "Custer Baker Middle School" };
    var firefighter = new Firefighter { Name = "Joel Clark",
                                FireStation = "Midtown" };
    var retired = new Retired { Name = "Joan Collins",
                                FullTimeHobby = "Scapbooking" };
    context.People.Add(teacher);
    context.People.Add(firefighter);
    context.People.Add(retired);
    context.SaveChanges();
    firefighter.Hero = teacher;
    teacher.Hero = retired;
    retired.Hero = firefighter;
    context.SaveChanges();
}

using (var context = new EF6RecipesContext())
{
    foreach(var person in context.People)
    {
        if (person.Hero != null)
            Console.WriteLine("\n{0}, Hero is: {1}", person.Name,
                                person.Hero.Name);
        else
            Console.WriteLine("{0}", person.Name);
```

```
        if (person is Firefighter)
            Console.WriteLine("Firefighter at station {0}",
                              ((Firefighter)person).FireStation);
        else if (person is Teacher)
            Console.WriteLine("Teacher at {0}", ((Teacher)person).School);
        else if (person is Retired)
            Console.WriteLine("Retired, hobby is {0}",
                              ((Retired)person).FullTimeHobby);
        Console.WriteLine("Fans:");
        foreach (var fan in person.Fans)
        {
            Console.WriteLine("\t{0}", fan.Name);
        }
    }
}
```

The output from the code in Listing 6-11 is as follows:

```
Susan Smith, Hero is: Joan Collins
Teacher at Custer Baker Middle School
Fans:
        Joel Clark

Joel Clark, Hero is: Susan Smith
Firefighter at station Midtown
Fans:
        Joan Collins

Joan Collins, Hero is: Joel Clark
Retired, hobby is Scapbooking
Fans:
        Susan Smith
```

6-5. Modeling a Self-Referencing Relationship and Retrieving a Complete Hierarchy
Problem

You are using a self-referencing table to store hierarchical data. Given a record, you want to retrieve all associated records that are part of that hierarchy at any level deep.

Solution

Suppose that you have a Category table like the one in the database diagram shown in Figure 6-6.

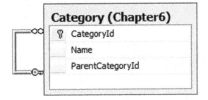

Figure 6-6. *Self-referencing Category table*

To create our model, do the following:

1. Create a new class in your project that inherits from DbContext.

2. Add a Category POCO entity class using the code in Listing 6-12.

   Listing 6-12. Creating the Category POCO Entity Class

   ```
   [Table("Category", Schema = "Chapter6")]
   public class Category
   {
       [Key]
       [DatabaseGenerated(DatabaseGeneratedOption.Identity)]
       public int CategoryId { get; set; }
       public string Name { get; set; }

       public virtual Category ParentCategory { get; set; }
       public virtual ICollection<Category> SubCategories { get; set; }
   }
   ```

3. Add an auto-property of type DbSet<Category> to the DbContext subclass.

4. Override the OnModelCreating method of DbContext in your subclass, as shown in Listing 6-13. In the override, we will create the ParentCategory and SubCategories associations and configure the foreign key constraint.

   Listing 6-13. Overriding OnModelCreating in the DbContext Subclass

   ```
   protected override void OnModelCreating(DbModelBuilder modelBuilder)
   {
       base.OnModelCreating(modelBuilder);

       modelBuilder.Entity<Category>()
                   .HasOptional(c => c.ParentCategory)
                   .WithMany(c => c.SubCategories)
                   .Map(m => m.MapKey("ParentCategoryId"));
   }
   ```

In our model, the Category entity has a Subcategories navigation property that we can use to get the collection of all of the immediate subcategories of the Category. However, to access them, we need to load them explicitly using either the Load()or the Include() methods. The Load() method requires an additional round trip to the database, while the Include() method provides only a predefined, limited depth.

We want to bring the entire hierarchy into the object graph as efficiently as possible. To do this, we use a Common Table Expression in a stored procedure.

To add the stored procedure to our model, do the following:

5. Create a stored procedure called GetSubCategories that makes use of a Common Table Expression to return all of the subcategories for a CategoryId recursively. The stored procedure is shown in Listing 6-14.

    Listing 6-14. The GetSubCategories() Stored Procedure That Returns Subcategories for a Given CategoryId

    ```
    create proc chapter6.GetSubCategories
    (@categoryid int)
    as
    begin
    with cats as
                    (
                    select c1.*
                    from chapter6.Category c1
                    where CategoryId = @categoryid
                    union all
                    select c2.*
                    from cats join  chapter6.Category c2 on cats.CategoryId =
                    c2.ParentCategoryId
                    )
                    select * from cats where CategoryId != @categoryid
    end
    ```

6. Add a method that takes an integer parameter and returns an ICollection<Category> to your DbContext subclass, as shown in Listing 6-15. Entity Framework 6 Code First does not yet support function imports in the way that the EF designer does, so in the method body we'll call our stored procedure with the SqlQuery method that's defined in the Database property of DbContext.

    Listing 6-15. Implementing the GetSubCategories Method in Our DbContext Subclass

    ```
    public ICollection<Category> GetSubCategories(int categoryId)
    {
        return this.Database.SqlQuery<Category>("exec Chapter6.GetSubCategories @catId",
                        new SqlParameter("@catId", categoryId)).ToList();
    }
    ```

We can use the GetSubCategories method that we've defined in our DbContext subclass to materialize our entire graph of categories and subcategories. The code in Listing 6-16 demonstrates the use of the GetSubCategories() method.

Listing 6-16. Retrieving the Entire Hierarchy Using the GetSubCategories() Method

```
using (var context = new EF6RecipesContext())
{
    var book = new Category { Name = "Books" };
    var fiction = new Category { Name = "Fiction", ParentCategory = book };
    var nonfiction = new Category { Name = "Non-Fiction", ParentCategory = book };
    var novel = new Category { Name = "Novel", ParentCategory = fiction };
    var history = new Category { Name = "History", ParentCategory = nonfiction };
```

```
    context.Categories.Add(novel);
    context.Categories.Add(history);
    context.SaveChanges();
}

using (var context = new EF6RecipesContext())
{
    var root = context.Categories.Where(o => o.Name == "Books").First();
    Console.WriteLine("Parent category is {0}, subcategories are:", root.Name);
    foreach (var sub in context.GetSubCategories(root.CategoryId))
    {
        Console.WriteLine("\t{0}", sub.Name);
    }
}
```

The output from the code in Listing 6-16 is as follows:

```
Parent category is Books, subcategories are:
        Fiction
        Non-Fiction
        History
        Novel
```

How It Works

Entity Framework supports self-referencing associations, as we have seen in Recipe 6.2 and Recipe 6.3. In these recipes, we directly loaded the entity references and collections using the Load() method. We cautioned, however, that each Load() results in a round trip to the database to retrieve an entity or entity collection. For larger object graphs, this database traffic may consume too many resources.

In this recipe, we demonstrated a slightly different approach. Rather than explicitly using Load() to materialize each entity or entity collection, we pushed the work off to the storage layer by using a stored procedure to enumerate recursively all of the subcategories and return the collection. We used a Common Table Expression in our stored procedure to implement the recursive query. In our example, we chose to enumerate all of the subcategories. You could, of course, modify the stored procedure to enumerate elements of the hierarchy selectively.

To use our stored procedure, we added a method to our DbContext subclass that calls the stored procedure through DbContext.Database.SqlQuery<T>() and called the method within our code. We use the SqlQuery<T>() method rather than the ExecuteSqlCommand() method because our stored procedure returns a result set.

6-6. Mapping Null Conditions in Derived Entities
Problem

You have a column in a table that allows null. You want to create a model using Table per Hierarchy inheritance with one derived type representing instances in which the column has a value and another derived type representing instances in which the column is null.

Solution

Let's say that you have a table describing experimental medical drugs. The table contains a column indicating when the drug was accepted for production. Until the drug is accepted for production, it is considered experimental. Once accepted, it is considered a medicine. We'll start with the Drug table in the database diagram in Figure 6-7.

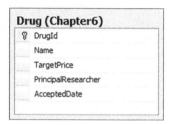

Figure 6-7. *Drug table with the nullable discriminator column, AcceptedDate*

To create a model using the Drug table, do the following:

1. Create a class in your project that inherits from DbContext.

2. Create Drug, Medicine, and Experimental POCO entity classes, as shown in Listing 6-17.

    Listing 6-17. Creating the Drug, Medicine, and Experimental POCO Entity Classes

```
[Table("Drug", Schema = "Chapter6")]
public abstract class Drug
{
    [Key]
    [DatabaseGenerated(DatabaseGeneratedOption.Identity)]
    public int DrugId { get; set; }
    public string Name { get; set; }
}

public class Experimental : Drug
{
    public string PrincipalResearcher { get; set; }

    public void PromoteToMedicine(DateTime acceptedDate, decimal targetPrice,
                        string marketingName)
    {
        var drug = new Medicine { DrugId = this.DrugId };
        using (var context = new DrugContext())
        {
            context.Drugs.Attach(drug);
            drug.AcceptedDate = acceptedDate;
            drug.TargetPrice = targetPrice;
            drug.Name = marketingName;
            context.SaveChanges();
        }
    }

}
```

```
public class Medicine : Drug
{
    public decimal? TargetPrice { get; set; }
    public DateTime AcceptedDate { get; set; }
}
```

3. Add an auto-property of type DbSet<Drug> to your DbContext subclass.

4. Override the OnModelCreating method of DbContext to configure the TPH mapping for Medicine and Experimental types, as shown in Listing 6-18.

Listing 6-18. Overriding OnModelCreating to Configure TPH Mapping

```
protected override void OnModelCreating(DbModelBuilder modelBuilder)
{
    base.OnModelCreating(modelBuilder);
    modelBuilder.Entity<Experimental>()
            .Map(m => m.Requires("AcceptedDate").HasValue((DateTime?)null));
    modelBuilder.Entity<Medicine>()
            .Map(m => m.Requires(d => d.AcceptedDate).HasValue());
}
```

How It Works

In this example, we made use of the null and is not null conditions to map a Drug without an AcceptedDate to an Experimental drug and a Drug with an AcceptedDate to a Medicine. As in many inheritance examples, we marked the base entity, Drug, as abstract because in our model we would never have an uncategorized drug.

It is interesting to note that, in the Medicine entity, we mapped the AcceptedDate discriminator column to a scalar property. In most scenarios, mapping the discriminator column to scalar property is prohibited. However, in this example, our use of the null and is not null conditions, as well as marking the AcceptedDate as not nullable, sufficiently constrains the values for property to allow the mapping.

In Listing 6-19, we insert a couple of Experimental drugs and query the results. We take the opportunity provided by the exposed AcceptedDate property to demonstrate one way to change an object from one derived type to another. In our case, we create a couple of Experimental drugs and then promote one of them to a Medicine.

Listing 6-19. Inserting and Retrieving Instances of Our Derived Types

```
class Program
{
    ...
    static void RunExample()
    {
        using (var context = new EF6RecipesContext())
        {
            var exDrug1 = new Experimental { Name = "Nanoxol",
                        PrincipalResearcher = "Dr. Susan James" };
            var exDrug2 = new Experimental { Name = "Percosol",
                        PrincipalResearcher = "Dr. Bill Minor" };
            context.Drugs.Add(exDrug1);
            context.Drugs.Add(exDrug2);
            context.SaveChanges();
```

```
        // Nanoxol just got approved!
        exDrug1.PromoteToMedicine(DateTime.Now, 19.99M, "Treatall");
        context.Entry(exDrug1).State = EntityState.Detached // better not use this instance any longer
    }

    using (var context = new EF6RecipesContext())
    {
        Console.WriteLine("Experimental Drugs");
        foreach (var d in context.Drugs.OfType<Experimental>())
        {
            Console.WriteLine("\t{0} ({1})", d.Name, d.PrincipalResearcher);
        }

        Console.WriteLine("Medicines");
        foreach (var d in context.Drugs.OfType<Medicine>())
        {
            Console.WriteLine("\t{0} Retails for {1}", d.Name,
                    d.TargetPrice.Value.ToString("C"));
        }
    }
}
}
```

Following is the output of the code in Listing 6-19:

```
Experimental Drugs
        Percosol (Dr. Bill Minor)
Medicines
        Treatall Retails for $19.99
```

We change an Experimental drug to a Medicine using the PromoteToMedicine()method. In the implementation of this method, we create a new Medicine instance, attach it to a new DbContext, and initialize it with the appropriate new values. Once the new instance is attached and initialized, we use the SaveChanges()method on the DbContext to save the new instance to the database. Because the instance has the same key (DrugId) as the Experimental drug, Entity Framework generates an update statement rather than an insert statement.

We implemented the PromoteToMedicine() method inside the POCO class Experimental. This allows us seamlessly to add the method to the class, and it provides for a much cleaner implementation. That being said, in the interest of creating persistence-ignorant POCO entities that can be used in multiple DbContexts, it might make more sense to implement a slightly altered version of this method in a helper class instead.

6-7. Modeling Table per Type Inheritance Using a Nonprimary Key Column
Problem

You have one or more tables in an existing schema that have a one-to-one relationship to a common table using keys that are not primary keys in the tables. You want to model this using Table per Type inheritance.

Solution

Let's say that your database contains the tables shown in the database diagram in Figure 6-8.

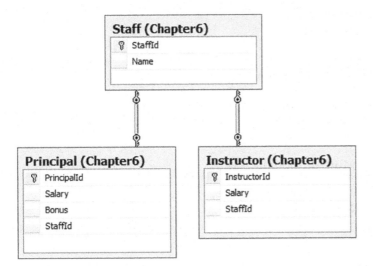

Figure 6-8. *A database diagram containing Staff, Principal, and Instructor tables*

In Figure 6-8, we have a Staff table containing the name of the staff member and two related tables containing information about Principals and Instructors. The important thing to notice here is that the Principal and Instructor tables have primary keys that are not the foreign keys for the Staff table. This type of relationship structure is not directly supported in Table per Type inheritance. For Table per Type, the related tables' primary keys must also be the foreign key for the primary (base) table. Also notice that the relationship is one-to-one. This is because we have constrained the StaffId columns in the Principal and Instructor tables to be unique by creating a unique index on this column in both tables.

To model the tables and relationships in Figure 6-8 using Table per Type inheritance, do the following:

1. Add a new ADO.NET Entity Data Model to your project, and import the Staff, Principal, and Instructor tables.

2. Delete the associations between the Principal and the Staff entities and between the Instructor and the Staff entities.

3. Right-click the Staff entity, and choose Add ➤ Inheritance. Select Staff as the base entity and Principal as the derived entity. Repeat this step by selecting Staff as the base entity and Instructor as the derived entity.

4. Delete the StaffId property from the Instructor and Principal entities.

5. Right-click the Staff entity, and choose Properties. Set the Abstract attribute to True. This marks the Staff entity as abstract.

6. Because the StaffId is not the primary key in either the Principal or the Instructor tables, we cannot use the default table mapping to map the Principal, Instructor, or Staff entities. Select each entity, view the Mapping Details window, and delete the table mapping. Repeat this for each entity.

7. Create the stored procedures in Listing 6-20. We will map these procedures to the Insert, Update, and Delete actions for the Principal and Instructor entities.

Listing 6-20. Stored Procedures for the Insert, Update, and Delete Actions for the Instructor and Principal Entities

```
create procedure [chapter6].[InsertInstructor]
(@Name varchar(50), @Salary decimal)
as
begin
                declare @staffid int
                insert into Chapter6.Staff(Name) values (@Name)
                set @staffid = SCOPE_IDENTITY()
                insert into Chapter6.Instructor(Salary,StaffId) values (@Salary,@staffid)
                select @staffid as StaffId,SCOPE_IDENTITY() as InstructorId
end
go

create procedure [chapter6].[UpdateInstructor]
(@Name varchar(50), @Salary decimal, @StaffId int, @InstructorId int)
as
begin
                update Chapter6.Staff set Name = @Name where StaffId = @StaffId
                update Chapter6.Instructor set Salary = @Salary where InstructorId = @InstructorId
end
go

create procedure [chapter6].[DeleteInstructor]
(@StaffId int)
as
begin
                delete Chapter6.Staff where StaffId = @StaffId
                delete Chapter6.Instructor where StaffId = @StaffId
end
go

create procedure [Chapter6].[InsertPrincipal]
(@Name varchar(50),@Salary decimal,@Bonus decimal)
as
begin
                declare @staffid int
                insert into Chapter6.Staff(Name) values (@Name)
                set @staffid = SCOPE_IDENTITY()
                insert into Chapter6.Principal(Salary,Bonus,StaffId) values
                (@Salary,@Bonus,@staffid)
                select @staffid as StaffId, SCOPE_IDENTITY() as PrincipalId
end
go

create procedure [Chapter6].[UpdatePrincipal]
(@Name varchar(50),@Salary decimal, @Bonus decimal, @StaffId int, @PrincipalId int)
as
```

```
begin
                update Chapter6.Staff set Name = @Name where StaffId = @StaffId
                update Chapter6.Principal set Salary = @Salary, Bonus = @Bonus where
                PrincipalId = @PrincipalId
end
go

create procedure [Chapter6].[DeletePrincipal]
(@StaffId int)
as
begin
                delete Chapter6.Staff where StaffId = @StaffId
                delete Chapter6.Principal where StaffId = @StaffId
end
```

8. Right-click the design surface, and select Update Model from Database. Add the stored procedures that you created in step 7.

9. Select the Principal entity, and view the Mapping Details window. Click the Map Entity to Functions button. This is the bottom button on the left side of the Mapping Details window. Map the Insert, Update, and Delete actions to the stored procedures. Make sure that you map the result columns StaffId and PrincipalId from the Insert action (see Figure 6-9).

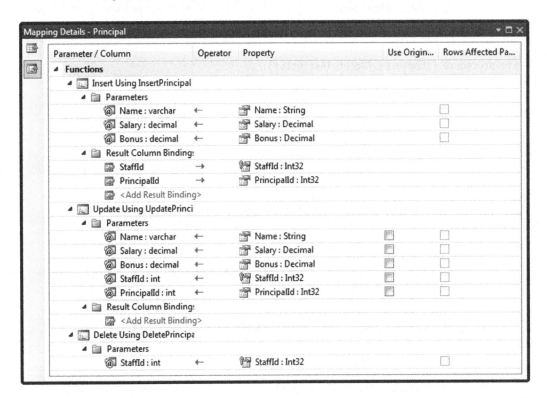

Figure 6-9. Insert, Update, and Delete actions mapped for the Principal entity

10. Repeat step 9 for the Instructor entity. Be sure to map the result columns StaffId and InstructorId from the Insert action.

Right-click the .edmx file in the Solution Explorer, and select Open With ➤ XML Editor. This will close the designer and open the .edmx file in the XML editor. Scroll down to `<EntityContainerMapping>` tag in the mapping layer. Insert the QueryView in Listing 6-21 into the `<EntitySetMapping>` tag.

Listing 6-21. QueryView for the Instructor and Principal Entities

```
<EntitySetMapping Name="Staffs">
    <QueryView>
        select value
        case
        when (i.StaffId is not null) then
        EFRecipesModel.Instructor(s.StaffId,s.Name,i.InstructorId,i.Salary)
        when (p.StaffId is not null) then
        EFRecipesModel.Principal(s.StaffId,s.Name,p.PrincipalId,p.Salary,p.Bonus)
        END
        from EFRecipesModelStoreContainer.Staff as s
        left join EFRecipesModelStoreContainer.Instructor as i
        on s.StaffId = i.StaffId
        left join EFRecipesModelStoreContainer.Principal as p
        on s.StaffId = p.StaffId
    </QueryView>
</EntitySetMapping>
```

How It Works

With Table per Type inheritance, Entity Framework requires that the foreign key for the base entity's table be the primary keys in the derived entity's table. In our example, each of the tables for the derived entities has separate primary keys.

To create a Table per Type inheritance model, we started at the conceptual level by deriving the Principal and Instructor entities from the Staff entity. Next we deleted the mappings that were created when we imported the table. We then used a QueryView expression to create the new mappings. Using QueryView pushed the responsibility for the Insert, Update, and Delete actions onto our code. To handle these actions, we used traditional stored procedures in the database.

We used QueryView to supply the mappings from our underlying tables to the scalar properties exposed by our derived entities. The key part of the QueryView is the case statement. There are two cases: either we have a Principal or we have an Instructor. We have an Instructor if the Instructor's StaffId is not null, or we have a Principal if the Principal's StaffId is not null. The remaining parts of the expression bring in the rows from the derived tables.

The code in Listing 6-22 inserts a couple of Principals and one Instructor into our database.

Listing 6-22. Inserting into and Retrieving from Our Model

```
using (var context = new EF6RecipesContext())
{
    var principal = new Principal { Name = "Robbie Smith",
                                    Bonus = 3500M, Salary = 48000M };
    var instructor = new Instructor { Name = "Joan Carlson",
                                      Salary = 39000M };
```

```
    context.Staffs.Add(principal);
    context.Staffs.Add(instructor);
    context.SaveChanges();
}

using (var context = new EF6RecipesContext())
{
    Console.WriteLine("Principals");
    Console.WriteLine("==========");
    foreach (var p in context.Staffs.OfType<Principal>())
    {
        Console.WriteLine("\t{0}, Salary: {1}, Bonus: {2}",
                        p.Name, p.Salary.ToString("C"),
                        p.Bonus.ToString("C"));
    }
    Console.WriteLine("Instructors");
    Console.WriteLine("===========");
    foreach (var i in context.Staffs.OfType<Instructor>())
    {
        Console.WriteLine("\t{0}, Salary: {1}", i.Name, i.Salary.ToString("C"));
    }
}
```

The following is the output of the code in Listing 6-22:

```
Principals
==========
        Robbie Smith, Salary: $48,000.00, Bonus: $3,500.00
Instructors
===========
        Joan Carlson, Salary: $39,000.00
```

6-8. Modeling Nested Table per Hierarchy Inheritance
Problem

You want to model a table using more than one level of Table per Hierarchy inheritance.

Solution

Suppose that we have an Employee table that contains various types of employees such as Hourly and Salaried Employee, as shown in Figure 6-10.

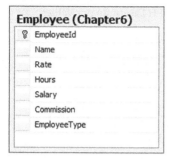

Figure 6-10. *The Employee table containing various types of employees*

The Employee table contains hourly employees, salaried employees, and commissioned employees, which is a subtype of salaried employees. To model this table with derived types for the hourly and salaried employees and a commissioned employee type derived from the salaried employee, do the following:

1. Create a new class in your project that inherits from DbContext.

2. Create POCO entity classes for Employee, HourlyEmployee, SalariedEmployee, and CommissionedEmployee, as shown in Listing 6-23.

   Listing 6-23. Creating the Employee, HourlyEmployee, SalariedEmployee, and CommissionedEmployee POCO Entities

   ```
   public abstract class Employee
   {

       public int EmployeeId { get; set; }
       public string Name { get; set; }
   }

   public class SalariedEmployee : Employee
   {
       public decimal? Salary { get; set; }
   }

   public class CommissionedEmployee : SalariedEmployee
   {
       public decimal? Commission { get; set; }
   }

   public class HourlyEmployee : Employee
   {
       public decimal? Rate { get; set; }
       public decimal? Hours { get; set; }
   }
   ```

3. Add an auto-property of type DbSet<Employee> to your DbContext subclass.

4. Override the OnModelCreating method of DbContext to configure the TPH discriminator values for each derived type, as shown in Listing 6-24.

Listing 6-24. Overriding OnModelCreating in Our DbContext Subclass to Configure TPH Discriminator Values

```
protected override void OnModelCreating(DbModelBuilder modelBuilder)
{
    base.OnModelCreating(modelBuilder);

    modelBuilder.Entity<Employee>()
                .HasKey(e => e.EmployeeId)
                .Property(e => e.EmployeeId)
                .HasDatabaseGeneratedOption(DatabaseGeneratedOption.Identity);

    modelBuilder.Entity<Employee>()
        .Map<HourlyEmployee>(m => m.Requires("EmployeeType").HasValue("hourly"))
        .Map<SalariedEmployee>(m => m.Requires("EmployeeType").HasValue("salaried"))
        .Map<CommissionedEmployee>(m => m.Requires("EmployeeType").HasValue("commissioned"))
        .ToTable("Employee", "Chapter6");
}
```

How It Works

Table per Hierarchy inheritance is a flexible modeling technique. The depth and breadth of the inheritance tree can be reasonably large and is easily implemented. This approach is efficient because no additional tables and their required joins are involved.

Implementing TPH with a Code-First approach is straightforward because object-oriented inheritance is hierarchical in nature.

Listing 6-25 demonstrates inserting into and retrieving from our model.

Listing 6-25. Inserting and Retrieving Derived Entities from Employee

```
using (var context = new EF6RecipesContext())
{
    var hourly = new HourlyEmployee { Name = "Will Smith", Hours = 39,
                                      Rate = 7.75M };
    var salaried = new SalariedEmployee { Name = "JoAnn Woodland",
                                          Salary = 65400M };
    var commissioned = new CommissionedEmployee { Name = "Joel Clark",
                                          Salary = 32500M, Commission = 20M };
    context.Employees.Add(hourly);
    context.Employees.Add(salaried);
    context.Employees.Add(commissioned);
    context.SaveChanges();
}

using (var context = new EF6RecipesContext())
{
    Console.WriteLine("All Employees");
    Console.WriteLine("=============");
    foreach (var emp in context.Employees)
```

```
{
    if (emp is HourlyEmployee)
        Console.WriteLine("{0} Hours = {1}, Rate = {2}/hour",
                              emp.Name,
                              ((HourlyEmployee)emp).Hours.Value.ToString(),
                              ((HourlyEmployee)emp).Rate.Value.ToString("C"));
    else if (emp is CommissionedEmployee)
        Console.WriteLine("{0} Salary = {1}, Commission = {2}%",
                          emp.Name,
                          ((CommissionedEmployee)emp).Salary.Value.ToString("C"),
                          ((CommissionedEmployee)emp).Commission.ToString());
    else if (emp is SalariedEmployee)
        Console.WriteLine("{0} Salary = {1}", emp.Name,
                          ((SalariedEmployee)emp).Salary.Value.ToString("C"));
}
}
```

The output of the code in Listing 6-25 is as follows:

```
All Employees
=============
Will Smith Hours = 39.00, Rate = $7.75/hour
JoAnn Woodland Salary = $65,400.00
Joel Clark Salary = $32,500.00, Commission = 20.00%
```

6-9. Applying Conditions in Table per Type Inheritance
Problem

You want to apply conditions while using Table per Type inheritance.

Solution

Let's say that you have the two tables depicted in Figure 6-11. The Toy table describes toys a company produces. Most toys manufactured by the company are for sale. Some toys are made just to donate to worthy charities. During the manufacturing process, a toy may be damaged. Damaged toys are refurbished, and an inspector determines the resulting quality of the refurbished toy.

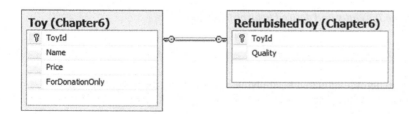

Figure 6-11. *Toy and RefurbishedToy tables with a one-to-one relationship*

The application that generates reports for the company has no need to access toys manufactured for donations. To create a model that filters out toys manufactured for donation while representing the Toy and RefurbishedToy tables using Table per Type inheritance, do the following:

1. Add a new ADO.NET Entity Data Model to your project, and import the Order and Lookup tables.

2. Delete the association between Toy and RefurbishedToy.

3. Right-click the Toy entity, and select Add ➤ Inheritance. Select Toy as the base entity and RefurbishedToy as the derived entity.

4. Delete the ToyId property in the RefurbishedToy entity.

5. Select the RefurbishedToy entity. In the Mapping Details window, map the ToyId column to the ToyId property. This value will come from the Toy base entity.

6. Delete the ForDonationOnly scalar property from the Toy entity.

7. Select the Toy entity, and view the Mapping Details window. Use Add a Table or View to map this entity to the Toy table. Add a condition When `ForDonationOnly` = 0.

The resulting model is shown in Figure 6-12.

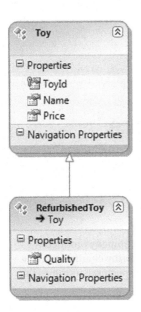

Figure 6-12. *The completed model with the Toy entity and derived RefurbishedToy entity*

How It Works

We limited the RefurbishedToy instances to nondonation toys by applying a condition on the base entity. This approach is useful in cases such as when we need to apply a permanent filter to an inheritance structure while using separate tables to implement some of the derived types.

The code in Listing 6-26 demonstrates inserting into and retrieving from our model.

Listing 6-26. *Inserting into and Retrieving from Our Model*

```
using (var context = new EF6RecipesContext())
{
    Context.Database.ExecuteSqlCommand(@"insert into chapter6.toy
            (Name,ForDonationOnly) values ('RagDoll',1)");
    var toy = new Toy { Name = "Fuzzy Bear", Price = 9.97M };
    var refurb = new RefurbishedToy { Name = "Derby Car", Price = 19.99M,
                                    Quality = "Ok to sell" };
    context.Toys.Add(toy);
    context.Toys.Add(refurb);
    context.SaveChanges();
}

using (var context = new EF6RecipesContext())
{
    Console.WriteLine("All Toys");
    Console.WriteLine("========");
    foreach (var toy in context.Toys)
    {
        Console.WriteLine("{0}", toy.Name);
    }
    Console.WriteLine("\nRefurbished Toys");
    foreach (var toy in context.Toys.OfType<RefurbishedToy>())
    {
        Console.WriteLine("{0}, Price = {1}, Quality = {2}", toy.Name,
                        toy.Price, ((RefurbishedToy)toy).Quality);
    }
}
```

The following is the output from Listing 6-26:

```
All Toys
========
Fuzzy Bear
Derby Car

Refurbished Toys
Derby Car, Price = 19.99, Quality = Ok to sell
```

6-10. Creating a Filter on Multiple Criteria
Problem

You want to filter rows for an entity based on multiple criteria.

Solution

Let's assume that we have a table that holds web orders, as shown in Figure 6-13.

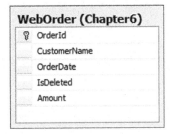

Figure 6-13. *The WebOrder table containing information about a web order*

Suppose that we have a business requirement, which defines instances of WebOrder as orders placed after the first day of 2012 or orders placed between 2010 and 2012 that are not deleted or orders placed before 2010 that have an order amount greater than $200. This kind of filter cannot be created using the rather limited conditions available in the Mapping Details window in the designer. One way to implement this complex filter is to use QueryView. To model this entity and implement a filter that satisfies the business requirement using QueryView, do the following:

1. Add a new ADO.NET Entity Data Model to your project, and import the WebOrder table.

   Create the stored procedures in Listing 6-27. In the next two steps, we'll map these to the insert, update, and delete actions for the WebOrder entity.

   Listing 6-27. Procedures Defined in the Database for the Insert, Update, and Delete Actions on the WebOrder Entity

```
create procedure [Chapter6].[InsertOrder]
(@CustomerName varchar(50),@OrderDate date,@IsDeleted bit,@Amount decimal)
as
begin
            insert into chapter6.WebOrder (CustomerName, OrderDate, IsDeleted, Amount)
            values (@CustomerName, @OrderDate, @IsDeleted, @Amount)
            select SCOPE_IDENTITY() as OrderId
end
go

create procedure [Chapter6].[UpdateOrder]
(@CustomerName varchar(50),@OrderDate date,@IsDeleted bit,
 @Amount decimal, @OrderId int)
as
begin
            update chapter6.WebOrder set CustomerName = @CustomerName,
        OrderDate = @OrderDate,IsDeleted = @IsDeleted,Amount = @Amount
            where OrderId = @OrderId
end
go

create procedure [Chapter6].[DeleteOrder]
(@OrderId int)
as
begin
            delete from Chapter6.WebOrder where OrderId = @OrderId
end
```

2.   Right-click the design surface, and select Update Model from Database. In the Update Wizard, select the InsertOrder, UpdateOrder, and DeleteOrder stored procedures.

3.   Select the WebOrder entity, and select the Map Entities to Functions button in the Mapping Details window. This button is the second of two buttons on the left side of the window. Map the InsertOrder procedure to the Insert action, the UpdateOrder procedure to the Update action, and the DeleteOrder procedure to the Delete action. The property/parameter mappings should automatically line up. However, the return value from the InsertOrder procedure must be mapped to the OrderId property. This is used by Entity Framework to get the value of the identity column OrderId after an insert. Figure 6-14 shows the correct mappings.

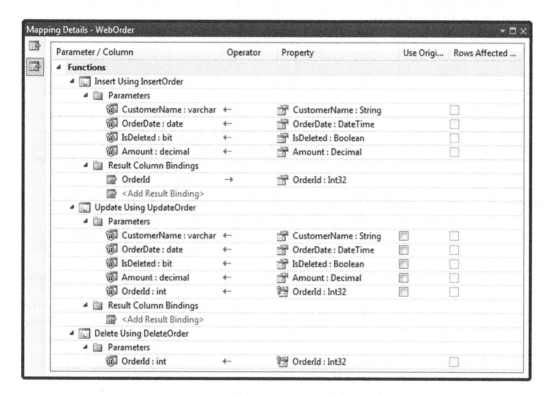

Figure 6-14. *Details for the stored procedure/action mappings*

4.   Select the table mapping (top button) in the Mapping Details window. Delete the mapping to the WebOrder table. We'll map this using QueryView.

Right-click the .edmx file in the Solution Explorer window, and select Open With ➤ XML Editor. In the C-S mapping layer, inside the `<EntitySetMapping>` tag, enter the code shown in Listing 6-28 This is the QueryView that will map our WebOrder entity.

Be careful! Changes made to the C-S mapping layer will be lost if you do another Update Model from Database.

Listing 6-28. Entity Set Mapping Using QueryView for the WebOrder Table

```
<EntitySetMapping Name="WebOrders">
  <QueryView>
    select value
    EFRecipesModel.WebOrder(o.OrderId,
    o.CustomerName,o.OrderDate,o.IsDeleted,o.Amount)
    from EFRecipesModelStoreContainer.WebOrder as o
    where (o.OrderDate > datetime'2007-01-01 00:00') ||
    (o.OrderDate between cast('2005-01-01' as Edm.DateTime) and
    cast('2007-01-01' as Edm.DateTime) and !o.IsDeleted) ||
    (o.Amount > 800 and o.OrderDate &lt;
    cast('2005-01-01' as Edm.DateTime))
  </QueryView>
</EntitySetMapping>
```

How It Works

QueryView is a read-only mapping that can be used instead of the default mapping offered by Entity Framework. When QueryView is inside of the `<EntitySetMapping>` tag of the mapping layer, it maps entities defined on the store model to entities defined on the conceptual model. When QueryView is inside of the `<AssociationSetMapping>` tag, it maps associations defined on the store model to associations defined on the conceptual model. One common use of QueryView inside of an `<AssociationSetMapping>` tag is to implement inheritance based on conditions that are not supported by the default condition mapping.

QueryView is expressed in Entity SQL. QueryView can query only entities defined on the store model. Additionally, eSQL in QueryView does not support group by and group aggregates.

When entities are mapped using QueryView, Entity Framework is unaware of the precise implementation of the mapping. Because Entity Framework does not know the underlying columns and tables used to create instances of the entities, it cannot generate the appropriate store-level actions to insert, update, or delete the entities. Entity Framework does track changes to these entities once they are materialized, but it does not know how to modify them in the underlying data store.

The burden of implementing the insert, update, and delete actions falls onto the developer. These actions can be implemented directly in the .edmx file or they can be implemented as stored procedures in the underlying database. To tie the procedures to the actions, you need to create a `<ModificationFunctionMapping>` section. We did this in step 4 using the designer rather than directly editing the .edmx file.

If an entity mapped using QueryView has associations with other entities, those associations, along with the related entities, also need to be mapped using QueryView. Of course, this can become rather tedious. QueryView is a powerful tool, but it can rapidly become burdensome.

Some of the common use cases for using QueryView are as follows.

1. To define filters that are not directly supported, such as greater than, less than, and so on

2. To map inheritance that is based on conditions other than is null, not null, or equal to

3. To map computed columns or return a subset of columns from a table, or to change a restriction or data type of a column, such as making it nullable, or to surface a string column as integer

4. To map Table per Type Inheritance based on different primary and foreign keys

5. To map the same column in the storage model to multiple types in the conceptual model

6. To map multiple types to the same table

Inside the QueryView in Listing 6-28, we have an Entity SQL statement that contains three parts. The first part is the select clause which instantiates an instance of the WebOrder entity with a constructor. The constructor takes the property values in precisely the same order as they are defined on the conceptual model in Listing 6-29.

Listing 6-29. The Definition of the WebOrder Entity in the Conceptual Model

```
<EntityType Name="WebOrder">
  <Key>
    <PropertyRef Name="OrderId" />
  </Key>
  <Property Name="OrderId" Type="Int32" Nullable="false"
            annotation:StoreGeneratedPattern="Identity" />
  <Property Name="CustomerName" Type="String" Nullable="false"
            MaxLength="50" Unicode="false" FixedLength="false" />
  <Property Name="OrderDate" Type="DateTime" Nullable="false" />
  <Property Name="IsDeleted" Type="Boolean" Nullable="false" />
  <Property Name="Amount" Type="Decimal" Nullable="false"
            Precision="18" Scale="2" />
</EntityType>
```

Notice that, in the Entity SQL in Listing 6-29 we fully qualified the conceptual namespace EFRecipesModel when creating an instance of the WebOrder entity. However, in the from clause we also fully qualified the store container, EFRecipesModelStoreContainer.

The final section of the Entity SQL expression includes the where clause that, of course, is the whole reason for using a QueryView in this example. Although the where clause can be arbitrarily complex, it is subject to the restrictions for Entity SQL in QueryView as noted above.

The code in Listing 6-30 demonstrates inserting and retrieving WebOrdersin our model.

Listing 6-30. Inserting and Retrieving WebOrder Entities

```
using (var context = new EF6RecipesContext())
{
    var order = new WebOrder {CustomerName = "Jim Allen",
                                OrderDate = DateTime.Parse("5/3/2012"),
                                IsDeleted = false, Amount = 200};
    context.WebOrders.Add(order);
    order = new WebOrder { CustomerName = "John Stevens",
                            OrderDate = DateTime.Parse("1/1/2011"),
                            IsDeleted = false, Amount = 400 };
    context.WebOrders.Add(order);
    order = new WebOrder { CustomerName = "Russel Smith",
                            OrderDate = DateTime.Parse("1/3/2011"),
                            IsDeleted = true, Amount = 500 };
    context.WebOrders.Add(order);
    order = new WebOrder { CustomerName = "Mike Hammer",
                            OrderDate = DateTime.Parse("6/3/2013"),
                            IsDeleted = true, Amount = 1800 };
    context.WebOrders.Add(order);
```

```
    order = new WebOrder { CustomerName = "Steve Jones",
                            OrderDate = DateTime.Parse("1/1/2008"),
                            IsDeleted = true, Amount = 600 };
    context.WebOrders.Add(order);
    context.SaveChanges();
}

using (var context = new EF6RecipesContext())
{
    Console.WriteLine("Orders");
    Console.WriteLine("======");
    foreach (var order in context.WebOrders)
    {
        Console.WriteLine("\nCustomer: {0}", order.CustomerName);
        Console.WriteLine("OrderDate: {0}", order.OrderDate.ToShortDateString());
        Console.WriteLine("Is Deleted: {0}", order.IsDeleted.ToString());
        Console.WriteLine("Amount: {0}", order.Amount.ToString("C"));
    }
}
```

The output of the code in Listing 6-30 follows. Notice that only customers that meet the criteria that we defined in the Entity SQL expression inside the QueryView are displayed.

```
Orders...

Customer: John Stevens
Order Date: 1/1/2011
Is Deleted: False
Amount: $400.00

Customer: Jim Allen
Order Date: 5/3/2012
Is Deleted: False
Amount: $200.00

Customer: Mike Hammer
Order Date: 6/3/2013
Is Deleted: True
Amount: $1,800.00
```

6-11. Using Complex Conditions with Table per Hierarchy Inheritance

Problem

You want to model a table using Table per Hierarchy inheritance by applying conditions more complex than those supported directly by Entity Framework.

Solution

Suppose that we have a Member table, as depicted in Figure 6-15. The Member table describes members in our club. In our model, we want to represent adult members, senior members, and teen members as derived types using Table per Type inheritance.

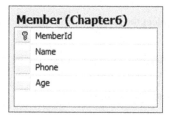

Figure 6-15. *The Member table describing members in our club*

Entity Framework supports Table per Hierarchy inheritance based on the conditions =, is null, and is not null. Simple expressions such as <, between, and > are not supported. In our case, a member whose age is less than 20 is a teen (the minimum age in our club is 13). A member between the ages of 20 and 55 is an adult. And, as you might expect, a member over the age of 55 is a senior. To create a model for the member table and the three derived types, do the following:

1. Add a new ADO.NET Entity Data Model to your project, and import the Member table.

2. Right-click the Member entity, and select Properties. Set the Abstract attribute to true. This marks the Member entity as abstract.

3. Create the stored procedures in Listing 6-31. We will use them to handle the Insert, Update, and Delete actions on the entities we'll derive from the Member entity.

Listing 6-31. Stored Procedures for the Insert, Update, and Delete Actions

```
create procedure [chapter6].[InsertMember]
(@Name varchar(50), @Phone varchar(50), @Age int)
as
begin
		insert into Chapter6.Member (Name, Phone, Age)
		values (@Name,@Phone,@Age)
		select SCOPE_IDENTITY() as MemberId
end
go

create procedure [chapter6].[UpdateMember]
(@Name varchar(50), @Phone varchar(50), @Age int, @MemberId int)
as
begin
		update Chapter6.Member set Name=@Name, Phone=@Phone, Age=@Age
		where MemberId = @MemberId
end
go
```

```
create procedure [chapter6].[DeleteMember]
(@MemberId int)
as
begin
                delete from Chapter6.Member where MemberId = @MemberId
end
```

4. Right-click the design surface, and select Update Model from Database. Select the stored procedures that you created in step 3.

5. Right-click the design surface, and select Add ➤ Entity. Name the new entity Teen, and set the base type to Member. Repeat this step, creating the derived entities Adult and Senior.

6. Select the Member entity, and view the Mapping Details window. Click Maps to Member, and select <Delete>. This deletes the mappings to the Member table.

7. Select the Teen entity, and view the Mapping Details window. Click the Map Entity to Functions button. This is the bottom button on the left of the Mapping Details window. Map the stored procedures to the corresponding Insert, Update, and Delete actions. The parameter/property mappings should automatically populate. Make sure that you set the Result Column Bindings to map the return value to the MemberId property for the Insert action. This identity column is generated on the database side (see Figure 6-16).

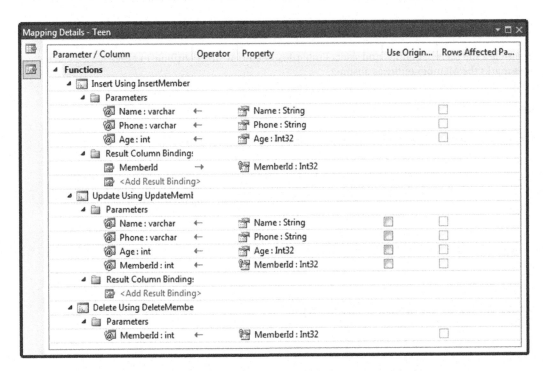

Figure 6-16. *Mapping the Insert, Update, and Delete actions for the Teen entity*

8. Repeat step 7 for the Adult and Senior entities.

Right-click the .edmx file in the Solution Explorer window, and select Open With ➤ XML Editor. This will open the .edmx file in the XML editor.

9. In the C-S mapping section, inside the `<EntityContainerMapping>` tag, enter the QueryView code shown in Listing 6-32.

Listing 6-32. *QueryView for Mapping the Member Table to the Derived Types Teen, Adult, and Senior*

```
<EntitySetMapping Name="Members">
  <QueryView>
    select value
    case
    when m.Age &lt; 20 then
    EFRecipesModel.Teen(m.MemberId,m.Name,m.Phone,m.Age)
    when m.Age between 20 and 55 then
    EFRecipesModel.Adult(m.MemberId,m.Name,m.Phone,m.Age)
    when m.Age > 55 then
    EFRecipesModel.Senior(m.MemberId,m.Name,m.Phone,m.Age)
    end
    from EFRecipesModelStoreContainer.Member as m
  </QueryView>
</EntitySetMapping>
```

The resulting model should look like the one in Figure 6-17.

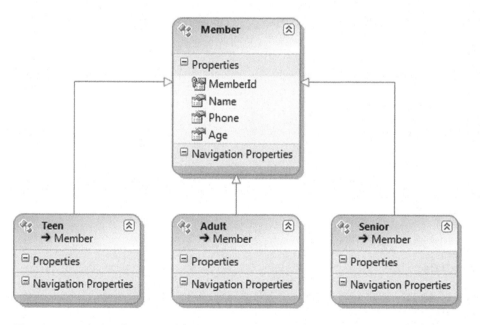

Figure 6-17. *The resulting model with Member and the three derived types: Senior, Adult, and Teen*

How It Works

Entity Framework supports only a limited set of conditions when modeling Table per Hierarchy inheritance. In this recipe, we extended the conditions using QueryView to define our own mappings between the underlying Member table and the derived types: Senior, Adult, and Teen. This is shown in Listing 6-32.

Unfortunately, QueryView comes at a price. Because we have defined the mappings ourselves, we also take on the responsibility for implementing the Insert, Update, and Delete actions for the derived types. This is not too difficult in our case.

In Listing 6-31, we defined the procedures to handle the Insert, Delete, and Update actions. We need to create only one set because these actions target the underlying Member table. In this recipe, we implemented them as stored procedures in the underlying database. We could have implemented in the .edmx file.

Using the designer, we mapped the procedures to the Insert, Update, and Delete actions for each of the derived types. This completes the extra work we need to do when we use QueryView.

The code in Listing 6-33 demonstrates inserting into and retrieving from our model. Here we insert one instance of each of our derived types. On the retrieval side, we print the members together with their phone number, unless the member is a Teen.

Listing 6-33. Inserting into and Retrieving from Our Model

```
using (var context = new EF6RecipesContext())
{
    var teen = new Teen { Name = "Steven Keller", Age = 17,
                          Phone = "817 867-5309" };
    var adult = new Adult { Name = "Margret Jones", Age = 53,
                            Phone = "913 294-6059" };
    var senior = new Senior { Name = "Roland Park", Age = 71,
                              Phone = "816 353-4458" };
    context.Members.Add(teen);
    context.Members.Add(adult);
    context.Members.Add(senior);
    context.SaveChanges();
}

using (var context = new EF6RecipesContext())
{
    Console.WriteLine("Club Members");
    Console.WriteLine("============");
    foreach(var member in context.Members)
    {
        bool printPhone = true;
        string str = string.Empty;
        if (member is Teen)
        {
            str = " a Teen";
            printPhone = false;
        }
        else if (member is Adult)
            str = "an Adult";
        else if (member is Senior)
            str = "a Senior";
        Console.WriteLine("{0} is {1} member, phone: {2}",member.Name,
                          str, printPhone ? member.Phone : "unavailable");
    }
}
```

The following is the output from the code in Listing 6-33:

```
Members of our club
====================
Steven Keller is a Teen member, phone: unavailable
Margret Jones is an Adult member, phone: 913 294-6059
Roland Park is a Senior member, phone: 816 353-4458
```

It is important to note here that no design time, or even runtime checking, is done to verify the ages for the derived types. It is entirely possible to create an instance of the Teen type and set the age property to 74—clearly not a teen. On the retrieval side, however, this row will be materialized as a Senior member—a situation likely to offend our Teen member.

We can introduce validation before changes are committed to the data store. To do this, register for the SavingChanges event when the context is created. We wire this event to our code that performs the validation. This code is shown in Listing 6-34.

Listing 6-34. Handling Validation in the SavingChanges Event

```
public partial class EF6RecipesContext
{
    partial void OnContextCreated()
    {
        this.SavingChanges += new EventHandler(Validate);
    }

    public void Validate(object sender, EventArgs e)
    {
        var entities = this.ObjectStateManager
                        .GetObjectStateEntries(EntityState.Added |
                                               EntityState.Modified)
                        .Select(et => et.Entity as Member);
        foreach (var member in entities) {
            if (member is Teen && member.Age > 19) {
                throw new ApplicationException("Entity validation failed");
            }
            else if (member is Adult && (member.Age < 20 || member.Age >= 55)) {
                throw new ApplicationException("Entity validation failed");
            }
            else if (member is Senior && member.Age < 55) {
                throw new ApplicationException("Entity validation failed");
            }
        }
    }
}
```

In Listing 6-34, when SaveChanges() is called, our Validate() method checks each entity that has either been added or modified. For each of these, we verify that the age property is appropriate for the type of the entity. When we find a validation error, we simply throw an exception.

We have several recipes in Chapter 12 that focus on handling events and validating objects before they are committed to the database.

6-12. Modeling Table per Concrete Type Inheritance

Problem

You have two or more tables with similar schema and data, and you want to model these tables as types derived from a common entity using Table per Concrete Type inheritance.

Solution

Let's assume that we have the tables shown in Figure 6-18.

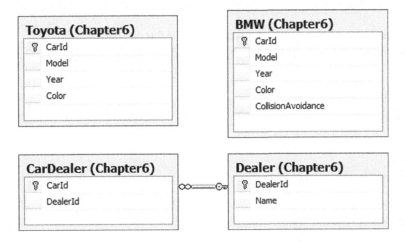

Figure 6-18. *Tables Toyota and BMW with similar structure that will become derived types of the Car entity*

In Figure 6-18, the tables Toyota and BMW have similar schema and represent similar data. The BMW table has an additional column with a bit value indicating whether the instance has the collision-avoidance feature. We want to create a model with a base entity holding the common properties of the Toyota and BMW tables. Additionally, we want to represent the one-to-many relationship between the car dealer and cars held in inventory. Figure 6-22 shows the final model.

To create the model, do the following:

1. Add a new ADO.NET Entity Data Model to your project, and import the Toyota, BMW, CarDealer, and Dealer tables.

2. Right-click the design surface, and select Add ➤ Entity. Name the new entity Car, and unselect the Create key property check box.

3. Right-click the Car entity, and view its properties. Set the Abstract property to `true`.

4. Move the common properties of the Toyota and BMW entities to the Car entity. You can use Cut/Paste to move these properties. Make sure that only the CollisionAvoidance property remains with the BMW entity and the Toyota entity has no properties. Both of these entities will inherit these common properties from the Car entity.

5. Right-click the Car entity, and select Add ➤ Inheritance. Set the base entity as Car and the derived entity as BMW.

6. Repeat step 5, but this time set the Toyota as the derived entity.

7. Right-click the CarDealer entity and select Delete. When prompted to delete the CarDealer table from the store model, select No.

8. Right-click the design surface, and select Add ➤ Association. Name the association CarDealer. Select Dealer on the left with a multiplicity of one. Select Car on the right with a multiplicity of many. Name the navigation property on the Car side Dealer. Name the navigation property on the Dealer side Cars. Be sure to uncheck the Add foreign key properties.

9. Select the association, and view the Mapping Details window. Select CarDealer in the Add a Table or View drop-down menu. Make sure that the DealerId property maps to the DealerId column, and the CarId property maps to the CarId column.

Right-click the .edmx file, and select Open With ➤ XML Editor. Edit the mapping section with the changes shown in Listing 6-35 for the BMW and Toyota entities.

Listing 6-35. Mapping the BMW and Toyota Tables

```
<EntitySetMapping Name="Cars">
  <EntityTypeMapping TypeName="IsTypeOf(EFRecipesModel.BMW)">
    <MappingFragment StoreEntitySet="BMW">
      <ScalarProperty Name="CollisionAvoidance"
                ColumnName="CollisionAvoidance" />
      <ScalarProperty Name="CarId" ColumnName="CarId"/>
      <ScalarProperty Name="Model" ColumnName="Model"/>
      <ScalarProperty Name="Year" ColumnName="Year"/>
      <ScalarProperty Name="Color" ColumnName="Color"/>
    </MappingFragment>
  </EntityTypeMapping>
  <EntityTypeMapping TypeName="IsTypeOf(EFRecipesModel.Toyota)">
    <MappingFragment StoreEntitySet="Toyota">
      <ScalarProperty Name="CarId" ColumnName="CarId"/>
      <ScalarProperty Name="Model" ColumnName="Model"/>
      <ScalarProperty Name="Year" ColumnName="Year"/>
      <ScalarProperty Name="Color" ColumnName="Color"/>
    </MappingFragment>
  </EntityTypeMapping>
</EntitySetMapping>
```

The resulting model is shown in Figure 6-19.

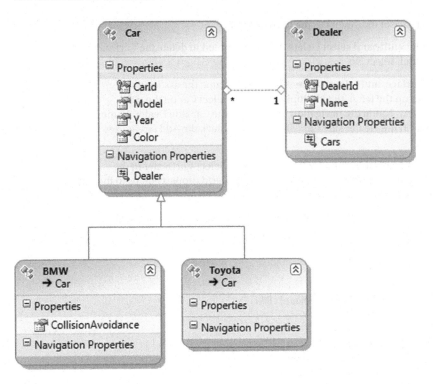

Figure 6-19. *The completed model with the derived entities BMW and Toyota represented in the database as separate tables*

How It Works

Table per Concrete Type is an interesting inheritance model in that it allows each derived entity to map to separate physical tables. From a practical perspective, the tables need to share at least some part of a common schema. This common schema is mapped in the base entity while the additional schema parts are mapped in the derived entities. For Table per Concrete Type inheritance to work properly, the entity key must be unique across the tables.

The base entity is marked abstract, and it is not mapped to any table. In Table per Concrete Type, only the derived entities are mapped to tables.

In our example, we marked the Car entity as abstract and we did not map it to any table. In the mapping shown in Listing 6-35, notice that we mapped only the derived entities BMW and Toyota. We moved all of the common properties (CarId, Model, Year, and Color) to the base entity. The derived entities contained only the properties unique to the entity. For instance, the BMW entity has the additional CollisionAvoidance property.

Because the entities Toyota and BMW derived from the Car entity, they became part of the same Cars entity set. This means that the CarId entity key must be unique within the entity set that now contains all of the derived entities. Because the entities are mapped to different tables, it is possible that we can have collisions in the keys. To avoid this, we set the CarId column in each table as an identity column. For the BMW table, we set the initial seed to 1 with an increment of 2. This will create odd values for the CarId key. For the Toyota table, we set the initial seed to 2 with an increment of 2. This will create event values for the CarId key.

When modeling relationships in Table per Concrete Type inheritance, it is better to define them at the derived type rather than at the base type. This is because the Entity Framework runtime would not know which physical table represents the other end of the association. In our example, of course, we provided a separate table (CarDealer) that contains the relationship. This allowed us to model the relationship at the base entity by mapping the association to the CarDealer table.

There are many practical applications of Table per Concrete Type inheritance Perhaps the most common is in working with archival data. Imagine that you have a several years worth of orders for your eCommerce site. At the end of each year, you archive the orders for the previous 12 months in an archive table and start the New Year with an empty table. With Table per Concrete Type inheritance, you can model the current and archived orders using the approach demonstrated here.

Table per Concrete Type inheritance has a particularly important performance advantage over other inheritance models When querying a derived type, the generated query targets the specific underlying table without the additional joins of Table per Type inheritance or the filtering of Table per Hierarchy. For large datasets or models with several derived types, this performance advantage can be significant.

The disadvantages of Table per Concrete Type inheritance include the overhead of potentially duplicate data across tables and the complexity of insuring unique keys across the tables. In an archival scenario, data is not duplicated but simply spread across multiple tables. In other scenarios, data (properties) may be duplicated across the tables.

The code in Listing 6-36 demonstrates inserting into and retrieving from our model.

Listing 6-36. Inserting into and Querying Our Model

```
using (var context = new EF6RecipesContext())
{
    var d1 = new Dealer { Name = "All Cities Toyota" };
    var d2 = new Dealer { Name = "Southtown Toyota" };
    var d3 = new Dealer { Name = "Luxury Auto World" };
    var c1 = new Toyota { Model = "Camry", Color = "Green",
                        Year = "2014", Dealer = d1 };
    var c2 = new BMW { Model = "310i", Color = "Blue",
                        CollisionAvoidance = true,
                        Year = "2014", Dealer = d3 };
    var c3 = new Toyota { Model = "Tundra", Color = "Blue",
                        Year = "2014", Dealer = d2 };
    context.Dealers.Add(d1);
    context.Dealers.Add(d2);
    context.Dealers.Add(d3);
    context.SaveChanges();
}

using (var context = new EF6RecipesContext())
{
    Console.WriteLine("Dealers and Their Cars");
    Console.WriteLine("======================");
    foreach (var dealer in context.Dealers)
    {
        Console.WriteLine("\nDealer: {0}", dealer.Name);
        foreach(var car in dealer.Cars)
        {
            string make = string.Empty;
            if (car is Toyota)
                make = "Toyota";
            else if (car is BMW)
                make = "BMW";
            Console.WriteLine("\t{0} {1} {2} {3}", car.Year,
                            car.Color, make, car.Model);
        }
    }
}
```

The output of the code in Listing 6-36 is as follows:

```
Dealers and Their Cars
=======================

Dealer: Luxury Auto World
        2014 Blue BMW 310i

Dealer: Southtown Toyota
        2014 Blue Toyota Tundra

Dealer: All Cities Toyota
        2014 Green Toyota Camry
```

6-13. Applying Conditions on a Base Entity

Problem

You want to derive a new entity from a base entity that currently exists in a model and continue to allow the base entity to be instantiated.

Solution

Let's assume that you have a model like the one shown in Figure 6-20.

Figure 6-20. *Our model with the Invoice entity*

This model contains a single Invoice entity. We want to derive a new entity that represents deleted invoices. This will allow us to separate more cleanly business logic that operates on active invoices differently than on deleted invoices. To add the derived entity, do the following:

1. View the Mapping Details window for the Invoice entity. Add a condition on the IsDeleted column to map the entity when the column is 0, as shown in Figure 6-21.

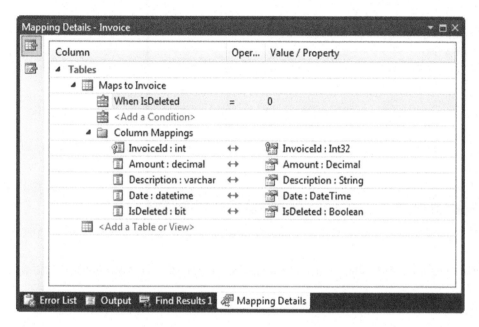

Figure 6-21. *Mapping the Invoice entity when the IsDeleted column is 0*

2. Now that the IsDeleted column is used in a condition, we need to remove it from the scalar properties for the entity. Right-click the IsDeleted property in the entity and select Delete.

3. Right-click the design surface, and select Add ➤ Entity. Name the new entity DeletedInvoice, and select Invoice as the base type.

4. View the Mapping Details window for the DeletedInvoice entity. Map the entity to the Invoice table. Add a condition on the IsDeleted column to map the entity when the column is 1, as shown in Figure 6-22.

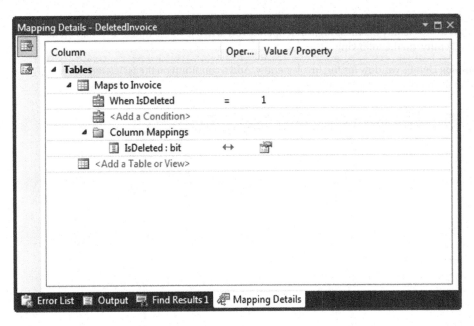

Figure 6-22. *Mapping the DeletedInvoice entity to the Invoice table when the IsDeleted column is 1*

The final model with the Invoice entity and the derived DeletedInvoice entity is shown in Figure 6-23.

Figure 6-23. *Our completed model with the Invoice entity and the DeletedInvoice entity*

How It Works

There are two different ways to model our invoices and deleted invoices. The approach we've shown here is only recommended if you have an existing model and code base, and you would like to add the DeletedInvoice derived type with as little impact as possible to the existing code. For a new model, it would be better to derive an ActiveInvoice type and a DeletedInvoice type from the Invoice base type. In this approach, you would mark the base type as abstract.

Using the approach we've shown here, you could can determine, as we do in the code in Listing 6-37, if the entity is a DeletedInvoice, either by casting or by using the OfType<>() method. However, you can't select for the Invoice entity alone. This is the critical drawback to the approach we've shown here.

The approach you should use for new code is to derive two new entities: ActiveInvoice and DeleteInvoice. With these two sibling types, you can use either casting or the OfType<>() method to operate on either type uniformly.

Listing 6-37. Using the as Operator to Determine If We Have an Invoice or DeletedInvoice

```
using (var context = new EF6RecipesContext())
{
    context.Invoices.Add(new Invoice { Amount = 19.95M,
                                    Description = "Oil Change",
                                    Date = DateTime.Parse("4/11/13") });
    context.Invoices.Add(new Invoice { Amount = 129.95M,
                                    Description = "Wheel Alignment",
                                    Date = DateTime.Parse("4/01/13") });
    context.Invoices.Add(new DeletedInvoice { Amount = 39.95M,
                                    Description = "Engine Diagnosis",
                                    Date = DateTime.Parse("4/01/13") });
    context.SaveChanges();
}

using (var context = new EF6RecipesContext())
{
    foreach (var invoice in context.Invoices)
    {
        var isDeleted = invoice as DeletedInvoice;
        Console.WriteLine("{0} Invoice",
                            isDeleted == null ? "Active" : "Deleted");
        Console.WriteLine("Description: {0}", invoice.Description);
        Console.WriteLine("Amount: {0}", invoice.Amount.ToString("C"));
        Console.WriteLine("Date: {0}", invoice.Date.ToShortDateString());
        Console.WriteLine();
    }
}
```

The following is the output of the code in Listing 6-37:

```
Active Invoice
Description: Oil Change
Amount: $19.95
Date: 4/11/2013

Active Invoice
Description: Wheel Alignment
Amount: $129.95
Date: 4/1/2013

Deleted Invoice
Description: Engine Diagnosis
Amount: $39.95
Date: 4/1/2013
```

6-14. Creating Independent and Foreign Key Associations

Problem

You want to use Model First to create both independent and foreign key associations.

Solution

Foreign keys and independent associations help us maintain referential integrity within the database schema and provide navigation paths to related entities. In order to create foreign keys and independent associations using Model First, do the following:

1. Add a new ADO.NET Entity Data Model to your project. Select Empty Model when prompted to choose the model contents. Click Finish. This will create an empty design surface.

2. Right-click the design surface, and select Add ➤ Entity. Name the new entity User and click OK.

3. Right-click the new entity, and add a scalar property for the UserName.

4. Right-click the design surface, and select Add ➤ Entity. Name the new entity PasswordHistory and click OK.

5. Right-click the new entity, and add a scalar property for the LastLogin. Right-click the LastLogin property, and change its type to DateTime.

6. Right-click the User entity, and select Add ➤ Association. To create a foreign key association, check the Add foreign key properties to the PasswordHistory entity check box. To create an independent association, uncheck this box.

7. Right-click the design surface, and select Generate Model from Database. Select a database connection, and complete the remainder of the wizard. This will generate the storage and mapping layers of the model and produce a script to generate the database for the model.

If you choose to create a foreign key association, the model should look like the one shown in Figure 6-24. If you choose to create an independent association, the model should look like the one shown in Figure 6-25.

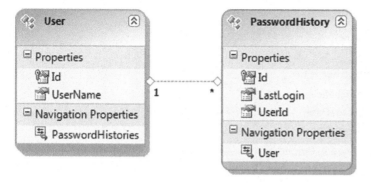

Figure 6-24. *A foreign key association between User and PasswordHistory*

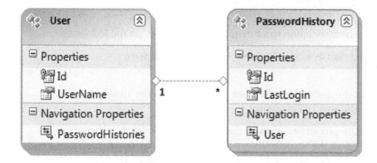

Figure 6-25. *An independent association between User and PasswordHistory*

How It Works

With a foreign key association, the foreign key is exposed as a property in the dependent entity. Exposing the foreign key allows many aspects of the association to be managed with the same code that manages the other property values. This is particularly helpful in disconnected scenarios, as we will see in Chapter 9. Foreign key associations are the default in Entity Framework.

For independent associations, the foreign keys are not exposed as properties. This makes the modeling at the conceptual layer somewhat cleaner because there is no noise introduced concerning the details of the association implementation. In the early versions of Entity Framework, only independent associations were supported.

6-15. Changing an Independent Association into a Foreign Key Association
Problem

You have a model that uses an independent association, and you want to change it to a foreign key association.

Solution

Let's say that you have a model like the one shown in Figure 6-26.

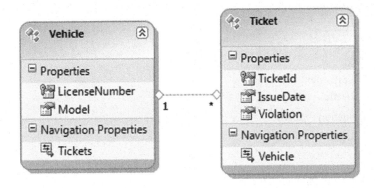

Figure 6-26. *A model for vehicles and tickets using an independent association*

To change the association from an independent association to a foreign key association, do the following:

1. Right-click the Ticket entity, and select Add ➤ Scalar Property. Rename the property LicenseNumber.

2. View the Mapping Details window for the association. Remove the mapping to the Ticket table by selecting <Delete> from the Maps to Ticket control.

3. Right-click the association, and view the properties. Click in the button in the Referential Constraint control. In the dialog box, select the Vehicle entity in the Principal drop-down control. The Principal Key and the Dependent Property should both be set to LicenseNumber, as shown in Figure 6-27.

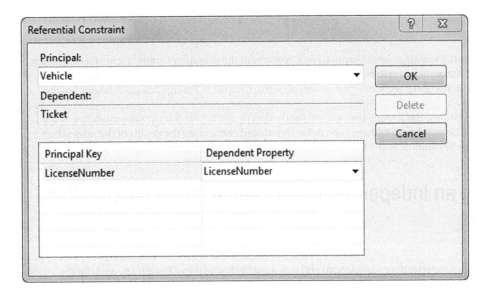

Figure 6-27. *Creating the referential constraint for the foreign key association*

4. View the Mapping Details window for the Ticket entity. Map the LicenseNumber column to the LicenseNumber property, as shown in Figure 6-28.

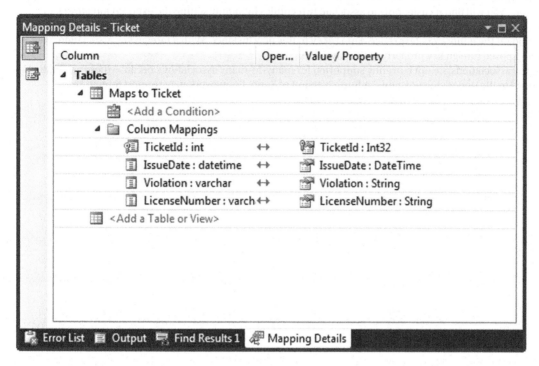

Figure 6-28. *Mapping the LicenseNumber column to the LicenseNumber property for the Ticket entity*

The final model is shown in Figure 6-29.

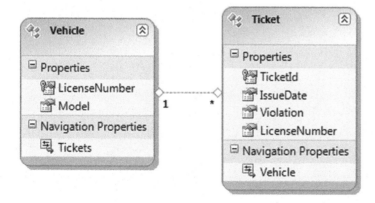

Figure 6-29. *The model with the independent association changed to a foreign key association*

How It Works

When you change an independent association into a foreign key association, most of your existing code will continue to work. You will find it easier now to associate two entities by simply setting the exposed foreign key to the appropriate value. To change a relationship with an independent association, you need to create a new instance of EntityKey and set the entity's xxxReference.EntityKey to this new instance. With a foreign key association, you simply set the exposed foreign key property to the key value.

Foreign key associations are not currently supported for many-to-many associations because these associations must be mapped to the underlying link table. A future version of Entity Framework may support foreign key associations, along with payloads, for many-to-many associations.

CHAPTER 7

Working with Object Services

This chapter contains a rather eclectic collection of recipes that provide practical solutions to common problems in real-world applications. We build our applications to tolerate changes in deployment environments, and we make our applications flexible enough so that few if any configuration details need to be hard-coded.

The first three recipes provide you with the tools to meet these challenges. The remaining recipes cover topics such as Entity Framework's Pluralization Service, using the edmgen.exe utility, working with identifying relationships, and retrieving objects from an object context.

7-1. Dynamically Building a Connection String
Problem

You want to build the connection string dynamically for your application.

Solution

Many real-world applications start out on a developer's desktop; move through one or more testing, integration, and staging environments; and finally end up in a production deployment. You want to configure the application's connection string dynamically depending on the current environment.

To build the connection string dynamically for your application, follow the pattern in Listing 7-1.

Listing 7-1. Dynamically Building a Connection String

```
public static class ConnectionStringManager
{
    public static string EFConnection = GetConnection();

    private static string GetConnection()
    {
        var sqlBuilder = new SqlConnectionStringBuilder();

        sqlBuilder.DataSource = ConfigurationManager.AppSettings["SqlDataSource"];

        // fill in the rest
        sqlBuilder.InitialCatalog = ConfigurationManager.AppSettings["SqlInitialCatalog"];
        sqlBuilder.IntegratedSecurity = true;
        sqlBuilder.MultipleActiveResultSets = true;
```

```
                var eBuilder = new EntityConnectionStringBuilder();
                eBuilder.Provider = "System.Data.SqlClient";
                eBuilder.Metadata =
                       "res://*/Recipe1.csdl|res://*/Recipe1.ssdl|res://*/Recipe1.msl";
                eBuilder.ProviderConnectionString = sqlBuilder.ToString();
                return eBuilder.ToString();      }
    }

public partial class EF6RecipesContainer
    {
        public EF6RecipesContainer(string nameOrConnectionString)
            : base(nameOrConnectionString)
        {

        }
    }
```

How It Works

When you add an ADO.NET Entity Data Model to your project, Entity Framework adds an entry to the <connectionStrings> section in your project's .config file. At runtime, the constructor for the object context is passed the key for this configuration entry (EF6RecipesContext for many of the recipes in this book). Given this key, the database context uses the connection string found in the .config file.

To create the connection string dynamically based on the environment in which our application is deployed, we created the ConnectionStringManager class (refer to Listing 7-1). In the GetConnection() method, we obtain the environment-specific values for data source and initial catalog from a config file. To use our ConnectionStringManager, we implemented an additional constructor that takes a string parameter representing the connection string or name inside the EF6RecipesContainer partial class.

When we instantiate EF6RecipesContainer, we can pass into it the value of ConnectionStringManager.EFConnection and, as a result, the instance will use the dynamically created connection string to connect to the database server.

7-2. Reading a Model from a Database
Problem

You want to read the CSDL, MSL, and SSDL definitions for your model from a database table.

Solution

Suppose that you have a model like the one shown in Figure 7-1.

Figure 7-1. *A model with a Customer entity*

Our model has just one entity: Customer. The conceptual layer (CSDL mapping layer (MSL and storage layer (SSDL definitions are typically found in the .edmx file in your project. We want to read these definitions from a database. To read these definitions from a database, do the following:

1. Right-click the design surface, and view the Properties. Change the Code Generation Strategy to None. We'll use POCO for our Customer class. See Chapter 8 for more recipes on using POCO.

2. Create the table shown in Figure 7-2. This table will hold the definitions for our project.

Definitions (Chapter7)

	Column Name	Data Type	Allow Nulls
🔑 Id	int	☐
	SSDL	xml	☐
	CSDL	xml	☐
	MSL	xml	☐
			☐

Figure 7-2. *The Definitions table holds the definitions for our SSDL, CSDL, and MSL. Note that the column data types for the definitions are XML*

3. Right-click the design surface, and view the Properties. Change the Metadata Artifact Processing to Copy to Output Directory. Rebuild your project. The build process will create three files in the output directory: `Recipe2.ssdl`, `Recipe2.csdl`, and `Recipe2.msl`.

4. Insert the contents of these files into the Definitions table in the corresponding columns. Use 1 for the Id column.

5. Follow the pattern in Listing 7-2 to read the metadata from the Definitions table, and create a MetadataWorkspacethat your application will use.

Listing 7-2. Reading the Metadata from the Definitions Table

```
using System;
using System.Collections.Generic;
using System.Linq;
using System.Text;
using System.Data.Metadata.Edm;
using System.Data.SqlClient;
using System.Data.EntityClient;
using System.Xml;
using System.Data.Mapping;
using System.Data.Objects;

namespace Recipe2
{
    class Program
    {
        static void Main(string[] args)
```

```csharp
        {
            RunExample();
        }

        static void RunExample()
        {
            using (var context = ContextFactory.CreateContext())
            {
                context.Customers.AddObject(
                        new Customer { Name = "Jill Nickels" });
                context.Customers.AddObject(
                        new Customer { Name = "Robert Cole" });
                context.SaveChanges();
            }

            using (var context = ContextFactory.CreateContext())
            {
                Console.WriteLine("Customers");
                Console.WriteLine("---------");
                foreach (var customer in context.Customers)
                {
                    Console.WriteLine("{0}", customer.Name);
                }
            }
        }
    }

    public class Customer
    {
        public virtual int CustomerId { get; set; }
        public virtual string Name { get; set; }
    }

    public class EFRecipesEntities : ObjectContext
    {
        private ObjectSet<Customer> customers;
        public EFRecipesEntities(EntityConnection cn)
            : base(cn)
        {
        }

        public ObjectSet<Customer> Customers
        {
            get
            {
                return customers ?? (customers = CreateObjectSet<Customer>());
            }
        }
    }
```

```
public static class ContextFactory
{
    static string connString = @"Data Source=localhost;
        Initial Catalog=EFRecipes;Integrated Security=True;";
    private static MetadataWorkspace workspace = CreateWorkSpace();

    public static EFRecipesEntities CreateContext()
    {
        var conn = new EntityConnection(workspace,
                        new SqlConnection(connString));
        return new EFRecipesEntities(conn);
    }

    private static MetadataWorkspace CreateWorkSpace()
    {
        string sql = @"select csdl,msl,ssdl from Chapter7.Definitions";
        XmlReader csdlReader = null;
        XmlReader mslReader = null;
        XmlReader ssdlReader = null;

        using (var cn = new SqlConnection(connString))
        {
            using (var cmd = new SqlCommand(sql, cn))
            {
                cn.Open();
                var reader = cmd.ExecuteReader();
                if (reader.Read())
                {
                    csdlReader = reader.GetSqlXml(0).CreateReader();
                    mslReader = reader.GetSqlXml(1).CreateReader();
                    ssdlReader = reader.GetSqlXml(2).CreateReader();
                }
            }
        }

        var workspace = new MetadataWorkspace();
        var edmCollection = new EdmItemCollection(new XmlReader[]
                                        { csdlReader });
        var ssdlCollection = new StoreItemCollection(new XmlReader[]
                                        { ssdlReader });
        var mappingCollection = new StorageMappingItemCollection(
            edmCollection, ssdlCollection, new XmlReader[] { mslReader });

        workspace.RegisterItemCollection(edmCollection);
        workspace.RegisterItemCollection(ssdlCollection);
        workspace.RegisterItemCollection(mappingCollection);
        return workspace;
    }
}
```

Following is the output of the code in Listing 7-2:

```
Customers
----------
Jill Nickels
Robert Cole
```

How It Works

The first part of the code in Listing 7-2 should be very familiar to you by now. We use Entity Framework to create a new context, create a few entities, and call SaveChanges() to persist the entities to the database. To retrieve the entities, we iterate through the collection and display each on the console. The only difference in this part is the call to ContextFactory.CreateContext().Normally, we would just use the new operator to get a new instance of our EFRecipesEntities context.

We've created the ContextFactory to create our context from the model metadata stored, not in the .edmx file, but in a table in a database. We do this in the CreateContext() method. The CreateContext() method creates a new EntityConnection based on two things: a workspace that we create with the CreateWorkSpace()method and a SQL connection string. The real work happens in how we create the workspace in the CreateWorkSpace() method.

The CreateWorkSpace() method opens a connection to the database where our metadata is stored. We construct a SQL statement that reads the one row from the Definitions table (refer to Figure 7-2) that holds our definitions for the conceptual layer, storage layer, and mapping layer. We read these definitions with XmlReaders. With these definitions, we create an instance of a MetadataWorkspace. A MetadataWorkspace is an in-memory representation of a model. Typically, this workspace is created by the default plumbing in Entity Framework from your .edmx file. In this recipe, we create this workspace from the definitions in a database. There are other ways to create this workspace including using embedded resources and an implementation with Code First.

The code in Listing 7-2 uses POCOs for our Customer entity. We cover POCO extensively in Chapter 8, but here we use POCO to simplify the code. With POCO, we don't use the classes generated by Entity Framework. Instead, we use our own classes that have no particular dependence on Entity Framework. In Listing 7-2, we created our own definition of the Customer entity in the Customer class. We also created our own object context: EFRecipesEntities. Our context, of course, does have a dependence on Entity Framework because it derives from ObjectContext.

7-3. Deploying a Model
Problem

You want to know the various options for deploying a model.

Solution

When you add a new ADO.NET Entity Data Model to your project, Entity Framework sets the Build Action property for the .edmx file to Entity Deploy. Additionally, the Metadata Artifact Processing property of the model is set to Embed in Output Assembly. When you build your project, the Entity Deploy action extracts three sections from the .edmx file into three separate files. The CSDL section is extracted into the Model.csdl file. The MSL section is extracted into the Model.msl file. The SSDL section is extracted into the Model.ssdl file. With the Embed in Output Assembly, these three files get embedded into the assembly as resources.

Changing the Metadata Artifact Processing property to Copy to Output Directory causes the three Model.* files to be copied to the same directory as the resulting assembly. The files are not embedded as a resource.

How It Works

The .edmx file contains all three model layers: conceptual, mapping, and storage. The file also contains additional data used by the designer to manage the design surface. At runtime, Entity Framework uses each of the layers separately. The .edmx file is just a convenient container for the design time user experience. The deployment of a model depends on model layers either embedded in the assembly, stored in files, or, as we saw in Recipe 7-2, retrieved from another source and used to complete a MetadataWorkspace.

If your Metadata Artifact Processing property is set to Embed in Output Assembly, you will notice that the connection string in your `App.config` or `web.config` file includes a `metadata` tag, which looks something like the following:

```
metadata=res://*/Recipe3.csdl|res://*/Recipe3.ssdl|res://*/Recipe3.msl;
```

This notation indicates a search path for each of the model layers embedded in the assembly. If you change the Metadata Artifact Processing property to Copy to Output Directory, you will see the connection string change to something like this:

```
metadata=.\Recipe3.csdl|.\Recipe3.ssdl|.\Recipe3.msl;
```

This notation indicates a file path to each of the model layers.

When embedding the model layers as resources in an assembly, you are not restricted by the connection string syntax to referencing only the executing assembly. Table 7-1 illustrates some of the possible constructions you can use to reference the embedded model layers in other assemblies.

Table 7-1. *Connection String Syntax for Loading Model Layers*

Syntax	Meaning
res://myassembly/file.ssdl	Loads the SSDL from myassembly
res://myassembly/	Loads the SSDL, CSDL, and MSL from myassembly
res://*/file.ssdl	Loads the SSDL from all assemblies in the AppDomain
res://*/	Loads the SSDL, CSDL, and MSL from all assemblies

7-4. Using the Pluralization Service

Problem

You want to use Entity Framework's Pluralization Service when you import a table from a database.

Solution

Suppose that you have a database with the tables shown in Figure 7-3.

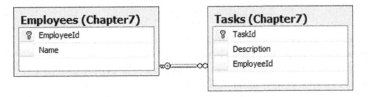

Figure 7-3. *Employees and Tasks tables in our database*

Notice that the tables in Figure 7-3 take the plural form. This is common in many databases. Some DBAs believe that all table names should be plural; other DBAs believe just the opposite. Of course, there are a few that don't seem to follow any particular view and mix things up. Depending on your perspective, you may want to use the singular form of the table names for your model's entities. Entity Framework provides a Pluralization Service that can automatically generate the singular form of a table name to use as the corresponding entity name.

To use the Pluralization Service when importing your tables, check the Pluralize or singularize generated object names box in the last step of the Entity Data Model Wizard (see Figure 7-4). By default, this box is checked.

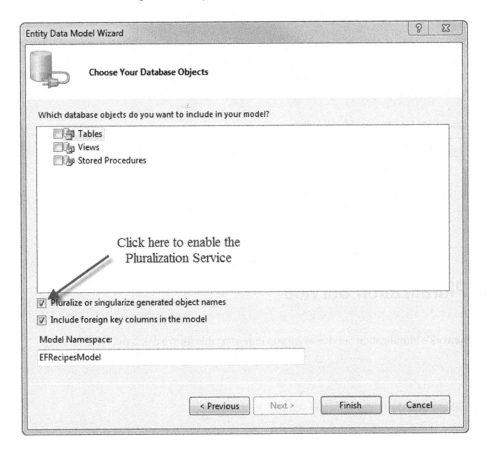

Figure 7-4. *Enabling the Pluralization Service*

Figure 7-5 shows a model created when we import the table in Figure 7-3 without the Pluralization Service enabled. Notice that entity names are taken directly from the table names and retain the plural form. Figure 7-6 shows the same tables imported with the Pluralization Service enabled. These entities use the singular forms of the table names.

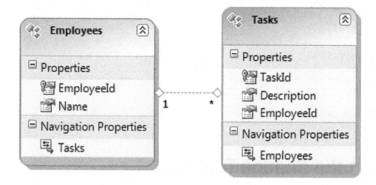

Figure 7-5. *The model created from the tables in Figure 7-3 without the Pluralization Service*

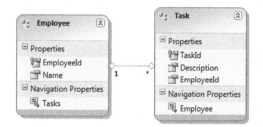

Figure 7-6. *The model created from the tables in Figure 7-3 with the Pluralization Service*

How It Works

Most developers prefer the entity names in the model in Figure 7-6. (Look at the names in boldface at the top of each entity.) Not only are the entity names singular, but the Employee navigation property in the Task entity also makes more sense than the Employees navigation property in the Tasks entity in Figure 7-5. In both cases, this navigation property is an EntityReference, not a collection. The plural form in Figure 7-5 seems somewhat confusing.

If our table names were singular to start with, the Pluralization Service would correctly pluralize the collection-based navigation properties and pluralize the underlying entity set names. This takes cares of the other half of the DBA community that uses singular names for tables.

You can set the default on/off state of the Pluralization Service for new entities in your model by changing the Pluralize New Objects property When you add new entities to your model, this setting will change the default on/off state for the Pluralization Service.

You can use the Pluralization Service outside of the context of Entity Framework. This service is available in the System.Data.Entity.Design namespace To add a reference to the System.Data.Entity.Design.dll, you will need to change your project's Target framework from the default .NET Framework 4 Client Profile to the more expansive .NET Framework 4. This setting is changed in the properties of the project. The code in Listing 7-3 demonstrates using the Pluralization Service to pluralize and singularize the words "Person" and "People."

Listing 7-3. Using the Pluralization Service

```
var service = PluralizationService.CreateService(new CultureInfo("en-US"));
string person = "Person";
string people = "People";
Console.WriteLine("The plural of {0} is {1}", person,
                  service.Pluralize(person));
```

243

```
Console.WriteLine("The singular of {0} is {1}", people,
                  service.Singularize(people));
```

Following is the output of the code in Listing 7-3:

```
The plural of Person is People
The singular of People is Person
```

7-5. Retrieving Entities from the Change Tracker

Problem

You want to create an extension method that retrieves entities from the change tracker in order to perform some operation before the data is saved.

Solution

Suppose that you have a model like the one shown in Figure 7-7.

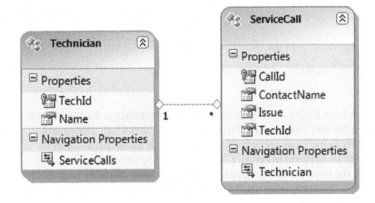

Figure 7-7. *Our model with technicians and their service calls*

In this model, each technician has service calls that include the contact name and issue for the call. You want to create an extension method that retrieves all entities in the model that are in the Added, Modified, or Unchanged state. To do this, follow the pattern in Listing 7-4.

Listing 7-4. Creating an Extension Method That Retrieves All of the Entities in the Added, Modified, or Unchanged State

```
class Program
{
    static void Main(string[] args)
    {
        RunExample();
    }
}
```

```csharp
static void RunExample()
{
    using (var context = new EF6RecipesContext())
    {
        var tech1 = new Technician { Name = "Julie Kerns" };
        var tech2 = new Technician { Name = "Robert Allison" };
        context.ServiceCalls.Add(new ServiceCall {
            ContactName = "Robin Rosen",
            Issue = "Can't get satellite signal.",
            Technician = tech1 });
        context.ServiceCalls.Add(new ServiceCall {
            ContactName = "Phillip Marlowe",
            Issue = "Channel not available",
            Technician = tech2 });

        // now get the entities we've added
        foreach (var tech in
                context.ChangeTracker.GetEntities<Technician>())
        {
            Console.WriteLine("Technician: {0}", tech.Name);
            foreach (var call in tech.ServiceCalls)
            {
                Console.WriteLine("\tService Call: Contact {0} about {1}",
                                call.ContactName, call.Issue);
            }
        }
    }
}

public static class ChangeTrackerExtensions
{
    public static IEnumerable<T> GetEntities<T>(this DbChangeTracker tracker)
    {
        var entities = tracker
                .Entries<T>()
                .Where(entry => entry.State != EntityState.Detached && entry.Entity != null)
                .Select(entry => entry.Entity)();
        return entities;
    }
}
```

Following is the output of the code in Listing 7-4:

```
Technician: Julie Kerns
        Service Call: Contact Robin Rosen about Can't get satellite signal.
Technician: Robert Allison
        Service Call: Contact Phillip Marlowe about Channel not available
```

How It Works

In Listing 7-4, we implemented the GetEntities<T>() extension method to retrieve all of the entities in the object context that are in the Added, Modified, or Unchanged state. Because this may be a common activity in your application, it makes sense to implement this just once in an extension method. In the implementation of the GetEntities<T>() method, we use LINQ-to-Entities to filter the set of entries returned by the Entries<T>() method. The method returns all entries that are not in the Detached state. From these, we filter out relationships and null entries. From the remaining entries, we select only those of the given type.

There are some important scenarios in which you might want to implement a method like GetEntities<T>(). For example, in the SavingChanges event, you may want to validate entities that are about to be inserted, modified, or deleted.

7-6. Generating a Model from the Command Line

Problem

You want to generate a model from the command line.

Solution

To generate a model for a given database from the command line, use the edmgen.exe program. To access the Visual Studio Command Prompt click Visual Studio 2012 Command Prompt under Microsoft Visual Studio 2012 from the Start menu.

The Microsoft documentation for the edmgen command provides a complete list of the command line options. The edmgen command supports a lot of useful command line options The following command, for example, will generate a model from all of the tables in the given Test database:

```
edmgen /mode:FullGeneration /project:Test /provider:"System.Data.SqlClient"
/c:"server=localhost;integrated security=true;database=Test;"
```

Other /mode options are available. One that can be particularly useful in a continuous integration build process is /mode:ValidateArtifacts. With this option, one or more of the generated layers are validated. You need to use one or both of the /inssdl or /incsdl options. If you are validating the mapping layer, all three layers must be specified.

You can use one of the /out options to specify the name of the generated file for specific model layers. For example, using /outcsdl:MyProject.csdl will create the conceptual layer definitions in a file named MyProject.csdl. There are similar options for the other layers.

How It Works

The edmgen command provides a convenient way to automate some of the build processes, and it is a useful tool for pregenerating query views and generating separate files for the model layers. One restriction of edmgen is that it does not provide a way to generate a model based on a subset of the tables in a database.

Using the edmgen command to pregenerate views can be tremendously helpful for application performance. Before a query can be executed, Entity Framework must build a set of views that it uses to access and query the database. Without using the edmgen utility, view generation takes place on the first Entity Framework call. If the data model is relatively small this initialization at first call may pose minimal risk; however, if the data model is large or particularly complex, then such a performance hit might not be acceptable. In a case such as the latter it may make sense to pregenerate query views using the edmgen command-line utility.

7-7. Working with Dependent Entities in an Identifying Relationship

Problem

You want to insert, update, and delete a dependent entity in an identifying relationship.

Solution

Suppose that you have a model like the one shown in Figure 7-8. The LineItem's entity key is a composite key comprised of InvoiceNumber and ItemNumber. InvoiceNumber is also a foreign key to the Invoice entity.

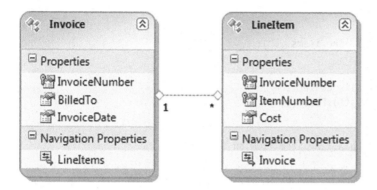

Figure 7-8. *Invoice and LineItem in an identifying relationship because of the composite entity key in the LineItem entity*

When one of the properties of an entity key is both the primary key and the foreign key, the entity is said to be participating in an *identifying relationship*. In our model, LineItem's entity key, its identity, is also a foreign key to the Invoice entity. The LineItem entity is referred to as the *dependent entity*, while Invoice is the *principal entity*.

There is a subtle difference in how Entity Framework handles the deletion of dependent entities in an identifying relationship. Because the dependent entity cannot exist without participating in the relationship, simply removing the dependent entity from the principal's collection will result in Entity Framework marking the dependent entity for deletion. Additionally, deleting the principal entity will also mark the dependent for deletion. This is reminiscent of the cascading deletes common in database systems. Of course, Entity Framework allows you to delete the dependent entity explicitly. The code in Listing 7-5 demonstrates all three of these scenarios.

Listing 7-5. Deleting the Dependent Entity

```
static void Main(string[] args)
{
    RunExample();
}

static void RunExample()
{
    using (var context = new EF6RecipesContext())
    {

        var invoice1 = new Invoice { BilledTo = "Julie Kerns",
                         InvoiceDate = DateTime.Parse("9/19/2013") };
```

```csharp
        var invoice2 = new Invoice { BilledTo = "Jim Stevens",
                        InvoiceDate = DateTime.Parse("9/21/2013") };
        var invoice3 = new Invoice { BilledTo = "Juanita James",
                        InvoiceDate = DateTime.Parse("9/23/2013") };
        context.LineItems.Add(new LineItem { Cost = 99.29M,
                                        Invoice = invoice1 });
        context.LineItems.Add(new LineItem { Cost = 29.95M,
                                        Invoice = invoice1 });
        context.LineItems.Add(new LineItem { Cost = 109.95M,
                                        Invoice = invoice2 });
        context.LineItems.Add(new LineItem { Cost = 49.95M,
                                        Invoice = invoice3 });
        context.SaveChanges();

        // display the line items
        Console.WriteLine("Original set of line items...");
        DisplayLineItems();

        // remove a line item from invoice1's collection
        var item = invoice1.LineItems.ToList().First();
        invoice1.LineItems.Remove(item);
        context.SaveChanges();
        Console.WriteLine("\nAfter removing a line item from an invoice...");
        DisplayLineItems();

        // remove invoice2
        context.Invoices.Remove(invoice2);
        context.SaveChanges();
        Console.WriteLine("\nAfter removing an invoice...");
        DisplayLineItems();

        // remove a single line item
        context.LineItems.Remove(invoice1.LineItems.First());
        context.SaveChanges();
        Console.WriteLine("\nAfter removing a line item...");
        DisplayLineItems();

        // update a single line item
        var item2 = invoice3.LineItems.ToList().First();
        item2.Cost = 39.95M;
        context.SaveChanges();
        Console.WriteLine("\nAfter updating a line item from an invoice...");
        DisplayLineItems();
    }
}
```

```
static void DisplayLineItems()
{
    bool found = false;
    using (var context = new EF6RecipesContext())
    {
        foreach (var lineitem in context.LineItems)
        {
            Console.WriteLine("Line item: Cost {0}",
                                lineitem.Cost.ToString("C"));
            found = true;
        }
    }
    if (!found)
        Console.WriteLine("No line items found!");
}
```

Following is the output of the code in Listing 7-5:

```
Original set of line items...
Line item: Cost $99.29
Line item: Cost $29.95
Line item: Cost $109.95
Line item: Cost $49.95

After removing a line item from an invoice...
Line item: Cost $29.95
Line item: Cost $109.95
Line item: Cost $49.95

After removing an invoice...
Line item: Cost $29.95
After removing a line item...
Line item: Cost $49.95
After updating a line item...
Line item: Cost $39.95
```

How It Works

The code in Listing 7-5 deletes line items in three ways. First it deletes a line item from an invoice's collection. Because a line item is dependent on the invoice for its identity, Entity Framework marks the referenced line item for deletion. Next it deletes an invoice. Entity Framework marks all of the dependent line items for deletion. Finally, the code deletes the last remaining line item directly by calling Remove() on the context's LineItems entity set.

You can modify all of the properties of a dependent entity except for properties that participate in the identifying relationship. In our model, we can modify the Cost property in a line item, but we can't change the Invoice navigation property.

When a principal object in an identifying relationship is saved to the database, the key that is generated at the database (for store-generated values) is written to the principal entity and to all of its dependent entities. This ensures that all are synchronized in the database context.

7-8. Inserting Entities Using a Database Context

Problem

You want to insert entities in your model to the database using a database context.

Solution

Suppose that you have a model like the one shown in Figure 7-9.

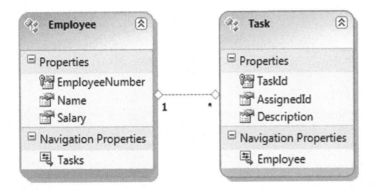

Figure 7-9. *A model with employees and their tasks*

The model in Figure 7-9 represents employees and their tasks. You want to insert new employees and their tasks into the underlying database. To insert an Employee, create a new instance of Employee and call the Add() method available on the Employees entity set in the context. To add a Task for an employee, create a new instance of Task and add it to the Tasks collection of the employee. You must also call Add() to add either the employee or the task to the database context. To persist the changes to the database, call the SaveChanges() method.

The code in Listing 7-6 demonstrates using Add() to add new objects to the database context and persist them to the database with SaveChanges().

Listing 7-6. Inserting New Entities into the Database

```
using (var context = new EF6RecipesContext())
{
    var employee1 = new Employee {EmployeeNumber = 629,
                                  Name = "Robin Rosen", Salary = 106000M };
    var employee2 = new Employee {EmployeeNumber = 147,
                                  Name = "Bill Moore", Salary = 62500M };
    var task1 = new Task { Description = "Report 3rd Qtr Accounting" };
    var task2 = new Task { Description = "Forecast 4th Qtr Sales" };
    var task3 = new Task { Description = "Prepare Sales Tax Report" };

    // use Add() on the Employees entity set
    context.Employees.Add(employee1);

    // add two new tasks to employee1's tasks
    employee1.Tasks.Add(task1);
    employee1.Tasks.Add(task2);
```

```
    // add a task to the employee and use
    // Add() to add the task to the database context
    employee2.Tasks.Add(task3);
    context.Tasks.Add(task3);

    // persist all of these to the database
    context.SaveChanges();
}

using (var context = new EF6RecipesContext())
{
    foreach (var employee in context.Employees)
    {
        Console.WriteLine("Employee: {0}'s Tasks", employee.Name);
        foreach (var task in employee.Tasks)
        {
            Console.WriteLine("\t{0}", task.Description);
        }
    }
}
```

Following is the output of the code in Listing 7-6:

```
Employee: Bill Moore's Tasks
        Prepare Sales Tax Report
Employee: Robin Rosen's Tasks
        Report 3rd Qtr Accounting
        Forecast 4th Qtr Sales
```

How It Works

In Listing 7-6, we used the Add() method available on the Employees and Tasks entity sets to add entities to the database context.

When you add an entity to the database context, Entity Framework creates a temporary entity key for the newly added entity. Entity Framework uses this temporary key to uniquely identify the entity. This temporary key is replaced by a real key after the object is persisted to the database. If saving two entities to the database results in both entities being assigned the same entity key, Entity Framework will throw an exception. This can happen if the keys are assigned the same value by the client or by some store-generating process.

For foreign key associations, you can assign the foreign key property of an entity the value of the entity key of a related entity. Although temporary keys are involved, Entity Framework will fix up the keys and relationships correctly when the entities are saved to the database.

You can also use the Attach() method to add an entity to a database context. This is a two-step process. First call Attach() with the entity. This adds it to the database context, but the change tracker initially marks the entity as Unchanged. Calling SaveChanges() at this point will not save the entity to the database. The second step is to pass the entity into the database context's Entry() method to obtain a DbEntityEntry instance and set its State property to the new state: EntityState.Added. Calling SaveChanges() at this point will save the new entity to the database.

7-9. Querying and Saving Asynchronously
Problem

You need to maintain the responsiveness of your application while performing queries and persisting changes to the database.

Solution

Suppose that you have Account and Transactions POCO entities, which you've written using the Code-First modeling strategy, like the ones shown in Listing 7-7.

Listing 7-7. Account and Transaction POCO Entities

```
public class Account
{
    public int AccountNumber { get; set; }
    public string AccountHolder { get; set; }

    public virtual ICollection<Transaction> Transactions { get; set; }
}

public class Transaction
{
    public int AccountNumber { get; set; }
    public int TransactionNumber { get; set; }
    public DateTime TransactionDate { get; set; }
    public decimal Amount { get; set; }
}
```

The Transaction entity is clearly a dependent entity of the Account entity, so we'll configure that relationship by creating EntityTypeConfiguration subclasses for each entity type, as shown in Listing 7-8.

Listing 7-8. Configuring the Account and Transaction Entity Types

```
public class AccountTypeConfiguration : EntityTypeConfiguration<Account>
{
    public AccountTypeConfiguration()
    {
        HasKey(a => a.AccountNumber);

        Property(a => a.AccountNumber)
            .HasDatabaseGeneratedOption(DatabaseGeneratedOption.Identity);

        HasMany(a => a.Transactions)
            .WithRequired();
    }
}
```

```csharp
public class TransactionTypeConfiguration : EntityTypeConfiguration<Transaction>
{
    public TransactionTypeConfiguration()
    {
        HasKey(t => new {t.AccountNumber, t.TransactionNumber});

        Property(t => t.TransactionNumber)
            .HasDatabaseGeneratedOption(DatabaseGeneratedOption.Identity);
    }
}
```

Finally, in Listing 7-9, we set up the DbContext subclass and implement an override of the OnModelCreating method in which we add the entity configurations to the model builder's Configurations collection.

Listing 7-9. Creating the DbContext Subclass

```csharp
public class EF6RecipesContext : DbContext
{
    public DbSet<Account> Accounts { get; set; }
    public DbSet<Transaction> Transactions { get; set; }

    public EF6RecipesContext() : base("name=EF6CodeFirstRecipesContext")
    {

    }

    protected override void OnModelCreating(DbModelBuilder modelBuilder)
    {
        base.OnModelCreating(modelBuilder);

        modelBuilder.Configurations.Add(new AccountTypeConfiguration());
        modelBuilder.Configurations.Add(new TransactionTypeConfiguration());
    }
}
```

In order to query and save asynchronously, we will use the ForEachAsync() LINQ-to-Entities method and the SaveChangesAsync() DbContext method respectively. The code in Listing 7-10 demonstrates the usage of each method.

Listing 7-10. Querying and Saving Entities Asynchronously

```csharp
static void Main(string[] args)
{
    RunExample().Wait();
    Console.ReadKey(true);
}

static async Task RunExample()
{
    using (var context = new EF6RecipesContext())
    {
        var account1 = new Account
```

```
        {
            AccountHolder = "Robert Dewey",
            Transactions = new HashSet<Transaction>
                {
                    new Transaction
                        {
                            TransactionDate = Convert.ToDateTime("07/05/2013"),
                            Amount = 104.00M
                        },
                    new Transaction
                        {
                            TransactionDate = Convert.ToDateTime("07/12/2013"),
                            Amount = 104.00M
                        },
                    new Transaction
                        {
                            TransactionDate = Convert.ToDateTime("07/19/2013"),
                            Amount = 104.00M
                        }
                }
        };
    var account2 = new Account
        {
            AccountHolder = "James Cheatham",
            Transactions = new List<Transaction>
                {
                    new Transaction
                        {
                            TransactionDate = Convert.ToDateTime("08/01/2013"),
                            Amount = 900.00M
                        },
                    new Transaction
                        {
                            TransactionDate = Convert.ToDateTime("08/02/2013"),
                            Amount = -42.00M
                        }
                }
        };
    var account3 = new Account
        {
            AccountHolder = "Thurston Howe",
            Transactions = new List<Transaction>
                {
                    new Transaction
                        {
                            TransactionDate = Convert.ToDateTime("08/05/2013"),
                            Amount = 100.00M
                        }
                }
        };
```

```
context.Accounts.Add(account1);
context.Accounts.Add(account2);
context.Accounts.Add(account3);
context.SaveChanges();

// Add monthly service charges for each account.
foreach (var account in context.Accounts)
{
    var transactions = new List<Transaction>
        {
            new Transaction
                {
                    TransactionDate = Convert.ToDateTime("08/09/2013"),
                    Amount = -5.00M
                },
            new Transaction
                {
                    TransactionDate = Convert.ToDateTime("08/09/2013"),
                    Amount = -2.00M
                }
        };

    Task saveTask = SaveAccountTransactionsAsync(account.AccountNumber, transactions);

    Console.WriteLine("Account Transactions for the account belonging to {0}
    (acct# {1})", account.AccountHolder, account.AccountNumber);

    await saveTask;
    await ShowAccountTransactionsAsync(account.AccountNumber);
}


    }
}

private static async Task SaveAccountTransactionsAsync(int accountNumber,
ICollection<Transaction> transactions)
{
    using (var context = new EF6RecipesContext())
    {
        var account = new Account { AccountNumber = accountNumber };
        context.Accounts.Attach(account);
        context.Entry(account).Collection(a => a.Transactions).Load();
        foreach (var transaction in transactions.OrderBy(t => t.TransactionDate))
        {
            account.Transactions.Add(transaction);
        }

        await context.SaveChangesAsync();
    }
}
```

```
private static async Task ShowAccountTransactionsAsync(int accountNumber)
{
    Console.WriteLine("TxNumber\tDate\tAmount");
    using (var context = new EF6RecipesContext())
    {
        var transactions = context.Transactions.Where(t => t.AccountNumber == accountNumber);
        await transactions.ForEachAsync(t => Console.WriteLine("{0}\t{1}\t{2}",
        t.TransactionNumber, t.TransactionDate, t.Amount));
    }
}
```

How It Works

Asynchronous constructs were introduced in .NET 4.5 to reduce the complexity normally associated with writing asynchronous code. When we call SaveAccountTransactionsAsync(), we assign it to a Task object, which calls the method and then returns execution control to the caller while the asynchronous portion of the SaveAccountTransactionsAsync() method is executing. The code that calls ShowAccountTransactionsAsync() is structured in much the same way. When the awaited calls in each of these two methods return, execution returns to the line following the caller's await statement.

It's important to know that the async model in .NET 4.5 is single-threaded rather than multi-threaded, so the code that follows await SaveAccountTransactionsAsync() is suspended until SaveAccountTransactionsAsync() returns. It's additionally important to know that any method that calls an async method must itself be marked with the async modifier and have Task or Task<T> as its return type.

The output of the code in Listing 7-10 is shown below.

```
Account Transactions for the account belonging to Robert Dewey (acct# 1)
TxNumber        Date                    Amount
1               7/5/2013 12:00:00 AM    104.00
2               7/12/2013 12:00:00 AM   104.00
3               7/19/2013 12:00:00 AM   104.00
7               8/9/2013 12:00:00 AM    -5.00
8               8/9/2013 12:00:00 AM    -2.00

Account Transactions for the account belonging to James Cheatham (acct# 2)
TxNumber        Date                    Amount
4               8/1/2013 12:00:00 AM    900.00
5               8/2/2013 12:00:00 AM    -42.00
9               8/9/2013 12:00:00 AM    -5.00
10              8/9/2013 12:00:00 AM    -2.00

Account Transactions for the account belonging to Thurston Howe (acct# 3)
TxNumber        Date                    Amount
6               8/5/2013 12:00:00 AM    100.00
11              8/9/2013 12:00:00 AM    -5.00
12              8/9/2013 12:00:00 AM    -2.00
```

CHAPTER 8

Plain Old CLR Objects

Objects should not know how to save themselves, load themselves, or filter themselves. That's a familiar mantra in software development, and especially in Domain Driven Development. There is a good bit of wisdom in this mantra. Having persistence knowledge bound too tightly to domain objects complicates testing, refactoring, and reuse. In ObjectContext, the classes generated by Entity Framework for model entities are heavily dependent on the plumbing of Entity Framework. For some developers, these classes know too much about the persistence mechanism, and they are too closely tied to the concerns of models and mapping. There is another option, however.

Entity Framework also supports using your own classes for the entities in the model. The term Plain Old CLR Object, often simply referred to as POCO, isn't meant to imply that your classes are either plain or old. It merely means that they don't contain any reference at all to specialized frameworks, they don't need to derive from third-party code, they don't need to implement any special interface, and they don't need to live in any special assembly or namespace. You may implement your domain objects however you see fit and tie them to the model with a custom object context. With that being said, you are ready to leverage all of the power of Entity Framework and follow just about any architectural pattern you choose. You can also use DbContext to generate the POCO classes for you.

This chapter covers a wide variety of recipes specific to POCO. The first recipe shows you the basics of using POCO. The remaining recipes focus on loading entities and keeping Entity Framework in sync with the state of your objects.

In this chapter, we've intentionally focused on writing most of the POCO-related code by hand to demonstrate how things work. All of the work involved in building the POCO plumbing goes away if you use the POCO T4 template available from the ADO.NET development team at Microsoft.

8-1. Using POCO

Problem

You want to use Plain Old CLR Objects (POCO) in your application.

Solution

Let's say that you have a data model like the one shown in Figure 8-1.

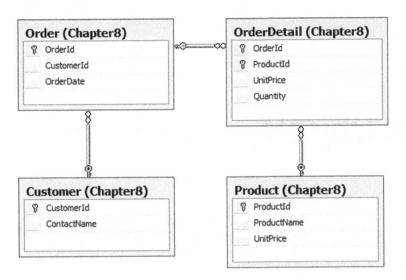

Figure 8-1. *A database model for customers and their orders*

To create an Entity Framework model based on the database tables in Figure 8-1, and using the POCO classes generated by Entity Framework representing an Order, OrderDetail, Customer, and Product, follow the steps below:

1. Right-click your project, and select Add ➤ New Item.

2. From the Visual C# Items Data templates, select ADO.NET Entity Data Model.

3. Select Generate from database to create the model from our existing tables.

4. Select the Order, OrderDetail, Customer, and Product tables, and click Next. In the generated model, the Product entity has an OrderDetails navigation property for all of the order details associated with this product. This is unnecessary here, so delete this navigation property. The completed model is shown in Figure 8-2.

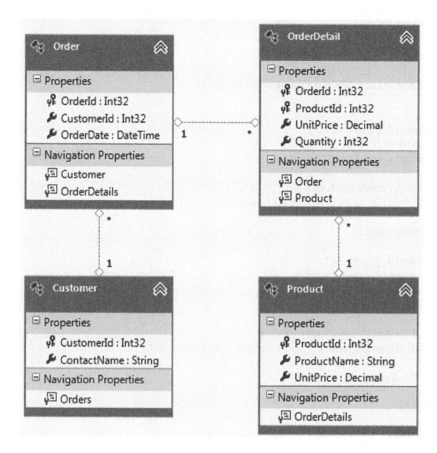

Figure 8-2. *The model for our customers' orders*

5. We will be using generated classes for our entities. By default, Entity Framework 6 generates entity classes in the form of POCO. Thus all of the database access code is in a separate class, and entities are generated in separate plain classes. It will yield the same implementation result as would have been created manually in previous Entity Framework versions by turning off code generation for the model. In this version, Code Generation Strategy is already set to None. The code in Listing 8-1 shows the classes for our model.

Listing 8-1. The Plain Old CLR classes for Our Model

```csharp
public partial class Customer
    {
        public Customer()
        {
            this.Orders = new HashSet<Order>();
        }
        public int CustomerId { get; set; }
        public string ContactName { get; set; }
        public virtual ICollection<Order> Orders { get; set; }
    }
```

```
public partial class Order
    {
        public Order()
        {
            this.OrderDetails = new HashSet<OrderDetail>();
        }

        public int OrderId { get; set; }
        public int CustomerId { get; set; }
        public System.DateTime OrderDate { get; set; }

        public virtual Customer Customer { get; set; }
        public virtual ICollection<OrderDetail> OrderDetails { get; set; }
    }
public partial class OrderDetail
    {
        public int OrderId { get; set; }
        public int ProductId { get; set; }
        public decimal UnitPrice { get; set; }
        public int Quantity { get; set; }

        public virtual Order Order { get; set; }
        public virtual Product Product { get; set; }
    }
public partial class Product
    {
        public Product()
        {
            this.OrderDetails = new HashSet<OrderDetail>();
        }

        public int ProductId { get; set; }
        public string ProductName { get; set; }
        public decimal UnitPrice { get; set; }

        public virtual ICollection<OrderDetail> OrderDetails { get; set; }
    }
```

Notice that there is no association from Product to OrderDetail, because we removed that navigation property in the designer.

6. To use POCO classes, Entity Framework also generated the class that is derived from DbContext. This class will expose an ObjectSet<T> for each of the entities in our model. The code in Listing 8-2 illustrates how we might define this class.

Listing 8-2. DbContext for Our Model Created While Generating an Entity Data Model

```
public partial class EFRecipesEntities : DbContext
    {
        public EFRecipesEntities()
            : base("name=EFRecipesEntities")
        {
        }
```

```
        protected override void OnModelCreating(DbModelBuilder modelBuilder)
        {
            throw new UnintentionalCodeFirstException();
        }
        public DbSet<Customer> Customers { get; set; }
        public DbSet<Order> Orders { get; set; }
        public DbSet<OrderDetail> OrderDetails { get; set; }
        public DbSet<Product> Products { get; set; }
    }
```

This completes the model with the generated POCO classes. The code in Listing 8-3 demonstrates inserting into and querying our model.

Listing 8-3. Using Our POCO Classes

```
using (var context = new EFRecipesEntities())
    {
        var tea = new Product { ProductName = "Green Tea", UnitPrice = 1.09M };
        var coffee = new Product
        {
            ProductName = "Colombian Coffee",
            UnitPrice = 2.15M
        };
        var customer = new Customer { ContactName = "Karen Marlowe" };
        var order1 = new Order { OrderDate = DateTime.Parse("10/06/13") };
        order1.OrderDetails.Add(new OrderDetail
        {
            Product = tea,
            Quantity = 4,
            UnitPrice = 1.00M
        });
        order1.OrderDetails.Add(new OrderDetail
        {
            Product = coffee,
            Quantity = 3,
            UnitPrice = 2.15M
        });
        customer.Orders.Add(order1);
        context.Customers.Add(customer);
        context.SaveChanges();
    }

    using (var context = new EFRecipesEntities())
    {
        var query = context.Customers.Include("Orders.OrderDetails.Product");
        foreach (var customer in query)
        {
            Console.WriteLine("Orders for {0}", customer.ContactName);
            foreach (var order in customer.Orders)
            {
                Console.WriteLine("--Order Date: {0}--",
                        order.OrderDate.ToShortDateString());
```

```
        foreach (var detail in order.OrderDetails)
        {
            Console.WriteLine(
                "\t{0}, {1} units at {2} each, unit discount: {3}",
                detail.Product.ProductName,
                detail.Quantity.ToString(),
                detail.UnitPrice.ToString("C"),
                (detail.Product.UnitPrice - detail.UnitPrice).ToString("C"));
        }
      }
    }
  }
```

The following is the output of the code in Listing 8-3:

```
Orders for Karen Marlowe
--Order Date: 4/19/2010--
        Green Tea, 4 units at $1.00 each, unit discount: $0.09
        Colombian Coffee, 3 units at $2.15 each, unit discount: $0.00
```

How It Works

The POCO class generation is the default feature of current version of Entity Framework. Code generation property value is already set to None. The DbContext class is also generated separately, so no data access code is plugged into the POCO classes.

All of the classes corresponding to each of the entities in our model are created. They are pretty simple and clean. Of course, without code generation, no DbContext is generated. To implement a DbContext that is specific to our model and our entities, a new class derived from DbContext is created while generating the Entity Data Model, and this class provides properties of type DbSet<T> corresponding to each of the Db sets in our context. By default, our EFRecipesEntities DbContext has the constructor code that enables it to be connected to the underlying database.

8-2. Loading Related Entities with POCO
Problem

Using POCO, you want to eagerly load related entities.

Solution

Suppose that you have a model like the one in Figure 8-3.

Figure 8-3. *A model representing venues, their events, and the competitors in the events*

We're using POCO for our entities, and we want to eagerly load the related entities (navigation properties). To do this, we use the Include() method available on the object context. The code in Listing 8-4 illustrates using the Include() method to do this.

Listing 8-4. Using the Include() Method Explicitly to Load Navigation Properties

```
class Program
{
    static void Main(string[] args)
    {
        RunExample();
    }

    static void RunExample()
    {
using (var context = new EFRecipesEntities())
        {
            var venue = new Venue { Name = "Sports and Recreational Grounds" };
            var event1 = new Event { Name = "Inter-school Soccer" };
            event1.Competitors.Add(new Competitor { Name = "St. Mary's School" });
            event1.Competitors.Add(new Competitor { Name = "City School" });
            venue.Events.Add(event1);
            context.Venues.Add(venue);
            context.SaveChanges();
        }
        using (var context = new EFRecipesEntities())
        {
            foreach (var venue in context.Venues.Include("Events").Include("Events.Competitors"))
            {
                Console.WriteLine("Venue: {0}", venue.Name);
                foreach (var evt in venue.Events)
                {
                    Console.WriteLine("\tEvent: {0}", evt.Name);
                    Console.WriteLine("\t--- Competitors ---");
                    foreach (var competitor in evt.Competitors)
```

```
                {
                    Console.WriteLine("\t{0}", competitor.Name);
                }
            }
        }
    }
    }
}

public partial class Venue
    {
        public Venue()
        {
            this.Events = new HashSet<Event>();
        }
        public int VenueId { get; set; }
        public string Name { get; set; }

        public virtual ICollection<Event> Events { get; set; }
    }
public partial class Event
    {
        public Event()
        {
            this.Competitors = new HashSet<Competitor>();
        }

        public int EventId { get; set; }
        public string Name { get; set; }
        public int VenueId { get; set; }

        public virtual ICollection<Competitor> Competitors { get; set; }
        public virtual Venue Venue { get; set; }
    }
public partial class Competitor
    {
        public int CompetitorId { get; set; }
        public string Name { get; set; }
        public int EventId { get; set; }

        public virtual Event Event { get; set; }
    }
public partial class EFRecipesEntities : DbContext
    {
        public EFRecipesEntities()
            : base("name=EFRecipesEntities")
        {
            this.Configuration.LazyLoadingEnabled = false;
        }
```

```
    protected override void OnModelCreating(DbModelBuilder modelBuilder)
    {
        throw new UnintentionalCodeFirstException();
    }
    public DbSet<Competitor> Competitors { get; set; }
    public DbSet<Event> Events { get; set; }
    public DbSet<Venue> Venues { get; set; }
}
```

The following is the output of the code in Listing 8-4:

```
Venue: City Center Hall
        Event: All Star Boxing
        --- Competitors ---
        Big Joe Green
        Terminator Tim
Venue: Sports and Recreational Grounds
        Event: Inter-school Soccer
        --- Competitors ---
        St. Mary's School
        City School
```

How It Works

When we're using code generated by Entity Framework for our model, we use the Include() method on the context query objects to load the related entities, and these related entities can be lists of entities or single objects. There are three methods of loading or querying related entities in Entity Framework: Eager Loading, Lazy Loading, and Explicit Loading. We have used the Include() method to demonstrate eagerly loading related entities. By default, Lazy Loading is enabled in Entity Framework, but we have disabled that here. To load a navigation property explicitly when using POCO, you need to use the Include() method exposed on the DbContext.

8-3. Lazy Loading with POCO
Problem

You are using Plain Old CLR Objects, and you want to lazy load related entities.

Solution

Let's say that you have a model like the one in Figure 8-4.

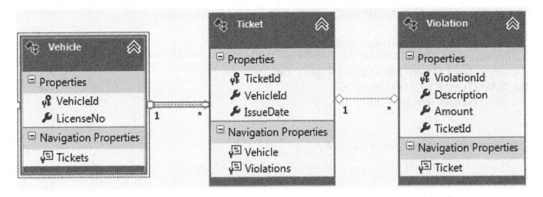

Figure 8-4. *A simple model for traffic tickets, the offending vehicles, and the details of the violation*

To enable lazy loading, you don't need to do anything. Lazy loading is enabled by default when an Entity Data Model is added into a Visual Studio project. The code in Listing 8-5 illustrates this approach.

Listing 8-5. Entity Classes Generation and Properties Set to Virtual: A Default Behavior of Entity Framework

```
class Program
{
    static void Main(string[] args)
    {
        RunExample();
    }

    static void RunExample()
    {
        using (var context = new EFRecipesEntities())
        {
            var vh1 = new Vehicle { LicenseNo = "BR-549" };
            var t1 = new Ticket { IssueDate = DateTime.Parse("06/10/13") };
            var v1 = new Violation
            {
                Description = "20 MPH over the speed limit",
                Amount = 125M
            };
            var v2 = new Violation
            {
                Description = "Broken tail light",
                Amount = 50M
            };
            t1.Violations.Add(v1);
            t1.Violations.Add(v2);
            t1.Vehicle = vh1;
            context.Tickets.Add(t1);
            var vh2 = new Vehicle { LicenseNo = "XJY-902" };
            var t2 = new Ticket { IssueDate = DateTime.Parse("06/12/13") };
            var v3 = new Violation
```

```csharp
                {
                    Description = "Parking in a no parking zone",
                    Amount = 35M
                };
                t2.Violations.Add(v3);
                t2.Vehicle = vh2;
                context.Tickets.Add(t2);
                context.SaveChanges();
            }
            using (var context = new EFRecipesEntities())
            {
                foreach (var ticket in context.Tickets)
                {
                    Console.WriteLine(" Ticket: {0}, Total Cost: {1}",
                      ticket.TicketId.ToString(),
                      ticket.Violations.Sum(v => v.Amount).ToString("C"));
                    foreach (var violation in ticket.Violations)
                    {
                        Console.WriteLine("\t{0}", violation.Description);
                    }
                }
            }

        }
    }

public partial class Ticket
    {
        public Ticket()
        {
            this.Violations = new HashSet<Violation>();
        }

        public int TicketId { get; set; }
        public int VehicleId { get; set; }
        public System.DateTime IssueDate { get; set; }

        public virtual Vehicle Vehicle { get; set; }
        public virtual ICollection<Violation> Violations { get; set; }
    }
public partial class Vehicle
    {
        public Vehicle()
        {
            this.Tickets = new HashSet<Ticket>();
        }

        public int VehicleId { get; set; }
        public string LicenseNo { get; set; }

        public virtual ICollection<Ticket> Tickets { get; set; }
    }
```

```
public partial class Violation
    {
        public int ViolationId { get; set; }
        public string Description { get; set; }
        public decimal Amount { get; set; }
        public int TicketId { get; set; }
        public virtual Ticket Ticket { get; set; }
    }
public partial class EFRecipesEntities : DbContext
    {
        public EFRecipesEntities()
            : base("name=EFRecipesEntities")
        {
        }

        protected override void OnModelCreating(DbModelBuilder modelBuilder)
        {
            throw new UnintentionalCodeFirstException();
        }

        public DbSet<Ticket> Tickets { get; set; }
        public DbSet<Vehicle> Vehicles { get; set; }
        public DbSet<Violation> Violations { get; set; }
```

The following is the output of the code in Listing 8-5:

```
Ticket: 1, Total Cost: $175.00
        20 MPH over the speed limit
        Broken tail light
Ticket: 2, Total Cost: $35.00
        Parking in a no parking zone
```

How It Works

Lazy loading is the default setting when generating an Entity Data Model. The navigation entity properties are also marked as virtual by default. You don't need to do anything explicitly to get this to work.

We have not done anything in the console program code to load the Violation object, which is related to the Ticket object when the ticket context is fetched. Lazy loading enables the access of related entity properties at the moment you access them in your code. It does not require you to query those properties at the time of the first loading of the context object of the main entity, as we did using Include() method in the previous recipe.

8-4. POCO with Complex Type Properties
Problem

You want to use a complex type in your POCO entity.

Solution

Suppose that your model looks like the one in Figure 8-5. In this model, the Name property is a complex type.

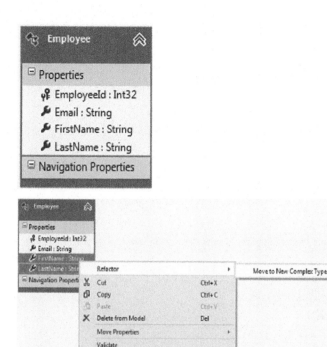

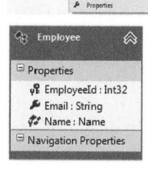

Figure 8-5. *A model for an employee. The Name property is a complex type, composed of FirstName and LastName*

Complex types are supported with POCO. When we refactor two or more entity properties to a new complex type, a new class is generated by default for that complex type. A property of the complex type class is also added into the main entity POCO class. Only classes are supported, as Entity Framework generates these while saving new complex types. The code in Listing 8-6 illustrates using the Name class for the complex type representing the employee's FirstName and LastName.

Listing 8-6. *Using a Complex Type with POCO*

```
class Program
{
    static void Main(string[] args)
    {
        RunExample();
    }

static void RunExample()
    {
        using (var context = new EFRecipesEntities())
        {
            context.Employees.Add(new Employee
            {
                Name = new Name
                {
                    FirstName = "Annie",
                    LastName = "Oakley"
                },
                Email = "aoakley@wildwestshow.com"
            });
            context.Employees.Add(new Employee
            {
                Name = new Name
                {
                    FirstName = "Bill",
                    LastName = "Jordan"
                },
                Email = "BJordan@wildwestshow.com"
            });
            context.SaveChanges();
        }

        using (var context = new EFRecipesEntities())
        {
            foreach (var employee in
                    context.Employees.OrderBy(e => e.Name.LastName))
            {
                Console.WriteLine("{0}, {1} email: {2}",
                            employee.Name.LastName,
                            employee.Name.FirstName,
                            employee.Email);
            }
        }
    }
}}
```

```csharp
public partial class Employee
    {
        public Employee()
        {
            this.Name = new Name();
        }

        public int EmployeeId { get; set; }
        public string Email { get; set; }

        public Name Name { get; set; }
    }
public partial class Name
    {
        public string FirstName { get; set; }
        public string LastName { get; set; }
    }
public partial class EFRecipesEntities : DbContext
    {
        public EFRecipesEntities()
            : base("name=EFRecipesEntities")
        {
        }

        protected override void OnModelCreating(DbModelBuilder modelBuilder)
        {
            throw new UnintentionalCodeFirstException();

        }

        public DbSet<Employee> Employees { get; set; }
    }
```

The following is the output of the code in Listing 8-6:

```
Jordan, Bill email: BJordan@wildwestshow.com
Oakley, Annie email: aoakley@wildwestshow.com
```

How It Works

When you use complex types with POCO, keep in mind the following two rules:

- The complex type must be a class.

- Inheritance cannot be used with complex type classes.

In Entity Framework, complex types do not leverage change tracking. Changes to complex types will not be reflected in change tracking. This means that if you mark the properties on a complex type as virtual, there is no change-tracking proxy support. All change tracking is snapshot-based.

When you delete or update a POCO entity with a complex type without first loading it from the database, you need to be careful to create an instance of the complex type. In Entity Framework, instances of complex types are structurally part of the entity, and null values are not supported. The code in Listing 8-7 illustrates one way to handle deletes.

Listing 8-7. *Deleting a POCO Entity with a Complex Type*

```
int id = 0;
        using (var context = new EFRecipesEntities())
        {
            var emp = context.Employees.Where(e =>
                    e.Name.FirstName.StartsWith("Bill")).FirstOrDefault();
            id = emp.EmployeeId;
        }

        using (var context = new EFRecipesEntities())
        {
            var empDelete = new Employee
            {
                EmployeeId = id,

            };
            context.Employees.Attach(empDelete);
            context.Employees.Remove(empDelete);
            context.SaveChanges();
        }
```

In Listing 8-7, we first have to find the EmployeeId of Bill Jordan. Because we are trying to show how we would delete Bill without first loading the entity into the context, we create a new context to illustrate deleting Bill given just his EmployeeId. We need to create an instance of the Employee entity complete with the Name type. Because we are deleting, it doesn't matter much what values we put in for FirstName and LastName. The key is that the Name property is not null. We satisfy this requirement by assigning a new (dummy) instance of Name. We then Attach() the entity and call Remove() and SaveChanges(). This deletes the entity.

8-5. Notifying Entity Framework About Object Changes
Problem
You are using POCO, and you want to have Entity Framework and the object state manager notified of changes to your objects.

Solution
Let's say that you have a model like the one in Figure 8-6.

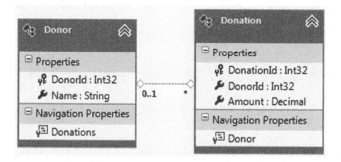

Figure 8-6. *A model for donors and their donations*

This model represents donations and donors. Because some donations are anonymous, the relationship between donor and donation is 0..1 to *.

We want to make changes to our entities, such as moving a donation from one donor to another, and have Entity Framework and the object state manager notified of these changes. In addition, we want Entity Framework to leverage this notification to fix up any relationships that are affected by such changes. In our case, if we change the Donor on a Donation, we want Entity Framework to fix up both sides of the relationship. The code in Listing 8-8 demonstrates how to do this.

The key part of Listing 8-8 is that we marked each property as virtual and each collection a type of ICollection<T>. This allows Entity Framework to create proxies for our POCO entities that enable change tracking. When creating instances of POCO entity types, Entity Framework often creates instances of a dynamically generated derived type that acts as a proxy for the entity. This proxy overrides some virtual properties of the entity that inserts hooks for performing actions automatically when the property is accessed. This mechanism is used to support lazy loading of relationships and change tracking of objects. Note that Entity Framework will not create proxies for types where there is nothing for the proxy to do. This means that you can also avoid proxies by having types that are sealed and/or have no virtual properties.

Listing 8-8. By Marking Each Property as virtual and Each Collection a Type of ICollection<T>, We Get Proxies That Enable Change Tracking

```
class Program
{
    static void Main(string[] args)
    {
        RunExample();
    }
}

static void RunExample()
    {
        using (var context = new EFRecipesEntities())
        {
            var donation = context.Donations.Create();
            donation.Amount = 5000M;

            var donor1 = context.Donors.Create();
            donor1.Name = "Jill Rosenberg";
            var donor2 = context.Donors.Create();
            donor2.Name = "Robert Hewitt";
```

273

```
                // give Jill the credit for the donation and save
                donor1.Donations.Add(donation);
                context.Donors.Add(donor1);
                context.Donors.Add(donor2);
                context.SaveChanges();

                // now give Robert the credit
                donation.Donor = donor2;

                // report
                foreach (var donor in context.Donors)
                {
                    Console.WriteLine("{0} has given {1} donation(s)", donor.Name,
                                    donor.Donations.Count().ToString());
                }
                Console.WriteLine("Original Donor Id: {0}",
                    context.Entry(donation).OriginalValues["DonorId"]);
                Console.WriteLine("Current Donor Id: {0}",
                                context.Entry(donation).CurrentValues["DonorId"]);
            }
        }}

public partial class Donor
    {
        public Donor()
        {
            this.Donations = new HashSet<Donation>();
        }

        public virtual int DonorId { get; set; }
        public virtual string Name { get; set; }

        public virtual ICollection<Donation> Donations { get; set; }
    }

public partial class Donation
    {
        public virtual int DonationId { get; set; }
        public virtual Nullable<int> DonorId { get; set; }
        public virtual decimal Amount { get; set; }

        public virtual Donor Donor { get; set; }
    }

public partial class EFRecipesEntities : DbContext
    {
        public EFRecipesEntities()
            : base("name=EFRecipesEntities")
        {
        }
```

```
protected override void OnModelCreating(DbModelBuilder modelBuilder)
{
    throw new UnintentionalCodeFirstException();
}

public DbSet<Donation> Donations { get; set; }
public DbSet<Donor> Donors { get; set; }
}
```

The following is the output of the code in Listing 8-8:

```
Jill Rosenberg has given 0 donation(s)
Robert Hewitt has given 1 donation(s)
Original Donor Id: 1
Current Donor Id: 2
```

How It Works

By default, Entity Framework uses a snapshot-based approach for detecting changes made to POCO entities. If you make some minor code changes to your POCO entities, Entity Framework can create change-tracking proxies that keep the DbContext synchronized with the runtime changes in your POCO entities.

There are two important benefits that come with change-tracking proxies. First, the DbContext stays informed of the changes, and it can keep the entity object graph state information synchronized with your POCO entities. This means that no time need be spent detecting changes using the snapshot-based approach.

Additionally, when the DbContext is notified of changes on one side of a relationship, it can mirror the change on the other side of the relationship if necessary. In Listing 8-8, when we moved a Donation from one Donor to another, Entity Framework also fixed up the Donations collections of both Donors.

For the Entity Framework to create the change-tracking proxies for your POCO classes, the following conditions must be met.

- The class must be public, nonabstract, and nonsealed.

- The class must implement virtual getters and setters for all properties that are persisted.

- You must declare collection-based relationships navigation properties as ICollection<T>. They cannot be a concrete implementation or another interface that derives from ICollection<T>.

Once your POCO classes have met these requirements, Entity Framework will return instances of the proxies for your POCO classes. If you need to create instances, as we have in Listing 8-8, you will need to use the Create() method on the DbContext. This method creates the instance of the proxy for your POCO entity, and it initializes all of the collections as instances of EntityCollection. It is this initialization of your POCO class's collections as instances of EntityCollection that enables fixing up relationships.

8-6. Retrieving the Original (POCO) Object
Problem

You are using POCO, and you want to retrieve the original object from a database.

Solution

Let's say that you are using a model like the one in Figure 8-7, and you are working in a disconnected scenario. You want to use a Where clause with FirstOrDefault() to retrieve the original object from the database before you apply changes received from a client.

Figure 8-7. *A model with a single Item entity*

To update the entity with new values after retrieving the entity and then to apply changes to save in database, follow the pattern in Listing 8-9.

Listing 8-9. Retrieving the Newly Added Entity and Replacing Its Values Using the Entry() Method

```
class Program
    {
        static void Main(string[] args)
        {
            RunExample();
        }

        static void RunExample()
        {
            int itemId = 0;
            using (var context = new EFRecipesEntities())
            {
                var item = new Item
                {
                    Name = "Xcel Camping Tent",
                    UnitPrice = 99.95M
                };
                context.Items.Add(item);
                context.SaveChanges();

                // keep the item id for the next step
                itemId = item.ItemId;
                Console.WriteLine("Item: {0}, UnitPrice: {1}",
                        item.Name, item.UnitPrice.ToString("C"));
            }

            using (var context = new EFRecipesEntities())
            {
                // pretend this is the updated
                // item we received with the new price
                var item = new Item
```

```
            {
                ItemId = itemId,
                Name = "Xcel Camping Tent",
                UnitPrice = 129.95M
            };
            var originalItem = context.Items.Where(x => x.ItemId == itemId).FirstOrDefault<Item>();
            context.Entry(originalItem).CurrentValues.SetValues(item);
            context.SaveChanges();
        }
        using (var context = new EFRecipesEntities())
        {
            var item = context.Items.Single();
            Console.WriteLine("Item: {0}, UnitPrice: {1}", item.Name,
                        item.UnitPrice.ToString("C"));
        }
    }
}
public partial class Item
    {
        public int ItemId { get; set; }
        public string Name { get; set; }
        public decimal UnitPrice { get; set; }
    }
public partial class EFRecipesEntities : DbContext
    {
        public EFRecipesEntities()
            : base("name=EFRecipesEntities")
        {

        }

        protected override void OnModelCreating(DbModelBuilder modelBuilder)
        {
            throw new UnintentionalCodeFirstException();
        }
        public DbSet<Item> Items { get; set; }
    }
```

The following is the output of the code in Listing 8-9:

```
Item: Xcel Camping Tent, UnitPrice: $99.95
Item: Xcel Camping Tent, UnitPrice: $129.95
```

How It Works

In Listing 8-9, we inserted an item into the model and saved it to the database. Then we pretended to receive an updated item, perhaps from a Silverlight client.

Next we need to update the item in the database. To do this, we need to get the entity from the database into the context. To get the entity, we used a Where clause with FirstorDefault and checked with the ID of the item. After that, we used the Entry() method of the context, which enables access to entire entity to apply any methods on that entity. Thus we used CurrentValues.SetValues to replace the original values with new values that come through the client. Finally, SaveChanges is called on the DbContext.

8-7. Manually Synchronizing the Object Graph and the Change Tracker

Problem

You want to control manually the synchronization between your POCO classes and the Change Tracker.

Change Tracker has access to the information that Entity Framework is storing about the entities that it is tracking. This information goes beyond the values stored in the properties of your entities and includes the current state of the entity, the original values from the database, which properties have been modified, and other data. The Change Tracker also gives access to additional operations that can be performed on an entity, such as reloading its values from the database to ensure that you have the latest data.

There are two different ways that Entity Framework can track changes to your objects: snapshot change tracking and change-tracking proxies.

Snapshot Change Tracking

POCO classes don't contain any logic to notify Entity Framework when a property value is changed. Because there is no way to be notified when a property value changes, Entity Framework will take a snapshot of the values in each property when it first sees an object and store the values in memory. This snapshot occurs when the object is returned from a query or when we add it to a DbSet. When Entity Framework needs to know what changes have been made, it will scan each object and compare its current values to the snapshot. This process of scanning each object is triggered through a method of Change Tracker called *DetectChanges*.

Change-Tracking Proxies

The other mechanism for tracking changes is through *change-tracking proxies*, which allow Entity Framework to be notified of changes as they are made. Change-tracking proxies are created using the mechanism of dynamic proxies that are created for lazy loading, but in addition to providing for lazy loading, they also have the ability to communicate changes to the context. To use change-tracking proxies, you need to structure your classes in such a way that Entity Framework can create a dynamic type at runtime that derives from your POCO class and overrides every property. This dynamic type, known as a *dynamic proxy*, includes logic in the overridden properties to notify Entity Framework when those properties are changed.

Snapshot change tracking depends on Entity Framework being able to detect when changes occur. The default behavior of the DbContext API is to perform this detection automatically as the result of many events on the DbContext. DetectChanges not only updates the context's state management information so that changes can be persisted to the database, but it also performs relationship fix-up when you have a combination of reference navigation properties, collection navigation properties, and foreign keys. It's important to have a clear understanding of how and when changes are detected, what to expect from them, and how to control them.

The most obvious time that Entity Framework needs to know about changes is during SaveChanges, but there are many others. For example, if we ask the Change Tracker for the current state of an object, it will need to scan and check if anything has changed. Scanning isn't just restricted to the object in question either—many of the operations you perform on the DbContext API will cause DetectChanges to be run. In most cases, DetectChanges is fast enough that it doesn't cause performance issues. However, if you have a very large number of objects in memory or you are performing a lot of operations on DbContext in quick succession, the automatic DetectChanges behavior may be a performance concern. Fortunately, you have the option of switching off the automatic DetectChanges behavior and calling it manually when you know that it needs to be called. Failure to do this can result in unexpected side effects. DbContext takes care of this requirement for you, provided that you leave automatic DetectChanges enabled. If you switch it off, you are responsible for calling DetectChanges for poorly performing sections of code and to reenable it once the section in question has finished executing. Automatic DetectChanges can be toggled on and off via the `DbContext.Configuration.AutoDetectChangesEnabled` Boolean flag.

Solution

Suppose that we have a model for speakers and the talks prepared for various conferences. The model might look something like the one in Figure 8-8.

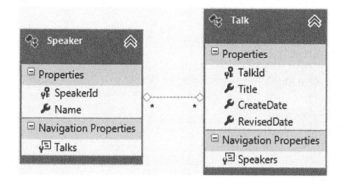

Figure 8-8. *A model with a many-to-many association between speakers and the talks they prepare*

The first thing to note in our model is that Speaker and Talk are in a many-to-many association. We have, through an independent association (and in an intermediate SpeakerTalk table in the database), a model that supports many speakers for any given talk and many talks for any given speaker.

We want to control manually the synchronization between our object graph and the Change Tracker. We will do this by calling the DetectChanges() method. Along the way, we'll illustrate how the synchronization is progressing.

Follow the pattern in Listing 8-10 to synchronize manually your POCO object graph with the Change Tracker.

Listing 8-10. Using DetectChanges() Explicitly When Required to Synchronize the Change Tracker Manually

```
class Program
{
    static void Main(string[] args)
    {
        RunExample();
    }
}

static void RunExample()
    {
        using (var context = new EFRecipesEntities())
        {
            context.Configuration.AutoDetectChangesEnabled = false;
            var speaker1 = new Speaker { Name = "Karen Stanfield" };
            var talk1 = new Talk { Title = "Simulated Annealing in C#" };
            speaker1.Talks = new List<Talk> { talk1 };

            // associations not yet complete
            Console.WriteLine("talk1.Speaker is null: {0}",
                        talk1.Speakers == null);

            context.Speakers.Add(speaker1);
```

```
                // now it's fixed up
                Console.WriteLine("talk1.Speaker is null: {0}",
                            talk1.Speakers == null);
                Console.WriteLine("Number of added entries tracked: {0}",
                            context.ChangeTracker.Entries().Where(e => e.State ==
System.Data.Entity.EntityState.Added).Count());
                context.SaveChanges();
                // change the talk's title
                talk1.Title = "AI with C# in 3 Easy Steps";
                Console.WriteLine("talk1's state is: {0}",
                            context.Entry(talk1).State);
                context.ChangeTracker.DetectChanges();
                Console.WriteLine("talk1's state is: {0}",
                            context.Entry(talk1).State);
                context.SaveChanges();
            }

        using (var context = new EFRecipesEntities())
        {
            foreach (var speaker in context.Speakers.Include("Talks"))
            {
                Console.WriteLine("Speaker: {0}", speaker.Name);
                foreach (var talk in speaker.Talks)
                {
                    Console.WriteLine("\tTalk Title: {0}", talk.Title);
                }
            }
        }
    }
}

public partial class Speaker
    {
        public int SpeakerId { get; set; }
        public string Name { get; set; }
        public ICollection<Talk> Talks { get; set; }
    }

public partial class Talk
    {
        public int TalkId { get; set; }
        public string Title { get; set; }
        public System.DateTime CreateDate { get; set; }
        public System.DateTime RevisedDate { get; set; }
        public ICollection<Speaker> Speakers { get; set; }
    }

public partial class EFRecipesEntities : DbContext
    {
        public EFRecipesEntities()
            : base("name=EFRecipesEntities")
        {
        }
```

```
        protected override void OnModelCreating(DbModelBuilder modelBuilder)
        {
            throw new UnintentionalCodeFirstException();
        }


        public DbSet<Speaker> Speakers { get; set; }
        public DbSet<Talk> Talks { get; set; }

    public override int SaveChanges()
    {
        var changeSet = this.ChangeTracker.Entries().Where(e => e.Entity is Talk);
        if (changeSet != null)
        {
            foreach (var entry in changeSet.Where(c => c.State ==
System.Data.Entity.EntityState.Added).Select(a => a.Entity as Talk))
            {
                entry.CreateDate = DateTime.UtcNow;
                entry.RevisedDate = DateTime.UtcNow;
            }
            foreach (var entry in changeSet.Where(c => c.State ==
System.Data.Entity.EntityState.Modified).Select(a => a.Entity as Talk))
            {
                entry.RevisedDate = DateTime.UtcNow;
            }
        }
        return base.SaveChanges();
    }
}
```

The following is the output of the code in Listing 8-10:

```
talk1.Speaker is null: True
talk1.Speaker is null: False
Number of added entries tracked: 2
talk1's state is: Unchanged
talk1's state is: Modified
Speaker: Karen Stanfield
        Talk Title: AI with C# in 3 Easy Steps
```

How It Works

The code in Listing 8-10 is a little involved, so let's take it one step at a time. First off, we create a speaker and a talk. Then we add the talk to the speaker's collection. At this point, the talk is part of the speaker's collection, but the speaker is not part of the talk's collection. The other side of the association has not been fixed up just yet.

Next we add the speaker to the DbContext with Add(speaker1). The second line of the output shows now that the talk's speaker collection is correct. Entity Framework has fixed up the other side of the association. Here Entity Framework did two things. It notified the object state manager that there are three entries to be created, although it is not shown in the result of number of entities added by Entity Framework, as it considers many-to-many relationships as independent relationships and not as separate entities. Thus it is only showing the entries as two: one of these entries is for the speaker and the other is for the talk. No entry is made for the many-to-many association entry, because Change Tracker does not return the state of independent relationships. The second thing that Entity Framework did was to fix up the talk's speaker collection.

When we call SaveChanges(), Entity Framework raises the overridden SaveChanges event. Inside this event, we update the CreateDate and RevisedDate properties. Before the SaveChanges() method is called, Entity Framework calls DetectChanges() to find any changes that occurred before. In Listing 8-10, we override the SaveChanges() method.

The DetectChanges() method relies on a snapshot base comparison of the original and current values for each property on each entity. This process determines what has changed in the object graph. For large object graphs, this comparison process may be time consuming.

8-8. Testing Domain Objects

Problem

You want to create unit tests for the business rules you have defined for your entities.

This type of recipe is often used when unit testing of specific data access functionality has to be performed.

Solution

For this solution, you'll use the POCO template to generate the classes for your entities. Using the POCO template will reduce the amount of code you need to write, and it will make the solution a more clear. Of course, you will use the remaining steps in this solution with your handcrafted POCO classes.

Suppose you have a model like the one shown in Figure 8-9.

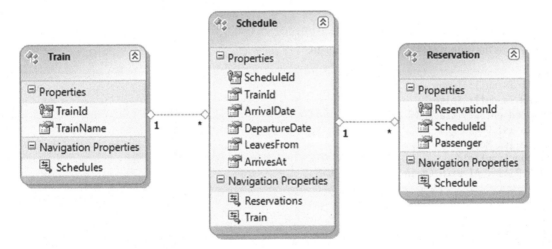

Figure 8-9. *A model of reservations, schedules, and trains*

This model represents reservations for train travel. Each reservation is for a particular scheduled train departure. To create the model and prepare the application for unit testing, do the following:

1. Create an empty solution. Right-click the solution in the Solution Explorer, and select Add ➤ New Project. Add a new Class Library project. Name this new project `TrainReservation`.

2. Right-click the `TrainReservation` project, and select Add ➤ New Item. Add a new ADO. NET Entity Data Model. Import the Train, Schedule, and Reservation tables. The resulting model should look like the one in Figure 8-9.

3. Add the IValidate interface and ChangeAction enum in Listing 8-11 to the project.

Listing 8-11. The IValidate Interface

```
public enum ChangeAction
{
    Insert,
    Update,
    Delete
}

interface IValidate
{
    void Validate(ChangeAction action);
}
```

4. Add the code in Listing 8-12 to the project. This code adds the validation code (the implementation of IValidate) to the Reservation and Schedule classes.

Listing 8-12. Implementation of the IValidate Interface for the Reservation and Schedule Classes

```
public partial class Reservation : IValidate
{
    public void Validate(ChangeAction action)
    {
        if (action == ChangeAction.Insert)
        {
            if (Schedule.Reservations.Count(r =>
                        r.ReservationId != ReservationId &&
                        r.Passenger == this.Passenger) > 0)
                throw new InvalidOperationException(
                        "Reservation for the passenger already exists");
        }
    }
}

public partial class Schedule : IValidate
{
    public void Validate(ChangeAction action)
    {
        if (action == ChangeAction.Insert)
        {
            if (ArrivalDate < DepartureDate)
```

```
                {
                    throw new InvalidOperationException(
                            "Arrival date cannot be before departure date");
                }

                if (LeavesFrom == ArrivesAt)
                {
                    throw new InvalidOperationException(
                            "Can't leave from and arrive at the same location");
                }
            }
        }
    }
```

5. Override the SaveChanges() method in the DbContext with the code in Listing 8-13. This will allow you to validate the changes before they are saved to the database.

Listing 8-13. Overriding the SaveChanges() Method

```
public partial class EFRecipesEntities
{

public override int SaveChanges()
    {
        this.ChangeTracker.DetectChanges();
        var entries = from e in this.ChangeTracker.Entries().Where(e => e.State ==
(System.Data.Entity.EntityState.Added | EntityState.Modified | EntityState.Deleted))
                where (e.Entity != null) &&
                    (e.Entity is IValidate)
                select e;
        foreach (var entry in entries)
        {
            switch (entry.State)
            {
                case EntityState.Added:
                    ((IValidate)entry.Entity).Validate(ChangeAction.Insert);
                    break;
                case EntityState.Modified:
                    ((IValidate)entry.Entity).Validate(ChangeAction.Update);
                    break;
                case EntityState.Deleted:
                    ((IValidate)entry.Entity).Validate(ChangeAction.Delete);
                    break;
            }
        }
        return base.SaveChanges();
    }
}
```

6. Create the IReservationContext interface in Listing 8-14. We'll use this interface to help us test against a fake DbContext so that changes are not saved to the real database.

Listing 8-14. Use this IReservationContext to Define the Methods You'll Need from the DbContext

```
public interface IReservationContext : IDisposable
{
    IDbSet<Train> Trains { get; }
    IDbSet<Schedule> Schedules { get; }
    IDbSet<Reservation> Reservations { get; }

    int SaveChanges();
}
```

7. The POCO template generates both the POCO classes and the class that implements the object context. We'll need this object context class to implement the IReservationContext interface. To do this, edit the Recipe8.Context.tt template file and add IReservationContext at the end of the line that generates the name of the object context class. The complete line should look like the following:

```
<#=Accessibility.ForType(container)#> partial class <#=code.Escape(container)#> :
DbContext,IReservationContext
```

8. Create the repository class in Listing 8-15. This class takes an IReservationContext in the constructor.

Listing 8-15. The ReservationRepository Class That Takes an IReservationContext in the Constructor

```
public class ReservationRepository: IDisposable
    {
        private IReservationContext _context;

        public ReservationRepository(IReservationContext context)
        {
          if (context == null)
             throw new ArgumentNullException("context is null");
          _context = context;
        }
        public void AddTrain(Train train)
        {
           _context.Trains.Add(train);
        }

        public void AddSchedule(Schedule schedule)
        {
           _context.Schedules.Add(schedule);
        }

        public void AddReservation(Reservation reservation)
        {
           _context.Reservations.Add(reservation);
        }
```

```
        public void SaveChanegs()
        {
            _context.SaveChanges();
        }

        public List<Schedule> GetActiveSchedulesForTrain(int trainId)
        {
            var schedules = from r in _context.Schedules
                        where r.ArrivalDate.Date >= DateTime.Today &&
                            r.TrainId == trainId
                        select r;
            return schedules.ToList();
        }
    }
```

9. Right-click the solution, and select Add ➤ New Project. Add a Test Project to the solution. Name this new project Tests. Add a reference to System.Data.Entity.

10. Create a fake object set and fake DbContext so that you can test your business rules in isolation without interacting with the database. Use the code in Listing 8-16.

Listing 8-16. The Implementation of the Fake Object Set and Fake Object Context

```
public class FakeDbSet<T> : IDbSet<T>
    where T : class
{
    HashSet<T> _data;
    IQueryable _query;

    public FakeDbSet()
    {
        _data = new HashSet<T>();
        _query = _data.AsQueryable();
    }

    public virtual T Find(params object[] keyValues)
    {
        throw new NotImplementedException("Derive from FakeDbSet<T> and override Find");
    }

    public void Add(T item)
    {
        _data.Add(item);
    }

    public void Remove(T item)
    {
        _data.Remove(item);
    }
```

```csharp
        public void Attach(T item)
        {
            _data.Add(item);
        }
        public void Detach(T item)
        {
            _data.Remove(item);
        }
        Type IQueryable.ElementType
        {
            get { return _query.ElementType; }
        }
        System.Linq.Expressions.Expression IQueryable.Expression
        {
            get { return _query.Expression; }
        }

        IQueryProvider IQueryable.Provider
        {
            get { return _query.Provider; }
        }
        System.Collections.IEnumerator System.Collections.IEnumerable.GetEnumerator()
        {
            return _data.GetEnumerator();
        }
        IEnumerator<T> IEnumerable<T>.GetEnumerator()
        {
            return _data.GetEnumerator();
        }
    }

public class FakeReservationContext : IReservationContext, IDisposable
    {
        private IDbSet<Train> trains;
        private IDbSet<Schedule> schedules;
        private IDbSet<Reservation> reservations;
        public FakeReservationContext()
        {
            trains = new FakeDbSet<Train>();
            schedules = new FakeDbSet<Schedule>();
            reservations = new FakeDbSet<Reservation>();
        }

        public IDbSet<Train> Trains
        {
            get { return trains; }
        }
```

```csharp
        public IDbSet<Schedule> Schedules
        {
            get { return schedules; }
        }

        public IDbSet<Reservation> Reservations
        {
            get { return reservations; }
        }

        public int SaveChanges()
        {
            foreach (var schedule in Schedules.Cast<IValidate>())
            {
                schedule.Validate(ChangeAction.Insert);
            }
            foreach (var reservation in Reservations.Cast<IValidate>())
            {
                reservation.Validate(ChangeAction.Insert);
            }
            return 1;
        }
        public void Dispose()
        {
        }
    }
```

11. We don't want to test against our real database, so we need to create a fake DbContext that simulates the DbContext with in-memory collections acting as our data store. Add the unit test code in Listing 8-17 to the Tests project.

Listing 8-17. The Unit Tests for Our Tests Project

```csharp
[TestClass]
public class ReservationTest: IDisposable
{
    private IReservationContext _context;

    [TestInitialize]
    public void TestSetup()
    {
        var train = new Train { TrainId = 1, TrainName = "Polar Express" };
        var schedule = new Schedule { ScheduleId = 1, Train = train,
                                      ArrivalDate = DateTime.Now,
                                      DepartureDate = DateTime.Today,
                                      LeavesFrom = "Dallas",
                                      ArrivesAt = "New York" };
        var reservation = new Reservation { ReservationId = 1,
                                            Passenger = "Phil Marlowe",
                                            Schedule = schedule };
        _context = new FakeReservationContext();
        var repository = new ReservationRepository(_context);
```

```
    repository.AddTrain(train);
    repository.AddSchedule(schedule);
    repository.AddReservation(reservation);
    repository.SaveChanges();
}

[TestMethod]
[ExpectedException(typeof(InvalidOperationException))]
public void TestForDuplicateReservation()
{
    var repository = new ReservationRepository(_context);
    var schedule = repository.GetActiveSchedulesForTrain(1).First();
    var reservation = new Reservation { ReservationId = 2,
                                        Schedule = schedule,
                                        Passenger = "Phil Marlowe" };
    repository.AddReservation(reservation);
    repository.SaveChanges();
}

[TestMethod]
[ExpectedException(typeof(InvalidOperationException))]
public void TestForArrivalDateGreaterThanDepartureDate()
{
    var repository = new ReservationRepository(_context);
    var schedule = new Schedule { ScheduleId = 2, TrainId = 1,
                                  ArrivalDate = DateTime.Today,
                                  DepartureDate = DateTime.Now,
                                  ArrivesAt = "New York",
                                  LeavesFrom = "Chicago" };
    repository.AddSchedule(schedule);
    repository.SaveChanges();
}

[TestMethod]
[ExpectedException(typeof(InvalidOperationException))]
public void TestForArrivesAndLeavesFromSameLocation()
{
    var repository = new ReservationRepository(_context);
    var schedule = new Schedule { ScheduleId = 3, TrainId = 1,
                                  ArrivalDate = DateTime.Now,
                                  DepartureDate = DateTime.Today,
                                  ArrivesAt = "Dallas",
                                  LeavesFrom = "Dallas" };
    repository.AddSchedule(schedule);
    repository.SaveChanges();
}
}
```

The Test project now has three unit tests that exercise the following business rules:

- A passenger cannot have more than one reservation for a scheduled departure.

- The arrival date and time for a schedule must be after the departure date and time.

- The departure location cannot be the same as the arrival location.

How It Works

With quite a lot of code, we've managed to build a complete solution that includes an interface (IReservationContext) that we can use to abstractly reference a DbContext, a fake DbSet (FakeDbSet<T>), a fake DbContext (FakeReservationContext), and a small set of unit tests. We use the fake DbContext so that our tests don't interact with the database. The purpose of the tests is to validate our business rules, not to test the database interactions.

One key to the solution is that we created a simplified repository that managed the inserting and selecting of our objects. The constructor for this repository takes an IReservationContext. This subtle abstraction allows us to pass in an instance of any class that implements IReservationContext. To test our domain objects, we pass in an instance of FakeReservationContext. To allow our domain objects to be persisted to the database, we would pass in an instance of our real DbContext: EFRecipesEntities.

We need the DbSets returned by our fake DbContext to match the DbSets returned by the real EFRecipesEntities DbContext. To do this, we changed the T4 template that generates the context to return IDbSet<T> in place of DbSet<T>. We made sure our fake DbContext also returned DbSets of type IDbSet<T>. With this in place, we implemented our FakeDbSet<T> and derived it from IDbSet<T>.

In the Tests project, we set up the tests by creating a Reservation Repository based on an instance of the FakeReservationContext. The unit tests interact with the FakeReservationContext in place of the real DbContext.

Best Practice

There are two testing approaches that seem to work well for Entity Framework: Define a repository interface that both the real repository and one or more "testing" repositories implement. By hiding all of the interactions with the persistence framework behind the implementation of the repository interface, there is no need to create fake versions of any of the other infrastructure parts. This can simplify the implementation of the testing code, but it may leave parts of the repository itself untested.

Define an interface for the DbContext that exposes properties of type IDbSet<T> and a SaveChanges() method, as we have done in this recipe. The real DbContext and all of the fake DbContexts must implement this interface. Using this approach, you don't need to fake the entire repository, which may be difficult in some cases. Your fake DbContexts don't need to mimic the behavior of the entire DbContext class; that would be a real challenge. You do need to limit your code to just what is available on the interfaces.

8-9. Testing a Repository Against a Database
Problem

You want to test your repository against the database.

This type of recipe is often used when integration testing of whole-data access functionality has to be performed.

Solution

You have created a repository that manages all of the queries, inserts, updates, and deletes. You want to test this repository against a real instance of the underlying database. Suppose that you have a model like the one shown in Figure 8-10. Because we will create and drop the database during the tests, let's start from the beginning in a test database.

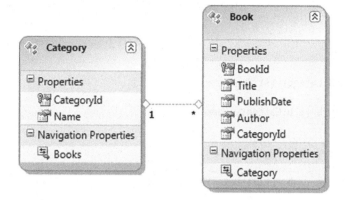

Figure 8-10. *A model of books in categories*

To test your repository, do the following:

1. Create an empty solution. Right-click the solution in the Solution Explorer, and select Add ➤ New Project. Add a new Class Library project. Name this new project BookRepository.

2. Create a new database. Call the database Test. We'll create and drop this database in the unit tests, so make sure you create a new empty database.

3. Add the Book and Category tables along with the relation corresponding to the model in Figure 8-10. Import these tables into a new model. Alternatively, you can use Model First to create the model and then generate the database script to create the database.

4. Add the code in Listing 8-18. This will create a BookRepository class that handles inserts and queries against the model.

    Listing 8-18. The BookRepository Class That Handles Inserts and Queries Against the Model

    ```
    namespace BookRepository
    {
        public class BookRepository
        {
            private TestEntities _context;

            public BookRepository(TestEntities context)
            {
                _context = context;
            }

            public void InsertBook(Book book)
            {
                _context.Books.Add(book);
            }

            public void InsertCategory(Category category)
            {
                _context.Categories.Add(category);
            }
    ```

```
        public void SaveChanges()
        {
            _context.SaveChanges();
        }

        public IQueryable<Book> BooksByCategory(string name)
        {
            return _context.Books.Where(b => b.Category.Name == name);
        }

        public IQueryable<Book> BooksByYear(int year)
        {
            return _context.Books.Where(b => b.PublishDate.Year == year);
        }
    }

}
```

5. Right-click the solution, and select Add ➤ New Project. Select Test Project from the installed templates. Add a reference to System.Data.Entity and a project reference to BookRepository.

6. Right-click the Test project, and select Add ➤ New Test. Add a Unit Test to the Test project. Add the code in Listing 8-19 to create the tests.

Listing 8-19. BookRepositoryTest Class with the Unit Tests

```
[TestClass]
public class BookRepositoryTest
{
    private TestEntities _context;

    [ClassInitialize]
    public void TestSetup()
    {
        _context = new TestEntities();
        if (_context.DatabaseExists())
        {
            _context.DeleteDatabase();
        }
        _context.CreateDatabase();
    }

    [TestMethod]
    public void TestsBooksInCategory()
    {
        var repository = new BookRepository.BookRepository(_context);
        var construction = new Category { Name = "Construction" };
        var book = new Book { Title = "Building with Masonary",
                              Author = "Dick Kreh",
                              PublishDate = new DateTime(1998, 1, 1) };
        book.Category = construction;
        repository.InsertCategory(construction);
        repository.InsertBook(book);
        repository.SaveChanges();
```

```
        // test
        var books = repository.BooksByCategory("Construction");
        Assert.AreEqual(books.Count(), 1);
    }

    [TestMethod]
    public void TestBooksPublishedInTheYear()
    {
        var repository = new BookRepository.BookRepository(_context);
        var construction = new Category { Name = "Construction" };
        var book = new Book { Title = "Building with Masonary",
                              Author = "Dick Kreh",
                              PublishDate = new DateTime(1998, 1, 1) };
        book.Category = construction;
        repository.InsertCategory(construction);
        repository.InsertBook(book);
        repository.SaveChanges();

        // test
        var books = repository.BooksByYear(1998);
        Assert.AreEqual(books.Count(), 1);
    }
}
```

7. Right-click the Test project, and select Add ➤ New Item. Select Application Configuration File from the General templates. Copy the `<connectionStrings>` section from the `App.config` file in the `BookRepository` project, and insert it into the new `App.config` file in the Test project.

8. Right-click the Test project, and select Set as Startup Project. Select Debug ➤ Start Debugging, or press F5 to execute the tests. Make sure that there are no active connections to the Test database. Active connections will cause the `DropDatabase()` method to fail.

How It Works

There are two common approaches to testing that are used with Entity Framework. The first approach is to test the business logic implemented in your objects. For this approach, you test against a "fake" database layer because your focus is on the business logic that governs the interactions of the objects and the rules that apply just before objects are persisted to the database. We illustrated this approach in Recipe 8-8.

A second approach is to test both the business logic and the persistence layer by interacting with the real database. This approach is more extensive, and also more costly in terms of time and resources. When it is implemented in an automated test harness, like the ones often used in a continuous integration environment, you need to automate the creation and dropping of the test database.

Each test iteration should start with a database in a known clean state. Subsequent test runs should not be affected by residue left in the database by previous tests. Dropping and creating databases together with the end-to-end code exercise requires more resources than the business logic only testing, as illustrated in Recipe 8-8.

In the unit tests in Listing 8-19, we checked to see whether the database exists in the Test Initialize phase. If the database exists, it is dropped with the `DropDatabase()` method. Next we create the database with the `CreateDatabase()` method. These methods use the connection string contained in the `App.config` file. This connection string would likely be different from the development database connection string. For simplicity, we used the same connection string for both.

CHAPTER 9

■ ■ ■

Using the Entity Framework in N-Tier Applications

Not all applications can be neatly bundled into a single process (that is, reside on a single physical server). In fact, in this ever-increasingly networked world, many application architectures support the classic logical layers of presentation, application, and data and also are physically deployed across multiple computers. While *logically layering* an application on a single computer can be accommodated in a single Application Domain without much concern for proxies, marshalling, serialization, and network protocols, applications that span from something as small as a mobile device to an enterprise application server found in a data center need to take all of these considerations into account. Fortunately, the Entity Framework together with technologies like Microsoft's Windows Communication Foundation, or the Microsoft Web API framework, are well suited for these types of n-Tier applications.

In this chapter, we'll cover a wide range of recipes for using the Entity Framework with n-Tier applications. To be clear, *n-Tier* is defined as an application architecture in which the presentation, business logic, and data access processing tiers are physically separated across multiple servers. This physical separation can help improve the scalability, maintainability, and future extensibility of an application, but often can have a negative impact on performance, as we are now crossing physical machine boundaries when processing application operations.

N-Tier architecture adds some special challenges to the change-tracking features of Entity Framework. Initially, data is fetched with an Entity Framework context object that is destroyed after the data is sent to the client. While on the client, changes made to the data are not tracked. Upon an update, a new context object must be created to process the submitted data. Obviously, the new context object knows nothing of the previous context object, nor the values of the original entities. In this chapter, we'll look at some approaches that you can implement to help bridge this gap.

In past versions of Entity Framework, a developer could leverage a special template entitled Self-Tracking Entities, which provided built-in plumbing to help track changes to disconnected entity objects. However, in Entity Framework 6, the self-tracking entity approach has been deprecated. While the legacy ObjectContext will support self-tracking entities, the more recent DbContext object does not. The recipes in this chapter focus on basic create, read, update, and delete operations you'll typically use in your n-Tier applications. Additionally, we'll take a deep dive into entity and proxy serialization, concurrency, and working with the unique challenges of tracking entity changes outside the scope of an object context.

9-1. Updating Single Disconnected Entities with the Web API
Problem

You want to leverage REST-based Web API services for inserts, deletes, and updates to a data store. Additionally, you want to implement the code-first approach for Entity Framework 6 to manage data access.

In this example, we emulate an n-Tier scenario where a stand-alone client application (Console Application) is calling a stand-alone website (Web API Project) that exposes REST-based services. Note that each tier is contained in a separate Visual Studio Solution, so as to allow for easier configuring, debugging, and simulation of an n-Tier application.

Solution

Let's say that you have a model like the one shown in Figure 9-1.

Figure 9-1. *A model for orders*

Our model represents Orders. We want to put the model and database code behind a Web API service so that any client that consumes HTTP can insert, update, and delete data into orders. To create the service, perform the following steps:

1. Create a new ASP.NET MVC 4 Web Application project, selecting the Web API template from the Project Templates wizard. Name the project `Recipe1.Service`.

2. Add a new Web API Controller to the project entitled `OrderController`.

3. As shown in Listing 9-1, add the Order entity class.

    Listing 9-1. Order Entity Class

    ```
    public class Order
    {
        public int OrderId { get; set; }
        public string Product { get; set; }
        public int Quantity { get; set; }
        public string Status { get; set; }
        public byte[] TimeStamp { get; set; }
    }
    ```

4. Add a reference in the `Recipe1.Service` project to the Entity Framework 6 libraries. Leveraging the NuGet Package Manager does this best. Right-click on Reference, and select Manage NuGet Packages. From the Online tab, locate and install the Entity Framework 6 package. Doing so will download, install and configure the Entity Framework 6 libraries in your project.

5. Then add a new class entitled `Recipe1Context`, and add the code from Listing 9-2 to it, ensuring that the class derives from the Entity Framework DbContext class.

Listing 9-2. Context Class

```
public class Recipe1Context : DbContext
{
    public Recipe1Context() : base("Recipe1ConnectionString") { }

    public DbSet<Order> Orders { get; set; }

    protected override void OnModelCreating(DbModelBuilder modelBuilder)
    {
        modelBuilder.Entity<Order>().ToTable("Chapter9.Order");
        // Following configuration enables timestamp to be concurrency token
        modelBuilder.Entity<Order>().Property(x => x.TimeStamp)
            .IsConcurrencyToken()
            .HasDatabaseGeneratedOption(DatabaseGeneratedOption.Computed);
    }
}
```

6. Next, from Listing 9-3, add the RecipeConnectionString connection string to the Web.Config file under the ConnectionStrings section.

Listing 9-3. Connection String for the Recipe1 Web API Service

```
<connectionStrings>
  <add name="Recipe1ConnectionString"
    connectionString="Data Source=.;
      Initial Catalog=EFRecipes;
      Integrated Security=True;
      MultipleActiveResultSets=True"
    providerName="System.Data.SqlClient" />
</connectionStrings>
```

7. Then add the code in Listing 9-4 to the Application_Start method in the Global.asax file. This code will disable the Entity Framework Model Compatibility check.

Listing 9-4. Disable the Entity Framework Model Compatibility Check

```
protected void Application_Start()
{
    // Disable Entity Framework Model Compatibilty
    Database.SetInitializer<Recipe1Context>(null);
    ...
}
```

8. Finally, replace the code in the OrderController with that from Listing 9-5.

Listing 9-5. Code for the OrderController

```
public class OrderController : ApiController
{
    // GET api/order
    public IEnumerable<Order> Get()
```

```
{
    using (var context = new Recipe1Context())
    {
        return context.Orders.ToList();
    }
}

// GET api/order/5
public Order Get(int id)
{
    using (var context = new Recipe1Context())
    {
        return context.Orders.FirstOrDefault(x => x.OrderId == id);
    }
}

// POST api/order
public HttpResponseMessage Post(Order order)
{
    // Cleanup data from previous requests
    Cleanup();

    using (var context = new Recipe1Context())
    {
        context.Orders.Add(order);
        context.SaveChanges();

        // create HttpResponseMessage to wrap result, assigning Http Status code of 201,
        // which informs client that resource created successfully
        var response = Request.CreateResponse(HttpStatusCode.Created, order);

        // add location of newly-created resource to response header
                        response.Headers.Location = new Uri(Url.Link("DefaultApi",
new { id = order.OrderId }));

        return response;
    }
}

// PUT api/order/5
public HttpResponseMessage Put(Order order)
{
    using (var context = new Recipe1Context())
    {
        context.Entry(order).State = EntityState.Modified;
        context.SaveChanges();

// return Http Status code of 200, informing client that resouce updated successfully
        return Request.CreateResponse(HttpStatusCode.OK, order);
    }
}
```

```
// DELETE api/order/5
public HttpResponseMessage Delete(int id)
{
    using (var context = new Recipe1Context())
    {
            var order = context.Orders.FirstOrDefault(x => x.OrderId == id);
            context.Orders.Remove(order);
            context.SaveChanges();

        // Return Http Status code of 200, informing client that resouce removed successfully
        return Request.CreateResponse(HttpStatusCode.OK);
    }
}

private void Cleanup()
{
    using (var context = new Recipe1Context())
    {
        context.Database.ExecuteSqlCommand("delete from chapter9.[order]");
    }
}
}
```

It's important to point out that when using Entity Framework with MVC or Web API, these ASP.NET frameworks contain a great deal of scaffolding (i.e., code generation tempates) that can generate a functioning controller that contains Entity Framework plumbing code for you, saving you the effort of constructing it manually.

Next we create the client solution, which will consume the Web API service.

9. Create a new Visual Studio solution that contains a Console application entitled Recipe1.Client.

10. Add the same Order entity class to the client that we added to the service back in Listing 9-1.

Finally, replace the code in the program.cs file with that from Listing 9-6.

Listing 9-6. Our Windows Console Application That Serves as Our Test Client

```
private HttpClient _client;
private Order _order;

private static void Main()
{
    Task t = Run();
    t.Wait();
    Console.WriteLine("\nPress <enter> to continue...");
    Console.ReadLine();
}

private static async Task Run()
{
    // create instance of the program class
    var program = new Program();
    program.ServiceSetup();
```

```
        program.CreateOrder();
        // do not proceed until order is added
        await program.PostOrderAsync();
        program.ChangeOrder();
        // do not proceed until order is changed
         await program.PutOrderAsync();
        // do not proceed until order is removed
      await  program.RemoveOrderAsync();
}

private void ServiceSetup()
{
    // map URL for Web API cal
    _client = new HttpClient { BaseAddress = new Uri("http://localhost:3237/") };

    // add Accept Header to request Web API content
    // negotiation to return resource in JSON format
    _client.DefaultRequestHeaders.Accept.
        Add(new MediaTypeWithQualityHeaderValue("application/json"));
}

private void CreateOrder()
{
    // Create new order
    _order = new Order { Product = "Camping Tent", Quantity = 3, Status = "Received" };
}

private async Task PostOrderAsync()
{
    // leverage Web API client side API to call service
    var response = await _client.PostAsJsonAsync("api/order", _order);
    Uri newOrderUri;

    if (response.IsSuccessStatusCode)
    {
        // Capture Uri of new resource
        newOrderUri = response.Headers.Location;

        // capture newly-created order returned from service,
        // which will now include the database-generated Id value
        _order = await response.Content.ReadAsAsync<Order>();
        Console.WriteLine("Successfully created order. Here is URL to new resource: {0}", newOrderUri);
    }
    else
        Console.WriteLine("{0} ({1})", (int)response.StatusCode, response.ReasonPhrase);
}

private void ChangeOrder()
{
    // update order
    _order.Quantity = 10;
}
```

```
private async Task PutOrderAsync()
{
    // construct call to generate HttpPut verb and dispatch
    // to corresponding Put method in the Web API Service
    var response = await _client.PutAsJsonAsync("api/order", _order);

    if (response.IsSuccessStatusCode)
    {
        // capture updated order returned from service, which will include new quanity
        _order = await response.Content.ReadAsAsync<Order>();
        Console.WriteLine("Successfully updated order: {0}", response.StatusCode);
    }
    else
        Console.WriteLine("{0} ({1})", (int)response.StatusCode, response.ReasonPhrase);
}

private async Task RemoveOrderAsync()
{
    // remove order
    var uri = "api/order/" + _order.OrderId;
    var response = await _client.DeleteAsync(uri);

    if (response.IsSuccessStatusCode)
        Console.WriteLine("Sucessfully deleted order: {0}", response.StatusCode);
    else
        Console.WriteLine("{0} ({1})", (int)response.StatusCode, response.ReasonPhrase);
}
```

The following is the output of our test client from Listing 9-6:

```
Successfully created order: http://localhost:3237/api/order/1054
Successfully updated order: OK
Sucessfully deleted order: OK
```

How It Works

Start by running the Web API application. The Web API application contains an MVC Web Controller that, when started, will bring up a home page. At this point, the site is running and its services are available.

Next open the console application, set a breakpoint on the first line of code in the program.cs file, and run the console application. First we establish some basic plumbing—mapping the Web API service URI and configuring the Accept Header—that will ask the Web API service to return the data in a JSON format. Then we create an Order object, which we send to the Web API service by calling the PostAsJsonAsync method from the HttpClient object. If you place a breakpoint in the Post Action Method in the Order Web API controller class, you'll see that it receives the order object as a parameter and adds it to the Order entity in the context object. Doing so marks the object as added and causes the context to start tracking it. Finally, we call the SaveChanges method to insert the new data into the underlying data store. We then wrap a HTTP status code of 201 and the URI location of the newly created resource into an HttpResponseMessage object and return it to the calling application. When using the ASP.NET Web API, we want to ensure that our client generates an HTTP Post verb when inserting new data. The HTTP Post verb will invoke the corresponding Post action method in the Web API controller.

Back in the client, we execute our next operation, changing the quantity of order and sending the entity back to the Web API service by calling the `PutAsJsonAsync` method from the `HttpClient` object. If you place a breakpoint in the `Put` Action Method in the Order Web API controller class, you'll see that it receives the order object as a parameter in the service. From the context object, we invoke the `Entry` method, passing in the Order entity reference. Then, by setting the `State` property to `Modified` attaches the entity of the underlying context object. The subsequent call to `SaveChanges` generates a SQL Update statement. In this case, we update all columns for order. In later recipes, we'll see how we can update only those properties that have changed. We complete the operation by sending an `HttpResponseMethod` to caller with a HTTP status code of 200.

Back in the client, we invoke our final operation, which will delete the Order entity from the underlying data store. We append the Id for the order as an additional URI segment and call the Web API service with the `DeleteAsync` method from the `HttpClient` object. In the service, we retrieve the target order from the data store and pass its reference to the `Remove` method, called from the Order entity and context object. Doing so marks the entity as deleted. The subsequent call to `SaveChanges` generates a SQL Delete statement that removes the order from the underlying data store.

In this recipe, we've seen that we can encapsulate Entity Framework data operations behind a Web API service. The client can consume the service by using the HttpClient object that is exposed by the Web API client API. Adhering to the Web API's HTTP verb-based dispatch, we leverage the `Post` action method to add a new record, the `Put` action method to update a record, and the `Delete` action method to remove a record. Also in the recipe, we implement Entity Framework using the code-first approach.

In a production application, we would most likely create a separate layer (Visual Studio class project) to separate the Entity Framework data access code from the Web API service.

9-2. Updating Disconnected Entities with WCF
Problem

You want to use a Windows Communication Foundation (WCF) service to expose selects, inserts, deletes, and updates for a data store and keep the database operations as simple as possible. Additionally, you want to implement the code-first approach for Entity Framework 6 to manage data access.

Solution

Let's say that you have a model like the one shown in Figure 9-2.

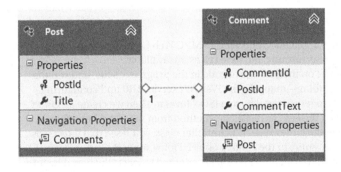

Figure 9-2. *A model for blog posts and comments*

Our model represents blog posts and the comments that readers have about the posts. To make things clearer, we've stripped out most of the properties that we would normally have, such as the body of the post, the author, the date and time of the post, and so on.

We want to put all of the database code behind a WCF service so that clients can read, update, and delete posts and comments, as well as insert new ones. To create the service, do the following:

1. Create a new Visual Studio solution, adding a c# class library project. Name the class library Recipe2.

2. Add a reference to the Entity Framework 6 libraries in the new project. Leveraging the NuGet Package Manager does this best. Right-click on Reference, and select Manage NuGet Packages. From the Online tab, locate and install the Entity Framework 6 package.

3. Add three classes to the Recipe2 project: Post, Comment, and Recipe2Context. Post and Comment represent POCO entity classes that will directly map to the corresponding Post and Comment tables. Recipe2Context is the DbContext object that will serve as the gateway to Entity Framework functionality. Make sure that you include the required WCF DataContract and DataMember attributes in the entity classes as shown in Listing 9-7.

Listing 9-7. Our POCO Classes Post, Comment, and Our Recipe2Context Context Object

```
[DataContract(IsReference = true)]
public class Post
{
    public Post()
    {
        comments = new HashSet<Comments>();
    }

    [DataMember]
    public int PostId { get; set; }
    [DataMember]
    public string Title { get; set; }
    [DataMember]
    public virtual ICollection<Comment> Comments { get; set; }
}

[DataContract(IsReference=true)]
public class Comment
{
    [DataMember]
    public int CommentId { get; set; }
    [DataMember]
    public int PostId { get; set; }
    [DataMember]
    public string CommentText { get; set; }
    [DataMember]
    public virtual Post Post { get; set; }
}

public class EFRecipesEntities : DbContext
{
    public EFRecipesEntities()
        : base("name=EFRecipesEntities")
```

```
    {
    }

    public DbSet<Post> posts;
    public DbSet<Comment> comments;

}
```

4. Add an App.config file to the Recipe2 project, and copy the connection string from Listing 9-8.

Listing 9-8. The Connection String for the Recipe1 Class Library

```
<connectionStrings>
  <add name="Recipe2ConnectionString"
  connectionString="Data Source=.;
      Initial Catalog=EFRecipes;
      Integrated Security=True;
      MultipleActiveResultSets=True"
  providerName="System.Data.SqlClient" />
</connectionStrings>
```

5. Next add a WCF service project to the solution. Use the default name Service1 just to keep things simple. Change the IService1.cs file to reflect the new IService1 interface in Listing 9-9.

Listing 9-9. The Service Contract for Our Service

```
[ServiceContract]
public interface IService1
{
    [OperationContract]
    void Cleanup();

    [OperationContract]
    Post GetPostByTitle(string title);

    [OperationContract]
    Post SubmitPost(Post post);

    [OperationContract]
    Comment SubmitComment(Comment comment);

    [OperationContract]
    void DeleteComment(Comment comment);
}
```

6. Change the service application code in the Service1.svc.cs file using the code from Listing 9-10. Add a project reference to the Recipe2 class library and a using statement so that the references to the POCO classes resolve correctly. You will also need to add a reference to Entity Framework 6 libraries.

Listing 9-10. The Implementation of the Service Contract in Listing 9-9. (Be sure to add references to System.Data.Entity and System.Security to this project.)

```
public class Service1 : IService
{
    public void Cleanup()
    {
        using (var context = new EFRecipesEntities())
        {
            context.Database.ExecuteSqlCommand("delete from chapter9.comment");
            context. Database.ExecuteSqlCommand ("delete from chapter9.post");
        }
    }

    public Post GetPostByTitle(string title)
    {
        using (var context = new EFRecipesEntities())
        {
            context.Configuration.ProxyCreationEnabled = false;
            var post = context.Posts.Include(p => p.Comments)
                               .Single(p => p.Title == title);
            return post;
        }
    }

    public Post SubmitPost(Post post)
    {
            context.Entry(post).State =
                // if Id equal to 0, must be insert; otherwise, it's an update
            post.PostId == 0 ? EntityState.Added : EntityState.Modified;
            context.SaveChanges();
            return post;
    }

    public Comment SubmitComment(Comment comment)
    {
        using (var context = new EFRecipesEntities())
        {
            context.Comments.Attach(comment);
            if (comment.CommentId == 0)
            {
                // this is an insert
                context.Entry(comment).State = EntityState.Added);
            }
            else
            {
                // set single property to modified, which sets state of entity to modified, but
                // only updates the single property - not the entire entity
                context.entry(comment).Property(x => x.CommentText).IsModified = true;
            }
```

```
            context.SaveChanges();
            return comment;
        }
    }

    public void DeleteComment(Comment comment)
    {
        using (var context = new EFRecipesEntities())
        {
            context.Entry(comment).State = EntityState.Deleted;
            context.SaveChanges();
        }
    }
}
```

7. Finally, add a Windows Console Application to the service project. We'll use this for our client to test the WCF service. Copy the code from Listing 9-11 into the Program class in the Console application. Right-click the console application project, select Add Service Reference, and add a reference to the Service1 service. You will also need to add a project reference to the class library created in step 1 or expose it through a proxy class from the service.

Listing 9-11. *Our Windows Console Application That Serves as Our Test Client*

```
class Program
{
    static void Main(string[] args)
    {
        using (var client = new ServiceReference2.Service1Client())
        {
            // cleanup previous data
            client.Cleanup();

            // insert a post
            var post = new Post { Title = "POCO Proxies" };
            post = client.SubmitPost(post);

            // update the post
            post.Title = "Change Tracking Proxies";
            client.SubmitPost(post);

            // add a comment
            var comment1 = new Comment {
                CommentText = "Virtual Properties are cool!",
                PostId = post.PostId };
            var comment2 = new Comment {
                CommentText = "I use ICollection<T> all the time",
                PostId = post.PostId };
            comment1 = client.SubmitComment(comment1);
            comment2 = client.SubmitComment(comment2);
```

```
            // update a comment
            comment1.CommentText = "How do I use ICollection<T>?";
            client.SubmitComment(comment1);

            // delete comment 1
            client.DeleteComment(comment1);

            // get posts with comments
            var p = client.GetPostByTitle("Change Tracking Proxies");
            Console.WriteLine("Comments for post: {0}", p.Title);
            foreach (var comment in p.Comments)
            {
                Console.WriteLine("\tComment: {0}", comment.CommentText);
            }
        }
    }
}
```

The following is the output of our test client from Listing 9-11:

```
Comments for post: Change Tracking Proxies
        Comment: I use ICollection<T> all the time
```

How It Works

Let's start with the Windows console application, which is our test client for the service. We create an instance of our service client in a using {} block. Just as we've done when creating an instance of an Entity Framework context in a using {} block, this ensures that Dispose() is implicitly called when we leave the block, either normally or via an exception.

Once we have an instance of our service client, the first thing we do is call the Cleanup() method. We do this to remove any previous test data we might have.

With the next couple of lines, we call the service's SubmitPost() method. In this method's implementation (see Listing 9-10), we interrogate the value of PostId. If the PostId is 0, we then assume it's a new post and set the Entity State to Added. Otherwise, we assume the entity exists and we are modifying it, thus setting the Entity State to Modified. Although somewhat crude, this approach can determine the state (new or existing) of the post entity, depending on the domain of the valid Ids for a post as well as the runtime initializing integers to 0. A better approach might involve sending an additional parameter to the method or creating a separate InsertPost() method. The best approach depends on the structure of your application.

If the post is to be inserted, we change the object state of the post to EntityState.Added. Otherwise, we change its object state to EntityState.Modified. The EntityState value drives whether an insert or update statement is generated. If the post is inserted, the post instance's PostId is updated with the new correct value. The post is returned.

Inserting and updating a single property on the Comment entity is similar to inserting and updating a post with one significant difference: as a business rule, when we update a comment, we want to make sure only to update the CommentText property. This property holds the body of the comment, and we don't want to update any other part of the Comment entity object. To do this, we mark just the CommentText property as modified. Entity Framework will generate a simple update statement that changes just the CommentText column in the database. Note that this works as we are just changing a *single property* of the entity. If we were changing multiple properties on the Comment entity, we would then need some way to track which properties were changed on the client. In cases where multiple properties can change, it is often more efficient to update the entity object, without need for complex client-side change tracking.

To delete a comment, we call the Entity() method on the context object, passing in the comment entity as an argument and set the EntityState to Deleted, which marks the comment for deletion and generates a SQL Delete statement.

Finally, the GetPostByTitle() method eagerly loads the comments for each post and returns an object graph of posts and related comments. Because we have implemented POCO classes, Entity Framework returns what is called a dynamic proxy object that wraps the underlying post and comments class. Unfortunately, WCF cannot serialize a proxy object. However, with the line ProxyCreationEnabled = false, we simply disable proxy class generation for the query and Entity Framework returns the actual objects. If we attempted to serialize the proxy object, we would receive the following error message:

```
The underlying connection was closed: The connection was closed unexpectedly
```

We could even move the ProxyCreationEnabled = false to the constructor of the service to enforce it for all the service methods.

In this recipe, we've seen that we can use POCO objects to handle CRUD operations with WCF. Because there is no state information stored on the client, we've built separate methods for inserting, updating, and deleting posts and comments. Other recipes in this chapter will demonstrate techniques used to reduce the number of methods our service must implement and to simplify the communication between the client and the server.

9-3. Finding Out What Has Changed with Web API
Problem

You want to leverage REST-based Web API services for database insert, delete, and update operations for an object graph without having to expose a separate method for updating each entity class. Additionally, you want to implement the code-first approach for Entity Framework 6 to manage data access.

In this example, we emulate an n-Tier scenario where a stand-alone client application (Console Application) is calling a stand-alone website (Web API Project) that exposes REST-based services. Note that each tier is contained in a separate Visual Studio Solution, to allow for easier configuring, debugging and simulation of an n-Tier application. Let's say that you have a model like the one shown in Figure 9-3.

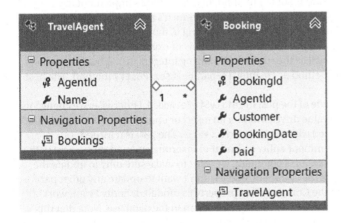

Figure 9-3. *A model for Travel Agents and Bookings*

Our model represents Travel Agents and their corresponding Bookings. We want to put the model and database code behind a Web API service so that any client that consumes HTTP can insert, update, and delete orders. To create the service, perform the following steps:

1. Create a new ASP.NET MVC 4 Web Application project, selecting the Web API template from the Project Templates wizard. Name the project Recipe3.Service.

2. Add a new Web API Controller to the project entitled TravelAgentController.

3. Next, from Listing 9-12 add the TravelAgent and Booking entity classes.

Listing 9-12. Travel Agent and Booking Entity Classes

```
public class TravelAgent
{
    public TravelAgent()
    {
        this.Bookings = new HashSet<Booking>();
    }

    public int AgentId { get; set; }
    public string Name { get; set; }

    public virtual ICollection<Booking> Bookings { get; set; }
}

public class Booking
{
    public int BookingId { get; set; }
    public int AgentId { get; set; }
    public string Customer { get; set; }
    public DateTime BookingDate { get; set; }
    public bool Paid { get; set; }

    public virtual TravelAgent TravelAgent { get; set; }
}
```

4. Add a reference in the Recipe3.Service project to the Entity Framework 6 libraries. Leveraging the NuGet Package Manager does this best. Right-click on Reference, and select Manage NuGet Packages. From the Online tab, locate and install the Entity Framework 6 package.

5. Then add a new class entitled Recipe3Context, and add the code from Listing 9-13 to it, ensuring that the class derives from the Entity Framework DbContext class.

Listing 9-13. Context Class

```
public class Recipe3Context : DbContext
{
    public Recipe3Context() : base("Recipe3ConnectionString") { }

    public DbSet<TravelAgent> TravelAgents { get; set; }
    public DbSet<Booking> Bookings { get; set; }
```

```
protected override void OnModelCreating(DbModelBuilder modelBuilder)
{
    modelBuilder.Entity<TravelAgent>().HasKey(x => x.AgentId);
    modelBuilder.Entity<TravelAgent>().ToTable("Chapter9.TravelAgent");
    modelBuilder.Entity<Booking>().ToTable("Chapter9.Booking");
}
}
```

6. Next, from Listing 9-14, add the Recipe3ConnectionString connection string to the Web.Config file under the ConnectionStrings section.

Listing 9-14. Connection String for the Recipe1 Web API Service

```
<connectionStrings>
  <add name="Recipe3ConnectionString"
    connectionString="Data Source=.;
        Initial Catalog=EFRecipes;
        Integrated Security=True;
        MultipleActiveResultSets=True"
    providerName="System.Data.SqlClient" />
</connectionStrings>
```

7. Then add the code in Listing 9-15 to the Application_Start method in the Global.asax file. This code will disable the Entity Framework Model Compatibility check and instruct the JSON serializer to ignore the self-referencing loop caused by navigation properties being bidirectional between TravelAgent and Booking.

Listing 9-15. Disable the Entity Framework Model Compatibility Check

```
protected void Application_Start()
{
    // Disable Entity Framework Model Compatibilty
    Database.SetInitializer<Recipe1Context>(null);

    // The bidirectional navigation properties between related entities
    // create a self-referencing loop that breaks Web API's effort to
    // serialize the objects as JSON. By default, Json.NET is configured
    // to error when a reference loop is detected. To resolve problem,
    // simply configure JSON serializer to ignore self-referencing loops.
    GlobalConfiguration.Configuration.Formatters.JsonFormatter
        .SerializerSettings.ReferenceLoopHandling =
            Newtonsoft.Json.ReferenceLoopHandling.Ignore;
    ...
}
```

8. Modify the Web API routing by changing the code in RouteConfig.cs file to match that of Listing 9-16.

Listing 9-16. Modifications to RouteConfig Class to Accommodate RPC-Style Routing

```
public static void Register(HttpConfiguration config)
{
    config.Routes.MapHttpRoute(
        name: "ActionMethodSave",
        routeTemplate: "api/{controller}/{action}/{id}",
        defaults: new { id = RouteParameter.Optional }
    );
}
```

9. Finally, replace the code in the TravelAgentController with that from Listing 9-17.

Listing 9-17. Travel Agent Web API Controller

```
public class TravelAgentController : ApiController
{
    // GET api/travelagent
    [HttpGet]
    public IEnumerable<TravelAgent> Retrieve()
    {
        using (var context = new Recipe3Context())
        {
            return context.TravelAgents.Include(x => x.Bookings).ToList();
        }
    }


    /// <summary>
    /// Update changes to TravelAgent, implementing Action-Based Routing in Web API
    /// </summary>
    public HttpResponseMessage Update(TravelAgent travelAgent)
    {
        using (var context = new Recipe3Context())
        {
            var newParentEntity = true;

            // adding the object graph makes the context aware of entire
            // object graph (parent and child entities) and assigns a state
            // of added to each entity.
            context.TravelAgents.Add(travelAgent);

            if (travelAgent.AgentId > 0)
            {
                // as the Id property has a value greater than 0, we assume
                // that travel agent already exists and set entity state to
                // be updated.
                context.Entry(travelAgent).State = EntityState.Modified;
                newParentEntity = false;
            }
```

```
                    // iterate through child entities, assigning correct state.
                    foreach (var booking in travelAgent.Bookings)
                    {
                        if (booking.BookingId > 0)
                            // assume booking already exists if ID is greater than zero.
                            // set entity to be updated.
                            context.Entry(booking).State = EntityState.Modified;
                    }

                    context.SaveChanges();

                    HttpResponseMessage response;

                    // set Http Status code based on operation type
                    response = Request.CreateResponse(newParentEntity
                        ? HttpStatusCode.Created : HttpStatusCode.OK, travelAgent);

                    return response;
                }
            }

        [HttpDelete]
        public HttpResponseMessage Cleanup()
        {
            using (var context = new Recipe3Context())
            {
                context.Database.ExecuteSqlCommand("delete from chapter9.booking");
                context.Database.ExecuteSqlCommand("delete from chapter9.travelagent");
            }

            return Request.CreateResponse(HttpStatusCode.OK);
        }

    }
```

Next we create the client Visual Studio solution that will consume the Web API service.

10. Create a new Visual Studio solution that contains a Console application entitled `Recipe3.Client`.

11. Replace the code in the program.cs file with that from Listing 9-18.

Listing 9-18. Our Windows Console Application That Serves as Our Test Client

```
internal class Program
{
    private HttpClient _client;
    private TravelAgent _agent1, _agent2;
    private Booking _booking1, _booking2, _booking3;
    private HttpResponseMessage _response;
```

```csharp
private static void Main()
{
    Task t = Run();
    t.Wait();
    Console.WriteLine("\nPress <enter> to continue...");
    Console.ReadLine();
}

private static async Task Run()
{
    var program = new Program();
    program.ServiceSetup();
    // do not proceed until clean-up is completed
    await program.CleanupAsync();
    program.CreateFirstAgent();
    // do not proceed until agent is created
    await program.AddAgentAsync();
    program.CreateSecondAgent();
    // do not proceed until agent is created
    await program.AddSecondAgentAsync();
    program.ModifyAgent();
    // do not proceed until agent is updated
    await program.UpdateAgentAsync();
    // do not proceed until agents are fetched
    await program.FetchAgentsAsync();
}

private void ServiceSetup()
{
    // set up infrastructure for Web API call
    _client = new HttpClient {BaseAddress = new Uri("http://localhost:6687/")};

    // add Accept Header to request Web API content negotiation to return resource in JSON format
    _client.DefaultRequestHeaders.Accept.Add(new MediaTypeWithQualityHeaderValue("application/json"));
}

private async Task CleanupAsync()
{
    // call cleanup method in service
    _response = await _client.DeleteAsync("api/travelagent/cleanup/");
}

private void CreateFirstAgent()
{
    // create new Travel Agent and booking
    _agent1 = new TravelAgent {Name = "John Tate"};
    _booking1 = new Booking
    {
        Customer = "Karen Stevens",
        Paid = false,
        BookingDate = DateTime.Parse("2/2/2010")
    };
```

313

```
        _booking2 = new Booking
        {
            Customer = "Dolly Parton",
            Paid = true,
            BookingDate = DateTime.Parse("3/10/2010")
        };
        _agent1.Bookings.Add(_booking1);
        _agent1.Bookings.Add(_booking2);
    }

    private async Task AddAgentAsync()
    {
        // call generic update method in Web API service to add agent and bookings
        _response = await _client.PostAsync("api/travelagent/update/",
            _agent1, new JsonMediaTypeFormatter());

        if (_response.IsSuccessStatusCode)
        {
            // capture newly created travel agent from service, which will include
            // database-generated Ids for each entity
            _agent1 = await _response.Content.ReadAsAsync<TravelAgent>();
            _booking1 = _agent1.Bookings.FirstOrDefault(x => x.Customer == "Karen Stevens");
            _booking2 = _agent1.Bookings.FirstOrDefault(x => x.Customer == "Dolly Parton");

            Console.WriteLine("Successfully created Travel Agent {0} and {1} Booking(s)",
                _agent1.Name, _agent1.Bookings.Count);
        }
        else
            Console.WriteLine("{0} ({1})", (int) _response.StatusCode, _response.ReasonPhrase);
    }

    private void CreateSecondAgent()
    {
        // add new agent and booking
        _agent2 = new TravelAgent {Name = "Perry Como"};
        _booking3 = new Booking
        {
            Customer = "Loretta Lynn",
            Paid = true,
            BookingDate = DateTime.Parse("3/15/2010")
        };
        _agent2.Bookings.Add(_booking3);
    }

    private async Task AddSecondAgentAsync()
    {
        // call generic update method in Web API service to add agent and booking
        _response = await _client.PostAsync("api/travelagent/update/",
            _agent2, new JsonMediaTypeFormatter());
```

```csharp
        if (_response.IsSuccessStatusCode)
        {
            // capture newly created travel agent from service
            _agent2 = await _response.Content.ReadAsAsync<TravelAgent>();
            _booking3 = _agent2.Bookings.FirstOrDefault(x => x.Customer == "Loretta Lynn");

            Console.WriteLine("Successfully created Travel Agent {0} and {1} Booking(s)",
                _agent2.Name, _agent2.Bookings.Count);
        }
        else
            Console.WriteLine("{0} ({1})", (int) _response.StatusCode, _response.ReasonPhrase);
    }

    private void ModifyAgent()
    {
        // modify agent 2 by changing agent name and assigning booking 1 to him from agent 1
        _agent2.Name = "Perry Como, Jr.";
        _agent2.Bookings.Add(_booking1);
    }

    private async Task UpdateAgentAsync()
    {
        // call generic update method in Web API service to update agent 2
        _response = await _client.PostAsync("api/travelagent/update/",
            _agent2, new JsonMediaTypeFormatter());

        if (_response.IsSuccessStatusCode)
        {
            // capture newly created travel agent from service, which will include Ids
            _agent1 = _response.Content.ReadAsAsync<TravelAgent>().Result;
            Console.WriteLine("Successfully updated Travel Agent {0} and {1} Booking(s)",
                _agent1.Name, _agent1.Bookings.Count);
        }
        else
            Console.WriteLine("{0} ({1})", (int) _response.StatusCode, _response.ReasonPhrase);
    }

    private async Task FetchAgentsAsync()
    {
        // call Get method on service to fetch all Travel Agents and Bookings
        _response = _client.GetAsync("api/travelagent/retrieve").Result;

        if (_response.IsSuccessStatusCode)
        {
            // capture newly created travel agent from service, which will include Ids
            var agents = await _response.Content.ReadAsAsync<IEnumerable<TravelAgent>>();

            foreach (var agent in agents)
            {
                Console.WriteLine("Travel Agent {0} has {1} Booking(s)", agent.Name,
agent.Bookings.Count());
            }
        }
```

```
        else
            Console.WriteLine("{0} ({1})", (int) _response.StatusCode, _response.ReasonPhrase);
    }
}
```

12. Finally, add the TravelAgent and Booking classes to this project just as we added to the service in Listing 9-12.

Following is the output of the test client from Listing 9-18:

```
Successfully created Travel Agent John Tate and 2 Booking(s)
Successfully created Travel Agent Perry Como and 1 Booking(s)
Successfully updated Travel Agent Perry Como, Jr. and 2 Booking(s)
Travel Agent John Tate has 1 Booking(s)
Travel Agent Perry Como, Jr. has 2 Booking(s)
```

How It Works

Start by running the Web API application. The Web API application contains an MVC Web Controller, which, when started, will bring up a home page. At this point, the site is running and its services are available.

Next open the console application, set a breakpoint on the first line of code in the program.cs file, and run the console application. First we establish some basic plumbing—mapping the Web API service URI and configuring the Accept Header—that will ask the Web API service to return data in a JSON format.

We then call the Cleanup action method on the TravelAgent Web API controller using the Client.DeleteAsync method exposed by the HttpClient object. Cleanup truncates the database tables to clear data from any previous operations.

Back in the client, we create a new travel agent and two bookings and then send these three new entities to the service by calling the PostAsync from the HttpClient object. If you place a breakpoint in the Update Action Method in the TravelAgent Web API controller class, you'll see that it receives the TravelAgent object as a parameter and adds it to the TravelAgents entity in the context object. Doing so marks the object and all its related child entity objects as added and causes the context to start tracking them.

■ **Note** It's worthwhile to mention that you should *Add* rather *Attach* a set of objects if there are multiple added entities with the same value in the Primary Key property (in this case, multiple Bookings with an Id = 0). If using *Attach* in this scenario, Entity Framework will throw an exception because of the Primary Key conflicts (multiple entities with a primary key = 0) in the non-added entities.

We next check the Id property and make a somewhat crude determination that if it is greater than 0, then this is an existing entity, and we set the entity state property to Modified by calling the Entry method on the Context object. Additionally, we set a flag entitled newParentEntity, so that we can return the correct Http Status Code later in the operation. In the event that the Id property of TravelAgent is equal to 1, then we leave the state property as Added.

We next iterate through each of the child booking objects applying the exact same logic. Upon completion, we call the SaveChanges method, which generates SQL Update statements for Modified entities and Sql Insert statements for Added entities. Then we return an Http Status Code of 201 for inserted entities and 200 for modified entities. The 200 Http Status Code informs the calling program that the operation completed successfully; while 201 informs the client that an insert operation completed successfully. When exposing REST-based services, it is a best practice to return an Http Status Code to the calling program to verify the outcome of the operation.

Subsequently in the client, we add another new travel agent and booking, using the PostAsync method to call the Update action method in the service, using the PostAsync method which again inserts each of the new objects into the database.

Next, we modify the name of the second agent and move one the bookings from the first agent to the second. This time, when we call the Update method, each of the entities has an Id property with a value greater than 1, and thus we set the entity state as modified, causing SQL Updates to be issued by the Entity Framework.

Finally, the client calls the Retrieve Action Method on the service leveraging the GetAsync method exposed by the HttpClient API. The Retrieve method is invoked, and returns all of the travel agent and booking entities. Here we simply implement eager loading with the Include() method, which returns all of the properties in each child booking entity.

Be aware that the JSON serializer will return all public properties in an entity object, even if you only project (for example, select) a subset of the properties.

In this recipe, we've seen that we can encapsulate Entity Framework data operations behind a Web API service. The client can consume the service by using the HttpClient object that is exposed by the Web API client API. In this example, we moved away from the Web API's preferred *HTTP verb-based dispatch* and implemented more of an *RPC-based routing approach*. In production applications, you'd most likely want to utilize the HTTP verb-based approach, as it fits into the underlying intent of the ASP.NET Web API, which is to expose REST-based services.

In a production application, we would most likely create another layer (Visual Studio class project) to separate the Entity Framework data access code from the Web API service.

9-4. Implementing Client-Side Change Tracking with Web API
Problem

You want to leverage REST-based Web API services for database insert, delete, and update operations to an object graph while implementing a reusable client-side approach to updating entity classes. Additionally, you want to leverage the code-first approach for Entity Framework 6 to manage data access.

In this example, we emulate an n-Tier scenario where a stand-alone client application (Console Application) is calling a stand-alone website (Web API Project) that exposes REST-based services.

Note that each tier is contained in a separate Visual Studio Solution, so as to allow for easier configuring, debugging, and simulation of an n-Tier application.

Solution

Let's say that you have a model like the one shown in Figure 9-4.

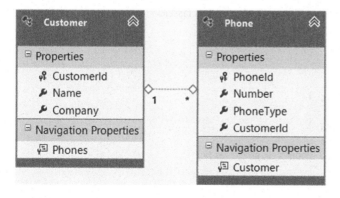

Figure 9-4. *A Customer and Phone Numbers model*

Our model represents Customers and their corresponding Phone Numbers. We want to put the model and database code behind a Web API service so that any client that consumes HTTP can insert, update, and delete orders. To create the service, perform the following steps:

1. Create a new ASP.NET MVC 4 Web Application project, selecting the Web API template from the Project Templates wizard. Name the project `Recipe4.Service`.

2. Add a new Web API Controller to the project entitled `CustomerController`.

3. Next, from Listing 9-19 add the entity base class entitled `BaseEntity` and the enum type entitled `TrackingState`. The base class extends each entity, adding a TrackingState property that the client is required to set when manipulating entity objects. The TrackingState property is driven from the TrackingState enum. Note that the TrackingState is not persisted to the database. Creating our own internal tracking state enum class lets us keep the client free of Entity Framework dependencies that would be required if we were to expose the Entity Framework tracking states to the client. In the DbContext file, note how we will instruct Entity Framework not to map the TrackingState property to the underlying database tables in the `OnModelCreating` method.

Listing 9-19. Entity Base Class and TrackingState Enum Type

```
public abstract class BaseEntity
{
    protected BaseEntity()
    {
        TrackingState = TrackingState.Nochange;
    }

    public TrackingState TrackingState { get; set; }
}

public enum TrackingState
{
    Nochange,
    Add,
    Update,
    Remove,
}
```

4. Next, from Listing 9-20, add the Customer and PhoneNumber entity classes.

Listing 9-20. Customer and Phone Entity Classes

```
public class Customer : BaseEntity
{
    public int CustomerId { get; set; }
    public string Name { get; set; }
    public string Company { get; set; }

    public virtual ICollection<Phone> Phones { get; set; }
}
```

```
public class Phone : BaseEntity
{
    public int PhoneId { get; set; }
    public string Number { get; set; }
    public string PhoneType { get; set; }
    public int CustomerId { get; set; }

    public virtual Customer Customer { get; set; }
}
```

5. Add a reference in the Recipe4.Service project to the Entity Framework 6 libraries. Leveraging the NuGet Package Manager does this best. Right-click on Reference, and select Manage NuGet Packages. From the Online tab, locate and install the Entity Framework 6 package.

6. Then add a new class entitled Recipe4Context, and add the code from Listing 9-21 to it, ensuring that the class derives from the Entity Framework DbContext class. Note closely how we leverage a new Entity Framework 6 features entitled "*Configuring Unmapped Base Types.*" In Listing 9-21, we define a convention that instructs each entity class to "ignore" (i.e., not map to the underlying database) the TrackingState property from the BaseEntity base class which we include only to track the state of the disconnected entities in operations that cross service boundaries.

■ **Note**   Rowan Martin, Microsoft Program Manager for the Entity Framework Team has published a helpful blog post about Configuring Unmapped Base Types: http://romiller.com/2013/01/29/ef6-code-first-configuring-unmapped-base-types/. Be certain to check out Rowan's other outstanding blog posts on the Entity Framework.

Listing 9-21. Context Class

```
public class Recipe4Context : DbContext
{
    public Recipe4Context() : base("Recipe4ConnectionString") { }

    public DbSet<Customer> Customers { get; set; }
    public DbSet<Phone> Phones { get; set; }

    protected override void OnModelCreating(DbModelBuilder modelBuilder)
    {
        // Do not persist TrackingState property to data store
        // This property is used internally to track state of
        // disconnected entities across service boundaries.
        // Leverage the Custom Code First Conventions features from Entity Framework 6.
        // Define a convention that performs a configuration for every entity
        // that derives from a base entity class.
        modelBuilder.Types<BaseEntity>().Configure(x => x.Ignore(y => y.TrackingState));
        modelBuilder.Entity<Customer>().ToTable("Chapter9.Customer");
        modelBuilder.Entity<Phone>().ToTable("Chapter9.Phone");
    }
}
```

7. Next, from Listing 9-22, add the Recipe4ConnectionString connection string to the Web.Config file under the ConnectionStrings section.

Listing 9-22. Connection string for the Recipe1 Web API Service

```
<connectionStrings>
  <add name="Recipe4ConnectionString"
    connectionString="Data Source=.;
      Initial Catalog=EFRecipes;
      Integrated Security=True;
      MultipleActiveResultSets=True"
    providerName="System.Data.SqlClient" />
</connectionStrings>
```

8. Then add the code in Listing 9-23 to the Application_Start method in the Global.asax file. This code will disable the Entity Framework Model Compatibility check and instruct the JSON serializer to ignore the self-referencing loop caused by navigation properties being bidirectional between Customer and PhoneNumber.

Listing 9-23. Disable the Entity Framework Model Compatibility Check

```
 protected void Application_Start()
 {
            // Disable Entity Framework Model Compatibilty
            Database.SetInitializer<Recipe1Context>(null);

            // The bidirectional navigation properties between related entities
            // create a self-referencing loop that breaks Web API's effort to
            // serialize the objects as JSON. By default, Json.NET is configured
            // to error when a reference loop is detected. To resolve problem,
            // simply configure JSON serializer to ignore self-referencing loops.
            GlobalConfiguration.Configuration.Formatters.JsonFormatter
                .SerializerSettings.ReferenceLoopHandling =
                    Newtonsoft.Json.ReferenceLoopHandling.Ignore;

            ...
 }
```

9. Next add a class entitled EntityStateFactory, and add the code from Listing 9-24 to it. The factory will translate the TrackingState enum values exposed to the client to Entity Framework state value required by the change tracking components.

Listing 9-24. Customer Web API Controller

```
public static EntityState Set(TrackingState trackingState)
{
    switch (trackingState)
    {
        case TrackingState.Add:
            return EntityState.Added;
        case TrackingState.Update:
            return EntityState.Modified;
        case TrackingState.Remove:
            return EntityState.Deleted;
```

```
            default:
                return EntityState.Unchanged;
        }
    }
```

Finally, replace the code in the CustomerController with that from Listing 9-25.

Listing 9-25. Customer Web API Controller

```
public class CustomerController : ApiController
{
    // GET api/customer
    public IEnumerable<Customer> Get()
    {
        using (var context = new Recipe4Context())
        {
            return context.Customers.Include(x => x.Phones).ToList();
        }
    }

    // GET api/customer/5
    public Customer Get(int id)
    {
        using (var context = new Recipe4Context())
        {
            return context.Customers.Include(x => x.Phones)
                .FirstOrDefault(x => x.CustomerId == id);
        }
    }

    [ActionName("Update")]
    public HttpResponseMessage UpdateCustomer(Customer customer)
    {
        using (var context = new Recipe4Context())
        {
            // Add object graph to context setting default state of 'Added'.
            // Adding parent to context automatically attaches entire graph
            // (parent and child entities) to context and sets state to 'Added'
            // for all entities.
            context.Customers.Add(customer);

            foreach (var entry in context.ChangeTracker.Entries<BaseEntity>())
            {
                entry.State = EntityStateFactory.Set(entry.Entity.TrackingState);

                if (entry.State == EntityState.Modified)
                {
                    // For entity updates, we fetch a current copy of the entity
                    // from the database and assign the values to the orginal values
                    // property from the Entry object. OriginalValues wrap a dictionary
                    // that represents the values of the entity before applying changes.
                    // The Entity Framework change tracker will detect
                    // differences between the current and original values and mark
```

```
                            // each property and the entity as modified. Start by setting
                            // the state for the entity as 'Unchanged'.
                            entry.State = EntityState.Unchanged;
                            var databaseValues = entry.GetDatabaseValues();
                            entry.OriginalValues.SetValues(databaseValues);
                        }
                    }

                    context.SaveChanges();
                }

                return Request.CreateResponse(HttpStatusCode.OK, customer);
            }

            [HttpDelete]
            [ActionName("Cleanup")]
            public HttpResponseMessage Cleanup()
            {
                using (var context = new Recipe4Context())
                {
                    context.Database.ExecuteSqlCommand("delete from chapter9.phone");
                    context.Database.ExecuteSqlCommand("delete from chapter9.customer");

                    return Request.CreateResponse(HttpStatusCode.OK);
                }
            }
        }
    }
```

Next we create the Visual Studio solution that will contain the client project that will consume the Web API service.

10. Create a new Visual Studio solution that contains a Console application entitled Recipe3.Client.

11. Replace the code in the program.cs file with that from Listing 9-26.

Listing 9-26. Our Windows Console Application That Serves as Our Test Client

```
internal class Program
{
    private HttpClient _client;
    private Customer _bush, _obama;
    private Phone _whiteHousePhone, _bushMobilePhone, _obamaMobilePhone;
    private HttpResponseMessage _response;

    private static void Main()
    {
        Task t = Run();
        t.Wait();
        Console.WriteLine("\nPress <enter> to continue...");
        Console.ReadLine();
    }
```

```
    private static async Task Run()
    {
        var program = new Program();
        program.ServiceSetup();
        // do not proceed until clean-up completes
        await program.CleanupAsync();
        program.CreateFirstCustomer();
        // do not proceed until customer is added
        await program.AddCustomerAsync();
        program.CreateSecondCustomer();
        // do not proceed until customer is added
        await program.AddSecondCustomerAsync();
        // do not proceed until customer is removed
        await program.RemoveFirstCustomerAsync();
        // do not proceed until customers are fetched
        await program.FetchCustomersAsync();
    }

    private void ServiceSetup()
    {
        // set up infrastructure for Web API call
        _client = new HttpClient {BaseAddress = new Uri("http://localhost:62799/")};

        // add Accept Header to request Web API content negotiation to return resource in JSON format
        _client.DefaultRequestHeaders.Accept.Add(new MediaTypeWithQualityHeaderValue
("application/json"));
    }

    private async Task CleanupAsync()
    {
        // call the cleanup method from the service
        _response = await _client.DeleteAsync("api/customer/cleanup/");
    }

    private void CreateFirstCustomer()
    {
        // create customer #1 and two phone numbers
        _bush = new Customer
        {
            Name = "George Bush",
            Company = "Ex President",
            // set tracking state to 'Add' to generate a SQL Insert statement
            TrackingState = TrackingState.Add,
        };

        _whiteHousePhone = new Phone
        {
            Number = "212 222-2222",
            PhoneType = "White House Red Phone",
            // set tracking state to 'Add' to generate a SQL Insert statement
            TrackingState = TrackingState.Add,
        };
```

```
        _bushMobilePhone = new Phone
        {
            Number = "212 333-3333",
            PhoneType = "Bush Mobile Phone",
            // set tracking state to 'Add' to generate a SQL Insert statement
            TrackingState = TrackingState.Add,
        };

        _bush.Phones.Add(_whiteHousePhone);
        _bush.Phones.Add(_bushMobilePhone);
    }

    private async Task AddCustomerAsync()
    {
        // construct call to invoke UpdateCustomer action method in Web API service
        _response = await _client.PostAsync("api/customer/updatecustomer/", _bush,
new JsonMediaTypeFormatter());

        if (_response.IsSuccessStatusCode)
        {
            // capture newly created customer entity from service, which will include
            // database-generated Ids for all entities
            _bush = await _response.Content.ReadAsAsync<Customer>();
            _whiteHousePhone = _bush.Phones.FirstOrDefault(x => x.CustomerId == _bush.CustomerId);
            _bushMobilePhone = _bush.Phones.FirstOrDefault(x => x.CustomerId == _bush.CustomerId);

            Console.WriteLine("Successfully created Customer {0} and {1} Phone Numbers(s)",
                _bush.Name, _bush.Phones.Count);
            foreach (var phoneType in _bush.Phones)
            {
                Console.WriteLine("Added Phone Type: {0}", phoneType.PhoneType);
            }
        }
        else
            Console.WriteLine("{0} ({1})", (int) _response.StatusCode, _response.ReasonPhrase);
    }

    private void CreateSecondCustomer()
    {
        // create customer #2 and phone numbers
        _obama = new Customer
        {
            Name = "Barack Obama",
            Company = "President",
            // set tracking state to 'Add' to generate a SQL Insert statement
            TrackingState = TrackingState.Add,
        };
```

```
    _obamaMobilePhone = new Phone
    {
        Number = "212 444-4444",
        PhoneType = "Obama Mobile Phone",
        // set tracking state to 'Add' to generate a SQL Insert statement
        TrackingState = TrackingState.Add,
    };

    // set tracking state to 'Modifed' to generate a SQL Update statement
    _whiteHousePhone.TrackingState = TrackingState.Update;

    _obama.Phones.Add(_obamaMobilePhone);
    _obama.Phones.Add(_whiteHousePhone);
}

private async Task AddSecondCustomerAsync()
{
    // construct call to invoke UpdateCustomer action method in Web API service
    _response = await _client.PostAsync("api/customer/updatecustomer/",
        _obama, new JsonMediaTypeFormatter());

    if (_response.IsSuccessStatusCode)
    {
        // capture newly created customer entity from service, which will include
        // database-generated Ids for all entities
        _obama = await _response.Content.ReadAsAsync<Customer>();
        _whiteHousePhone = _bush.Phones.FirstOrDefault(x => x.CustomerId == _obama.CustomerId);
        _bushMobilePhone = _bush.Phones.FirstOrDefault(x => x.CustomerId == _obama.CustomerId);

        Console.WriteLine("Successfully created Customer {0} and {1} Phone Numbers(s)",
            _obama.Name, _obama.Phones.Count);

        foreach (var phoneType in _obama.Phones)
        {
            Console.WriteLine("Added Phone Type: {0}", phoneType.PhoneType);
        }
    }
    else
        Console.WriteLine("{0} ({1})", (int) _response.StatusCode, _response.ReasonPhrase);
}

private async Task RemoveFirstCustomerAsync()
{
    // remove George Bush from underlying data store.
    // first, fetch George Bush entity, demonstrating a call to the
    // get action method on the service while passing a parameter
    var query = "api/customer/" + _bush.CustomerId;
    _response = _client.GetAsync(query).Result;
```

```
        if (_response.IsSuccessStatusCode)
        {
            _bush = await _response.Content.ReadAsAsync<Customer>();

            // set tracking state to 'Remove' to generate a SQL Delete statement
            _bush.TrackingState = TrackingState.Remove;

            // must also remove bush's mobile number -- must delete child before removing parent
            foreach (var phoneType in _bush.Phones)
            {
                // set tracking state to 'Remove' to generate a SQL Delete statement
                phoneType.TrackingState = TrackingState.Remove;
            }

            // construct call to remove Bush from underlying database table
            _response = await _client.PostAsync("api/customer/updatecustomer/", _bush,
new JsonMediaTypeFormatter());

            if (_response.IsSuccessStatusCode)
            {
                Console.WriteLine("Removed {0} from database", _bush.Name);
                foreach (var phoneType in _bush.Phones)
                {
                    Console.WriteLine("Remove {0} from data store", phoneType.PhoneType);
                }
            }
            else
                Console.WriteLine("{0} ({1})", (int) _response.StatusCode, _response.ReasonPhrase);
        }
        else
        {
            Console.WriteLine("{0} ({1})", (int) _response.StatusCode, _response.ReasonPhrase);
        }
    }

    private async Task FetchCustomersAsync()
    {

        // finally, return remaining customers from underlying data store
        _response = await _client.GetAsync("api/customer/");

        if (_response.IsSuccessStatusCode)
        {
            var customers = await _response.Content.ReadAsAsync<IEnumerable<Customer>>();

            foreach (var customer in customers)
            {
                Console.WriteLine("Customer {0} has {1} Phone Numbers(s)",
                    customer.Name, customer.Phones.Count());
```

```
            foreach (var phoneType in customer.Phones)
            {
                Console.WriteLine("Phone Type: {0}", phoneType.PhoneType);
            }
        }
    }
    else
    {
        Console.WriteLine("{0} ({1})", (int) _response.StatusCode, _response.ReasonPhrase);
    }
  }
}
```

12. Finally, add the same Customer, Phone, BaseEntity, and TrackingState classes that we added to service in Listings 9-19 and 9-20.

Following is the output of our test client from Listing 9-26:

```
Successfully created Customer Geroge Bush and 2 Phone Numbers(s)
Added Phone Type: White House Red Phone
Added Phone Type: Bush Mobile Phone
Successfully created Customer Barrack Obama and 2 Phone Numbers(s)
Added Phone Type: Obama Mobile Phone
Added Phone Type: White House Red Phone
Removed Geroge Bush from database
Remove Bush Mobile Phone from data store
Customer Barrack Obama has 2 Phone Numbers(s)
Phone Type: White House Red Phone
Phone Type: Obama Mobile Phone
```

How It Works

Start by running the Web API application. The Web API application contains an MVC Web Controller that, when started, will bring up a home page. At this point, the site is running and its services are available.

Next open the console application, set a breakpoint on the first line of code in the program.cs file, and run the console application. We first establish some basic plumbing—mapping the Web API service URI and configuring the Accept Header—that will ask the Web API service to return the data in a JSON format.

We then call the Cleanup action method on the Customer Web API controller using the Client.DeleteAsync method exposed by the HttpClient object. This call invokes the Cleanup action method in the service and truncates data from the database tables for any previous operations.

Back in the client, we create a new customer and two phone number objects. Note how we *explicitly* set the TrackingState property for each entity in the client to instruct the Entity Framework Change Tracking Components of the SQL operation required for each entity.

We then invoke the UpdateCustomer action method from the service by making a call to the PostAsync method from the HttpClient object. If you place a breakpoint in the UpdateCustomer Action Method in the Customer Web API controller class, you'll see that it receives the Customer object as a parameter and immediately adds it to the context object. Doing so marks the object graph as added, and it causes the context to start tracking it.

Interestingly, we next hook into the underlying DbChangeTracker, which is exposed as a property of the context object. DbChangeTracker exposes a generic IEnumerable type of <DbEntityEntry> entitled Entries. We simply assign the base EntityType to it. Doing so allows us to enumerate through each of the entities in the context that are of type BaseEntity (the base type from which our entity classes derive in this recipe). For each iteration, we make a call to the EntityStateFactory to translate our internal TrackingState enum value to a valid EntityState value used by Entity Framework to drive change tracking. If the client set the TrackingState to Modified, we do some additional processing. We set the state of the entity (from Modified) to Unchanged and call the GetDatabaseValues method on the Entry object, which returns the current values for the entity from the underlying data store. We then assign these current values to the OriginalValues collection in the Entry object. Under the hood, the Entity Framework change-tracking engine detects any differences between the original and submitted values, and it marks those individual properties as Modified and the entity as Modified. The subsequent SaveChanges operation will then only update those properties that we changed in the client—not all of the properties in the entity.

Back in the client, we demonstrate adding, modifying, and deleting entity objects by setting the TrackingState. The UpdateCustomer method in the service simply translates the TrackingState values to Entity Framework state properties and submits the objects to the change-tracking engine for the correct SQL operation.

In this recipe, we've seen that we can encapsulate Entity Framework data operations behind a Web API service. The client can consume the service by using the HttpClient object that is exposed by the Web API client API. By requiring each entity object to derive from a base entity type, we can expose a *TrackingState* value that the client can set to communicate the needed SQL operation to the Entity Framework change-tracking engine.

In a production application, we would most likely create another layer (Visual Studio class project) to separate the Entity Framework data access code from the Web API service. More importantly, it would not be difficult to take the client-side tracking approach used in this recipe and implement it using generic types. Doing so would allow us to reuse the base functionality across all of our entity types, thus reducing large amounts of redundant code.

9-5. Deleting an Entity When Disconnected
Problem

You have an object that you have retrieved from a WCF service and you want to mark it for deletion.

Solution

Suppose that you have a model like the one shown in Figure 9-5.

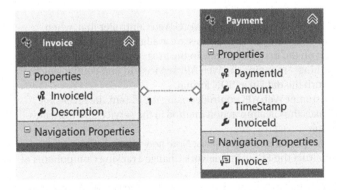

Figure 9-5. *A model for payments on invoices*

Our model represents payments on invoices. In our application, we have implemented a WCF service to handle the database interactions from a client. We want to delete an object, in our case a Payment entity, using the service. To keep the solution as simple as possible, we'll build a WCF service library and define the model inside of it by doing the following:

1. Create a WCF Service Library by right-clicking the solution and selecting Add New Project. Select WCF ➤ WCF Service Library. Name the WCF library Recipe5.

2. Right-click the Recipe5 project, and select Add New Item. Select Data ➤ ADO.NET Entity Data Model. Use the wizard to add a model with the Invoice and Payment tables. For simplicity, we've removed the Payments navigation property on the Invoice entity. (Right-click on the Payments navigation property in the Invoice entity in the Entity Framework designer, and click Delete From Model.) Right-click the TimeStamp property in the Payment entity, select Properties, and set its Concurrency Mode to Fixed. Doing so will engage the TimeStamp property in concurrency control, sending the value as part of the WHERE clauses in all subsequent SQL update and delete operations.

3. In the IService1.cs file, change the service definition as shown in Listing 9-27.

Listing 9-27. *The Service Contract for Our WCF Service*

```
[ServiceContract]
public interface IService1
{
    [OperationContract]
    Payment InsertPayment();

    [OperationContract]
    void DeletePayment(Payment payment);
}
```

4. In the Service1.cs file, implement the service as shown in Listing 9-28.

Listing 9-28. *The Implementation of Our Service Contract*

```
public class Service1 : IService1
{
    public Payment InsertPayment()
    {
        using (var context = new EFRecipesEntities())
        {
            // delete the previous test data
            context.Database.ExecuteSqlCommand("delete from chapter9.payment");
            context.Database.ExecuteSqlCommand("delete from chapter9.invoice");

            var payment = new Payment { Amount = 99.95M, Invoice =
                            new Invoice { Description = "Auto Repair" } };
            context.Payments.Add(payment);
            context.SaveChanges();
            return payment;
        }
    }
}
```

```
        public void DeletePayment(Payment payment)
        {
            using (var context = new EFRecipesEntities())
            {
                context.Entry(payment).State = EntityState.Deleted;
                context.SaveChanges();
            }
        }
    }
```

5. To test our service, we'll need a client. Add a new Windows Console Application project to the solution. Use the code in Listing 9-29 for the client. Add a service reference to the client by right-clicking the client project and selecting Add Service Reference. You may need to right-click the service project and select Debug ➤ Start Instance to start an instance of your service before you can add a service reference in the client.

Listing 9-29. A Simple Console Application to Test Our WCF Service

```
class Program
{
    static void Main()
    {
        var client = new Service1Client();
        var payment = client.InsertPayment();
        client.DeletePayment(payment);
    }
}
```

If you set a breakpoint on the first line in the Main() method of the client and debug the application, you can step through the insertion and deletion of a Payment entity.

How It Works

In this recipe, we demonstrate a common pattern for updating disconnected entities where the client is consuming WCF or Web API services that expose data from Entity Framework.

In the client, we use the InsertPayment() method to insert a new payment into the database. The method returns the payment that was inserted. The payment that is returned to the client is disconnected from the DbContext. In fact, in a situation such as this, the context object may be in a different process space or on an entirely different computer.

We use the DeletePayment() method to delete the Payment entity from the database. In the implementation of this method (see Listing 9-28), we call the Entry() method from the DbContext object passing in an argument of payment. We then set the State property for this entity to EntityState.Deleted, which marks the object for deletion. SaveChanges() deletes the payment from the database.

The payment object that we attached for deletion had all its properties set as they were when the object was inserted into the database. However, because we're using *foreign key association*, only the entity key, concurrency property, and TimeStamp property are needed for Entity Framework to generate the appropriate where clause to delete the entity. The one exception to this rule is when your POCO class has one or more properties that are complex types. Because complex types are considered structural parts of an entity, they cannot be null. To keep things simple, you could simply create a dummy instance of the complex type, as Entity Framework is building its SQL Delete statement from the entity key and concurrency property only. If you leave the complex type property null, SaveChanges() will throw an exception.

If you are using an *independent association* in which the multiplicity of the related entity is one or 0..1, then Entity Framework requires the entity keys of those references to be set correctly in order to generate the appropriate where clause of an update or delete statement. In our example, if we had an independent association between Invoice and Payment, we would need to set the Invoice navigation property to an *instance* of Invoice with the correct value for the InvoiceId property. The resulting where clause would include the PaymentId, TimeStamp, and InvoiceId.

■ **Note**   When implementing an N-Tier architecture with Entity Framework, serious consideration should be given to using the Foreign Key Association approach for related entities. The Independent Association approach is difficult to implement and can make your code quite complex. For a great explanation of these approaches, including their benefits and drawbacks, check out the following blog post from Arthur Vickers, Developer on the Entity Framework Team: **whats-the-deal-with-mapping-foreign-keys-using-the-entity-framework**. Be certain to check out Arthur's other outstanding blog posts on the Entity Framework.

If your entity object contains several independent associations, setting all of them can quickly become tedious. You might find it simpler just to retrieve the instance from the database and mark it for deletion. This makes your code a little simpler, but when you retrieve the object from the database, Entity Framework will rewrite the query to bring in all of the relationships that are one or 0..1, unless, of course, you are using the *NoTracking* context option. If this Recipe were implementing the Independent Association approach, when we load the Payment entity prior to marking for deletion, Entity Framework would create an object state entry for the Payment entity and a relationship entry for the relationship between Payment and Invoice. When we marked the Payment entity for deletion, Entity Framework would also mark the relationship entry for deletion. Like previously, the resulting where clause would include the PaymentId, TimeStamp, and InvoiceId.

Another option for deleting entities in independent associations is to eagerly load the related entities and transport the entire object graph back to the WCF or Web API service for deletion. In this example, we could eagerly load the related Invoice entity with the Payment entity. If we were to delete the Payment entity, we could send back the graph containing both entities to the service. But, be forewarned that this approach consumes more network bandwidth and processing time for serialization, so the cost may outweigh the benefit of more clarity in the code.

9-6. Managing Concurrency When Disconnected
Problem

You want to make sure that changes made on an entity by a WCF client are applied only if the concurrency token has not changed.

Solution

Let's suppose that you have a model like the one shown in Figure 9-6.

Figure 9-6. *Our model with a single Order entity*

We want to update an order using a WCF service while guaranteeing that the order we're updating has not changed since the last time we retrieved the order. We'll show two slightly different ways to handle this. In both approaches, we use a concurrency column, in our case, the TimeStamp column.

1. Create a WCF Service Library by right-clicking the solution and selecting Add New Project. Select WCF ➤ WCF Service Library. Name the project `Recipe6`.

2. Right-click the project, and select Add New Item. Select Data ➤ ADO.NET Entity Data Model. Use the wizard to add a model with the Order table. In the Entity Framework designer, right-click the TimeStamp property, select Properties, and set its Concurrency Mode to Fixed.

3. In the `IService1.cs` file, change the service definition as shown in Listing 9-30.

Listing 9-30. Our WCF Service Contract

```
[ServiceContract]
public interface IService1
{
    [OperationContract]
    Order InsertOrder();

    [OperationContract]
    void UpdateOrderWithoutRetrieving(Order order);

    [OperationContract]
    void UpdateOrderByRetrieving(Order order);
}
```

4. In the `Service1.cs` file, implement the service as shown in Listing 9-31.

Listing 9-31. The Implementation of Our Service Contract

```
public class Service1 : IService1
{
    public Order InsertOrder()
    {
        using (var context = new EFRecipesEntities())
        {
            // remove previous test data
            context.Database.ExecuteSqlCommand("delete from chapter9.[order]");
```

```
            var order = new Order { Product = "Camping Tent",
                           Quantity = 3, Status = "Received" };
            context.Orders.Add(order);
            context.SaveChanges();
            return order;
        }
    }

    public void UpdateOrderWithoutRetrieving(Order order)
    {
        using (var context = new EFRecipesEntities())
        {
            try
            {
                context.Orders.Attach(order);
                if (order.Status == "Received")
                {
                    context.Entry(order).Property(x => x.Quantity).IsModified = true;
                    context.SaveChanges();
                }
            }
            catch (OptimisticConcurrencyException ex)
            {
                // Handle OptimisticConcurrencyException

            }
        }
    }

    public void UpdateOrderByRetrieving(Order order)
    {
        using (var context = new EFRecipesEntities())
        {
            // fetch current entity from database
            var dbOrder = context.Orders
                        .Single(o => o.OrderId == order.OrderId);
            if (dbOrder != null &&
                // execute concurrency check
              StructuralComparisons.StructuralEqualityComparer.Equals(order.TimeStamp, dbOrder.TimeStamp))
            {
                dbOrder.Quantity = order.Quantity;
                context.SaveChanges();
            }
      else
      {
        // Add code to handle concurrency issue
      }
        }
    }
}
```

5. To test our service, we'll need a client. Add a new Windows Console Application project to the solution. Use the code in Listing 9-32 for the client. Add a service reference to the client by right-clicking the client project and selecting Add Service Reference. You may need to right-click the service project and select Debug ➤ Start Instance to start an instance of your service before you can add a service reference in the client.

Listing 9-32. The Client We Use to Test Our WCF Service

```
class Program
{
    static void Main(string[] args)
    {
        var service = new Service1Client();
        var order = service.InsertOrder();
        order.Quantity = 5;
        service.UpdateOrderWithoutRetrieving(order);
        order = service.InsertOrder();
        order.Quantity = 3;
        service.UpdateOrderByRetrieving(order);
    }
}
```

If you set a breakpoint on the first line in the Main() method of the client and debug the application, you can step through inserting the order and updating the order using both methods.

How It Works

Our InsertOrder() method (see Listing 9-31) deletes any previous test data, inserts a new order, and returns the order. The order returned has both the database generated OrderId and TimeStamp properties. In our client, we use two slightly different approaches to update this order.

In the first approach, UpdateOrderWithoutRetrieving(), we Attach() the order from the client and check whether the order status is Received, and, if it is, we mark the entity's Quantity property as modified and call SaveChanges(). Entity Framework will generate an update statement setting the new quantity with a where clause that includes both the OrderId and the TimeStamp values from the Order entity. If the TimeStamp value has changed by some intermediate update to the database, this update will fail. To capture and handle such a concurrency exception, we wrap the operation with Try/Catch construct, trap for an OptimisticConcurrencyException, and handle the exception. This ensures that the Order entity we are updating has not been modified between the time we obtained it from the InsertOrder() method and the time we updated it in the database. Note in the example how all entity properties are updated, whether they have changed or not.

Alternately, you could explicitly check the concurrency of an entity before performing an update. Here you could retrieve the target entity from the database and manually compare the TimeStamp properties to determine whether an intervening change has occurred. This approach is illustrated in Listing 9-31 with a fresh order by calling the UpdateOrderByRetrieving() method. Although not foolproof (the order could be changed by another client between the time you retrieve the order from the database, compare TimeStamp values, and call SaveChanges()), this approach does provide valuable insight into what properties or associations have changed on an entity. Although not efficient as the first approach, this method might be useful if the object graph or entities are large or complex.

9-7. Serializing Proxies in a WCF Service

Problem

You have a dynamic proxy object returned from a query. You want to serialize the proxy as a plain old CLR object. When Implementing POCO-based entity objects (Plain-Old CLR Objects), Entity Framework automatically generates a dynamically generated derived type at runtime, known as a *dynamic proxy* object, for each POCO entity object. The proxy object overrides many of the virtual properties of the POCO class to inject hooks for performing actions such as change tracking and the lazy loading of related entities.

Solution

Let's suppose that you have a model like the one shown in Figure 9-7.

Figure 9-7. *A model with a Client entity*

We'll use the *ProxyDataContractResolver class* to deserialize a proxy object on the server to a POCO object on the WCF client. Do the following:

1. Create a new WCF Service Application. Add an ADO.NET Entity Data Model with the Client table. The model should look like the one shown in Figure 9-7.

2. Open the Client POCO class that Entity Framework generated, and add the virtual keyword to each property, as shown in Listing 9-33. Doing so will cause Entity Framework to generate dynamic proxy classes.

■ **Note** Keep in mind that if you make any changes to the EDMX file, Entity Framework will automatically regenerate your underlying classes and overwrite your changes from Step #2. You could repeat your changes or even consider modifying the underlying T4 template that generates the entity code.

Listing 9-33. Our Client POCO Class and Our Object Vontext

```
public class Client
{
    public virtual int ClientId { get; set; }
    public virtual string Name { get; set; }
    public virtual string Email { get; set; }
}
```

3. We need the DataContractSerializer to use a ProxyDataContractResolver class to transform the client proxy to the client entity for the WCF service's client. For this, we'll create an operation behavior attribute and apply the attribute on the GetClient() service method. Add the code in Listing 9-34 to create the new attribute. Keep in mind that the ProxyDataContractResolver class resides in the Entity Framework namespace.

Listing 9-34. Our Custom Operation Behavior Attribute

```
using System.ServiceModel.Description;
using System.ServiceModel.Channels;
using System.ServiceModel.Dispatcher;
using System.Data.Objects;

namespace Recipe8
{
    public class ApplyProxyDataContractResolverAttribute : Attribute,
                IOperationBehavior
    {
        public void AddBindingParameters(OperationDescription description,
                                            BindingParameterCollection parameters)
        {
        }

        public void ApplyClientBehavior(OperationDescription description,
                                            ClientOperation proxy)
        {
            DataContractSerializerOperationBehavior
                dataContractSerializerOperationBehavior =
                    description.Behaviors
                     .Find<DataContractSerializerOperationBehavior>();
            dataContractSerializerOperationBehavior.DataContractResolver =
                    new ProxyDataContractResolver();
        }

        public void ApplyDispatchBehavior(OperationDescription description,
                DispatchOperation dispatch)
        {
            DataContractSerializerOperationBehavior
                dataContractSerializerOperationBehavior =
                    description.Behaviors
                     .Find<DataContractSerializerOperationBehavior>();
            dataContractSerializerOperationBehavior.DataContractResolver =
                    new ProxyDataContractResolver();
        }

        public void Validate(OperationDescription description)
        {
        }
    }
}
```

4. Change the IService1.cs interface using the code in Listing 9-35.

    Listing 9-35. *Our IService1 Interface Definition, Which Replaces the Code in IService1.cs*

    ```
    [ServiceContract]
    public interface IService1
    {
        [OperationContract]
        void InsertTestRecord();

        [OperationContract]
        Client GetClient();

        [OperationContract]
        void Update(Client client);
    }
    ```

5. Change the implementation of the IService1 interface in the IService1.svc.cs file with the
    code shown in Listing 9-36.

    Listing 9-36. *The Implementation of the IService1 Interface, Which Replaces the Code in IService1.svc.cs*

    ```
    public class Client
    {
        [ApplyProxyDataContractResolver]
        public Client GetClient()
        {
            using (var context = new EFRecipesEntities())
            {
                context.Cofiguration.LazyLoadingEnabled = false;
                return context.Clients.Single();
            }
        }

        public void Update(Client client)
        {
            using (var context = new EFRecipesEntities())
            {
                context.Entry(client).State =
                        EntityState.Modified;
                context.SaveChanges();
            }
        }

        public void InsertTestRecord()
        {
            using (var context = new EFRecipesEntities())
            {
                // delete previous test data
                context.ExecuteSqlCommand("delete from chapter9.client");
    ```

```
                    // insert new test data
                    context.ExecuteStoreCommand(@"insert into
                            chapter9.client(Name, Email)
                            values ('Jerry Jones','jjones@gmail.com')");
                }
            }
        }
```

6. Add a Windows Console Application to the solution. This will be our test client. Use the
    code shown in Listing 9-37 to implement our test client. Add a service reference to our
    WCF service.

    Listing 9-37. Our Windows console application test client

```
using Recipe8Client.ServiceReference1;

namespace Recipe8Client
{
    class Program
    {
        static void Main(string[] args)
        {
            using (var serviceClient = new Service1Client())
            {
                serviceClient.InsertTestRecord();
                var client = serviceClient.GetClient();
                Console.WriteLine("Client is: {0} at {1}",
                                    client.Name, client.Email);
                client.Name = "Alex Park";
                client.Email = "AlexP@hotmail.com";
                serviceClient.Update(client);
                client = serviceClient.GetClient();
                Console.WriteLine("Client changed to: {0} at {1}",
                                    client.Name, client.Email);
            }
        }
    }
}
```

Following is the output of our test client:

```
Client is: Jerry Jones at jjones@gmail.com
Client changed to: Alex Park at AlexP@hotmail.com
```

How It Works

Microsoft recommends using POCO objects with WCF to simplify serialization of the entity object. However, if your
application is using POCO objects with *changed-based notification* (you have marked properties as virtual and
navigation property collections are of type ICollection), then Entity Framework will create *dynamic proxies* for entities
returned from queries.

There are two problems with dynamic proxies and WCF. The first problem has to do with the serialization of the proxy. The DataContractSerializer can only serialize and deserialize known types, such as the Client entity in our example. However, as Entity Framework generates a dynamic proxy class for the Client entity, we need to serialize the proxy class, not the Client. Here is where DataContractResolver comes to the rescue. It can map one type to another during serialization. ProxyDataContractResolver derives from DataContractResolver and maps proxy types to POCO classes, such as our Client entity. To use the ProxyDataContractResolver, we created an attribute (see Listing 9-34) to resolve proxies into POCO classes. We applied this attribute to the `GetClient()` method in Listing 9-36. This causes the dynamic proxy for the Client entity returned by the `GetClient()` to be correctly serialized for its journey to the user of the WCF service.

The second problem with dynamic proxies and WCF has to do with lazy loading. When the DataContractSerializer serializes the entity, it accesses each of the properties of the entity that would trigger lazy loading of navigation properties. This, of course, is not what we want. To prevent this, we explicitly turned off lazy loading in Listing 9-36.

CHAPTER 10

Stored Procedures

Stored procedures are fixtures in the life of just about anyone who uses modern relational database systems such as Microsoft's SQL Server. A *stored procedure* is a bit of code that lives on the database server and often acts as an abstraction layer isolating the code consuming the data from many of the details of the physical organization of the data. Stored procedures can increase performance by moving data-intensive computations closer to the data, and they can act as a data-side repository for business and security logic. The bottom line is that if you use data, you will consume it at some point through a stored procedure.

In this chapter, we explore a number of recipes specifically focused on using stored procedures with Entity Framework. We used stored procedures in other recipes throughout this book, but usually they were in the context of implementing Insert, Update, and Delete actions. In this chapter, we'll show you several ways to consume the data exposed by stored procedures.

10-1. Returning an Entity Collection with Code Second

Problem

You want to get an entity collection from a stored procedure using a code-second approach.

Solution

Code second refers to the practice of applying Code-First techniques to model an existing database schema.

Let's say that you have a POCO model like the one shown in Listing 10-1.

Listing 10-1. The Customer POCO Model

```
public class Customer
{
    public int CustomerId { get; set; }
    public string Name { get; set; }
    public string Company { get; set; }
    public string ContactTitle { get; set; }
}
```

We've set up our DbContext subclass and have configured our Customer entities in Listing 10-2.

Listing 10-2. The DbContext Subclass for Customer Entities

```
public class EF6RecipesContext : DbContext
{
    public DbSet<Customer> Customers { get; set; }

    public EF6RecipesContext() : base("name=EF6CodeFirstRecipesContext")
    {

    }

    protected override void OnModelCreating(DbModelBuilder modelBuilder)
    {
        base.OnModelCreating(modelBuilder);

        modelBuilder.Types<Customer>()
                    .Configure(c =>
                    {
                        c.HasKey(cust => cust.CustomerId);

                        c.Property(cust => cust.CustomerId)
.HasDatabaseGeneratedOption(DatabaseGeneratedOption.Identity);

                        c.Property(cust => cust.Name)
                         .HasMaxLength(50);

                        c.Property(cust => cust.Company)
                         .HasMaxLength(50);

                        c.Property(cust => cust.ContactTitle)
                         .HasMaxLength(50);

                        c.ToTable("Customer", "Chapter10");
                    });
    }
}
```

In the database, we have defined the stored procedure in Listing 10-3, which returns customers for given a company name and customer title.

Listing 10-3. GetCustomers Returns All of the Customers with the Given Title in the Given Company.

```
create procedure Chapter10.GetCustomers
(@Company varchar(50),@ContactTitle varchar(50))
as
begin
select * from
chapter10.Customer where
(@Company is null or Company = @Company) and
(@ContactTitle is null or ContactTitle = @ContactTitle)
End
```

To use the GetCustomers stored procedure in the model, do the following.

1. Create a new public method called GetCustomers in the DbContext subclass that takes two string parameters and returns a collection of Customer objects, as shown in Listing 10-4.

Listing 10-4. A New Method to Return a Collection of Customer Objects

```
public ICollection<Customer> GetCustomers(string company, string contactTitle)
{
    throw new NotImplementedException();
}
```

2. Implement the GetCustomers() method by calling SqlQuery on the DbContext.Database object (see Listing 10-5).

Listing 10-5. DbContext Subclass with GetCustomers() Implementation

```
public class EF6RecipesContext : DbContext
{
    public DbSet<Customer> Customers { get; set; }

    public EF6RecipesContext() : base("name=EF6CodeFirstRecipesContext")
    {

    }

    protected override void OnModelCreating(DbModelBuilder modelBuilder)
    {
        base.OnModelCreating(modelBuilder);

        modelBuilder.Types<Customer>()
                .Configure(c =>
                    {
                        c.HasKey(cust => cust.CustomerId);

                        c.Property(cust => cust.CustomerId)
                         .HasDatabaseGeneratedOption(DatabaseGeneratedOption.Identity);

                        c.Property(cust => cust.Name)
                         .HasMaxLength(50);

                        c.Property(cust => cust.Company)
                         .HasMaxLength(50);

                        c.Property(cust => cust.ContactTitle)
                         .HasMaxLength(50);

                        c.ToTable("Customer", "Chapter10");
                    });
    }
}
```

```
        public ICollection<Customer> GetCustomers(string company, string contactTitle)
        {
            return Database.SqlQuery<Customer>("EXEC Chapter10.GetCustomers @Company,
                                                            @ContactTitle"
                              , new SqlParameter("Company", company)
                              , new SqlParameter("ContactTitle", contactTitle))
                              .ToList();
        }
    }
```

3. Follow the pattern in Listing 10-6 to use the GetCustomers stored procedure.

    Listing 10-6. Querying the Model with the GetCustomers Stored Procedure via the GetCustomers()
    Method

```
//Add customers to the database that we will query with our stored procedure.
using (var context = new EF6RecipesContext())
{
    var c1 = new Customer {Name = "Robin Steele", Company = "GoShopNow.com",
                        ContactTitle="CEO"};
    var c2 = new Customer {Name = "Orin Torrey", Company = "GoShopNow.com",
                        ContactTitle="Sales Manager"};
    var c3 = new Customer {Name = "Robert Lancaster", Company = "GoShopNow.com",
                        ContactTitle = "Sales Manager"};
    var c4 = new Customer { Name = "Julie Stevens", Company = "GoShopNow.com",
                        ContactTitle = "Sales Manager" };
    context.Customers.Add(c1);
    context.Customers.Add(c2);
    context.Customers.Add(c3);
    context.Customers.Add(c4);
    context.SaveChanges();
}

using (var context = new EF6RecipesContext())
{
    var allCustomers = context.GetCustomers("GoShopNow.com", "Sales Manager");
    Console.WriteLine("Customers that are Sales Managers at GoShopNow.com");
    foreach (var c in allCustomers)
    {
        Console.WriteLine("Customer: {0}", c.Name);
    }
}
```

The following is the output of the code in Listing 10-6:

```
Customers that are Sales Managers at GoShopNow.com
Customer: Orin Torrey
Customer: Robert Lancaster
Customer: Julie Stevens
```

How It Works

To retrieve an entity collection from a stored procedure in the database, we implemented a new method in the DbContext subclass called GetCustomers(). Within the method implementation, we call DbContext.Database.SqlQuery<T>() to execute the GetCustomers stored procedure, which we defined in Listing 10-3.

The SqlQuery() method can be used to execute nearly any DML statement that returns a result set. The method takes a string parameter to specify the query to execute, as well as additional SQL parameters to be substituted in the query itself. The SqlQuery<T>() generic method will return a strongly-typed collection of *T* entities, which allows the developer to avoid enumerating and casting a collection of objects.

10-2. Returning Output Parameters
Problem

You want to retrieve values from one or more output parameters of a stored procedure.

Solution

Let's say you have a model like the one shown in Figure 10-1.

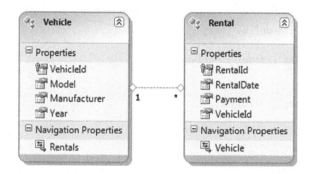

Figure 10-1. *A simple model for vehicle rental*

For a given date, you want to know the total number of rentals, the total rental payments made, and the vehicles rented. The stored procedure in Listing 10-7 is one way to get the information you want.

Listing 10-7. A Stored Procedure for the Vehicles Rented, the Number of Rentals, and the Total Rental Payments

```
create procedure [chapter10].[GetVehiclesWithRentals]
(@date date,
@TotalRentals int output,
@TotalPayments decimal(18,2) output)
as
begin
  select @TotalRentals = COUNT(*), @TotalPayments = SUM(payment)
  from chapter10.Rental
  where RentalDate = @date
```

```
  select distinct v.*
  from chapter10.Vehicle v join chapter10.Rental r
  on v.VehicleId = r.VehicleId
end
```

To use the stored procedure in Listing 10-7 in the model, do the following.

1. Right-click the design surface, and select Update Model From Database. In the dialog box, select the GetVehiclesWithRentals stored procedure. Click Finish to add the stored procedure to the model.

2. Right-click the design surface, and select Add ➤ Function Import. Select the GetVehiclesWithRentals stored procedure from the Stored Procedure Name drop-down. In the Function Import Name text box, enter GetVehiclesWithRentals. This will be the name used for the method in the model. Select the Entities Return Type, and select Vehicle in the drop-down. Click OK.

3. Follow the pattern in Listing 10-8 to use the GetVehiclesWithRentals stored procedure.

Listing 10-8. Querying the Model Using the GetVehiclesWithRentals Stored Procedure via the GetVehiclesWithRentals() method

```
using (var context = new EF6RecipesContext())
{
    var car1 = new Vehicle { Manufacturer = "Toyota", Model = "Camry",
                                Year = 2013 };
    var car2 = new Vehicle { Manufacturer = "Chevrolet", Model = "Corvette",
                                Year = 2013 };
    var r1 = new Rental { Vehicle = car1,
                            RentalDate = DateTime.Parse("5/7/2013"),
                            Payment = 59.95M };
    var r2 = new Rental { Vehicle = car2,
                            RentalDate = DateTime.Parse("5/7/2013"),
                            Payment = 139.95M };
    context.AddToRentals(r1);
    context.AddToRentals(r2);
    context.SaveChanges();
}

using (var context = new EF6RecipesContext())
{
    string reportDate = "5/7/2013";
    var totalRentals = new ObjectParameter("TotalRentals", typeof(int));
    var totalPayments = new ObjectParameter("TotalPayments", typeof(decimal));
    var vehicles = context.GetVehiclesWithRentals(DateTime.Parse(reportDate),
                        totalRentals, totalPayments);
    Console.WriteLine("Rental Activity for {0}",reportDate);
    Console.WriteLine("Vehicles Rented");
    foreach(var vehicle in vehicles)
    {
        Console.WriteLine("{0} {1} {2}",vehicle.Year.ToString(),
                            vehicle.Manufacturer, vehicle.Model);
    }
}
```

```
Console.WriteLine("Total Rentals: {0}",
                    ((int)totalRentals.Value).ToString());
Console.WriteLine("Total Payments: {0}",
                    ((decimal)totalPayments.Value).ToString("C"));
}
```

The following is the output of the code in Listing 10-8:

```
Rental Activity for 5/7/2013
Vehicles Rented
2013 Toyota Camry
2013 Chevrolet Corvette
Total Rentals: 2
Total Payments: $200.00
```

How It Works

When we updated the model with the GetVehiclesWithRentals stored procedure, the wizard updated the store model with the stored procedure. By importing the function (in Step 2), we updated the conceptual model. The result is that the stored procedure is exposed as the GetVehiclesWithRentals() method, which has a signature semantically similar to the stored procedure.

There is one important thing to note when calling the GetVehiclesWithRentals() method: the returned entity collection must be materialized before the output parameters will become available. This should not be too surprising to those who have used multiple result sets in ADO.NET. The data reader must be advanced (with the NextResult() method) to the next result set. Similarly, the entire returned entity collection must be accessed or disposed before the output parameters can be accessed.

In our example, it is not enough to materialize the first vehicle for the output parameters to become available. The entire collection must be materialized. This means moving the lines that print the total rentals and total payments to a position after the foreach loop. Alternatively, we could materialize the entire collection with the ToList() method and then iterate through the list. This would allow us to access the output parameters prior to iterating through the collection.

10-3. Returning a Scalar Value Result Set

Problem

You want to use a stored procedure that returns a result set containing a single scalar value.

Solution

Let's say you have a model like the one shown in Figure 10-2.

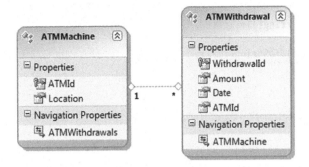

Figure 10-2. *A model representing ATM machines and withdrawal transactions*

You want to use a stored procedure that returns the total amount withdrawn from a given ATM on a given date. The code in Listing 10-9 is one way to implement this stored procedure.

Listing 10-9. The GetWithdrawals Stored Procedure That Returns the Total Amount Withdrawn from a Given ATM on a Given Date

```
create procedure [Chapter10].[GetWithdrawals]
(@ATMId int, @WithdrawalDate date)
as
begin
        select SUM(amount) TotalWithdrawals
        from Chapter10.ATMWithdrawal
        where ATMId = @ATMId and [date] = @WithdrawalDate
end
```

To use the stored procedure in Listing 10-9 in the model, do the following:

1. Right-click the design surface, and select Update Model From Database. In the dialog box, select the GetWithdrawals stored procedure. Click Finish to add the stored procedure to the model.

2. Right-click the design surface, and select Add ➤ Function Import. Select the GetWithdrawals stored procedure from the Stored Procedure Name drop-down. In the Function Import Name text box, enter GetWithdrawals. This will be the name used for the method in the model. Select the Scalars Return Type, and select Decimal in the drop-down. Click OK.

3. Follow the pattern in Listing 10-10 to use the GetWithdrawals stored procedure.

    Listing 10-10. Querying the Model with the GetWithdrawals Stored Procedure via the GetWithdrawals() Method

    ```
    DateTime today = DateTime.Parse("5/7/2013");
    DateTime yesterday = DateTime.Parse("5/6/2013");
    using (var context = new EF6RecipesContext())
    {
        var atm = new ATMMachine { ATMId = 17, Location = "12th and Main" };
        atm.ATMWithdrawals.Add(new ATMWithdrawal {Amount = 20.00M, Date= today});
        atm.ATMWithdrawals.Add(new ATMWithdrawal {Amount = 100.00M, Date = today});
    ```

```
            atm.ATMWithdrawals.Add(new ATMWithdrawal {Amount = 75.00M, Date = yesterday});
            atm.ATMWithdrawals.Add(new ATMWithdrawal {Amount = 50.00M, Date=  today});
            context.ATMMachines.Add(atm);
            context.SaveChanges();
        }

        using (var context = new EF6RecipesContext())
        {
            var forToday = context.GetWithdrawals(17, today).FirstOrDefault();
            var forYesterday = context.GetWithdrawals(17, yesterday).FirstOrDefault();
            var atm = context.ATMMachines.Where(o => o.ATMId == 17).FirstOrDefault();
            Console.WriteLine("ATM Withdrawals for ATM at {0} at {1}",
                    atm.ATMId.ToString(), atm.Location);
            Console.WriteLine("\t{0} Total Withdrawn = {1}",
                    yesterday.ToShortDateString(), forYesterday.Value.ToString("C"));
            Console.WriteLine("\t{0} Total Withdrawn = {1}", today.ToShortDateString(),
                    forToday.Value.ToString("C"));
        }
```

The following is the output from the code in Listing 10-10:

```
ATM Withdrawals for ATM at 17 at 12th and Main
        5/6/2013 Total Withdrawn = $75.00
        5/7/2013 Total Withdrawn = $170.00
```

How It Works

Notice that Entity Framework expects the stored procedure to return a collection of scalar values. In our example, our store procedure returns just one decimal value. We use the `FirstOrDefault()` method to extract this scalar from the collection.

10-4. Returning a Complex Type from a Stored Procedure

Problem

You want to use a stored procedure that returns a complex type in the model.

Solution

Let's say that you have a model with an Employee entity. Employee contains the employee's ID, name, and a complex address type that holds the address, city, state, and ZIP code for the employee. The name of the complex type is EmployeeAddress. The property in the Employee entity is simply Address. The Employee entity is shown in Figure 10-3.

Figure 10-3. *An Employee entity with an Address property of type EmployeeAddress, which is a complex type*

You want to use a stored procedure to return a collection of instances of the EmployeeAddress complex type. The stored procedure that returns the addresses might look like the one shown in Listing 10-11.

Listing 10-11. A Stored Procedure to Return the Addresses for Employees in a Given City

```
create procedure [Chapter10].[GetEmployeeAddresses]
(@city varchar(50))
as
begin
        select [address], city, [state], ZIP
        from Chapter10.Employee where city = @city
end
```

To use the stored procedure in Listing 10-11 in the model, do the following.

1. Right-click the design surface, and select Update Model From Database. In the dialog box, select the GetEmployeeAddresses stored procedure. Click Finish to add the stored procedure to the model.

2. Right-click the design surface, and select Add ➤ Function Import. Select the GetEmployeeAddresses stored procedure from the Stored Procedure Name drop-down. In the Function Import Name text box, enter GetEmployeeAddresses. This will be the name used for the method in the model. Select the Complex Return Type, and select EmployeeAddress in the drop-down. Click OK.

3. Follow the pattern in Listing 10-12 to use the GetEmployeeAddresses stored procedure.

Listing 10-12. Querying the Model Using the GetEmployeeAddresses Stored Procedure via the GetEmployeeAddresses() Method

```
using (var context = new EF6RecipesContext())
{
    var emp1 = new Employee { Name = "Lisa Jefferies",
                    Address = new EmployeeAddress {
                                Address = "100 E. Main",
                                City = "Fort Worth", State = "TX",
                                ZIP = "76106" } };
    var emp2 = new Employee { Name = "Robert Jones",
```

```
                       Address = new EmployeeAddress {
                                   Address = "3920 South Beach",
                                   City = "Fort Worth", State = "TX",
                                   ZIP = "76102" } };
      var emp3 = new Employee { Name = "Steven Chue",
                     Address = new EmployeeAddress {
                                 Address = "129 Barker",
                                 City = "Euless", State = "TX",
                                 ZIP = "76092" } };
      var emp4 = new Employee { Name = "Karen Stevens",
                     Address = new EmployeeAddress {
                                 Address = "108 W. Parker",
                                 City = "Fort Worth", State = "TX",
                                 ZIP = "76102" } };
      context.Employees.Add(emp1);
      context.Employees.Add(emp2);
      context.Employees.Add(emp3);
      context.Employees.Add(emp4);
      context.SaveChanges();
}

using (var context = new EF6RecipesContext())
{
    Console.WriteLine("Employee addresses in Fort Worth, TX");
    foreach (var address in context.GetEmployeeAddresses("Fort Worth"))
    {
        Console.WriteLine("{0}, {1}, {2}, {3}", address.Address,
                         address.City, address.State, address.ZIP);
    }
}
```

The following is the output of the code in Listing 10-12:

```
Employee addresses in Fort Worth, TX
100 E. Main, Fort Worth, TX, 76106
3920 South Beach, Fort Worth, TX, 76102
108 W. Parker, Fort Worth, TX, 76102
```

How It Works

Complex types offer a convenient way to refactor repeated groups of properties into a single type that can be reused across many entities. In this recipe, we created a stored procedure that returned the address information for employees in a given city. In the model, we mapped these returned columns to the fields of the EmployeeAddress complex type. The GetEmployeeAdresses() method is defined by the Function Import Wizard to return a collection of instances of the EmployeeAddress type.

Complex types are often used to hold arbitrarily shaped data returned from a stored procedure. The data is not required to map to any entity in the model. Because complex types are not tracked by the object context, they are both a lightweight and efficient alternative to handling shaped data in the model.

10-5. Defining a Custom Function in the Storage Model

Problem

You want to define a custom function inside the model rather than a stored procedure in the database.

Solution

Let's say that you have a database that keeps track of members and the messages they have sent. Figure 10-4 shows one representation of this database.

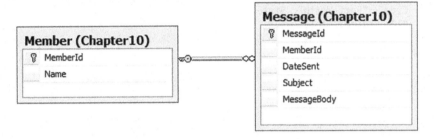

Figure 10-4. *A simple database of members and their messages*

It may be the case that, as an entry-level programmer, you have not been granted access to the database to create stored procedures. However, being wise and productive, you want to encapsulate the query logic for finding the members with the highest number of messages into a reusable custom function in the storage model procedure. The model looks like the one shown in Figure 10-5.

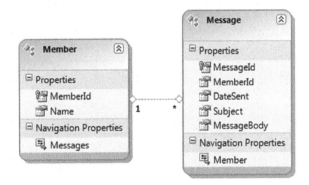

Figure 10-5. *The model for members and their messages*

To define the custom function in the storage model, do the following:

1. Right-click the .edmx file, and select Open With ➤ XML (Text) Editor. This will open the .edmx file in the XML editor.

   Add the code in Listing 10-13 into the <Schema> element. This defines the custom function.

Listing 10-13. The Definition of the Custom Function MembersWithTheMostMessages

```
<Function Name="MembersWithTheMostMessages" IsComposable="false">
  <CommandText>
    select m.*
    from chapter10.member m
    join
    (
    select msg.MemberId, count(msg.MessageId) as MessageCount
    from chapter10.message msg where datesent = @datesent
    group by msg.MemberId
    ) temp on m.MemberId = temp.MemberId
    order by temp.MessageCount desc
  </CommandText>
  <Parameter Name="datesent" Type="datetime" />
</Function>
```

2. Open the .edmx file in the Designer. Right-click the design surface, and select Add ➤ Function Import. In the dialog box, select the MembersWithTheMostMessages in the Stored Procedure Name drop-down. Enter MembersWithTheMostMessages in the Function Import Name text box. Finally, select Entities as the return type and choose Member as the entity type. Click OK.

3. Follow the pattern in Listing 10-14 to use the MembersWithTheMostMessages() method, which exposes the MembersWithTheMostMessages custom function.

Listing 10-14. Using the MembersWithTheMostMessages Function via the MembersWithTheMostMessages() method

```
DateTime today = DateTime.Parse("5/7/2013");
using (var context = new EF6RecipesContext())
{
    var mem1 = new Member { Name = "Jill Robertson" };
    var mem2 = new Member { Name = "Steven Rhodes" };
    mem1.Messages.Add(new Message { DateSent = today,
                                    MessageBody = "Hello Jim",
                                    Subject = "Hello" });
    mem1.Messages.Add(new Message { DateSent = today,
                                    MessageBody = "Wonderful weather!",
                                    Subject = "Weather" });
    mem1.Messages.Add(new Message { DateSent = today,
                                    MessageBody = "Meet me for lunch",
                                    Subject = "Lunch plans" });
    mem2.Messages.Add(new Message { DateSent = today,
                                    MessageBody = "Going to class today?",
                                    Subject = "What's up?" });
    context.Members.Add(mem1);
    context.Members.Add(mem2);
    context.SaveChanges();
}
```

```
using (var context = new EF6RecipesContext())
{
    Console.WriteLine("Members by message count for {0}",
                      today.ToShortDateString());
    var members = context.MembersWithTheMostMessages(today);
    foreach (var member in members)
    {
        Console.WriteLine("Member: {0}", member.Name);
    }
}
```

Following is the output of the code in Listing 10-14:

```
Members by message count for 5/7/2013
Member: Jill Robertson
Member: Steven Rhodes
```

How It Works

A custom function is different from a model-defined function (see Chapter 11) in that a *custom function* is defined in the storage model. This makes the custom function much more like a traditional stored procedure in a database. Just like a DefiningQuery in the storage model defines a "virtual" table that doesn't really exist in the database, a custom function in the storage model is like a "virtual" stored procedure. Some in the Entity Framework community refer to custom functions as *native functions*. The Microsoft documentation uses the term "custom function," so we'll go with that.

The code in Listing 10-13 defines our custom function. We put this in the storage model section of the .edmx file by directly editing the file using the XML editor. Note that if you use the Update From Database Wizard to update the model with new objects from your database, the wizard will overwrite this section. So be careful to save out any changes that you've made to the storage model before you use the Update From Database Wizard.

Just like with the stored procedures in the previous recipes, we used the Function Import Wizard to map the custom function to a CLR method. This defines the name of the CLR method and the expected return type. In our case, the Custom Function returns a collection of instances of the Member entity.

In Listing 10-14, the code uses the MembersWithTheMostMessages() method to invoke the custom function. This is the same pattern we used with stored procedures.

Custom functions can be helpful in the following scenarios:

- You don't have permissions to create the stored procedures you need in the database.

- You want to manage deployments of the code and the database separately. Using one or more custom functions, you can deploy your code without deploying new stored procedures for the database.

- The existing stored procedures in the database have parameters that are incompatible with your entities. Using custom functions, you can create an abstraction layer that drops, adds, or changes types between the stored procedure parameters and the properties on your entity.

10-6. Populating Entities in a Table per Type Inheritance Model

Problem

You want to use a stored procedure to populate entities in a Table per Type inheritance model.

Solution

Let's say the model looks like the one shown in Figure 10-6. In this model, the entities Magazine and DVD extend the base entity Media. In the underlying database, we have a table for each of these entities. We have modeled these tables using Table per Type inheritance. We want to use a stored procedure to obtain the data for this model from the database.

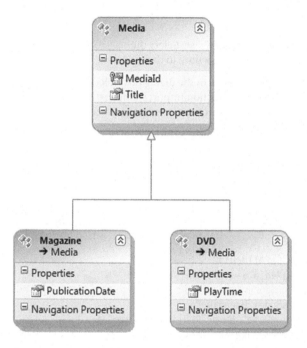

Figure 10-6. *A model using Table per Type inheritance. The model represents some information about magazines and DVDs*

■ **Tip**   Need to brush up on Table per Type modeling and its performance implications? Check out Recipe 2-8 in Chapter 2.

To create and use a stored procedure that returns these entities, do the following.

1. In your database, create the stored procedure in Listing 10-15.

    Listing 10-15. The GetAllMedia Stored Procedure That Returns a Rowset with a Discriminator Column

    ```
    create procedure [Chapter10].[GetAllMedia]
    as
    begin
    select m.MediaId,c.Title,m.PublicationDate, null PlayTime,'Magazine' MediaType
    from chapter10.Media c join chapter10.Magazine m on c.MediaId = m.MediaId
    union
    select d.MediaId,c.Title,null,d.PlayTime,'DVD'
    from chapter10.Media c join chapter10.DVD d on c.MediaId = d.MediaId
    end
    ```

2. Right-click the design surface, and select Update Model from Database. Select the GetAllMedia stored procedure. Click Finish to add the stored procedure to the model.

3. Right-click the design surface, and select Add ➤ Function Import. In the dialog box, select the GetAllMedia stored procedure. Enter GetAllMedia in the Function Import Name text box. Select Entities as the type of collection and Media as the type of entity returned. Click OK. This will create the skeleton <FunctionImportMapping>.

4. Right-click the .edmx file, and select Open With ➤ XML Editor. Edit the <FunctionImportMapping> tag in the mapping section of the .edmx file to match the code in Listing 10-16. This maps the rows returned by the stored procedure either to the Magazine or to the DVD entity based on the MediaType column.

    Listing 10-16. This FunctionImportMapping Conditionally Maps the Returned Rows to Either the Magazine or the DVD Entity.

    ```
    <FunctionImportMapping FunctionImportName="GetAllMedia"
     FunctionName="EF6RecipesModel.Store.GetAllMedia">
      <ResultMapping>
        <EntityTypeMapping TypeName="EF6RecipesModel.Magazine">
          <ScalarProperty ColumnName="PublicationDate" Name="PublicationDate"/>
          <Condition ColumnName="MediaType" Value="Magazine"/>
        </EntityTypeMapping>
        <EntityTypeMapping TypeName="EF6RecipesModel.DVD">
          <ScalarProperty ColumnName="PlayTime" Name="PlayTime"/>
          <Condition ColumnName="MediaType" Value="DVD"/>
        </EntityTypeMapping>
      </ResultMapping>
    </FunctionImportMapping>
    ```

5. Follow the pattern in Listing 10-17 to use the GetAllMedia stored procedure via the GetAllMedia() method.

Listing 10-17. Using the GetAllMedia Stored Procedure via the GetAllMedia() Method

```
Using (var context = new EF6RecipesContext())
{
    context.MediaSet.Add(new Magazine { Title = "Field and Stream",
                        PublicationDate = DateTime.Parse("6/12/1945") });
    context.MediaSet.Add(new Magazine { Title = "National Geographic",
                        PublicationDate = DateTime.Parse("7/15/1976") });
    context.MediaSet.Add(new DVD { Title = "Harmony Road",
                        PlayTime = "2 hours, 30 minutes" });
    context.SaveChanges();
}

using (var context = new EF6RecipesContext())
{
    var allMedia = context.GetAllMedia();
    Console.WriteLine("All Media");
    Console.WriteLine("=========");
    foreach (var m in allMedia)
    {
        if (m is Magazine)
            Console.WriteLine("{0} Published: {1}", m.Title,
                            ((Magazine)m).PublicationDate.ToShortDateString());
        else if (m is DVD)
            Console.WriteLine("{0} Play Time: {1}", m.Title, ((DVD)m).PlayTime);
    }
}
```

The following is the output of the code in Listing 10-17:

```
All Media
=========
Field and Stream Published: 6/12/1945
National Geographic Published: 7/15/1976
Harmony Road Play Time: 2 hours, 30 minutes
```

How It Works

The two key parts to the solution are the discriminator column injected into the result set by the stored procedure and the conditional mapping of the results to the Magazine and DVD entities.

■ **Note**   The discriminator column is a metadata column that specifies the type of object represented by the database record.

The stored procedure in Listing 10-15 forms a union of rows from the Magazine and DVD tables, and it injects the strings Magazine or DVD into the MediaType discriminator column. For each select, we join to the Media table, which is represented in the model by the base entity, to include the Title column. All of the rows from all three tables are now in the result set with each row tagged to indicate the table from where it came.

With each row tagged with either Magazine or DVD, we conditionally map the rows either to the Magazine or DVD entities based on the tag or value in the discriminator column. This is done in the <FunctionImportMapping> section.

In Listing 10-17, we call the CLR method GetAllMedia(), which we mapped to the GetAllMedia stored procedure when we added the Function Import. When we call GetAllMedia(), the entire object graph is materialized with the inheritance hierarchy intact. We iterate through the collection, alternately printing out the Magazine and DVD entities.

10-7. Populating Entities in a Table per Hierarchy Inheritance Model

Problem

You want to use a stored procedure to populate entities in a Table per Hierarchy inheritance model.

Solution

Suppose you have a model like the one shown in Figure 10-7. We have two derived entities: Instructor and Student. Because this model is using Table per Hierarchy inheritance, we have just one table in the database. The Person table has a discriminator column that is used to map the table to the derived entities. You want to populate the entities with a stored procedure.

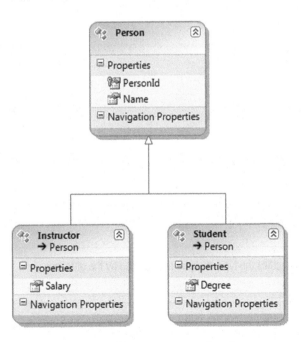

Figure 10-7. *A model for instructors and students*

To create and use a stored procedure that returns these entities, do the following:

1. In your database, create the stored procedure in Listing 10-18. This stored procedure returns all of the people in the hierarchy.

    Listing 10-18. The GetAllPeople Stored Procedure, Which Returns All the People, Both Students and Instructors, in the Model

    ```
    create procedure [Chapter10].[GetAllPeople]
    as
    begin
    select * from chapter10.Person
    end
    ```

2. Right-click the design surface, and select Update Model from Database. Select the GetAllPeople stored procedure. Click Finish to add the stored procedure to the model.

3. Right-click the design surface, and select Add ➤ Function Import. In the dialog box, select the GetAllPeople stored procedure. Enter GetAllPeople in the Function Import Name text box. Select Entities as the type of collection and Person as the type of entity returned. Click OK. This will create the skeleton <FunctionImportMapping> section.

4. Right-click the .edmx file, and select Open With ➤ XML Editor. Edit the <FunctionImportMapping> tag in the mapping section of the .edmx file to match the code in Listing 10-19. This maps the rows returned by the stored procedure either to the Instructor or to Student entity based on the PersonType column.

    Listing 10-19. The FunctionImportMapping Conditionally Maps Rows to Either the Instructor or Student Entity

    ```
    <FunctionImportMapping FunctionImportName="GetAllPeople"
            FunctionName="EF6RecipesModel.Store.GetAllPeople">
      <ResultMapping>
        <EntityTypeMapping TypeName="EFRecipesModel.Student">
          <ScalarProperty Name="Degree" ColumnName="Degree" />
          <Condition ColumnName="PersonType" Value="Student"/>
        </EntityTypeMapping>
        <EntityTypeMapping TypeName="EF6RecipesModel.Instructor">
          <ScalarProperty Name="Salary" ColumnName="Salary"/>
          <Condition ColumnName="PersonType" Value="Instructor"/>
        </EntityTypeMapping>
      </ResultMapping>
    </FunctionImportMapping>
    ```

5. Follow the pattern in Listing 10-20 to use the GetAllPeople stored procedure via the GetAllPeople() method

    Listing 10-20. Querying the Model Using the GetAllPeople Stored Procedure via the GetAllPeople() Method.

    ```
    using (var context = new EF6RecipesContext())
    {
        context.People.Add(new Instructor { Name = "Karen Stanford",
                                            Salary = 62500M });
        context.People.Add(new Instructor { Name = "Robert Morris",
                                            Salary = 61800M });
    ```

```
                context.People.Add(new Student { Name = "Jill Mathers",
                                                Degree = "Computer Science" });
                context.People.Add(new Student { Name = "Steven Kennedy",
                                                Degree = "Math" });
                context.SaveChanges();
        }

        using (var context = new EF6RecipesContext())
        {
            Console.WriteLine("Instructors and Students");
            var allPeople = context.GetAllPeople();
            foreach (var person in allPeople)
            {
                if (person is Instructor)
                    Console.WriteLine("Instructor {0} makes {1}/year",
                                        person.Name,
                                        ((Instructor)person).Salary.ToString("C"));
                else if (person is Student)
                    Console.WriteLine("Student {0}'s major is {1}",
                                        person.Name, ((Student)person).Degree);
            }
        }
    }
```

The following is the output of the code in Listing 10-20:

```
Instructors and Students
Instructor Karen Stanford makes $62,500.00/year
Instructor Robert Morris makes $61,800.00/year
Student Jill Mathers's major is Computer Science
Student Steven Kennedy's major is Math
```

How It Works

Using a stored procedure to populate entities in a Table per Hierarchy inheritance model turns out to be a little easier than for Table per Type (see Recipe 10-6). Here the stored procedure just selected all rows in the Person table. The PersonType column contains the discriminator value that we use in <FunctionImportMapping> in Listing 10-19 to map the rows conditionally either to the Student or to the Instructor entity. In Recipe 10-6, the stored procedure had to create the column. In this recipe as well as in Recipe 10-6, the key part is the conditional mapping in the <FunctionImportMapping> tag.

10-8. Mapping the Insert, Update, and Delete Actions to Stored Procedures

Problem

You want to map the Insert, Update, and Delete actions to stored procedures.

Solution

Let's say you have a model with the Athlete entity shown in Figure 10-8. The underlying database has the Athlete table shown in Figure 10-9. You want to use stored procedures for the Insert, Update, and Delete actions.

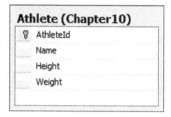

Figure 10-8. *The Athlete entity in the model*

Figure 10-9. *The Athlete table with some basic information about athletes*

To map stored procedures to the Insert, Update, and Delete actions for the Athlete entity, do the following:

1. In your database, create the stored procedures in Listing 10-21.

Listing 10-21. The Stored Procedures for the Insert, Update, and Delete Actions

```
create procedure [chapter10].[InsertAthlete]
(@Name varchar(50), @Height int, @Weight int)
as
begin
        insert into Chapter10.Athlete values (@Name, @Height, @Weight)
        select SCOPE_IDENTITY() as AthleteId
end
go

create procedure [chapter10].[UpdateAthlete]
(@AthleteId int, @Name varchar(50), @Height int, @Weight int)
as
begin
        update Chapter10.Athlete set Name = @Name, Height = @Height, [Weight] = @Weight
        where AthleteId = @AthleteId
```

```
end
go

create procedure [chapter10].[DeleteAthlete]
(@AthleteId int)
as
begin
        delete from Chapter10.Athlete where AthleteId = @AthleteId
end
```

2. Right-click the design surface and select Update Model from Database. Select the new stored procedures from Listing 10-19 and click Finish. This will add the stored procedures to the model.

3. Right-click the Athlete Entity, and select Stored Procedure Mapping. Select the stored procedures for each of the actions. For the Insert action, map the return column AthleteId for the Insert action to the AthleteId property (see Figure 10-10).

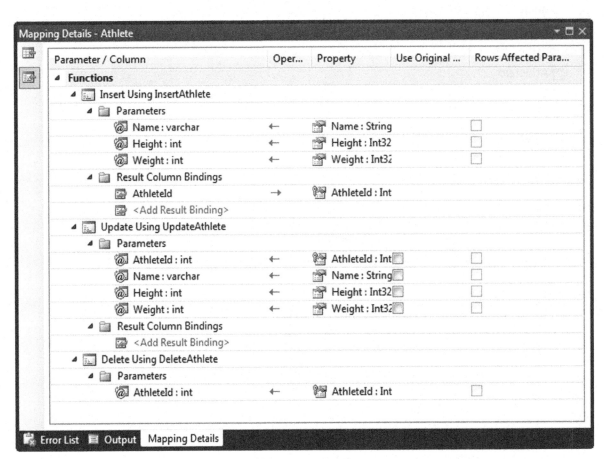

Figure 10-10. Mapping the stored procedures, parameters, and return values for the Insert, Update, and Delete actions

How It Works

We updated the model with the stored procedures we created in the database. This makes the stored procedures available for use in the model. Once we have the stored procedures available in the model, we mapped them to the Insert, Update, and Delete actions for the entity.

In this recipe, the stored procedures are about as simple as you can get. They take in properties as parameters and perform the action. For the Insert stored procedure, we need to return the stored generated key for the entity. In this recipe, the stored generated key is just an identity column. We need to return this from the stored procedure for the Insert action and map this returned value to the AthleteId property. This is an important step. Without this, Entity Framework would not be able to get the entity key for the instance of the Athlete entity just inserted.

You may ask, "When do I map stored procedures to the actions?" In most cases, Entity Framework will generate efficient code for the Insert, Update, and Delete actions. You may also be wondering, "When would I ever need to replace this with my own stored procedures?" Here are the best-practice answers to this question.

- Your company requires you to use stored procedures for some or all of the Insert, Update, or Delete activity for certain tables.

- You have additional tasks to do during one or more of the actions. For example, you might want to manage an audit trail or perform some complex business logic, or perhaps you need to leverage a user's privileges to execute stored procedures for security checking.

- Your entity is based on a QueryView (see Chapter 6 and Chapter 15) that requires you to map some or all of the actions to stored procedures.

The code in Listing 10-22 demonstrates inserting, deleting, and updating in the model. The code isn't any different because of the mapping of the actions, and that's fine. The fact that we have replaced the code that Entity Framework would have dynamically generated with our own stored procedures will not affect the code that uses the entity.

Listing 10-22. Executing the Insert, Update, and Delete Actions

```
using (var context = new EF6RecipesContext())
{
    context.Athletes.Add(new Athlete { Name = "Nancy Steward",
                            Height = 167, Weight = 53 });
    context.Athletes.Add(new Athlete { Name = "Rob Achers",
                            Height = 170, Weight = 77 });
    context.Athletes.Add(new Athlete { Name = "Chuck Sanders",
                            Height = 171, Weight = 82 });
    context.Athletes.Add(new Athlete { Name = "Nancy Rodgers",
                            Height = 166, Weight = 59 });
    context.SaveChanges();
}
using (var context = new EF6RecipesContext())
{
    // do a delete and an update
    var all = context.Athletes;
    context.Delete(all.First(o => o.Name == "Nancy Steward"));
    all.First(o => o.Name == "Rob Achers").Weight = 80;
    context.SaveChanges();
}
```

```
using (var context = new EF6RecipesContext())
{
    Console.WriteLine("All Athletes");
    Console.WriteLine("============");
    foreach (var athlete in context.Athletes)
    {
        Console.WriteLine("{0} weighs {1} Kg and is {2} cm in height",
          athlete.Name, athlete.Weight, athlete.Height);
    }
}
```

The following is the output of the code in Listing 10-22:

```
All Athletes
============
Rob Achers weighs 80 Kg and is 170 cm in height
Chuck Sanders weighs 82 Kg and is 171 cm in height
Nancy Rodgers weighs 59 Kg and is 166 cm in height
```

10-9. Using Stored Procedures for the Insert and Delete Actions in a Many-to-Many Association

Problem

You want to use stored procedures for the Insert and Delete actions in a payload-free, many-to-many association. These stored procedures affect only the link table in the association and not the associated entities.

Solution

Let's say that you have a many-to-many relationship between an Author table and a Book table. The link table, AuthorBook, is used as part of the relationship, as shown in Figure 10-11.

Figure 10-11. *A payload-free, many-to-many relationship between an Author and a Book*

When you import these tables into a model, you get a model that looks like the one shown in Figure 10-12.

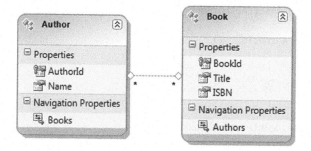

Figure 10-12. *The model created by importing the tables in Figure 10-11*

To use stored procedures for the Insert and Delete actions, do the following.

1. In your database, create the stored procedures in Listing 10-23.

    Listing 10-23. The stored Procedures for the Insert and Delete Actions

    ```
    create procedure [chapter10].[InsertAuthorBook]
    (@AuthorId int,@BookId int)
    as
    begin
            insert into chapter10.AuthorBook(AuthorId,BookId) values (@AuthorId,@BookId)
    end
    go

    create procedure [chapter10].[DeleteAuthorBook]
    (@AuthorId int,@BookId int)
    as
    begin
            delete chapter10.AuthorBook where AuthorId = @AuthorId and BookId = @BookId
    end
    ```

2. Right-click the design surface, and select Update Model from Database. Select the new stored procedures from Listing 10-23 and click Finish. This will add the stored procedures to the model.

3. The current release of Entity Framework does not have designer support for mapping stored procedures to the Insert and Delete actions for an association. To perform this mapping manually, right-click the .edmx file and select Open With † XML Editor. Add the code in Listing 10-24 in the Mappings section inside the <AssociationSetMapping> tag.

Listing 10-24. Mapping the Stored Procedures to the Insert and Delete Actions for the Many-to-Many Association

```
<ModificationFunctionMapping>
  <InsertFunction FunctionName="EF6RecipesModel.Store.InsertAuthorBook">
    <EndProperty Name="Author">
      <ScalarProperty Name="AuthorId" ParameterName="AuthorId"  />
    </EndProperty>
    <EndProperty Name="Book">
      <ScalarProperty Name="BookId" ParameterName="BookId" />
    </EndProperty>
  </InsertFunction>
  <DeleteFunction FunctionName="EF6RecipesModel.Store.DeleteAuthorBook">
    <EndProperty Name="Author">
      <ScalarProperty Name="AuthorId" ParameterName="AuthorId"  />
    </EndProperty>
    <EndProperty Name="Book">
      <ScalarProperty Name="BookId" ParameterName="BookId" />
    </EndProperty>
  </DeleteFunction>
</ModificationFunctionMapping>
```

The code in Listing 10-25 demonstrates inserting into and deleting from the model. As you can see from the SQL Profiler output that follows, our InsertAuthorBook and DeleteAuthorBook stored procedures are called when Entity Framework updates the many-to-many association.

Listing 10-25. Inserting into the Model

```
using (var context = new EF6RecipesContext())
{
    var auth1 = new Author { Name = "Jane Austin"};
    var book1 = new Book { Title = "Pride and Prejudice",
                           ISBN = "1848373104" };
    var book2 = new Book { Title = "Sense and Sensibility",
                           ISBN = "1440469563" };
    auth1.Books.Add(book1);
    auth1.Books.Add(book2);
    var auth2 = new Author { Name = "Audrey Niffenegger" };
    var book3 = new Book { Title = "The Time Traveler's Wife",
                           ISBN = "015602943X" };
    auth2.Books.Add(book3);
    context.Authors.Add(auth1);
    context.Authors.Add(auth2);
    context.SaveChanges();
    context.Delete(book1);
    context.SaveChanges();
}
```

Here is the output of the SQL Profiler showing the SQL statements that are executed by the code in Listing 10-25:

```
exec sp_executesql N'insert [Chapter10].[Author]([Name])
values (@0)
select [AuthorId]
from [Chapter10].[Author]
where @@ROWCOUNT > 0 and [AuthorId] = scope_identity()',N'@0 varchar(50)',
 @0='Jane Austin'

exec sp_executesql N'insert [Chapter10].[Author]([Name])
values (@0)
select [AuthorId]
from [Chapter10].[Author]
where @@ROWCOUNT > 0 and [AuthorId] = scope_identity()',N'@0 varchar(50)',
 @0='Audrey Niffenegger'

exec sp_executesql N'insert [Chapter10].[Book]([Title], [ISBN])
values (@0, @1)
select [BookId]
from [Chapter10].[Book]
where @@ROWCOUNT > 0 and [BookId] = scope_identity()',N'@0 varchar(50),
 @1 varchar(50)',@0='Pride and Prejudice',@1='1848373104'
exec sp_executesql N'insert [Chapter10].[Book]([Title], [ISBN])
values (@0, @1)
select [BookId]
from [Chapter10].[Book]
where @@ROWCOUNT > 0 and [BookId] = scope_identity()',N'@0 varchar(50),
 @1 varchar(50)',@0='Sense and Sensibility',@1='1440469563'

exec sp_executesql N'insert [Chapter10].[Book]([Title], [ISBN])
values (@0, @1)
select [BookId]
from [Chapter10].[Book]
where @@ROWCOUNT > 0 and [BookId] = scope_identity()',N'@0 varchar(50),
 @1 varchar(50)',@0='The Time Traveler''s Wife',@1='015602943X'

exec [Chapter10].[InsertAuthorBook] @AuthorId=1,@BookId=1

exec [Chapter10].[InsertAuthorBook] @AuthorId=1,@BookId=2

exec [Chapter10].[InsertAuthorBook] @AuthorId=2,@BookId=3

exec [Chapter10].[DeleteAuthorBook] @AuthorId=1,@BookId=1

exec sp_executesql N'delete [Chapter10].[Book]
 where ([BookId] = @0)',N'@0 int',@0=7
```

How It Works

To map the stored procedures to the Insert and Delete actions for the many-to-many association, we created the stored procedures in our database and then updated the model with the stored procedures.

Because Entity Framework's designer does not currently support mapping stored procedures to the Insert and Delete actions for associations, we need to edit the .edmx file directly. In the Mappings section, we added a `<ModificationFunctionMapping>` tag that maps the Insert and Delete actions for the association to our stored procedures. In this tag, we refer to the `InsertAuthorBook` and `DeleteAuthorBook` stored procedures, which are defined in the Store model because we updated the model with these stored procedures from the database.

In the trace from Listing 10-25, we can see not only the expected inserts for the Author and Book tables, but we can also see that our stored procedures are used to insert and delete the association.

10-10. Mapping the Insert, Update, and Delete Actions to Stored Procedures for Table per Hierarchy Inheritance

Problems

You have a model that uses Table per Hierarchy inheritance, and you want to map the Insert, Update, and Delete actions to stored procedures.

Solution

Let's say that your database contains a Product table that describes a couple of different kinds of products (see Figure 10-14). You have created a model with derived types for each of the product types represented in the Product table. The model looks like the one shown in Figure 10-14.

Product (Chapter10)		
Column Name	Data Type	Allow Nulls
🔑 ProductId	int	☐
Title	varchar(50)	☐
ProductType	varchar(50)	☐
Publisher	varchar(50)	☑
Rating	varchar(50)	☑
		☐

Figure 10-13. *A Product table with a discriminator column, ProductType, that indicates the type of product described by the row in the table*

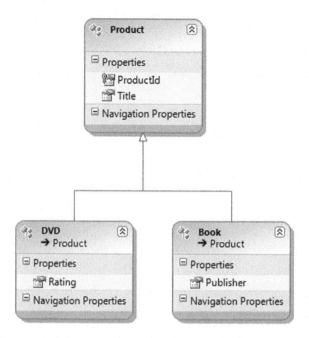

Figure 10-14. *A model using Table per Hierarchy inheritance with a derived type for each of the products*

To map stored procedures to the Insert, Update, and Delete actions for this model, do the following:

1. In your database, create the stored procedures in Listing 10-26. These stored procedures will handle the Insert, Update, and Delete actions for the Book and DVD entities.

Listing 10-26. The Stored Procedure We Map to the Insert, Update, and Delete Actions for the Model

```
create procedure [chapter10].[InsertBook]
(@Title varchar(50), @Publisher varchar(50))
as
begin
        insert into Chapter10.Product (Title, Publisher, ProductType) values
            (@Title,@Publisher, 'Book')
        select SCOPE_IDENTITY() as ProductId
end
go
create procedure [chapter10].[UpdateBook]
(@Title varchar(50), @Publisher varchar(50), @ProductId int)
as
begin
        update Chapter10.Product set Title = @Title, Publisher = @Publisher
            where ProductId = @ProductId
end
go

create procedure [chapter10].[DeleteBook]
(@ProductId int)
```

```
as
begin
        delete from Chapter10.Product where ProductId = @ProductId
end
go

create procedure [chapter10].[InsertDVD]
(@Title varchar(50), @Rating varchar(50))
as
begin
        insert into Chapter10.Product (Title, Rating, ProductType) values
           (@Title, @Rating, 'DVD')
        select SCOPE_IDENTITY() as ProductId
end
go

create procedure [chapter10].[DeleteDVD]
(@ProductId int)
as
begin
        delete from Chapter10.Product where ProductId = @ProductId
end
go

create procedure [chapter10].[UpdateDVD]
(@Title varchar(50), @Rating varchar(50), @ProductId int)
as
begin
        update Chapter10.Product set Title = @Title, Rating = @Rating
           where ProductId = @ProductId
end
```

2. Right-click the design surface, and select Update Model from Database. Select the newly created stored procedures, and click Finish to add them to the model.

3. Right-click the Book entity and select Stored Procedure Mapping. Map the InsertBook, UpdateBook, and DeleteBook stored procedures to the corresponding actions for the entity. Map the Result Column Binding for the Insert action to the ProductId property (see Figure 10-15).

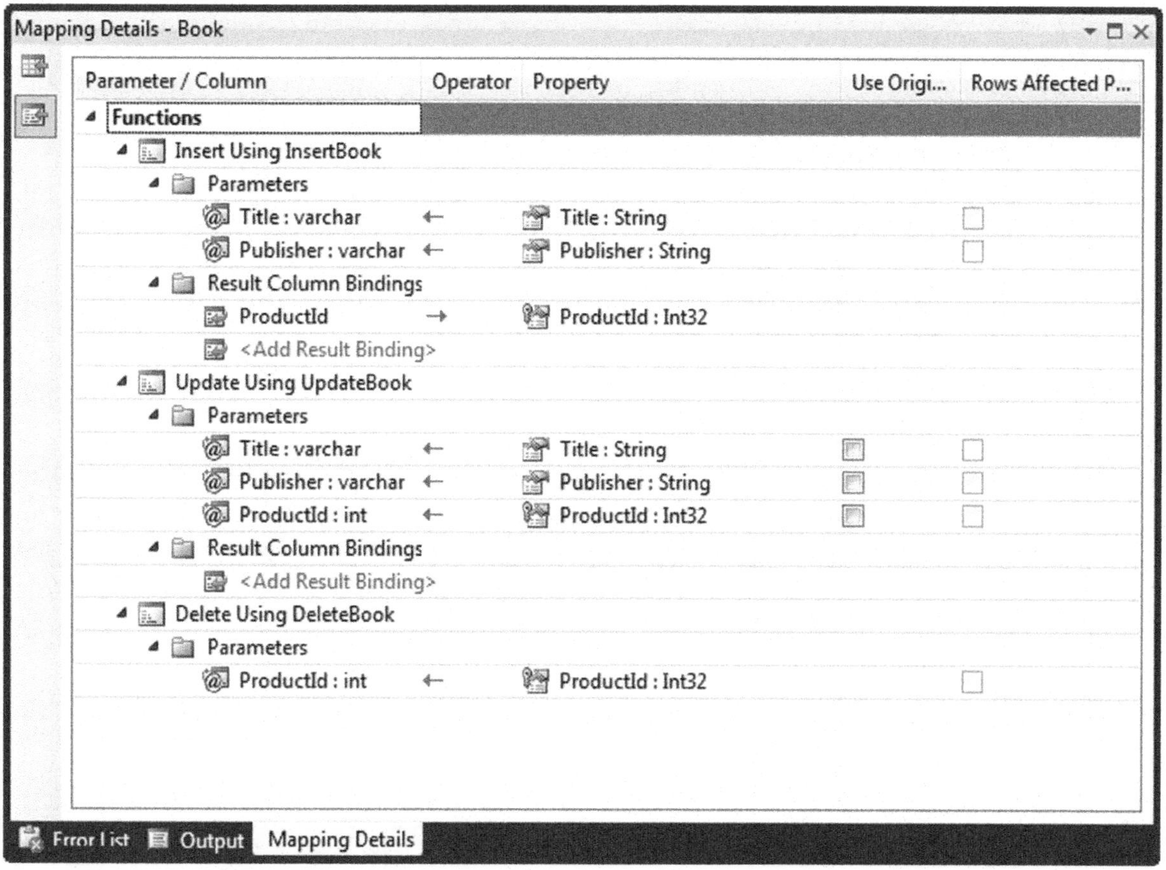

Figure 10-15. *Mapping the stored procedures to the Insert, Update, and Delete actions for the Book entity. Be particularly careful to map the Result Column Binding to the ProductId property for the Insert action*

4. Right-click the DVD entity, and select Stored Procedure Mapping. Map the InsertDVD, UpdateDVD, and DeleteDVD stored procedures to the corresponding actions for the entity. Map the Result Column Binding for the Insert action to the ProductId property (see Figure 10-16).

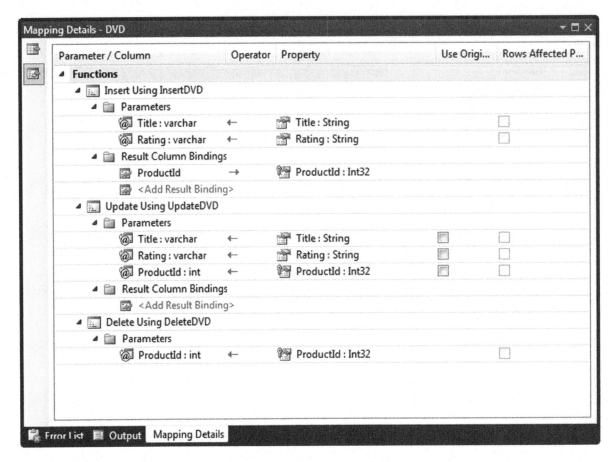

Figure 10-16. *Mapping the stored procedures to the Insert, Update, and Delete actions for the DVD entity*

How It Works

We created the stored procedures for the Insert, Update, and Delete actions for both the Book and DVD entities and imported them into the model. Once we have these stored procedures in the model, we mapped them to the corresponding actions, being careful to map the Result Column Binding for the Insert action to the ProductId property. This ensures that the store generated key for the Product is mapped to the ProductId property.

The Table per Hierarchy inheritance is supported by the implementation of the Insert stored procedures. Each of them inserts the correct ProductType value. Given these values in the tables, Entity Framework can correctly materialize the derived entities.

The code in Listing 10-27 demonstrates inserting, updating, deleting, and querying the model.

Listing 10-27. Exercising the Insert, Update, and Delete Actions

```
using (var context = new EF6RecipesContext())
{
    var book1 = new Book { Title = "A Day in the Life",
                           Publisher = "Colorful Press" };
    var book2 = new Book { Title = "Spring in October",
                           Publisher = "AnimalCover Press" };
```

```
    var dvd1 = new DVD { Title = "Saving Sergeant Pepper", Rating = "G" };
    var dvd2 = new DVD { Title = "Around The Block", Rating = "PG-13" };
    context.Products.Add(book1);
    context.Products.Add(book2);
    context.Products.Add(dvd1);
    context.Products.Add(dvd2);
    context.SaveChanges();

    // update a book and delete a dvd
    book1.Title = "A Day in the Life of Sergeant Pepper";
    context.Delete(dvd2);
    context.SaveChanges();
}

using (var context = new EF6RecipesContext())
{
    Console.WriteLine("All Products");
    Console.WriteLine("============");
    foreach (var product in context.Products)
    {
        if (product is Book)
            Console.WriteLine("'{0}' published by {1}",
                    product.Title, ((Book)product).Publisher);
        else if (product is DVD)
            Console.WriteLine("'{0}' is rated {1}",
                    product.Title, ((DVD)product).Rating);
    }
}
```

The following is the output of the code in Listing 10-27:

```
All Products
============
'Spring in October' published by AnimalCover Press
'A Day in the Life of Sergeant Pepper' published by Colorful Press
'Saving Sergeant Pepper' is rated G
```

CHAPTER 11

Functions

Functions provide a power mechanism for code reuse, and offer you a good way to make your code cleaner and more understandable. They can also be used to leverage code in the Entity Framework runtime as well as in the database layer. Functions are of various types: Rowset Functions, Aggregate Functions, Ranking Functions, and Scalar Functions. Functions are either deterministic or nondeterministic. Functions are deterministic when they always return the same result any time that they are called by using a specific set of input values. Functions are nondeterministic when they could return different results every time they are called, even with the same specific set of input values.

In the first seven recipes, we explore *model-defined functions*. These functions allow you to create functions at the conceptual layer. These functions are defined in terms of Entity Framework types and your model entities. This makes them portable across data store implementations.

In the remaining recipes, we show you how to use functions defined by Entity Framework and the database layer. These functions are implemented for you, and they allow you to leverage existing code either in Entity Framework's runtime or, closer to your data, in the database layer.

11-1. Returning a Scalar Value from a Model-Defined Function
Problem

You want to define a function in the conceptual model that takes an instance of an entity and returns a scalar value.

Solution

Suppose that you have a model like the one shown in Figure 11-1.

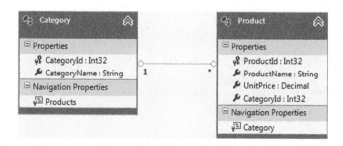

Figure 11-1. *A model for products and categories*

To create a model-defined function that takes an instance of the Category entity and returns the average unit price for all of the products in the given category, do the following:

1. Right-click the .edmx file in the Solution Explorer, and select Open With ➤ XML Editor.

2. Insert the code in Listing 11-1 just below the <Schema> tag in the conceptual models section of the .edmx file. This defines the function in the model.

Listing 11-1. Definition of the AverageUnitPrice() Function in the Model

```
<Function Name="AverageUnitPrice" ReturnType="Edm.Decimal">
            <Parameter Name="category" Type="EFRecipesModel.Category" />
            <DefiningExpression>
                ANYELEMENT(Select VALUE Avg(p.UnitPrice)
                from EFRecipesEntities.Products as p where p.Category == category

                )
            </DefiningExpression>
        </Function>
```

3. Insert into and query the model using code similar to the pattern shown in Listing 11-2.

Listing 11-2. Inserting into and Querying the Model Using the Model-Defined Function AverageUnitPrice()

```
class Program
{
    static void Main(string[] args)
    {
        RunExample();
    }

    static void RunExample()
    {
        using (var context = new EFRecipesEntities())
        {
            var c1 = new Category { CategoryName = "Backpacking Tents" };
            var p1 = new Product
            {
                ProductName = "Hooligan",
                UnitPrice = 89.99M,
                Category = c1
            };

            var p2 = new Product
            {
                ProductName = "Kraz",
                UnitPrice = 99.99M,
                Category = c1
            };
```

```
        var p3 = new Product
        {
            ProductName = "Sundome",
            UnitPrice = 49.99M,
            Category = c1
        };
        context.Categories.Add(c1);
        context.Products.Add(p1);
        context.Products.Add(p2);
        context.Products.Add(p3);

        var c2 = new Category { CategoryName = "Family Tents" };
        var p4 = new Product
        {
            ProductName = "Evanston",
            UnitPrice = 169.99M,
            Category = c2
        };
        var p5 = new Product
        {
            ProductName = "Montana",
            UnitPrice = 149.99M,
            Category = c2
        };
        context.Categories.Add(c2);
        context.Products.Add(p4);
        context.Products.Add(p5);
        context.SaveChanges();
    }
    // with eSQL
    using (var context = new EFRecipesEntities())
    {
        Console.WriteLine("Using eSQL for the query...");
        Console.WriteLine();
        string sql = @"Select c.CategoryName, EFRecipesModel
                    .AverageUnitPrice(c) as AveragePrice from
                    EFRecipesEntities.Categories as c";
        var objectContext = (context as IObjectContextAdapter).ObjectContext;
        var cats = objectContext.CreateQuery<DbDataRecord>(sql);
        foreach (var cat in cats)
        {
            Console.WriteLine("Category '{0}' has an average price of {1}",
                    cat["CategoryName"], ((decimal)cat["AveragePrice"]).ToString("C"));
        }
    }

    // with LINQ
    using (var context = new EFRecipesEntities())
    {
        Console.WriteLine();
        Console.WriteLine("Using LINQ for the query...");
        Console.WriteLine();
```

```
                    var cats = from c in context.Categories
                        select new
                        {
                            Name = c.CategoryName,
                            AveragePrice = MyFunctions.AverageUnitPrice(c)
                        };
                    foreach (var cat in cats)
                    {
                        Console.WriteLine("Category '{0}' has an average price of {1}",
                                    cat.Name, cat.AveragePrice.ToString("C"));
                    }
                }
            }
        }
        public class MyFunctions
        {
            [EdmFunction("EFRecipesModel", "AverageUnitPrice")]
            public static decimal AverageUnitPrice(Category category)
            {
                throw new NotSupportedException("Direct calls are not supported!");
            }
        }
```

Following is the output of the code in Listing 11-2:

```
Using eSQL for the query...

Category 'Backpacking Tents' has an average price of $79.99
Category 'Family Tents' has an average price of $159.99

Using LINQ for the query...

Category 'Backpacking Tents' has an average price of $79.99
Category 'Family Tents' has an average price of $159.99
```

How It Works

Model-defined functions are created in the conceptual layer and written in eSQL. Of course, this allows you to program against the entities in your model as we have done here, referencing the Category and Product entities and their association in the function's implementation. The added benefit is that we are not tied to a specific storage layer. We could swap out the lower layers, even the database provider, and our program would still work.

The designer currently provides no support for model-defined functions. Unlike stored procedures, which are supported by the designer, model-defined functions do not show up in the model browser nor anywhere else in the designer. The designer will not check for syntax errors in the eSQL. You will find out about these at runtime. However, the designer will at least tolerate model-defined functions enough to open the .edmx file. Model-defined functions are evaluated in Entity Framework and not in the back-end database.

In Listing 11-2, the code starts off by inserting a couple of categories and a few products for each. Once we have the data in place, we query it using two slightly different approaches.

In the first query example, we build an eSQL statement that calls the AverageUnitPrice() function. We create and execute the query. For each row in the results, we pull out the data for the first column, which is the category name, and the data for the second column, which is the average unit price for the category. We display them for each row.

The second query example is a little more interesting. Here we use the AverageUnitPrice() function in a LINQ query. To do this, we need to add a stub method in a separate class. The method is decorated with the [EdmFunction()] attribute, which marks it as an implementation of a model-defined function. This CLR method will not actually be called, which is evident by the exception we throw in the body of the method. Because we return a scalar value, the method's implementation here is simply for the signature (the parameter number, types, and return type). In the LINQ query, we grab each category and reshape the results into an anonymous type that holds the category name and the result of calling the AverageUnitPrice() method in the MyFunction class. This is the stub we created that is tied to the AverageUnitPrice() model-defined function. For each of the resulting objects, we display the category name and the category's average unit price.

DbContext is the light version of ObjectContext. Whenever a CreateQuery is to be used to execute a Sql (Entity SQL), then ObjectContext is required. Thus ObjectContext is fetched through DbContext using (context as IObjectContextAdapter) ObjectContext.

The parameters for model-defined functions can be scalar, entity types, complex types, anonymous types, or collections of these. In many of the recipes in this chapter, we'll show you how to create and use model-defined functions with these parameter types.

The parameters for model-defined functions don't show direction. There are no "out" parameters, only implied "in" parameters. The reason for this is that model-defined functions are composable and can be used as part of LINQ queries. This prevents them from returning values in output parameters.

In this example, we returned a single scalar decimal value. To do this, we had to explicitly return a scalar using the AnyElement operator. Entity Framework does not know how to map a collection to a scalar value. We help out here by using the AnyElement operator, which signals that only a single value will result from the query. It just so happens that we return a collection of just one element from which the AnyElement operator selects just one element.

Best Practice

Model-defined functions provide a clean and practical way to implement parts of a conceptual model that would be tedious if not impossible any other way. Here are some best practices and uses for model-defined functions.

> Model-defined functions are written in eSQL and defined at the conceptual layer. This provides a level of abstraction from the details of the store layer and allows you to leverage a more complete model independent of the store layer.

> You can define functions for expressions that you commonly use in your LINQ or eSQL queries. This provides better code organization and allows code reuse. Also, if you use LINQ, then due to the nature of IntelliSense and compile-time checks, there will be fewer code issues because of typos.

> Model-defined functions are composable, which allows you to implement functions that serve as building blocks for more complex expressions. This can both simplify your code and make it more maintainable.

> Model-defined functions can be used in places where you have computed properties. A *computed property*, like a function, is a read-only value. For properties, you incur the cost of computing the value when the entity is materialized, whether or not you need the computed property. With a model-defined function, the cost of computing the value is incurred only when you actually need the value.

11-2. Filtering an Entity Collection Using a Model-Defined Function

Problem

You want to create a model-defined function that filters a collection.

Solution

Suppose that we have a model with Customers and Invoices, as shown in Figure 11-2.

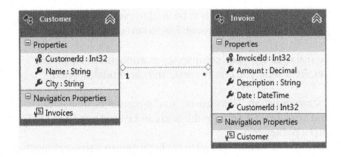

Figure 11-2. *Customer and Invoice in a model*

Let's say that we want to create a model-defined function that takes a collection of invoices and filters the collection to those invoices that have an amount greater than $300. Just for fun, let's use this model-defined function in a query that further filters this collection to just those invoices created after 5/1/2013. Of course, we'll want to load all of the customers associated with these invoices.

To get started, do the following:

1. Right-click the .edmx file in the Solution Explorer, and select Open With ➤ XML Editor.

2. Insert the code in Listing 11-3 just below the <Schema> tag in the conceptual models section of the .edmx file. This defines the function in the model.

Listing 11-3. The GetInvoices() Model-Defined Function

```
<Function Name="GetInvoices" ReturnType="Collection(EFRecipesModel.Invoice)" >
        <Parameter Name="invoices" Type="Collection(EFRecipesModel.Invoice)">
        </Parameter>
        <DefiningExpression>
           Select VALUE i
           from invoices as i where i.Amount > 300M
        </DefiningExpression>
    </Function>
```

3. Insert into and query the model using code similar to the pattern shown in Listing 11-4.

Listing 11-4. *Querying the Model Using the GetInvoices() Model-Defined Function with Both eSQL and LINQ*

```csharp
class Program
    {
        static void Main(string[] args)
        {
            RunExample();
        }

        static void RunExample()
        {
            using (var context = new EFRecipesEntities())
            {
                DateTime d1 = DateTime.Parse("8/8/2013");
                DateTime d2 = DateTime.Parse("8/12/2012");
                var c1 = new Customer { Name = "Jill Robinson", City = "Dallas" };
                var c2 = new Customer { Name = "Jerry Jones", City = "Denver" };
                var c3 = new Customer { Name = "Janis Brady", City = "Dallas" };
                var c4 = new Customer { Name = "Steve Foster", City = "Dallas" };
                context.Invoices.Add(new Invoice
                {
                    Amount = 302.99M,
                    Description = "New Tires",
                    Date = d1,
                    Customer = c1
                });
                context.Invoices.Add(new Invoice
                {
                    Amount = 430.39M,
                    Description = "Brakes and Shocks",
                    Date = d1,
                    Customer = c2
                });
                context.Invoices.Add(new Invoice
                {
                    Amount = 102.28M,
                    Description = "Wheel Alignment",
                    Date = d1,
                    Customer = c3
                });
                context.Invoices.Add(new Invoice
                {
                    Amount = 629.82M,
                    Description = "A/C Repair",
                    Date = d2,
                    Customer = c4
                });
                context.SaveChanges();
            }
```

```
        using (var context = new EFRecipesEntities())
        {
            Console.WriteLine("Using eSQL query...");
            string sql = @"Select value i from
                    EFRecipesModel.GetInvoices(EFRecipesEntities.Invoices) as i
                    where i.Date > DATETIME'2013-05-1 00:00'
                    and i.Customer.City = @City";
            var objectContext = (context as IObjectContextAdapter).ObjectContext;
            var invoices = objectContext.CreateQuery<Invoice>(sql,
                    new ObjectParameter("City", "Dallas")).Include("Customer");
            foreach (var invoice in invoices)
            {
                Console.WriteLine("Customer: {0}\tInvoice for: {1}, Amount: {2}",
                    invoice.Customer.Name, invoice.Description, invoice.Amount);
            }
        }

        using (var context = new EFRecipesEntities())
        {
            Console.WriteLine();
            Console.WriteLine("Using LINQ query...");
            DateTime date = DateTime.Parse("5/1/2013");
            var invoices = from invoice in
                        MyFunctions.GetInvoices(context.Invoices)
                    where invoice.Date > date
                    where invoice.Customer.City == "Dallas"
                    select invoice;
            foreach (var invoice in ((DbQuery<Invoice>)invoices)
                                .Include("Customer"))
            {
                Console.WriteLine("Customer: {0}, Invoice for: {1}, Amount: {2}",
                    invoice.Customer.Name, invoice.Description, invoice.Amount);
            }
        }
    }
}

public class MyFunctions
{
    [EdmFunction("EFRecipesModel", "GetInvoices")]
    public static IQueryable<Invoice> GetInvoices(IQueryable<Invoice> invoices)
    {
        return invoices.Provider.CreateQuery<Invoice>(
            Expression.Call((MethodInfo) MethodInfo.GetCurrentMethod(),
                    Expression.Constant(invoices,
                                typeof(IQueryable<Invoice>))));
    }
}
```

Following is the output of the code in Listing 11-4:

```
Using eSQL for the query...
Customer: Jill Robinson Invoice for: New Tires, Amount: 302.99

Using LINQ for the query...
Customer: Jill Robinson, Invoice for: New Tires, Amount: 302.99
```

How It Works

From the definition of our GetInvoices() function in Listing 11-3, we see that it takes a collection of Invoices and returns a collection of Invoices. On the CLR side, this translates to taking an IQueryable<Invoice> and returning an IQueryable<Invoice>.

In the eSQL expression, we use the GetInvoices() function in the from clause. We pass in the unfiltered collection of Invoices and our GetInvoices() function returns the filtered collection. We further filter the collection by date and the customer's city using a where clause. Then we use CreateQuery<Invoice>() to build the ObjectQuery<Invoice>. In building the query, we pass in the parameter to filter by city and use the Include() method to include the related customers. Once we have the ObjectQuery<Invoice>, we iterate over the resulting collection and print out the invoices that matched the two filters that we applied.

For the LINQ query, the story is a little more interesting. Here we build the expression using the GetInvoices() method in the from clause and filter the resulting collection by date and city, much like we did with the eSQLexpression. However, to use our function in a LINQ query, we need to implement a CLR method that takes an IQueryable<Invoice> and returns an IQueryable<Invoice>. Unlike the stub method in Recipe 11-1, in which the model-defined function returned a scalar value, here we have to provide an implementation in the body of the method. Creating this method is often referred to as *bootstrapping*.

Here are some rules for bootstrapping:

- Bootstrapping is required when a model-defined function returns an IQueryable<T>.

- When a function returns an IQueryable<T> but does not take an IQueryable<T>, the bootstrapping method must be implemented in a partial class of the ObjectContext.

The second rule comes about because we can't return an IQueryable<T> that has meaning in our ObjectContext without starting with an IQueryable<T>. If we pass in an IQueryable<T>, then we can perform some operation in our bootstrapping method that returns a related IQueryable<T>. However, we can't manufacture an IQueryable<T> outside of a partial class of our ObjectContext. In our example, we received an IQueryable<T> as a parameter, so we are free to implement the bootstrapping code outside of a partial class of our ObjectContext.

In the implementation of our bootstrapping method, we get an instance of IQueryProvider from the IQueryable<Invoice> through the Provider property. IQueryProvider.CreateQuery<Invoice>() allows us to tack onto the expression tree for the IQueryable<T>. Here we add in the call to the GetInvoices() function, passing in the collection of invoices that we have.

11-3. Returning a Computed Column from a Model-Defined Function
Problem

You want to return a computed column from a model-defined function.

Solution

Suppose that we have an Employee entity containing the properties FirstName, LastName, and BirthDate, as shown in Figure 11-3.

***Figure 11-3.** An Employee entity with a few typical properties*

We want to create a model-defined function that returns the full name of the employee by combining the FirstName and LastName columns. We want to create another model-defined function that returns the age of the employee based on the value in the BirthDate column.

To create and use these functions, do the following:

1. Right-click the .edmx file in the Solution Explorer, and click Open With ➤ XML Editor. This will open the .edmx file in the XML Editor.

2. Insert the code in Listing 11-5 just below the <Schema> tag in the conceptual models section of the .edmx file. This defines the functions in the model.

   ***Listing 11-5.** Code for Model-Defined Functions*

   ```xml
   <Function Name="FullName" ReturnType="Edm.String">
           <Parameter Name="emp" Type="EFRecipesModel.Employee" />
           <DefiningExpression>
               Trim(emp.FirstName) + " " + Trim(emp.LastName)
           </DefiningExpression>
       </Function>
       <Function Name="Age" ReturnType="Edm.Int32">
           <Parameter Name="emp" Type="EFRecipesModel.Employee" />
           <DefiningExpression>
               Year(CurrentDateTime()) - Year(emp.BirthDate)
           </DefiningExpression>
       </Function>
   ```

3. Insert into and query the model using code similar to the pattern shown in Listing 11-6.

   ***Listing 11-6.** Inserting into and Querying the Model Invoking the Model-Defined Functions Using Both eSQL and LINQ*

   ```csharp
   class Program
       {
           static void Main(string[] args)
           {
               RunExample();
           }
   ```

```
static void RunExample()
{
    using (var context = new EFRecipesEntities())
    {
        context.Employees.Add(new Employee
        {
            FirstName = "Jill",
            LastName = "Robins",
            BirthDate = DateTime.Parse("3/2/1976")
        });
        context.Employees.Add(new Employee
        {
            FirstName = "Michael",
            LastName = "Kirk",
            BirthDate = DateTime.Parse("4/12/1985")
        });
        context.Employees.Add(new Employee
        {
            FirstName = "Karen",
            LastName = "Stanford",
            BirthDate = DateTime.Parse("7/6/1963")
        });
        context.SaveChanges();
    }

    using (var context = new EFRecipesEntities())
    {
        Console.WriteLine("Query using eSQL");
        var esql = @"Select EFRecipesModel.FullName(e) as Name,
                    EFRecipesModel.Age(e) as Age from
                    EFRecipesEntities.Employees as e";
        var objectContext = (context as IObjectContextAdapter).ObjectContext;
        var emps = objectContext.CreateQuery<DbDataRecord>(esql);
        foreach (var emp in emps)
        {
            Console.WriteLine("Employee: {0}, Age: {1}", emp["Name"],
                        emp["Age"]);
        }
    }

    using (var context = new EFRecipesEntities())
    {
        Console.WriteLine("\nQuery using LINQ");
        var emps = from e in context.Employees
                select new
                {
                    Name = MyFunctions.FullName(e),
                    Age = MyFunctions.Age(e)
                };
```

```
                foreach (var emp in emps)
                {
                    Console.WriteLine("Employee: {0}, Age: {1}", emp.Name,
                                emp.Age.ToString());
                }
            }
        }
    }

    public class MyFunctions
    {
        [EdmFunction("EFRecipesModel", "FullName")]
        public static string FullName(Employee employee)
        {
            throw new NotSupportedException("Direct calls are not supported.");
        }

        [EdmFunction("EFRecipesModel", "Age")]
        public static int Age(Employee employee)
        {
            throw new NotSupportedException("Direct calls are not supported.");
        }
    }
```

The output of the code from Listing 11-6 is as follows:

```
Query using eSQL
Employee: Jill Robins, Age: 37
Employee: Michael Kirk, Age: 28
Employee: Karen Stanford, Age: 50

Query using LINQ
Employee: Jill Robins, Age: 37
Employee: Michael Kirk, Age: 28
Employee: Karen Stanford, Age: 50
```

How It Works

Our model-defined functions return types Edm.String for the FullName() function and Edm.Int32 for the Age() function. These functions are defined on the conceptual level, so they don't directly refer to any type system outside of the Entity Data Model's type system. These primitive types are easily translated to the CLR type system.

In the <DefiningExpression> or body of the model-defined functions, we directly access the properties of the entities we received in the parameters. There is no need to use a select statement. However, the resulting expression must have a type that matches the type defined as the return type of the function.

After inserting a few employees into our model, we first query using eSQL. We construct an eSQL expression that invokes our two model-defined functions and projects the results to the Name and Age columns. Our eSQL expression results in a collection of anonymous types that contain just the Name and Age members. Because we're not returning one of the types defined in the model, we declare the type in CreateQuery<T>() to be DbDataRecord. We iterate over the collection resulting from the evaluation of the query and print out the employees' names and ages.

For the LINQ query, we select from the Employees entity set and project onto an anonymous type containing the Name and Age members. We set these members to the result of invoking our `FullName()` and `Age()` functions. As seen in the previous recipes in this chapter, we need to define the corresponding CLR methods. Because we are returning scalar values, these methods are never called and are used only for their signatures. The implementation of these methods reflects this.

We could have created read-only properties in a partial declaration of our Employee entity to implement the full name and age calculations. However, this would force the evaluation of these methods each time the entity is retrieved. With model-defined functions, we perform the calculations only when needed.

11-4. Calling a Model-Defined Function from a Model-Defined Function

Problem

You want to use a model-defined function in the implementation of another model-defined function.

Solution

Suppose that we have the model shown in Figure 11-4, representing the types of associates in a company along with their reporting structure

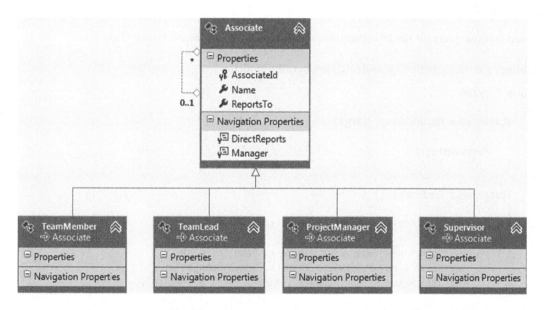

Figure 11-4. *A model representing the associate types in a company together with the reporting association*

In our fictional company, team members are managed by a team leader. Team leaders are managed by project managers. Supervisors manage project managers. Of course, there could be many other associate types, but for simplicity we'll stick with just these few.

If we wanted to return all of the team members for a given project manager or supervisor, we would need to drill down through the project managers and team leaders to get to the team members. To hide the complexity of navigating through these layers, we can create model-defined functions that allow easier and more direct access to these navigation properties.

To create and use these functions, do the following:

1. Right-click the .edmx file in the Solution Explorer, and click Open With ➤ XML Editor. This will open the .edmx file in the XML Editor.

2. Insert the code in Listing 11-7 just below the <Schema> tag in the conceptual models section of the .edmx file. This defines the functions in the model.

Listing 11-7. Model-Defined Functions for Navigating the Associate Hierarchy

```
<Function Name="GetProjectManager" ReturnType="EFRecipesModel.ProjectManager">
  <Parameter Name="teammember" Type="EFRecipesModel.TeamMember" />
  <DefiningExpression>
    treat(teammember.Manager.Manager as EFRecipesModel.ProjectManager)
  </DefiningExpression>
</Function>

<Function Name="GetSupervisor" ReturnType="EFRecipesModel.Supervisor">
  <Parameter Name="teammember" Type="EFRecipesModel.TeamMember" />
  <DefiningExpression>
    treat(EFRecipesModel.GetProjectManager(teammember).Manager as
        EFRecipesModel.Supervisor)
  </DefiningExpression>
</Function>
```

3. Insert into and query the model using code similar to the pattern shown in Listing 11-8.

Listing 11-8. Using Both eSQL and LINQ to Query the Model

```
class Program
{
    static void Main(string[] args)
    {
        RunExample();
    }

    static void RunExample()
    {
        using (var context = new EFRecipesEntities())
        {
            var john = new Supervisor { Name = "John Smith" };
            var steve = new Supervisor {Name = "Steve Johnson"};
            var jill = new ProjectManager { Name = "Jill Masterson",
                                            Manager = john };
            var karen = new ProjectManager { Name = "Karen Carns",
                                             Manager = steve };
            var bob = new TeamLead { Name = "Bob Richardson", Manager = karen };
            var tom = new TeamLead { Name = "Tom Landers", Manager = jill };
            var nancy = new TeamMember { Name = "Nancy Jones", Manager = tom };
            var stacy = new TeamMember { Name = "Stacy Rutgers",
                                         Manager = bob };
```

```
            context.Associates.Add(john);
            context.Associates.Add(steve);
            context.SaveChanges();
        }

        using (var context = new EFRecipesEntities())
        {
            Console.WriteLine("Using eSQL...");
            var emps = context.Associates.OfType<TeamMember>()
                .Where(@"EFRecipesModel.GetProjectManager(it).Name =
                        @projectManager ||
                        EFRecipesModel.GetSupervisor(it).Name == @supervisor",
                    new ObjectParameter("projectManager", "Jill Masterson"),
                    new ObjectParameter("supervisor", "Steve Johnson"));
            Console.WriteLine("Team members that report up to either");
            Console.WriteLine("Project Manager Jill Masterson ");
            Console.WriteLine("or Supervisor Steve Johnson");
            foreach (var emp in emps)
            {
                Console.WriteLine("\tAssociate: {0}", emp.Name);
            }
        }

        using (var context = new EFRecipesEntities())
        {
            Console.WriteLine();
            Console.WriteLine("Using LINQ...");
            var emps = from e in context.Associates.OfType<TeamMember>()
                        where MyFunctions.GetProjectManager(e).Name ==
                          "Jill Masterson" ||
                        MyFunctions.GetSupervisor(e).Name == "Steve Johnson"
                        select e;
            Console.WriteLine("Team members that report up to either");
            Console.WriteLine("Project Manager Jill Masterson ");
            Console.WriteLine("or Supervisor Steve Johnson");
            foreach (var emp in emps)
            {
                Console.WriteLine("\tAssociate: {0}", emp.Name);
            }
        }
    }
}

public class MyFunctions
{
    [EdmFunction("EFRecipesModel", "GetProjectManager")]
    public static ProjectManager GetProjectManager(TeamMember member)
    {
        throw new NotSupportedException("Direct calls not supported.");
    }
```

```
[EdmFunction("EFRecipesModel", "GetSupervisor")]
public static Supervisor GetSupervisor(TeamMember member)
{
    throw new NotSupportedException("Direct calls not supported.");
}
}
```

The output of the code from Listing 11-8 is as follows:

```
Using eSQL...
Team members that report up to either
Project Manager Jill Masterson
or Supervisor Steve Johnson
        Associate: Nancy Jones
        Associate: Stacy Rutgers
Using LINQ...
Team members that report up to either
Project Manager Jill Masterson
or Supervisor Steve Johnson
        Associate: Nancy Jones
        Associate: Stacy Rutgers
```

How It Works

In the GetSupervisor() function in Listing 11-7, we need to make three hops through the Manager navigation property. The first one gets the team lead from the team member, the second one gets the project manager from the team lead, and the final one gets the supervisor from the project manager. We already created the GetProjectManager() function in Listing 11-7, so we can leverage that function to simplify the implementation of the GetSupervisor() function.

We use the treat() eSQL operator to cast an instance of Associate to its concrete type, which is either ProjectManager or Supervisor. If we didn't use the treat() operator, Entity Framework would raise an exception complaining that it cannot map the instance of Associate to ProjectManager or Supervisor.

In Listing 11-8, using the GetProjectManager() and GetSupervisor() functions allows us to simplify the code by hiding all of the traversal through the object graph via the Manager navigation property.

Because we are not returning IQueryable<T> from our model-defined function, we didn't need to provide an implementation of the stubs we require to use these functions in the LINQ query.

11-5. Returning an Anonymous Type from a Model-Defined Function

Problem

You want to create a model-defined function that returns an anonymous type.

Solution

Let's say that you have a model for hotel reservations like the one shown in Figure 11-5.

Figure 11-5. *A model for hotel reservations*

You want to retrieve the total number of reservations and the total room revenue for each visitor. Because you will need this information in several places, you want to create a model-defined function that takes in a search parameter and returns a collection of anonymous types containing the summary information for each visitor.

To create and use this model-defined function, do the following:

1. Right-click the .edmx file in the Solution Explorer, and click Open With ➤ XML Editor. This will open the .edmx file in the XML Editor.

2. Insert the code in Listing 11-9 just below the <Schema> tag in the conceptual models section of the .edmx file. This defines the function in the model.

Listing 11-9. The VisitorSummary() Model-Defined Function

```
<Function Name="VisitorSummary">
  <Parameter Name="StartDate" Type="Edm.DateTime" />
  <Parameter Name="Days" Type="Edm.Int32" />
  <ReturnType>
    <CollectionType>
      <RowType>
        <Property Name="Name" Type="Edm.String" />
        <Property Name="TotalReservations" Type="Edm.Int32" />
        <Property Name="BusinessEarned" Type="Edm.Decimal" />
      </RowType>
    </CollectionType>
  </ReturnType>
  <DefiningExpression>
    Select
    r.Visitor.Name,
    COUNT(r.ReservationId) as TotalReservations,
    SUM(r.Cost) as BusinessEarned
    from EFRecipesEntities.Reservations as r
    where r.ReservationDate between StartDate and
    AddDays(StartDate,Days)
    group by r.Visitor.Name
  </DefiningExpression>
</Function>
```

3. Insert into and query the model using code similar to the pattern shown in Listing 11-10.

Listing 11-10. Querying the Model Using the VistorySummary() Model-Defined Function

```
class Program
{
    static void Main(string[] args)
    {
        RunExample();
    }

    static void RunExample()
    {
        using (var context = new EFRecipesEntities())
        {
            var hotel = new Hotel { Name = "Five Seasons Resort" };
            var v1 = new Visitor { Name = "Alex Stevens" };
            var v2 = new Visitor { Name = "Joan Hills" };
            var r1 = new Reservation { Cost = 79.99M, Hotel = hotel,
                ReservationDate = DateTime.Parse("2/19/2010"), Visitor = v1 };
            var r2 = new Reservation { Cost = 99.99M, Hotel = hotel,
                ReservationDate = DateTime.Parse("2/17/2010"), Visitor = v2 };
            var r3 = new Reservation { Cost = 109.99M, Hotel = hotel,
                ReservationDate = DateTime.Parse("2/18/2010"), Visitor = v1 };
            var r4 = new Reservation { Cost = 89.99M, Hotel = hotel,
                ReservationDate = DateTime.Parse("2/17/2010"), Visitor = v2 };
            context.Hotels.Add(hotel);
            context.SaveChanges();
        }

        using (var context = new EFRecipesEntities())
        {
            Console.WriteLine("Using eSQL...");
            var esql = @"Select value v from
                EFRecipesModel.VisitorSummary(DATETIME'2010-02-16 00:00', 7) as v";
            var objectContext = (context as IObjectContextAdapter).ObjectContext;
            var visitors = objectContext.CreateQuery<DbDataRecord>(esql);

            foreach (var visitor in visitors)
            {
                Console.WriteLine("{0}, Total Reservations: {1}, Revenue: {2:C}",
                    visitor["Name"], visitor["TotalReservations"],
                    visitor["BusinessEarned"]);
            }
        }

        using (var context = new EFRecipesEntities())
        {
            Console.WriteLine();
            Console.WriteLine("Using LINQ...");
            var visitors = from v in
```

```
                    context.VisitorSummary(DateTime.Parse("2/16/2010"), 7)
                    select v;
                foreach (var visitor in visitors)
                {
                    Console.WriteLine("{0}, Total Reservations: {1}, Revenue: {2:C}",
                        visitor["Name"], visitor["TotalReservations"],
                        visitor["BusinessEarned"]);
                }
            }
        }
    }

    partial class EFRecipesEntities
    {
        [EdmFunction("EFRecipesModel", "VisitorSummary")]
        public IQueryable<DbDataRecord> VisitorSummary(DateTime StartDate, int Days)
        {
            return this.QueryProvider.CreateQuery<DbDataRecord>(
                Expression.Call(
                Expression.Constant(this),
                (MethodInfo)MethodInfo.GetCurrentMethod(),
                new Expression[] { Expression.Constant(StartDate),
                                    Expression.Constant(Days) }
                ));
        }
    }
```

The output from the code in Listing 11-10 is as follows:

```
Using eSQL...
Alex Stevens, Total Reservations: 2, Revenue: $189.98
Joan Hills, Total Reservations: 2, Revenue: $189.98

Using LINQ...
Alex Stevens, Total Reservations: 2, Revenue: $189.98
Joan Hills, Total Reservations: 2, Revenue: $189.98
```

How It Works

In Listing 11-9, for the definition of the VisitorSummary() function, we group the results by visitor, which is the navigation property exposed on the entity. To get the total count of reservations for each visitor, we use the eSQL Count()function. To get the total revenue, we use the Sum() function.

In the function, we shape the results as a collection of rows of three values: Name, TotalReservations, and BusinessEarned. Here we use the <CollectionType> and <RowType> tags to indicate the return type. In CLR terms, this is a collection of DbDataRecords.

To use the function in a LINQ query, we create a CLR method that returns IQueryable<DbDataRecord>. As in the previous recipes, we decorated the method with the EdmFunction()attribute. However, because we are returning an IQueryable<T>, we need to implement the body of the method to include the function call in the expression tree. Furthermore, because we need access to the QueryProvider in our ObjectContext to return an IQueryable<T>, we need to implement this method inside the EFRecipesEntities class.

11-6. Returning a Complex Type from a Model-Defined Function

Problem

You want to return a complex type from a model-defined function.

Solution

Suppose that we have a model for patients and their visits to a local hospital. This model is shown in Figure 11-6.

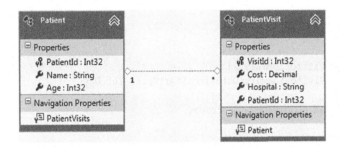

Figure 11-6. *A model for patient visits*

You want to create a model-defined function that returns summary information about the patient with their name, the total number of visits, and their accumulated bill. Additionally, you want to filter the results to include only patients over 40 years old.

To create and use the model-defined function, do the following:

1. Right-click the designer, and select Add ➤ Complex Type.

2. Right-click the new complex type in the Model Browser. Rename the type to VisitSummary, and add the following properties:

    a. Name of type String, not nullable

    b. TotalVisits of type Int32, not nullable

    c. TotalCost of type Decimal, not nullable

3. Right-click the .edmx file in the Solution Explorer, and click Open With ➤ XML Editor. This will open the .edmx file in the XML Editor.

4. Insert the code in Listing 11-11 just below the <Schema> tag in the conceptual models section of the .edmx file. This defines the function in the model.

Listing 11-11. The GetVisitSummary() Model-Defined Function

```
<Function Name="GetVisitSummary"  ReturnType="Collection(EFRecipesModel.VisitSummary)">
  <DefiningExpression>
    select VALUE EFRecipesModel.VisitSummary(pv.Patient.Name,
                 Count(pv.VisitId),Sum(pv.Cost))
    from EFRecipesEntities.PatientVisits as pv
    group by pv.Patient.PatientId
  </DefiningExpression>
</Function>
```

5. Insert into and query the model using code similar to the pattern shown in Listing 11-12.

Listing 11-12. Using eSQL and LINQ with the VisitSummary() Function to Query the Model

```csharp
class Program
{
    static void Main(string[] args)
    {
        RunExample();
    }

    static void RunExample()
    {
        using (var context = new EFRecipesEntities())
        {
            string hospital = "Oakland General";
            var p1 = new Patient { Name = "Robin Rosen", Age = 41 };
            var p2 = new Patient { Name = "Alex Jones", Age = 39 };
            var p3 = new Patient { Name = "Susan Kirby", Age = 54 };
            var v1 = new PatientVisit { Cost = 98.38M, Hospital = hospital,
                                        Patient = p1 };
            var v2 = new PatientVisit { Cost = 1122.98M, Hospital = hospital,
                                        Patient = p1 };
            var v3 = new PatientVisit { Cost = 2292.72M, Hospital = hospital,
                                        Patient = p2 };
            var v4 = new PatientVisit { Cost = 1145.73M, Hospital = hospital,
                                        Patient = p3 };
            var v5 = new PatientVisit { Cost = 2891.07M, Hospital = hospital,
                                        Patient = p3 };
            context.Patients.Add (p1);
            context.Patients.Add (p2);
            context.Patients.Add (p3);
            context.SaveChanges();
        }

        using (var context = new EFRecipesEntities())
        {
            Console.WriteLine("Query using eSQL...");
            var esql = @"Select value ps from EFRecipesEntities.Patients
                        as p join EFRecipesModel.GetVisitSummary()
                        as ps on p.Name = ps.Name where p.Age > 40";
            var objectContext = (context as IObjectContextAdapter).ObjectContext;
            var patients = objectContext.CreateQuery<VisitSummary>(esql);
            foreach (var patient in patients)
            {
                Console.WriteLine("{0}, Visits: {1}, Total Bill: {2}",
                    patient.Name, patient.TotalVisits.ToString(),
                    patient.TotalCost.ToString("C"));
            }
        }
```

```
using (var context = new EFRecipesEntities())
{
    Console.WriteLine();
    Console.WriteLine("Query using LINQ...");
    var patients = from p in context.Patients
                   join ps in context.GetVisitSummary() on p.Name equals
                     ps.Name
                   where p.Age >= 40
                   select ps;
    foreach (var patient in patients)
    {
        Console.WriteLine("{0}, Visits: {1}, Total Bill: {2}",
            patient.Name, patient.TotalVisits.ToString(),
            patient.TotalCost.ToString("C"));
    }
}
}
}

partial class EFRecipesEntities
{
    [EdmFunction("EFRecipesModel", "GetVisitSummary")]
    public IQueryable<VisitSummary> GetVisitSummary()
    {
        return this.QueryProvider.CreateQuery<VisitSummary>(
            Expression.Call(Expression.Constant(this),
              (MethodInfo)MethodInfo.GetCurrentMethod()));
    }
}
```

The code in Listing 11-12 produces the following output:

```
Query using eSQL...
Robin Rosen, Visits: 2, Total Bill: $1,221.36
Susan Kirby, Visits: 2, Total Bill: $4,036.80

Query using LINQ...
Robin Rosen, Visits: 2, Total Bill: $1,221.36
Susan Kirby, Visits: 2, Total Bill: $4,036.80
```

How It Works

We started by creating the complex type in the model. With the complex type created, we defined the
GetVisitSummary() function in Listing 11-11 as returning a collection of our newly created complex type. Notice that
the constructor for our complex type takes in parameters in the same order as those defined by our complex type. You
might need to double-check in the .edmx file to make sure that the designer created the complex type properties in
the order in which you created them interactively.

Because our function returns IQueryable<VisitSummary>, we need to implement the bootstrapping code. Also, because we need to get access to the QueryProvider inside our ObjectContext, we need to implement the method in a partial class of our EFRecipesEntities class, which is our ObjectContext.

You might be wondering when you would return a collection of complex types rather than a collection of anonymous types from a function. If you used the function in a LINQ query, the bootstrapping method would need to return IQueryable<DbDataRecord> for the anonymous type. However, although this collection could not be filtered further, a collection of complex types could be further filtered.

11-7. Returning a Collection of Entity References from a Model-Defined Function

Problem

You want to return a collection of entity references from a model-defined function.

Solution

Let's say that you have a model, such as the one shown in Figure 11-7, for events and their sponsors. Sponsors provide different levels of financial support for events. Platinum sponsors provide the highest level of financial support.

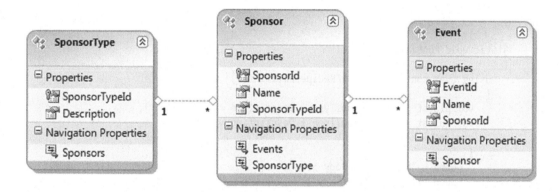

Figure 11-7. *A model for events and their sponsors*

You want to create a model-defined function that returns a collection of all the sponsors who are at the Platinum level. Because you need only the entity key information for the sponsor, the function needs to return only a collection of references to the sponsors.

To create and use the model-defined function, do the following:

1. Right-click the .edmx file in the Solution Explorer, and click Open With ➤ XML Editor. This will open the .edmx file in the XML Editor.

2. Insert the code in Listing 11-13 just below the <Schema> tag in the conceptual models section of the .edmx file. This defines the function in the model.

Listing 11-13. The Definition of the PlatinumSponsors() Function

```
<Function Name="PlatinumSponsors">
        <ReturnType>
          <CollectionType>
            <ReferenceType Type="EFRecipesModel.Sponsor" />
          </CollectionType>
        </ReturnType>
        <DefiningExpression>
          select value ref(s)
          from EFRecipesEntities.Sponsors as s
          where s.SponsorType.Description == 'Platinum'
        </DefiningExpression>
      </Function>
```

3. Insert into and query the model using code similar to the pattern shown in Listing 11-14.

Listing 11-14. Using eSQL and Our PlatinumSponsors() Function to Find All Events with Platinum-Level Sponsors

```
class Program
{
    static void Main(string[] args)
    {
        RunExample();
    }

    static void RunExample()
    {
        using (var context = new EFRecipesEntities())
        {
            var platst = new SponsorType { Description = "Platinum" };
            var goldst = new SponsorType { Description = "Gold" };
            var sp1 = new Sponsor
            {
                Name = "Rex's Auto Body Shop",
                SponsorType = goldst
            };
            var sp2 = new Sponsor
            {
                Name = "Midtown Eye Care Center",
                SponsorType = platst
            };
            var sp3 = new Sponsor
            {
                Name = "Tri-Cities Ford",
                SponsorType = platst
            };
            var ev1 = new Event { Name = "OctoberFest", Sponsor = sp1 };
            var ev2 = new Event { Name = "Concerts in the Park", Sponsor = sp2 };
            var ev3 = new Event { Name = "11th Street Art Festival", Sponsor = sp3 };
            context.Events.Add(ev1);
            context.Events.Add(ev2);
```

```
        context.Events.Add(ev3);
        context.SaveChanges();
    }

    using (var context = new EFRecipesEntities())
    {
        Console.WriteLine("Events with Platinum Sponsors");
        Console.WriteLine("=============================");
        var esql = @"select value e from EFRecipesEntities.Events as e where
            ref(e.Sponsor) in (EFRecipesModel.PlatinumSponsors())";

        var objectContext = (context as IObjectContextAdapter).ObjectContext;

        var events = objectContext.CreateQuery<Event>(esql);
        foreach (var ev in events)
        {
            Console.WriteLine(ev.Name);
        }
    }
}
}
```

The output of the code in Listing 11-14 is as follows:

```
Events with Platinum Sponsors
=============================
Concerts in the Park
11th Street Art Festival
```

How It Works

The <ReferenceType> element in the conceptual model denotes a reference to an entity type. This means that we are returning a reference to an entity, not the complete entity. Our model-defined function returns a collection of references to Platinum-level sponsors. To illustrate using our function, we created an eSQL expression in Listing 11-14 to get all of the events with Platinum-level sponsors. There are, of course, lots of different ways to get the events sponsored by Platinum-level sponsors, but by encapsulating the collection of Platinum-level sponsors in our model-defined function, we introduce a bit of code reusability.

We didn't show a corresponding use in a LINQ query because the bootstrapping code would need to return an IQueryable<EntityKey>, which is fine, but a subsequent Contains clause would not work because the result is not strongly typed.

11-8. Using Canonical Functions in eSQL
Problem

You want to call a canonical function in your eSQL query. A canonical function is an eSQL function that is natively supported by all data providers. Examples include Sum(), Count(), and Avg().

Solution

Suppose that we have a model for customers and their orders, as shown in Figure 11-8.

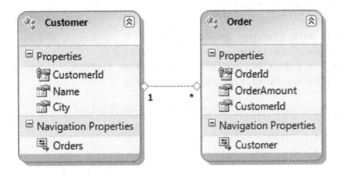

Figure 11-8. *A model for customers and their orders*

You want to retrieve the number of orders and the total purchase amount made by customers who have placed orders above the average order.

To create and use this query, follow the pattern shown in Listing 11-15.

Listing 11-15. *Querying the Model in eSQL Using the Sum(), Count(), and Avg() Functions*

```
class Program
{
    static void Main(string[] args)
    {
        RunExample();
    }

    static void RunExample()
    {
        using (var context = new EFRecipesEntities())
        {
            var c1 = new Customer { Name = "Jill Masters", City = "Raytown" };
            var c2 = new Customer { Name = "Bob Meyers", City = "Austin" };
            var c3 = new Customer { Name = "Robin Rosen", City = "Dallas" };
            var o1 = new Order { OrderAmount = 12.99M, Customer = c1 };
            var o2 = new Order { OrderAmount = 99.39M, Customer = c2 };
            var o3 = new Order { OrderAmount = 101.29M, Customer = c3 };
            context.Orders.Add(o1);
            context.Orders.Add(o2);
            context.Orders.Add(o3);
            context.SaveChanges();
        }

        using (var context = new EFRecipesEntities())
        {
            Console.WriteLine("Customers with above average total purchases");
            var esql = @"select o.Customer.Name, count(o.OrderId) as TotalOrders,
                Sum(o.OrderAmount) as TotalPurchases
```

```
        from EFRecipesEntities.Orders as o
        where o.OrderAmount >
          anyelement(select value Avg(o.OrderAmount) from
                    EFRecipesEntities.Orders as o)
        group by o.Customer.Name";

    var objectContext = (context as IObjectContextAdapter).ObjectContext;

    var summary = objectContext.CreateQuery<DbDataRecord>(esql);
    foreach (var item in summary)
    {
        Console.WriteLine("\t{0}, Total Orders: {1}, Total: {2:C}",
            item["Name"], item["TotalOrders"], item["TotalPurchases"]);
    }
  }
 }
}
```

The output of the code in Listing 11-15 is as follows:

```
Customers with above average total purchases
        Bob Meyers, Total Orders: 1, Total: $99.39
        Robin Rosen, Total Orders: 1, Total: $101.29
```

How It Works

In this recipe, we used the canonical functions Count(),Sum(),and Avg(). These functions are independent of the data store, which means that they are portable and return types in the EDM space rather than data store-specific or CLR types.

11-9. Using Canonical Functions in LINQ
Problem

You want to use canonical functions in a LINQ query.

Solution

Let's say that you have a model for movie rentals like the one shown in Figure 11-9. The MovieRental entity holds the date that the movie was rented and the date that it was returned, as well as any late fees that have been accumulated.

Figure 11-9. *The MovieRental entity that has the dates for a rental period along with any late fees*

You want to retrieve all of the movies that were returned more than 10 days after they were rented. These are the late movies.

To create and use this query, follow the pattern shown inListing 11-16.

Listing 11-16. Retrieving the Late Movies using the DateDiff() Function

```
class Program
    {
        static void Main(string[] args)
        {
            RunExample();
        }

        static void RunExample()
        {
            using (var context = new EFRecipesEntities())
            {
                var mr1 = new MovieRental
                {
                    Title = "A Day in the Life",
                    RentalDate = DateTime.Parse("2/19/2013"),
                    ReturnedDate = DateTime.Parse("3/4/2013"),
                    LateFees = 3M
                };
                var mr2 = new MovieRental
                {
                    Title = "The Shortest Yard",
                    RentalDate = DateTime.Parse("3/15/2013"),
                    ReturnedDate = DateTime.Parse("3/20/2013"),
                    LateFees = 0M
                };
                var mr3 = new MovieRental
                {
                    Title = "Jim's Story",
                    RentalDate = DateTime.Parse("3/2/2013"),
                    ReturnedDate = DateTime.Parse("3/19/2013"),
                    LateFees = 3M
                };
```

```
        context.MovieRentals.Add(mr1);
        context.MovieRentals.Add(mr2);
        context.MovieRentals.Add(mr3);
        context.SaveChanges();
    }

    using (var context = new EFRecipesEntities())
    {
        Console.WriteLine("Movie rentals late returns");
        Console.WriteLine("==========================");
        var late = from r in context.MovieRentals
                   where DbFunctions.DiffDays(r.RentalDate, r.ReturnedDate) > 10
                   select r;
        foreach (var rental in late)
        {
            Console.WriteLine("{0} was {1} days late, fee: {2}", rental.Title,
                    (rental.ReturnedDate - rental.RentalDate).Days - 10,
                    rental.LateFees.ToString("C"));
        }
    }
}
```

The output of the code in Listing 11-16 is the following:

```
Movie rentals late returns
==========================
A Day in the Life was 3 days late, fee: $3.00
Jim's Story was 7 days late, fee: $3.00
```

How It Works

Canonical functions, which are defined in Entity Framework, are data source-agnostic and supported by all data providers. The types returned from canonical functions are defined in terms of types from the Entity Data Model.

In this recipe, we used the DiffDays() function to calculate the number of days between the start and end of the rental period. Because DiffDays() is a canonical function, it will be implemented by all providers.

Best Practice

You may be asking yourself, "When should I use EntityFunctions?" Entity Framework provides translations for some expressions into the canonical functions, but the translation is limited. Not every CLR method will translate to the corresponding canonical function.

Here's the best practice. If there is a translation available, use it. It makes the code easier to read. If there is no translation available, use the EntityFunction class to call the canonical function explicitly, as in the following code snippet:

```
var laterentals = from r in context.MovieRentals
                  where (r.ReturnedDate - r.RentalDate).Days > 10
                  select r;
does not translate to the Canonical Function, so you should use,
var laterentals = from r in context.MovieRentals
                  where EntityFunctions.DiffDays(r.RentalDate,
                                                 r.ReturnedDate) > 10
                  select r;
```

11-10. Calling Database Functions in eSQL

Problem

You want to call a database function in an eSQL statement.

Solution

Let's say that you have an eCommerce website, and you need to find all of the customers within a certain distance of a given ZIP code. Your model might look like the one shown in Figure 11-10.

Figure 11-10. *WebCustomer and Zip entities in a model*

We'll need to pull out some basic math functions to get this to work. Unfortunately, Entity Framework does not have the canonical functions we need, so we'll have to use the functions available in the data store.

Use the pattern in Listing 11-17 to call the database functions from an eSQL expression.

Listing 11-17. Using Database Functions to Determine the Distance between a Customer and a Given Zip Code

```
class Program
    {
        static void Main(string[] args)
        {
            RunExample();
        }
```

```
static void RunExample()
{
    using (var context = new EFRecipesEntities())
    {
        var c1 = new WebCustomer { Name = "Alex Stevens", Zip = "76039" };
        var c2 = new WebCustomer { Name = "Janis Jones", Zip = "76040" };
        var c3 = new WebCustomer { Name = "Cathy Robins", Zip = "76111" };
        context.Zips.Add(new Zip
        {
            Latitude = 32.834298M,
            Longitude = -32.834298M,
            ZipCode = "76039"
        });
        context.Zips.Add(new Zip
        {
            Latitude = 32.835298M,
            Longitude = -32.834798M,
            ZipCode = "76040"
        });
        context.Zips.Add(new Zip
        {
            Latitude = 33.834298M,
            Longitude = -31.834298M,
            ZipCode = "76111"
        });
        context.WebCustomers.Add(c1);
        context.WebCustomers.Add(c2);
        context.WebCustomers.Add(c3);
        context.SaveChanges();
    }

    using (var context = new EFRecipesEntities())
    {
        string esql = @"select value c
                from EFRecipesEntities.WebCustomers as c
                join
                (SELECT z.ZipCode,
                  3958.75 * (SqlServer.Atan(SqlServer.Sqrt(1 -
                   SqlServer.power(((SqlServer.Sin(t2.Latitude/57.2958M) *
                       SqlServer.Sin(z.Latitude/57.2958M)) +
                       (SqlServer.Cos(t2.Latitude/57.2958M) *
                       SqlServer.Cos(z.Latitude/57.2958M) *
                        SqlServer.Cos((z.Longitude/57.2958M) -
                       (t2.Longitude/57.2958M)))), 2)) /(
                          ((SqlServer.Sin(t2.Latitude/57.2958M) *
                          SqlServer.Sin(z.Latitude/57.2958M)) +
                           (SqlServer.Cos(t2.Latitude/57.2958M) *
                            SqlServer.Cos(z.Latitude/57.2958M) *
                            SqlServer.Cos((z.Longitude/57.2958M) -
                              (t2.Longitude/57.2958M))))))
                    ) as DistanceInMiles
```

```
                          FROM EFRecipesEntities.Zips AS z join
                            (select top(1) z2.Latitude as Latitude,z2.Longitude as
                             Longitude
                             from EFRecipesEntities.Zips as z2
                             where z2.ZipCode = @Zip
                            ) as t2 on 1 = 1
                          ) as matchingzips on matchingzips.ZipCode = c.Zip
                         where matchingzips.DistanceInMiles <= @RadiusInMiles";

                 var objectContext = (context as IObjectContextAdapter).ObjectContext;

                 var custs = objectContext.CreateQuery<WebCustomer>(esql,
                           new ObjectParameter("Zip", "76039"),
                           new ObjectParameter("RadiusInMiles", 5));
                 Console.WriteLine("Customers within 5 miles of 76039");
                 foreach (var cust in custs)
                 {
                     Console.WriteLine("Customer: {0}", cust.Name);
                 }
             }
         }
     }
```

The output of the code in Listing 11-17 is as follows:

```
Customers within 5 miles of 76039
Customer: Alex Stevens
Customer: Janis Jones
```

How It Works

Okay, the eSQL is a little complex, but the complexity is because we're calling a bunch of database functions. Using the database functions in eSQL is fairly simple. These functions are available in the SqlServer namespace. Not all database functions are available in eSQL, so check the current Microsoft documentation to get a complete list. These functions are available only for SQL Server database.

In this example, the Zip entity has the latitude and longitude for each ZIP code. These values represent the geographic location of the center of the ZIP code. To calculate the distance between two ZIP codes involves a bit of math. Luckily, the database side provides the necessary functions to do the calculation.

11-11. Calling Database Functions in LINQ
Problem

You want to call a database function in a LINQ query.

Solution

Let's say that you have an Appointment entity in your model, and you want to query for all of the appointments that you have on a given day of the week. The Appointment entity might look like the one shown in Figure 11-11.

Figure 11-11. *An Appointment entity with the start and end times for appointments*

If we want to find all of the appointments for Thursday, we can't use the CLR enum DayOfWeek.Thursday to compare with the StartsAt property in a where clause because this does not translate to a data store statement. We need to use the pattern shown in Listing 11-18.

Listing 11-18. Using a Database Function in a LINQ Query

```
class Program
    {
        static void Main(string[] args)
        {
            RunExample();
        }

        static void RunExample()
        {
            using (var context = new EFRecipesEntities())
            {
                var app1 = new Appointment
                {
                    StartsAt = DateTime.Parse("7/23/2013 14:00"),
                        GoesTo = DateTime.Parse("7/23/2013 15:00")
                };
                var app2 = new Appointment
                {
                    StartsAt = DateTime.Parse("7/24/2013 9:00"),
                    GoesTo = DateTime.Parse("7/24/2013 11:00")
                };
                var app3 = new Appointment
                {
                    StartsAt = DateTime.Parse("7/24/2013 13:00"),
                        GoesTo = DateTime.Parse("7/23/2013 15:00")
                };
                context.Appointments.Add(app1);
                context.Appointments.Add(app2);
                context.Appointments.Add(app3);
                context.SaveChanges();
            }
```

```
using (var context = new EFRecipesEntities())
{
    var apps = from a in context.Appointments
               where SqlFunctions.DatePart("WEEKDAY", a.StartsAt) == 4
               select a;
    Console.WriteLine("Appointments for Thursday");
    Console.WriteLine("===========================");
    foreach (var appointment in apps)
    {
        Console.WriteLine("Appointment from {0} to {1}",
                appointment.StartsAt.ToShortTimeString(),
                appointment.GoesTo.ToShortTimeString());
    }
}
```

The output of the code in Listing 11-18 is as follows:

```
Appointments for Thursday
===========================
Appointment from 9:00 AM to 11:00 AM
Appointment from 1:00 PM to 3:00 PM
```

How It Works

Database functions are available for use in both eSQL and LINQ queries. These functions are exposed via methods in the SqlFunctions class. Because these functions execute on the database side, the behavior you get might differ slightly from what you would expect on the .NET side. For example, DayOfWeek.Thursday evaluates to 4 on the .NET side. On the database side, Thursday is the fifth day of the week, so we check for a value of 5.

As with database functions in eSQL, not all database functions are available for LINQ queries. Check the current documentation from Microsoft for a complete list of the available functions.

11-12. Defining Built-in Functions
Problem

You want to define a built-in function for use in an eSQL or LINQ query.

Solution

Let's say that you want to use the IsNull function in the database, but this function is not currently exposed by Entity Framework for either eSQL or LINQ. Suppose we have a WebProduct entity in our model like the one shown in Figure 11-12.

Figure 11-12. *A WebProduct entity in our model*

To expose this database function for your queries, do the following:

1. Right-click the .edmx file in the Solution Explorer, and click Open With ➤ XML Editor. This will open the .edmx file in the XML Editor.

2. Insert the code in Listing 11-19 just below the <Schema> tag in the storage models section of the .edmx file. This defines the functions in the storage layer.

Listing 11-19. Defining Our Function in the Storage Layer

```
<Function Name="ISNULL" ReturnType="varchar" BuiltIn="true" Schema="dbo">
    <Parameter Name="expr1" Type="varchar"  Mode="In" />
    <Parameter Name="expr2" Type="varchar"  Mode="In" />
</Function>
```

3. Insert into and query the model using code similar to the pattern shown in Listing 11-19.

Listing 11-20. Using the ISNULL() Function in an eSQL and LINQ Query

```
class Program
    {
        static void Main(string[] args)
        {
            RunExample();
        }

        static void RunExample()
        {
            using (var context = new EFRecipesEntities())
            {
                var w1 = new WebProduct
                {
                    Name = "Camping Tent",
                    Description = "Family Camping Tent, Color Green"
                };
                var w2 = new WebProduct { Name = "Chemical Light" };
                var w3 = new WebProduct
                {
                    Name = "Ground Cover",
                    Description = "Blue ground cover"
                };
```

```
                context.WebProducts.Add(w1);
                context.WebProducts.Add(w2);
                context.WebProducts.Add(w3);
                context.SaveChanges();
            }

            using (var context = new EFRecipesEntities())
            {
                Console.WriteLine("Query using eSQL...");
                var esql = @"select value
                    EFRecipesModel.Store.ISNULL(p.Description,p.Name)
                    from EFRecipesEntities.WebProducts as p";
                var objectContext = (context as IObjectContextAdapter).ObjectContext;
                var prods = objectContext.CreateQuery<string>(esql);
                foreach (var prod in prods)
                {
                    Console.WriteLine("Product Description: {0}", prod);
                }
            }

            using (var context = new EFRecipesEntities())
            {
                Console.WriteLine();
                Console.WriteLine("Query using LINQ...");
                var prods = from p in context.WebProducts
                            select BuiltinFunctions.ISNULL(p.Description, p.Name);
                foreach (var prod in prods)
                {
                    Console.WriteLine(prod);
                }
            }
        }
    }

    public class BuiltinFunctions
    {
        [EdmFunction("EFRecipesModel.Store", "ISNULL")]
        public static string ISNULL(string check_expression, string replacementvalue)
        {
            throw new NotSupportedException("Direct calls are not supported.");
        }
    }
```

The output from the code in Listing 11-20 is as follows:

```
Query using eSQL...
Product Description: Family Camping Tent, Color Green
Product Description: Chemical Light
Product Description: Blue ground cover

Query using LINQ...
Family Camping Tent, Color Green
Chemical Light
Blue ground cover
```

How It Works

In the definition of the ISNULL() function in Listing 11-18, we need to match the name of the database function with our function's name. Both have to be the same in spelling but not in case.

We defined the function not in the conceptual layer, as in previous recipes in this chapter, but in the store layer. This function is already available in the database; we are simply surfacing it in the store layer for our use.

When we use the function in the eSQL statement, we need to fully qualify the namespace for the function. Here that fully qualified name is EFRecipesModel.Store.ISNULL().

To use the function in a LINQ query, we need to create the bootstrapping method. We are not returning an IQueryable<T>, so no implementation of the method is required.

CHAPTER 12

Customizing Entity Framework Objects

The recipes in this chapter explore some of the customizations that can be applied to objects and to the processes in Entity Framework. These recipes cover many of the "behind the scenes" things that you can do to make your code more uniform by pushing concerns about things like business rule enforcement out of the details of your application to a central, application-wide implementation.

We start off this chapter with a recipe that shows you how to have your own code executable anytime SaveChanges() is called within your application. This recipe and a few others are particularly useful if you want to enforce business rules from a single point in your application.

In other recipes, we show you how to track database connections, how to automate responses to collection changes, how to implement cascading deletes, how to assign default values, and how to work with strongly typed XML properties.

The common thread of all of these recipes is extending the objects and processes in Entity Framework to make your code more resilient, uniform, and maintainable.

12-1. Executing Code When SaveChanges() Is Called

Problem

You want to execute code anytime SaveChanges() is called in a data context.

Solution

Let's say that you have a model that represents a job applicant. As part of the model, you want the file containing the applicant's resume to be deleted when the applicant's record is deleted. You could find every place in your application where you need to delete an applicant's record, but you want a more consistent and unified approach.

Your model looks like the one shown in Figure 12-1.

Figure 12-1. *A model for job applicant*

To ensure that the applicant's resume file is deleted when the applicant is deleted, we override the SavingChanges() method in the DbContext. In our overridden method, we need to scan the DbContext for changes that include deleting instances of the Applicant entity. Next we need to tell Entity Framework to save the changes by calling the real SaveChanges() method. Finally, for each of the deleted Applicants, we need to delete the associated resume file. The code in Listing 12-1 demonstrates this approach.

Listing 12-1. Overriding SaveChanges() to Delete the Resume File When the Applicant Is Deleted

```
class Program
    {
        static void Main(string[] args)
        {
            RunExample();
        }

        static void RunExample()
        {
            using (var context = new EFRecipesEntities())
            {
                var path1 = "AlexJones.txt";
                File.AppendAllText(path1, "Alex Jones\nResume\n...");
                var path2 = "JanisRogers.txt";
                File.AppendAllText(path2, "Janis Rodgers\nResume\n...");
                var app1 = new Applicant
                {
                    Name = "Alex Jones",
                    ResumePath = path1
                };
                var app2 = new Applicant
                {
                    Name = "Janis Rogers",
                    ResumePath = path2
                };
                context.Applicants.Add(app1);
                context.Applicants.Add(app2);
                context.SaveChanges();
```

```
            // delete Alex Jones
             context.Applicants.Remove(app1);
             context.SaveChanges();
        }
      }
   }
   public partial class EFRecipesEntities
   {
       public override int SaveChanges()
       {
           Console.WriteLine("Saving Changes...");
           var applicants = this.ChangeTracker.Entries().Where(e => e.State == System.Data.Entity.
EntityState.Deleted).Select(e => e.Entity).OfType<Applicant>().ToList();

           int changes = base.SaveChanges();
           Console.WriteLine("\n{0} applicants deleted",
                         applicants.Count().ToString());
           foreach (var app in applicants)
           {
              File.Delete(app.ResumePath);
              Console.WriteLine("\n{0}'s resume at {1} deleted",
                            app.Name, app.ResumePath);
           }
           return changes;
       }
   }
```

Following is the output from the code in Listing 12-1:

```
Saving Changes...
0 applicants deleted
Saving Changes...

1 applicants deleted

Alex Jones's resume at AlexJones.txt deleted
```

How It Works

The code in Listing 12-1 starts by inserting two applicants, each with the path to a resume file that we also created. The goal here is to delete the resume file in a structured way when the instance of the Applicant entity is deleted. We do this by overriding the SaveChanges() method.

In our SaveChanges() method, first we gather up all of the instances of Applicant that have been marked for deletion. These are the ones that will be deleted from the database when we call the real SaveChanges() method. We need to get them before we call SaveChanges(), because after we call SaveChanges() these instances will be detached from the context and we will no longer be able to use this query to retrieve them. Once we have the instances that will be deleted, we call SaveChanges() to do the real work of persisting objects to the database. Once the changes have been successfully committed, we can delete the resume files.

Entity Framework does not expose insert, update, and delete events for each entity. However, much of what we would do in these events can be handled, as we have demonstrated here, by overriding the SaveChanges() method.

12-2. Validating Property Changes

Problem

You want to validate a value being assigned to a property.

Solution

Let's say that you have a model with a User entity. The User entity has properties for the full name and user name for the user. You have a business rule that says that each user must have a UserName greater than five characters long. You want to enforce this business rule with code that sets the IsActive property to false if the UserName is set to a string less than or equal to five characters; otherwise the IsActive flag is set to true. This approach does not work in a Code-First approach. The model is shown in Figure 12-2.

Figure 12-2. *The User entity in our model*

To enforce our business rule, we need to implement the partial methods OnUserNameChanging() and OnUserNameChanged().These methods are called during the property change activity and after the property has been changed. The code in Listing 12-2 demonstrates one solution.

Listing 12-2. Monitoring the Changing of the UserName Property

```
class Program
{
    static void Main(string[] args)
    {
        RunExample();
    }

    static void RunExample()
    {
        using (var context = new EFRecipesEntities())
        {
            var user1 = new User { FullName = "Robert Meyers",
                                   UserName = "RM" };
            var user2 = new User { FullName = "Karen Kelley",
                                   UserName = "KKelley" };
            context.Users.AddObject(user1);
            context.Users.AddObject(user2);
```

```
                context.SaveChanges();
                Console.WriteLine("Users saved to database");
            }

            using (var context = new EFRecipesEntities())
            {
                Console.WriteLine();
                Console.WriteLine("Reading users from database");
                foreach (var user in context.Users)
                {
                    Console.WriteLine("{0} is {1}, UserName is {2}", user.FullName,
                            user.IsActive ? "Active" : "Inactive", user.UserName);
                }
            }
        }
    }
}

public partial class User
{
    partial void OnUserNameChanging(string value)
    {
        if (value.Length > 5)
            Console.WriteLine("{0}'s UserName changing to {1}, OK!",
                                this.FullName, value);
        else
            Console.WriteLine("{0}'s UserName changing to {1}, Too Short!",
                                this.FullName, value);
    }

    partial void OnUserNameChanged()
    {
        this.IsActive = (this.UserName.Length > 5);
    }
}
```

Following is the output of the code in Listing 12-2:

```
Robert Meyers's UserName changing to RM, Too Short!
Karen Kelley's UserName changing to KKelley, OK!
Users saved to database

Reading users from database
Robert Meyers's UserName changing to RM, Too Short!
Robert Meyers is Inactive, UserName is RM
Karen Kelley's UserName changing to KKelley, OK!
Karen Kelley is Active, UserName is KKelley
```

How It Works

In the solution, we implement the partial methods OnUserNameChanging() and OnUserNameChanged() to monitor the property change activity. The OnUserNameChanging() method is called when the property value is being set. Here we have an opportunity to throw an exception or, as in our example, simply report that the UserName is being set to a value of five characters or fewer.

The OnUserNameChanged() method is called after the property has been changed. Here we simply set the IsActive property based on the length of the final UserName property value.

These partial methods are created by Entity Framework as part of the code generation process. The names of the partial methods are derived from the property names. In our case, each method name included the name of the property. These partial methods are called inside the setter for each property.

You may be wondering a bit about the output of code. Notice that the partial methods are called twice in our example. They are called when the property value is set. They are also called when the User instances are materialized from the database. This second call happens, of course, because the materialization process involves setting the property value from the persisted value in the database.

In addition to these two partial methods, Entity Framework exposes two events for monitoring property changes. These events, PropertyChanging and PropertyChanged, are raised when any property on an Entity is changed. The sender of the event is the instance of the entity, and the PropertyEventArgs parameter contains a PropertyName that holds the name of the property that is changing or that has changed. Because these events are fired for any property change on the entity, they can be useful in some scenarios, particularly if you have an entity with many properties. They are somewhat less useful in practical terms because they don't readily expose the current and proposed values for the property.

When our UserName property value changes, the sequence is as follows:

1. OnUserNameChanging() method is called.

2. PropertyChanging event is raised.

3. PropertyChanged event is raised.

4. OnUserNameChanged() method is called.

The PropertyChanging and PropertyChanged events are not raised when a navigation property value is changed. The state of an entity changes only when a scalar or complex property changes.

12-3. Logging Database Connections
Problem

You want to create a log entry each time a connection is opened or closed to the database.

Solution

Entity Framework exposes a StateChange event on the connection for a DbContext. To create a log entry each time a connection is opened or closed, we need to handle this event.

Suppose our model looks like the one shown in Figure 12-3. In Listing 12-3, we create a few instances of a Donation and save them to the database. The code implements the override SaveChanges() method to wire in our handler for the StateChange event.

Figure 12-3. *The model with the Donation entity*

Listing 12-3. Code to Implement Logging of Open and Close of a Database Connection

```
class Program
    {
        static void Main(string[] args)
        {
            RunExample();
        }

        static void RunExample()
        {
            using (var context = new EFRecipesEntities())
            {
                context.Donations.Add(new Donation
                {
                    DonorName = "Robert Byrd",
                    Amount = 350M
                });
                context.Donations.Add(new Donation
                {
                    DonorName = "Nancy McVoid",
                    Amount = 250M
                });
                context.Donations.Add(new Donation
                {
                    DonorName = "Kim Kerns",
                    Amount = 750M
                });
                Console.WriteLine("About to SaveChanges()");
                context.SaveChanges();
            }

            using (var context = new EFRecipesEntities())
            {
                var list = context.Donations.Where(o => o.Amount > 300M);
                Console.WriteLine("Donations over $300");
                foreach (var donor in list)
```

```
            {
                Console.WriteLine("{0} gave {1}", donor.DonorName,
                            donor.Amount.ToString("C"));
            }
        }
        Console.WriteLine("Press any key to close...");
        Console.ReadLine();
    }
}

public partial class EFRecipesEntities
{
    public override int SaveChanges()
    {
        this.Database.Connection.StateChange += (s, e) =>
        {
            var conn = (DbConnection)s;
            Console.WriteLine("{0}: Database: {1}, State: {2}, was: {3}",
                DateTime.Now.ToShortTimeString(), conn.Database,
                e.CurrentState, e.OriginalState);
        };
        return base.SaveChanges();
    }
}
```

Following is the output from the code in Listing 12-3:

```
About to SaveChanges()
09:56 : Database: EFRecipes, State: Open, was: Closed
09:56: Database: EFRecipes, State: Closed, was: Open
Donations over $300
Robert Byrd gave $350.00
Kim Kerns gave $750.00
```

How It Works

To wire in the handler for the StateChange event, we implement the override SaveChanges() method.

Our event handler receives two parameters: the sender of the event and a StateChangeEventArgs. This second parameter provides access to the CurrentState of the connection and the OriginalState of the connection. We create a log entry indicating both of these states as well as the time of the event and the associated database.

If you are paying particularly close attention to the order of the log entries, you will notice that, in the second using block, the connection to the database occurs during the execution of the query in the foreach loop, and not when the query is constructed. This demonstrates the important concept that queries are executed only when explicitly required. In our case, this execution occurs during the iteration.

12-4. Recalculating a Property Value When an Entity Collection Changes

Problem

You want to recalculate a property value on the entity when its entity collection changes.

Solution

Both EntityCollection and EntityReference derive from RelatedEnd. RelatedEnd exposes an AssociationChanged event. This event is raised when the association is changed or modified. In particular, this event is raised when an element is added to, or removed from, a collection.

To recalculate a property values, we implement a handler for the AssociationChanged event.

Let's say that you have a model with a shopping cart and items for the cart. The model is shown in Figure 12-4.

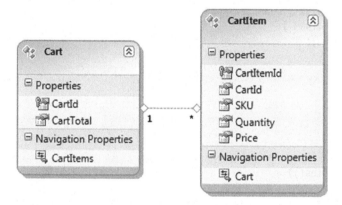

Figure 12-4a. *A model for a cart*

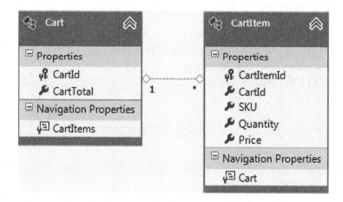

Figure 12-4b. *The cart's items*

The code in Listing 12-4 demonstrates using the AssociationChanged event to recalculate the CartTotal property on the Cart entity when items are added to, or removed from, the CartItems collection.

Listing 12-4. *Using the AssociationChanged Event to Keep the CartTotal in Sync with the Items in the Cart*

```
class Program
{
    static void Main(string[] args)
    {
        RunExample();
    }

    static void RunExample()
    {
        using (var context = new EFRecipesEntities())
        {
            var item1 = new CartItem { SKU = "AMM-223", Quantity = 3,
                                       Price = 19.95M };
            var item2 = new CartItem { SKU = "CAMP-12", Quantity = 1,
                                       Price = 59.95M };
            var item3 = new CartItem { SKU = "29292", Quantity = 2,
                                       Price = 4.95M };
            var cart = new Cart { CartTotal = 0 };
            cart.CartItems.Add(item1);
            cart.CartItems.Add(item2);
            cart.CartItems.Add(item3);
            context.Carts.AddObject(cart);
            item1.Quantity = 1;
            context.SaveChanges();
        }

        using (var context = new EFRecipesEntities())
        {
            foreach (var cart in context.Carts)
            {
                Console.WriteLine("Cart Total = {0}",
                                  cart.CartTotal.ToString("C"));
                foreach (var item in cart.CartItems)
                {
                    Console.WriteLine("\tSKU = {0}, Qty = {1}, Unit Price = {2}",
                                      item.SKU, item.Quantity.ToString(),
                                      item.Price.ToString("C"));
                }
            }
        }
    }
}

public partial class Cart
{
    public Cart()
    {
        this.CartItems.AssociationChanged += (s, e) =>
            {
                if (e.Action == CollectionChangeAction.Add)
```

```
            {
                var item = e.Element as CartItem;
                item.PropertyChanged += (ps, pe) =>
                    {
                        if (pe.PropertyName == "Quantity")
                        {
                            this.CartTotal =
                              this.CartItems.Sum(t => t.Price * t.Quantity);
                            Console.WriteLine("Qty changed, total = {0}",
                                this.CartTotal.ToString("C"));
                        }
                    };
            }
            this.CartTotal = this.CartItems.Sum(t => t.Price * t.Quantity);
            Console.WriteLine("New total = {0}",
                                this.CartTotal.ToString("C"));
        };
    }
}
```

Following is the output from the code in Listing 12-4:

```
New total = $59.85
New total = $119.80
New total = $129.70
Qty changed, total = $89.80
Cart Total = $89.80
New total = $89.80
        SKU = AMM-223, Qty = 1, Unit Price = $19.95
        SKU = CAMP-12, Qty = 1, Unit Price = $59.95
        SKU = 29292, Qty = 2, Unit Price = $4.95
```

How It Works

To keep the CartTotal property in sync with the items in the CartItems collection, we need to wire in a handler for the AssociationChanged event on the CartItems collection. We do this in the constructor for the Cart entity.

The event handler is a little complicated because we have to consider two cases. In the first case, we're simply adding or removing an item from the cart. Here we just recalculate the total by iterating through the collection and summing the price for each item multiplied by the quantity of the item. To get this sum, we use the Sum() method and pass in a lambda expression that multiplies the price and quantity.

In the second case, the entity collection remains the same, but one of the items has its quantity changed. This also affects the cart total and requires that we recalculate. For this case, we wire in a handler for the PropertyChanged event whenever we add an item to the cart. This second handler simply recalculates the cart total when the Quantity property changes.

To wire in this second handler, we depend on the Action property exposed in the CollectionChangedEventArgs, which is passed as the second parameter to our first event handler. The actions defined are Add, Remove, and Refresh.

Batch operations such as Load(), Clear(), and Attach() raise the CollectionChangedEvent just once regardless of how many elements are in the collection. This can be good if your collection contains lots of elements and you are interested in, as we are here, the entire collection. It can, of course, be annoying if you need to track collection changes at a more granular level.

423

12-5. Automatically Deleting Related Entities

Problem

When an entity is deleted, you want to delete the related entities automatically.

Solution

Suppose that you have a table structure that consists of a course, the classes for the course, and the enrollment in each class, as shown in Figure 12-5.

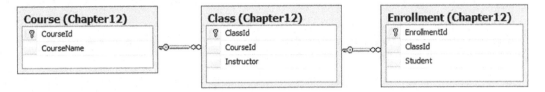

Figure 12-5. *The Course, Class, and Enrollment tables in our database*

Given these tables, you have created a model like the one shown in Figure 12-6.

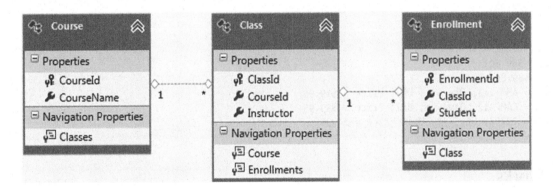

Figure 12-6. *A model with the Course, Class, and Enrollment entities and their associations*

When a course is deleted from the database, you want all of the classes for the course to be deleted and all of the enrollments for the classes to be deleted as well. To get this to work, we set a cascade delete rule in the database for the relationships. To set this rule, select the relationship in SQL Server Management Studio, view the properties, and select Cascade in the INSERT and UPDATE Specification's Delete Rule.

When these tables are imported into the model, these cascade delete rules will also be imported. You can see this by selecting the one-to-many association between Course and Class and viewing the properties (see Figure 12-7).

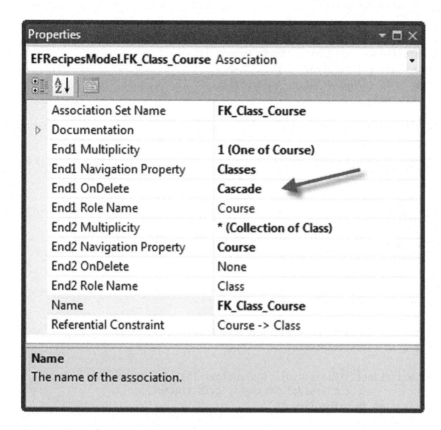

Figure 12-7. *The cascade delete rule from the database was imported into the model, and it is shown in the properties for the association*

The cascade delete shown in Figure 12-7 is in the conceptual layer. There is a similar rule present in the store layer. Both of these Entity Framework rules and the underlying database cascade delete rule are necessary to keep the object context and the database in sync when objects are deleted.

The code in Listing 12-5 demonstrates the cascade delete.

Listing 12-5. Using the Underlying Cascade Delete Rules to Delete the Related Objects

```
class Program
    {
        static void Main(string[] args)
        {
            RunExample();
        }

        static void RunExample()
        {
            using (var context = new EFRecipesEntities())
            {
                var course1 = new Course { CourseName = "CS 301" };
                var course2 = new Course { CourseName = "Math 455" };
                var en1 = new Enrollment { Student = "James Folk" };
```

425

```
                var en2 = new Enrollment { Student = "Scott Shores" };
                var en3 = new Enrollment { Student = "Jill Glass" };
                var en4 = new Enrollment { Student = "Robin Rosen" };
                var class1 = new Class { Instructor = "Bill Meyers" };
                var class2 = new Class { Instructor = "Norma Hall" };
                class1.Course = course1;
                class2.Course = course2;
                class1.Enrollments.Add(en1);
                class1.Enrollments.Add(en2);
                class2.Enrollments.Add(en3);
                class2.Enrollments.Add(en4);
                context.Classes.Add(class1);
                context.Classes.Add(class2);
                context.SaveChanges();
                context.Classes.Remove(class1);
                context.SaveChanges();
            }
            using (var context = new EFRecipesEntities())
            {
                foreach (var course in context.Courses)
                {
                    Console.WriteLine("Course: {0}", course.CourseName);
                    foreach (var c in course.Classes)
                    {
                        Console.WriteLine("\tClass: {0}, Instructor: {1}",
                                        c.ClassId.ToString(), c.Instructor);
                        foreach (var en in c.Enrollments)
                        {
                            Console.WriteLine("\t\tStudent: {0}", en.Student);
                        }
                    }
                }
            }

            Console.WriteLine("Press any key to close...");
            Console.ReadLine();
        }
    }
```

Following is the output from the code in Listing 12-5:

```
Course: CS 301
Course: Math 455
        Class: 8, Instructor: Norma Hall
                Student: Jill Glass
                Student: Robin Rosen
```

How It Works

This recipe has the cascade delete rule both in the database and in the model. In the model, the rule is represented both at the conceptual layer and in the store layer. To keep the object context in sync with the database, we defined the cascade delete in both the database and in the model.

Best Practice

Now you may be asking, "Why do we need this rule in both the model and in the database? Wouldn't it suffice to have the rule either in the database, or in the model?"

The reason cascade delete exists at the conceptual layer is to keep the objects loaded in the object context in sync with the cascade delete changes made by the database. For example, if we have classes and enrollments for a given course loaded in the object context and we mark the course for deletion, Entity Framework would also mark the course's classes and their enrollments for deletion. All of this happens before anything is sent to the database. At the model layer, cascade delete means to mark related entities for deletion. Ultimately, Entity Framework will issue redundant deletes for these entities.

Thus if Entity Framework will issue redundant deletes, why not just have the rules in the model and not in the database? Here's why: For Entity Framework to mark entities for deletion, they must be loaded into the DbContext. Imagine that we have a course in the DbContext, but we haven't loaded the related classes or the related enrollments. If we delete the course, the related classes and enrollments can't be marked for deletion because they are not in the DbContext. No commands will be sent to the database to delete these related rows. However, if we have the cascade delete rules in place in the database, the database will take care of deleting the rows.

The best practice here is to have the cascade delete rules both in the model and in the database.

If you have added a cascade delete rule to a model, Entity Framework will not overwrite it if you update the model from the database. Unfortunately, if you don't have a cascade delete rule in the model and you update the model from the database while the database has a newly created cascade delete rule, Entity Framework will not add a cascade delete rule in the conceptual layer. You will have to add it manually.

12-6. Deleting All Related Entities
Problem

You want to delete all of the related entities in the most generic way possible.

Solution

We want to delete all of the related entities in a generic way; that is, in a way that will work across all entities without specific reference to any particular entity type. To do this, we will create a method that uses the Relationship Manager to get all of the related ends. With these, we can use CreateSourceQuery() to retrieve the entities and delete them.

The code in Listing 12-6 demonstrates this method using the model in Figure 12-8. In this model, we have recipes with related ingredients and steps.

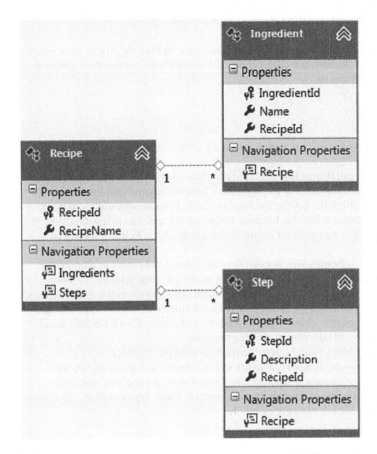

Figure 12-8. *A model with ingredients and steps for each recipe*

Listing 12-6. Demonstrating the DeleteRelatedEntities<>() Method

```
class Program
{
    static void Main(string[] args)
    {
        RunExample();
    }

    static void DeleteRelatedEntities<T>(T entity, EFRecipesEntities context)
            where T : EntityObject
    {
        var entities = ((IEntityWithRelationships)entity)
                    .RelationshipManager.GetAllRelatedEnds()
                    .SelectMany(e =>
                     e.CreateSourceQuery().OfType<EntityObject>()).ToList();
        foreach (var child in entities)
```

```
        {
            context.DeleteObject(child);
        }
        context.SaveChanges();
    }

    static void RunExample()
    {
        using (var context = new EFRecipesEntities())
        {
            var recipe1 = new Recipe { RecipeName = "Chicken Risotto" };
            var recipe2 = new Recipe { RecipeName = "Baked Chicken" };
            recipe1.Steps.Add(new Step { Description = "Bring Broth to a boil" });
            recipe1.Steps.Add(new Step { Description =
                                     "Slowly add Broth to Rice" });
            recipe1.Ingredients.Add(new Ingredient { Name = "1 Cup White Rice" });
            recipe1.Ingredients.Add(new Ingredient { Name =
                                     "6 Cups Chicken Broth"});
            recipe2.Steps.Add(new Step { Description =
                                     "Bake at 350 for 35 Minutes" });
            recipe2.Ingredients.Add(new Ingredient { Name = "1 lb Chicken" } );
            context.Recipes.AddObject(recipe1);
            context.Recipes.AddObject(recipe2);
            context.SaveChanges();
            Console.WriteLine("All the Related Entities...");
            ShowRecipes();
            DeleteRelatedEntities(recipe2, context);
            Console.WriteLine("\nAfter Related Entities are Deleted...");
            ShowRecipes();
        }
    }

    static void ShowRecipes()
    {
        using (var context = new EFRecipesEntities())
        {
            foreach (var recipe in context.Recipes)
            {
                Console.WriteLine("\n*** {0} ***", recipe.RecipeName);
                Console.WriteLine("Ingredients");
                foreach (var ingredient in recipe.Ingredients)
                {
                    Console.WriteLine("\t{0}", ingredient.Name);
                }
                Console.WriteLine("Steps");
                foreach (var step in recipe.Steps)
                {
                    Console.WriteLine("\t{0}", step.Description);
                }
            }
        }
    }
}
```

Following is the output of the code in Listing 12-6:

```
All the Related Entities...

*** Chicken Risotto ***
Ingredients
        1 Cup White Rice
        6 Cups Chicken Broth
Steps
        Bring Broth to a boil
        Slowly add Broth to Rice

*** Baked Chicken ***
Ingredients
        1 lb Chicken
Steps
        Bake at 350 for 35 Minutes

After Related Entities are Deleted...

*** Chicken Risotto ***
Ingredients
        1 Cup White Rice
        6 Cups Chicken Broth
Steps
        Bring Broth to a boil
        Slowly add Broth to Rice

*** Baked Chicken ***
Ingredients
Steps
```

How It Works

Of course, there is no real performance benefit using the code in Listing 12-6. What is useful about this approach is that it deletes all of the related entities without reference to any particular entity type. We could have loaded the second recipe and simply marked each of the ingredients and steps for deletion, but this code snippet would be specific to these entities in this model. The method in Listing 12-6 will work across all entity types and delete all related entities.

12-7. Assigning Default Values
Problem

You want to assign default values to the properties of an entity before it is saved to the database.

Solution

Let's say that you have a table similar to the one in Figure 12-9, which holds information about a purchase order. The key, PurchaseOrderId, is a GUID, and there are two columns holding the date and time for the creation and last modification of the object. There is also a comments column that is no longer used and should always be set to "N/A". Because we no longer use the comments, we don't have this property available on the entity. You want to initialize the PurchaseOrderId column, the date fields, the Paid column, and the comments column to default values. Our model is shown in Figure 12-10.

PurchaseOrder (Chapter12)

	Column Name	Data Type	Allow Nulls
🔑	PurchaseOrderId	uniqueidentifier	☐
	Amount	decimal(18, 2)	☐
	CreateDate	datetime	☐
	ModifiedDate	datetime	☐
	Paid	bit	☐
	Comments	varchar(8000)	☐
			☐

Figure 12-9. *The PurchaseOrder table with several columns that need default values*

Figure 12-10. *The model created from the PurchaseOrder table in Figure 12-9*

We will illustrate three different ways to set default values. Default values that don't need to be dynamically calculated can be set as the Default Value for the property in the conceptual model. Select the Paid property and view its Properties. Set the Default Value to false.

For properties that need to be calculated at runtime, we need to override the SaveChanges event. This is illustrated in Listing 12-7. In this event, if the object is in the Added state, we set the PurchaseOrderId to a new GUID and set the CreateDate and ModifiedDate fields.

To illustrate setting the default value outside of the conceptual model, we can modify the store layer to set a default value for the comments column. This approach would be useful if we didn't want to surface some properties in the model, yet wanted to set their default values. To set the default value through the store layer, right-click the .edmx file and select Open With ➤ XML Editor. Add DefaultValue="N/A" to the <Property> tag for the Comment property in the SSDL section of the .edmx file.

Listing 12-7. *Overriding the SaveChanges Event to Set the Default Values*

```
class Program
    {
        static void Main(string[] args)
        {
            RunExample();
        }

        static void RunExample()
        {
            using (var context = new EFRecipesEntities())
            {
                context.PurchaseOrders.Add(
                                new PurchaseOrder { Amount = 109.98M });
                context.PurchaseOrders.Add(
                                new PurchaseOrder { Amount = 20.99M });
                context.PurchaseOrders.Add(
                                new PurchaseOrder { Amount = 208.89M });
                context.SaveChanges();
            }

            using (var context = new EFRecipesEntities())
            {
                Console.WriteLine("Purchase Orders");
                foreach (var po in context.PurchaseOrders)
                {
                    Console.WriteLine("Purchase Order: {0}",
                                    po.PurchaseOrderId.ToString(""));
                    Console.WriteLine("\tPaid: {0}", po.Paid ? "Yes" : "No");
                    Console.WriteLine("\tAmount: {0}", po.Amount.ToString("C"));
                    Console.WriteLine("\tCreated On: {0}",
                                    po.CreateDate.ToShortTimeString());
                    Console.WriteLine("\tModified at: {0}",
                                    po.ModifiedDate.ToShortTimeString());
                }
            }
        }
    }

    public partial class EFRecipesEntities
    {
        public override int SaveChanges()
        {
            var changeSet = this.ChangeTracker.Entries().Where(e => e.Entity is PurchaseOrder);
            if (changeSet != null)
            {
                foreach (var order in changeSet.Where(c => c.State == System.Data.Entity.
                EntityState.Added).Select(a => a.Entity as PurchaseOrder))
```

```
            {
                order.PurchaseOrderId = Guid.NewGuid();
                order.CreateDate = DateTime.UtcNow;
                order.ModifiedDate = DateTime.UtcNow;
            }
            foreach (var order in changeSet.Where(c => c.State == System.Data.Entity.
            EntityState.Modified).Select(a => a.Entity as PurchaseOrder))
            {
                order.ModifiedDate = DateTime.UtcNow;
            }
        }
        return base.SaveChanges();
    }
}
```

Following is the output from the code in Listing 12-7:

```
Purchase Orders
Purchase Order: 1b4df3c6-6f72-4c6b-9ce2-331bad509be5
        Paid: No
        Amount: $208.89
        Created On: 3:15 PM
        Modified at: 3:15 PM
Purchase Order: c042f045-38af-4bfc-93c0-a870ffd36195
        Paid: No
        Amount: $20.99
        Created On: 3:15 PM
        Modified at: 3:15 PM
Purchase Order: 223faf4a-e128-4f5a-8dee-b9b104ed43b7
        Paid: No
        Amount: $109.98
        Created On: 3:15 PM
        Modified at: 3:15 PM
```

How It Works

We demonstrated three different ways to set default values. For values that are static and for which a property is exposed on the entity for the underlying column, we can use the designer's Default Value for the property. This is ideally suited for the Paid property. By default, we want to set this to false. New purchase orders are typically unpaid.

For columns that need dynamically calculated values, such as the CreateDate, ModifiedDate, and PurchaseOrderId columns, we override the SaveChanges event that computes these values and sets the column values just before the entity is saved to the database.

Finally, for columns that are not surfaced as properties on the entity and need a static default value, we can use the Default Value attribute in the store layer property definition. In this recipe, we set the comments column default value to "N/A" in the store layer property definition.

There is another option for assigning default values. You could assign them in the constructor for the entity. The constructor is called each time a new instance of the entity is created. This includes each time the instance is materialized from the database. You have to be careful not to overwrite previous values for the properties from the database.

12-8. Retrieving the Original Value of a Property

Problem

You want to retrieve the original value of a property before the entity is saved to the database.

Solution

Let's say that you have a model (see Figure 12-11) representing an Employee, and part of this entity includes the employee's salary. You have a business rule that an employee's salary cannot be increased by more than 10 percent. To enforce this rule, you want to check the new salary against the original salary for increases in excess of 10 percent. You want to do this check just before the entity is saved to the database.

Figure 12-11. *An Employee entity with the employee's salary*

To verify that a salary increase does not exceed 10 percent as required by our business rule, we override the SaveChanges event. In the overridden event, we retrieve the current and original values. If the new value is more than 110 percent of the original value, we throw an exception. This exception, of course, causes the saving of the entity to fail. The code in Listing 12-8 provides the details.

Listing 12-8. Overriding the SaveChanges Event to Enforce the Business Rule

```
class Program
    {
        static void Main(string[] args)
        {
            RunExample();
        }

        static void RunExample()
        {
            using (var context = new EFRecipesEntities())
            {
                var emp1 = new Employee { Name = "Roger Smith", Salary = 108000M };
                var emp2 = new Employee { Name = "Jane Hall", Salary = 81500M };
                context.Employees.Add(emp1);
                context.Employees.Add(emp2);
                context.SaveChanges();
                emp1.Salary = emp1.Salary * 1.5M;
                try
```

```
                {
                    context.SaveChanges();
                }
                catch (Exception)
                {
                    Console.WriteLine("Oops, tried to increase a salary too much!");
                }
            }

            using (var context = new EFRecipesEntities())
            {
                Console.WriteLine();
                Console.WriteLine("Employees");
                foreach (var emp in context.Employees)
                {
                    Console.WriteLine("{0} makes {1}/year", emp.Name,
                                        emp.Salary.ToString("C"));
                }
            }
            Console.WriteLine("Press any key to close...");
            Console.ReadLine();
        }
    }

    public partial class EFRecipesEntities
    {
        public override int SaveChanges()
        {
            var entries = this.ChangeTracker.Entries().Where(e => e.Entity is Employee && e.State ==
            System.Data.Entity.EntityState.Modified);
            foreach (var entry in entries)
            {
                var originalSalary = Convert.ToDecimal(
                                entry.OriginalValues["Salary"]);
                var currentSalary = Convert.ToDecimal(
                                entry.CurrentValues["Salary"]);
                if (originalSalary != currentSalary)
                {
                    if (currentSalary > originalSalary * 1.1M)
                        throw new ApplicationException(
                                    "Can't increase salary more than 10%");
                }
            }
            return base.SaveChanges();
        }
    }
}
```

Following is the output of the code in Listing 12-8:

```
Oops, tried to increase a salary too much!

Employees
Roger Smith makes $108,000.00/year
Jane Hall makes $81,500.00/year
```

How It Works

In the SaveChanges overridden event, we first retrieve all of the object state entries for the Employee entity that are in the modified state. For each of them, we look for a modified "Salary" property with both original and current value, which represents the value after modification. If they differ, we check to see if they differ by more than 10 percent. If they do, then we throw an ApplicationException. Otherwise, we simply call the SaveChanges of the DbContext and let Entity Framework save the changes to the database.

12-9. Retrieving the Original Association for Independent Associations
Problem

You have an independent association. You want to retrieve the original association prior to saving the changes to the database using ObjectContext.

Solution

Suppose that you have a model representing an order and the order's status (see Figure 12-12). The fulfillment of an order goes through three stages, as represented in the OrderStatus entity. First the order is assembled. Next the order is tested. Finally, the order is shipped. Your application has a business rule that confines all orders to this three-step process. You want to enforce this rule by throwing an exception if an order goes, for example, from assembly to shipped without first being tested. The association between Order and OrderStatus is an independent association.

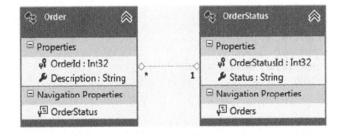

Figure 12-12. *A model with orders and their status*

To solve this problem, we wire in a handler for the SavingChanges event. In this handler, we check to verify that the order status changes follow the prescribed sequence. The code in Listing 12-9 provides the details.

Listing 12-9. *Enforcing the Sequence of Fulfillment Steps for an Order*

```
class Program
{
    static void Main(string[] args)
    {
        RunExample();
    }

    static void RunExample()
    {
        using (var context = new EFRecipesEntities())
        {
            // static order status
            var assemble = new OrderStatus { OrderStatusId = 1,
                                             Status = "Assemble" };
            var test = new OrderStatus { OrderStatusId = 2,
                                         Status = "Test" };
            var ship = new OrderStatus { OrderStatusId = 3,
                                         Status = "Ship" };
            context.OrderStatus.AddObject(assemble);
            context.OrderStatus.AddObject(test);
            context.OrderStatus.AddObject(ship);

            var order = new Order { Description = "HAL 9000 Supercomputer",
                                    OrderStatus = assemble };
            context.Orders.AddObject(order);
            context.SaveChanges();

            order.OrderStatus = ship;
            try
            {
                context.SaveChanges();
            }
            catch (Exception)
            {
                Console.WriteLine("Oops...better test first.");
            }
            order.OrderStatus = test;
            context.SaveChanges();
            order.OrderStatus = ship;
            context.SaveChanges();
        }

        using (var context = new EFRecipesEntities())
        {
            foreach (var order in context.Orders)
            {
                Console.WriteLine("Order {0} [{1}], status = {2}",
                                  order.OrderId.ToString(),
```

```
                              order.Description,
                              order.OrderStatus.Status);
            }
        }
    }
}

public partial class EFRecipesEntities
{
    partial void OnContextCreated()
    {
        this.SavingChanges += new EventHandler(EFRecipesEntities_SavingChanges);
    }

    void EFRecipesEntities_SavingChanges(object sender, EventArgs e)
    {
        // all the tracked orders
        var orders = this.ObjectStateManager.GetObjectStateEntries(
                        EntityState.Modified | EntityState.Unchanged)
                    .Where(entry => entry.Entity is Order)
                    .Select(entry => entry.Entity as Order);

        foreach (var order in orders)
        {
            var deletedEntry = this.ObjectStateManager
                    .GetObjectStateEntries(EntityState.Deleted)
                    .Where(entry => entry.IsRelationship &&
                        entry.EntitySet.Name == order
                            .OrderStatusReference
                            .RelationshipSet.Name).First();
            if (deletedEntry != null)
            {
                EntityKey deletedKey = null;
                if ((EntityKey)deletedEntry.OriginalValues[0] == order.EntityKey)
                {
                    deletedKey = deletedEntry.OriginalValues[1] as EntityKey;
                }
                else if ((EntityKey)deletedEntry.OriginalValues[1] ==
                        order.EntityKey)
                {
                    deletedKey = deletedEntry.OriginalValues[0] as EntityKey;
                }
                if (deletedKey != null)
                {
                    var oldStatus = this.GetObjectByKey(deletedKey)
                                    as OrderStatus;

                    // better be going to the next status
                    if (oldStatus.OrderStatusId + 1 !=
                        order.OrderStatus.OrderStatusId)
```

```
                              throw new ApplicationException(
                                  "Can't transition to that order status!");
                          }
                      }
                  }
              }
          }
```

Following is the output of the code in Listing 12-9:

```
Oops...better test first.
Order 2 [HAL 9000 Supercomputer], status = Ship
```

How It Works

We wired in a handler for the SavingChanges event. In this handler, we picked out the previous order status and the new (current) order status and verified that the new status ID is one greater than the previous ID. Of course, the code in Listing 12-9 doesn't look quite that simple. Here's how to find both the original order status and the new one.

For independent associations, in the object state manager there is an entry for the order, the order status, and a relationship entry with one end pointing to the order and the other end pointing to the order status. The relationship entry is identified by IsRelationship set to true.

First we get all of the orders tracked in the object context. To do this, we use the object state manager to get all of the entries that are either modified or unchanged. We use a Where clause to filter this down to just entities of type Order.

For each order, we get all object state entries that are deleted. Then we use a Where clause to pick out just the relationship entries (IsRelationship is true) in the OrderStatus relationship set. Because there should be at most one of these for any order, we pick the first. We look for the deleted relationships because when a relationship is changed, the original one is marked deleted and the new one is created. Because we're interested in the previous relationship, we look for a deleted relationship between the order and the order status.

Once we have the deleted relationship, we need to look at the original values for the entry to find both the order end and the order status end. Be careful not to reference the current values here. Because the relationship is deleted, referencing the current values will cause an exception. As we don't know which end of the relationship is the order and which end is the order status, we test both.

With the original order status entity in hand, we simply check whether the original OrderStatusId is one less than the new OrderStatusId. We created the OrderStatus objects so that their IDs would increment by one just to make the code a little easier.

12-10. Retrieving XML
Problem

You want to treat a scalar property of type string as XML data.

Solution

Let's say that you have an XML column in a table in your database. When you import this table into a model, Entity Framework interprets the data type as a string rather than XML (see Figure 12-13). The current version of Entity Framework does not expose XML data types from the database. You want to work with this property as if it were an XML data type.

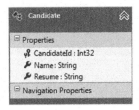

Figure 12-13. *A model with a Candidate entity. The Resume property is of type string in the model but of type XML in the database*

The Resume property of the Candidate entity is of type string in the model, but it is an XML type in the database. To manipulate the property as if it were of type XML, we'll make the property private and expose a CandidateResume property as XML.

Select the Resume property and view its properties. Change the setter and getter to private. Next, we need to expose a new property that will surface the resume as XML. The code in Listing 12-10 provides the details.

With the CandidateResume property, we can manipulate the Resume natively by using the XML API. In Listing 12-10, we create a strongly-typed resume using XElement class and assign it to the CandidateResume property, which assigns the original string Resume property inside the setter. After saving the Candidate entity to the database, we later update the Resume element inside the CandidateResume and update the changes made to the database.

Listing 12-10. Using the CandidateResume Property to Expose the Resume as XML

```
class Program
    {
        static void Main(string[] args)
        {
            RunExample();
        }

        static void RunExample()
        {
            using (var context = new EFRecipesEntities())
            {
                var resume = new XElement("Person",
                    new XElement("Name", "Robin St.James"),
                    new XElement("Phone", "817 867-5201"),
                    new XElement("FirstOffice", "Dog Catcher"),
                    new XElement("SecondOffice", "Mayor"),
                    new XElement("ThirdOffice", "State Senator"));
                var can = new Candidate
                {
                    Name = "Robin St.James",
                    CandidateResume = resume
                };
                context.Candidates.Add(can);
                context.SaveChanges();
                can.CandidateResume.SetElementValue("Phone", "817 555-5555");
                context.SaveChanges();
            }
```

```csharp
            using (var context = new EFRecipesEntities())
            {
                foreach (var can in context.Candidates)
                {
                    Console.WriteLine("{0}", can.Name);
                    Console.WriteLine("Phone: {0}",
                            can.CandidateResume.Element("Phone").Value);
                    Console.WriteLine("First Political Office: {0}",
                            can.CandidateResume.Element("FirstOffice").Value);
                    Console.WriteLine("Second Political Office: {0}",
                            can.CandidateResume.Element("SecondOffice").Value);
                    Console.WriteLine("Third Political Office: {0}",
                            can.CandidateResume.Element("ThirdOffice").Value);
                }
            }
            Console.WriteLine("Press any key to close...");
            Console.ReadLine();
        }
    }

    public partial class Candidate
    {
        private XElement candidateResume = null;

        public XElement CandidateResume
        {
            get
            {
                if (candidateResume == null)
                {
                    candidateResume = XElement.Parse(this.Resume);
                    candidateResume.Changed += (s, e) =>
                    {
                        this.Resume = candidateResume.ToString();
                    };
                }
                return candidateResume;
            }
            set
            {
                candidateResume = value;
                candidateResume.Changed += (s, e) =>
                {
                    this.Resume = candidateResume.ToString();
                };
                this.Resume = value.ToString();
            }
        }
    }
}
```

Following is the output of the code in Listing 12-10:

```
Robin St.James
Phone: 817 555-5555
First Political Office: Dog Catcher
Second Political Office: Mayor
Third Political Office: State Senator
```

How It Works

The current release of Entity Framework does not support the XML data type. Given the importance of XML, it is likely that some future version will provide full support. In this recipe, we created a new property, CandidateResume, which exposes the candidate's resume as XML.

The code in Listing 12-10 demonstrates using the CandidateResume property in place of the Resume property. For both the getter and setter, we wired in a handler for the Changed event on the XML. This handler keeps the Resume property in sync with the CandidateResume property. Entity Framework will look at the Resume property when it comes time to persist an instance of the Candidate entity. Only changes to the Resume property will be saved. We need to reflect changes in the CandidateResume property to the Resume property for the database to stay in sync (via Entity Framework).

12-11. Applying Server-Generated Values to Properties

Problem

You have several columns in a table whose values are generated by the database. You want to have Entity Framework set the corresponding entity properties after inserts and updates.

Solution

Suppose that you have a table like the one in Figure 12-14.

ParkingTicket (Chapter12)

	Column Name	Data Type	Allow Nulls
🔑	TicketId	int	☐
	Amount	money	☐
	CreateDate	date	☐
	Paid	bit	☐
	PaidDate	date	☑
	TimeStamp	timestamp	☐
			☐

Figure 12-14. *The ParkingTicket table with the TicketId, CreateDate, PaidDate, and TimeStamp columns generated by the database*

Also, let's say that you have created a trigger, like the one in Listing 12-11, so that the PaidDate column is populated when the Paid column is set to true. You've also set the TicketId to be an Identity column and CreateDate to default to the current date. With the trigger in Listing 12-11 and the automatically generated values, only the Amount and Paid columns are required for an insert.

Listing 12-11. A Trigger That Sets the PaidDate Column When the Paid Bit is Set to true.

```
CREATE TRIGGER UpdateParkingTicket
ON ParkingTicket
FOR UPDATE
AS
UPDATE ParkingTicket
  SET PaidDate = GETDATE()
  FROM ParkingTicket
   JOIN Inserted i ON
                      ParkingTicket.TicketId = i.TicketId
  WHERE i.Paid = 1
```

After an insert or an update, you want Entity Framework to populate the entity with the values generated by the database. To create the model that supports this, do the following:

1. Right-click the project, and select Add ➤ New Item. Add a new ADO.NET Entity Data Model. Import the ParkingTicket table. The resulting model should look like the one shown in Figure 12-15.

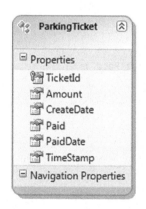

Figure 12-15. The model with the ParkingTicket entity

2. Right-click on each of the scalar properties in the ParkingTicket entity. View the properties of each. Notice that the StoreGeneratedPattern property is set to Identity for the TicketId. For TimeStamp, the StoreGeneratedPattern property is set to Computed. The StoreGeneratedPattern property for CreateDate and PaidDate is not set. Change both the values to Computed.

Listing 12-12. Code to Check if the Database-Generated Values Are Populated Back to the Properties on Inserts and Updates

```
class Program
    {
        static void Main(string[] args)
        {
            RunExample();
        }

        static void RunExample()
        {
            using (var context = new EFRecipesEntities())
            {
                context.ParkingTickets.Add(new ParkingTicket { Amount = 132.0M, Paid = false });
                context.ParkingTickets.Add(new ParkingTicket { Amount = 255.0M, Paid = false });
                context.SaveChanges();
            }

            using (var context = new EFRecipesEntities())
            {
                foreach (var ticket in context.ParkingTickets)
                {
                    Console.WriteLine("Ticket: {0}", ticket.TicketId);
                    Console.WriteLine("Date: {0}", ticket.CreateDate.ToShortDateString());
                    Console.WriteLine("Amount: {0}", ticket.Amount.ToString("C"));
                    Console.WriteLine("Paid: {0}",
                                ticket.PaidDate.HasValue ?
                                ticket.PaidDate.Value.ToShortDateString() : "Not Paid");
                    Console.WriteLine();
                    ticket.Paid = true; // just paid ticket!
                }

                // save all those Paid flags
                context.SaveChanges();
                foreach (var ticket in context.ParkingTickets)
                {
                    Console.WriteLine("Ticket: {0}", ticket.TicketId);
                    Console.WriteLine("Date: {0}", ticket.CreateDate.ToShortDateString());
                    Console.WriteLine("Amount: {0}", ticket.Amount.ToString("C"));
                    Console.WriteLine("Paid: {0}",
                                ticket.PaidDate.HasValue ?
                                ticket.PaidDate.Value.ToShortDateString() : "Not Paid");
                    Console.WriteLine();
                }
            }
            Console.WriteLine("Press any key to close...");
            Console.ReadLine();
        }
    }
```

Following is the output of the code in Listing 12-12:

```
Ticket: 5
Date: 7/3/2013
Amount: $132.00
Paid: Not Paid

Ticket: 6
Date: 7/3/2013
Amount: $255.00
Paid: Not Paid

Ticket: 5
Date: 7/3/2013
Amount: $132.00
Paid: 3/24/2010

Ticket: 6
Date: 7/3/2013
Amount: $255.00
Paid: 3/24/2010
```

How It Works

When you set a property's StoreGeneratedPattern to Identity or Computed, Entity Framework knows that the database will generate the value. Entity Framework will retrieve these columns from the database with a subsequent select statement.

When the StoreGeneratePattern is set to Identity, Entity Framework retrieves the database-generated value just once at the time of insert. When the StoreGeneratedPattern is set to Computed, Entity Framework will refresh the value on each insert and update. In this example, the PaidDate column was set by the trigger (because we set Paid to true) on update and Entity Framework acquired this value after the update.

12-12. Validating Entities on Saving Changes
Problem

You want to validate entities before they are saved to the database using an ObjectContext.

Solution

Suppose that you have a model like the one shown in Figure 12-16.

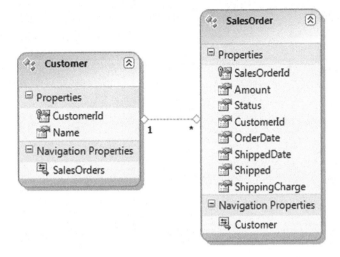

Figure 12-16. *A model for customers and their orders*

There are certain business rules around customers and their orders. You want to make sure that these rules are checked before an order is saved to the database. Let's say that you have the following rules:

- The order date on an order must be after the current date.

- The ship date on an order must be after the order date.

- An order cannot be shipped unless it is in an "Approved" status.

- If an order amount is over $5,000, there is no shipping charge.

- An order that has shipped cannot be deleted.

To check if changes to an entity violates any of these rules, we'll define an IValidatable interface that has just one method: Validate(). Any of our entity types can implement this interface. For this example, we'll show the implementation for the SalesOrder entity. We'll handle the SavingChanges event and call Validate() on all entities that implement IValidator. This will allow us to intercept and validate entities before they are saved to the database. The code in Listing 12-13 provides the details.

Listing 12-13. Validating SaleOrder Entities in the SavingeChanges Event

```
class Program
{
    static void Main(string[] args)
    {
        RunExample();
    }

    static void RunExample()
    {
        // bad order date
        using (var context = new EFRecipesEntities())
        {
            var customer = new Customer { Name = "Phil Marlowe" };
            var order = new SalesOrder { OrderDate = DateTime.Parse("3/12/18"),
```

```
                                 Amount = 19.95M, Status = "Approved",
                                 ShippingCharge = 3.95M,
                                 Customer = customer };
    context.Customers.AddObject(customer);
    try
    {
        context.SaveChanges();
    }
    catch (Exception ex)
    {
        Console.WriteLine(ex.Message);
    }
}

// order shipped before it was ordered
using (var context = new EFRecipesEntities())
{
    var customer = new Customer { Name = "Phil Marlowe" };
    var order = new SalesOrder { OrderDate = DateTime.Parse("3/12/10"),
                                 Amount = 19.95M, Status = "Approved",
                                 ShippingCharge = 3.95M,
                                 Customer = customer };
    context.Customers.AddObject(customer);
    context.SaveChanges();
    try
    {
        order.Shipped = true;
        order.ShippedDate = DateTime.Parse("3/10/10");
        context.SaveChanges();
    }
    catch (Exception ex)
    {
        Console.WriteLine(ex.Message);
    }
}

// order shipped, but not approved
using (var context = new EFRecipesEntities())
{
    var customer = new Customer { Name = "Phil Marlowe" };
    var order = new SalesOrder { OrderDate = DateTime.Parse("3/12/10"),
                                 Amount = 19.95M, Status = "Pending",
                                 ShippingCharge = 3.95M,
                                 Customer = customer };
    context.Customers.AddObject(customer);
    context.SaveChanges();
    try
    {
        order.Shipped = true;
        order.ShippedDate = DateTime.Parse("3/13/10");
        context.SaveChanges();
    }
```

```
        catch (Exception ex)
        {
            Console.WriteLine(ex.Message);
        }
    }

    // order over $5,000 and shipping not free
    using (var context = new EFRecipesEntities())
    {
        var customer = new Customer { Name = "Phil Marlowe" };
        var order = new SalesOrder { OrderDate = DateTime.Parse("3/12/10"),
                                     Amount = 6200M, Status = "Approved",
                                     ShippingCharge = 59.95M,
                                     Customer = customer };
        context.Customers.AddObject(customer);
        context.SaveChanges();
        try
        {
            order.Shipped = true;
            order.ShippedDate = DateTime.Parse("3/13/10");
            context.SaveChanges();
        }
        catch (Exception ex)
        {
            Console.WriteLine(ex.Message);
        }
    }

    // order deleted after it was shipped
    using (var context = new EFRecipesEntities())
    {
        var customer = new Customer { Name = "Phil Marlowe" };
        var order = new SalesOrder { OrderDate = DateTime.Parse("3/12/10"),
                                     Amount = 19.95M, Status = "Approved",
                                     ShippingCharge = 3.95M,
                                     Customer = customer };
        context.Customers.AddObject(customer);
        context.SaveChanges();
        order.Shipped = true;
        order.ShippedDate = DateTime.Parse("3/13/10");
        context.SaveChanges();
        try
        {
            context.DeleteObject(order);
            context.SaveChanges();
        }
        catch (Exception ex)
        {
            Console.WriteLine(ex.Message);
        }
    }
  }
}
}
```

```csharp
public partial class EFRecipesEntities
{
    partial void OnContextCreated()
    {
        this.SavingChanges +=new EventHandler(EFRecipesEntities_SavingChanges);
    }

    private void EFRecipesEntities_SavingChanges(object sender, EventArgs e)
    {
        var entries = this.ObjectStateManager
                    .GetObjectStateEntries(EntityState.Added |
                                           EntityState.Modified |
                                           EntityState.Deleted)
                    .Where(entry => entry.Entity is IValidator)
                    .Select(entry => entry).ToList();
        foreach (var entry in entries)
        {
            var entity = entry.Entity as IValidator;
            entity.Validate(entry);
        }
    }
}

public interface IValidator
{
    void Validate(ObjectStateEntry entry);
}

public partial class SalesOrder : IValidator
{
    public void Validate(ObjectStateEntry entry)
    {
        if (entry.State == EntityState.Added)
        {
            if (this.OrderDate > DateTime.Now)
                throw new ApplicationException(
                  "OrderDate cannot be after the current date");
        }
        else if (entry.State == EntityState.Modified)
        {
            if (this.ShippedDate < this.OrderDate)
            {
                throw new ApplicationException(
                  "ShippedDate cannot be before OrderDate");
            }
            if (this.Shipped.Value && this.Status != "Approved")
            {
                throw new ApplicationException(
                  "Order cannot be shipped unless it is Approved");
            }
```

```
        if (this.Amount > 5000M && this.ShippingCharge != 0)
        {
            throw new ApplicationException(
              "Orders over $5000 ship for free");
        }
    }
    else if (entry.State == EntityState.Deleted)
    {
        if (this.Shipped.Value)
            throw new ApplicationException(
                "Shipped orders cannot be deleted");
    }
  }
}
```

Following is the output of the code in Listing 12-13:

```
OrderDate cannot be after the current date
ShippedDate cannot be before OrderDate
Order cannot be shipped unless it is Approved
Orders over $5000 ship for free
Shipped orders cannot be deleted
```

How It Works

When you call SaveChanges(), Entity Framework raises the SavingChanges event before it saves the object changes to the database. We implemented the partial method OnContextCreated() so that we can wire in a handler for this event. When SavingChanges is raised, we handle the event by calling the Validate() method on every entity that implements the IValidator interface. We've shown an implementation of this interface that supports our business rules. If you have business rules for other entity types in your model, you could implement the IValidator interface for them.

Best Practice

Business rules in many applications almost always change over time. Industry or government regulation changes, continuous process improvement programs, evolving fraud prevention, and many other factors influence the introduction of new business rules as well as changes to existing rules. It's a best practice to organize your code base so that the concerns around business rule validation and enforcement are more easily maintained. Often, this means keeping all of this code in a separate assembly or in a separate folder in the project. Defining and implementing interfaces, such as the IValidator interface in this recipe, help to ensure that business rules validation is uniformly applied.

CHAPTER 13

Improving Performance

The recipes in this chapter cover a wide range of specific ways to improve the performance of your Entity Framework applications. In many cases, simple changes to a query or to the model, or even pushing startup overhead to a different part of application, can significantly improve some aspect of your application's performance.

13-1. Optimizing Queries in a Table per Type Inheritance Model
Problem

You want to improve the performance of a query in a model with Table per Type inheritance.

Solution

Let's say that you have a simple Table per Type inheritance model, like the one shown in Figure 13-1.

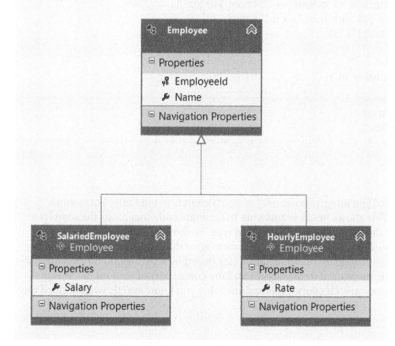

Figure 13-1. *A simple Table per Type inheritance model for Salaried and Hourly employees*

You want to query this model for a given employee. To improve the performance of the query when you know the type of employee, use the OfType<T>() operator to narrow the result to entities of the specific type, as shown in Listing 13-1.

Listing 13-1. Improving the Performance of a Query Against a Table per Type Inheritance Model When You Know the Entity Type

```
using (var context = new EFRecipesEntities())
{
    context.Employees.Add(new SalariedEmployee { Name = "Robin Rosen",
                                    Salary = 89900M });
    context.Employees.Add(new HourlyEmployee { Name = "Steven Fuller",
                                    Rate = 11.50M });
    context.Employees.Add(new HourlyEmployee { Name = "Karen Steele",
                                    Rate = 12.95m });
    context.SaveChanges();
}

using (var context = new EFRecipesEntities())
{
    // a typical way to get Steven Fuller's entity
    var emp1 = context.Employees.Single(e => e.Name == "Steven Fuller");
    Console.WriteLine("{0}'s rate is: {1} per hour", emp1.Name,
                    ((HourlyEmployee)emp1).Rate.ToString("C"));

    // slightly more efficient way if we know that Steven is an HourlyEmployee
    var emp2 = context.Employees.OfType<HourlyEmployee>()
                            .Single(e => e.Name == "Steven Fuller");
    Console.WriteLine("{0}'s rate is: {1} per hour", emp2.Name,
                    emp2.Rate.ToString("C"));
}
```

Following is the output of the code in Listing 13-1:

```
Steven Fuller's rate is: $11.50 per hour
Steven Fuller's rate is: $11.50 per hour
```

How It Works

The key to making the query in a Table per Type inheritance model more efficient is to tell Entity Framework explicitly the type of the expected result. This allows Entity Framework to generate code that limits the search to the specific tables that hold the values for the base type and the derived type. Without this information, Entity Framework has to generate a query that pulls together all of the results from all of the tables holding derived type values, and then it determines the appropriate type for materialization (for example, fetching and transformation of data to entity objects). Depending on the number of derived types and the complexity of your model, this may require substantially more work than is necessary. Of course, this assumes that you know exactly what derived type the query will return.

13-2. Retrieving a Single Entity Using an Entity Key

Problem

You want to retrieve a single entity using an entity key, regardless of whether you're implementing a Database-First, Model-First, or Code-First approach for Entity Framework. In this example, you want to implement the Code-First approach.

Solution

Suppose that you have a model with an entity type representing a painting. The model might look like the one shown in Figure 13-2.

Figure 13-2. *The Painting entity type in our model*

To start, this example leverages the Code-First approach for Entity Framework. In Listing 13-2, we create the entity class, Painting.

Listing 13-2. The Painting Entity Object

```
public class Painting
{
    public string AccessionNumber { get; set; }
    public string Name { get; set; }
    public string Artist { get; set; }
    public decimal LastSalePrice { get; set; }
}
```

Next, in Listing 13-3, we create the DbContext object, which is our gateway into Entity Framework functionality when leveraging the Code-First approach.

Listing 13-3. DbContext Object

```
public class Recipe2Context : DbContext
{
    public Recipe2Context()
        : base("Recipe2ConnectionString")
```

```
    {
        // Disable Entity Framework Model Compatibility
        Database.SetInitializer<Recipe2Context>(null);
    }

    protected override void OnModelCreating(DbModelBuilder modelBuilder)
    {
        // map AccessionNumber as primary key to table
        modelBuilder.Entity<Painting>().HasKey(x => x.AccessionNumber);
        modelBuilder.Entity<Painting>().ToTable("Chapter13.Painting");
    }

    public DbSet<Painting> Paintings { get; set; }
```

Next add an App.Config class to the project, and add to it the code from Listing 13-4, under the ConnectionStrings section.

Listing 13-4. Connection String

```
<connectionStrings>
  <add name="Recipe2ConnectionString"
       connectionString="Data Source=.;
       Initial Catalog=EFRecipes;
       Integrated Security=True;
       MultipleActiveResultSets=True"
       providerName="System.Data.SqlClient" />
</connectionStrings>
```

In Listing 13-5, we load data and demonstrate both fetching an entity with a LINQ query and then with the Find() method.

Listing 13-5. Retrieving an Entity with the Find() Method

```
private static void RunExample()
{
    using (var context = new Recipe2Context())
    {
        context.Paintings.Add(new Painting
        {
            AccessionNumber = "PN001",
            Name = "Sunflowers",
            Artist = "Rosemary Golden",
            LastSalePrice = 1250M
        });
    }

    using (var context = new Recipe2Context())
    {
// LINQ query always fetches entity from database, even if it already exists in context
        var paintingFromDatabase =
            context.Paintings.FirstOrDefault(x => x.AccessionNumber == "PN001");
```

```
        // Find() method fetches entity from context object
        var paintingFromContext = context.Paintings.Find("PN001");
    }

    Console.WriteLine("Press <enter> to continue...");
    Console.ReadLine();
}
```

How It Works

When issuing a LINQ query, a round trip will always be made to the database to retrieve the requested data, even if that data has already been loaded into the context object in memory. When the query completes, entity objects that do not exist in the context are added and then tracked. By default, if the entity object is already present in the context, it is not overwritten with the more recent database values.

However, the DbSet object, which wraps each of our entity objects, exposes a Find() method. Specifically, Find() expects a single argument that represents the primary key of the entity object. If necessary, an array of values can be passed into Find() to support a composite key. Find() is very efficient, as it will first search the underlying context for the target object. If found, Find() returns the entity directly from the context object. If not found, then it automatically queries the underlying data store. If still not found, Find() simply returns NULL to the caller. Additionally, Find() will return entities that have been added to the context (think of having a state of "Added"), but not yet saved to the underlying database. Fortunately, the Find() method is available with any of three modeling approaches: Database-First, Model-First, or Code-First.

In Listing 13-5, we invoke a LINQ query to retrieve a Painting. A LINQ query will always query the underlying database, even if the entity is already loaded into the context. Figure 13-3 shows the SQL query that is generated.

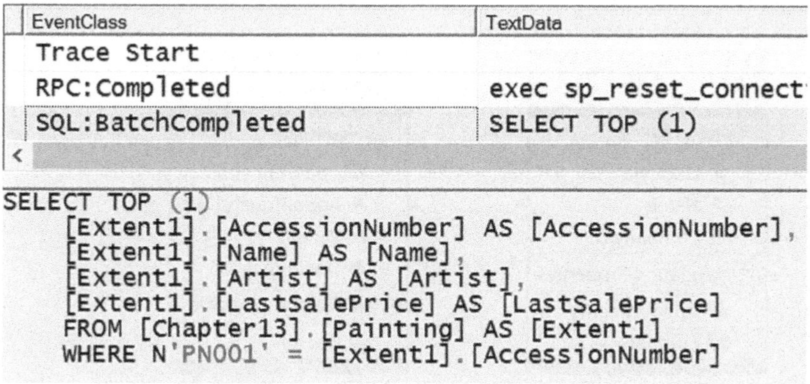

EventClass	TextData
Trace Start	
RPC: Completed	exec sp_reset_connect
SQL: BatchCompleted	SELECT TOP (1)

```
SELECT TOP (1)
    [Extent1].[AccessionNumber] AS [AccessionNumber],
    [Extent1].[Name] AS [Name],
    [Extent1].[Artist] AS [Artist],
    [Extent1].[LastSalePrice] AS [LastSalePrice]
    FROM [Chapter13].[Painting] AS [Extent1]
    WHERE N'PN001' = [Extent1].[AccessionNumber]
```

Figure 13-3. *SQL Query returning our painting*

In the next line of code, we once again search for the same painting. This time, however, we leverage the Find() method exposed by the DbSet Class. Since the Painting entity is a DbSet class, we simply call the Find() method on it and pass in the primary key of the entity as an argument. Find() first searches the context object in memory for "PN001," finds the object, and returns a reference to it, avoiding a round trip to the database. Note in Figure 13-4 how a SQL Query was *not* generated.

EventClass	TextData	ApplicationName

Figure 13-4. The Find() method locates the object in memory, not generating a database query

For a more detailed example of leveraging the Find() method in your application, take a look at Recipe 5-3.

13-3. Retrieving Entities for Read-Only Access
Problem

You want to retrieve some entities efficiently that you will only display and not need to update. Additionally, you want to implement the Entity Framework Code-First approach.

Solution

A very common activity in many applications, especially websites, is to let the user browse through data. In many cases, the user will never update the data. For these situations, you can make your code much more efficient if you avoid the overhead of caching and change tracking from the context object. You can easily do this using the AsNoTracking method.

Let's say that you have an application that manages appointments for doctors. Your model may look something like the one shown in Figure 13-5.

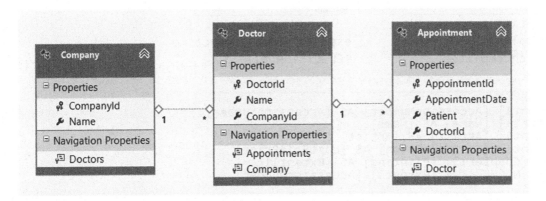

Figure 13-5. A model for managing doctors and their appointments

To start, this example leverages the Code-First approach for Entity Framework. In Listing 13-6, we create our entity classes, Company, Doctor, and Appointment.

Listing 13-6. The Painting Entity Object

```
public class Company
{
    public Company()
    {
        Doctors = new HashSet<Doctor>();
    }

    public int CompanyId { get; set; }
    public string Name { get; set; }

    public virtual ICollection<Doctor> Doctors { get; set; }
}

public class Doctor
{
    public Doctor()
    {
        Appointments = new HashSet<Appointment>();
    }

    public int DoctorId { get; set; }
    public string Name { get; set; }
    public int CompanyId { get; set; }

    public virtual ICollection<Appointment> Appointments { get; set; }
    public virtual Company Company { get; set; }
}

public class Appointment
{
    public int AppointmentId { get; set; }
    public System.DateTime AppointmentDate { get; set; }
    public string Patient { get; set; }
    public int DoctorId { get; set; }

    public virtual Doctor Doctor { get; set; }
}
```

Next, in Listing 13-7, we create the DbContext object, which is our gateway into Entity Framework functionality when leveraging the Code-First approach.

Listing 13-7. DbContext Object

```
public class Recipe3Context : DbContext
{
    public Recipe3Context()
        : base("Recipe3ConnectionString")
    {
        // Disable Entity Framework Model Compatibility
        Database.SetInitializer<Recipe3Context>(null);
    }
```

```
protected override void OnModelCreating(DbModelBuilder modelBuilder)
{
    modelBuilder.Entity<Appointment>().ToTable("Chapter13.Appointment");
    modelBuilder.Entity<Company>().ToTable("Chapter13.Company");
    modelBuilder.Entity<Doctor>().ToTable("Chapter13.Doctor");
}

public DbSet<Appointment> Appointments { get; set; }
public DbSet<Company> Companies { get; set; }
public DbSet<Doctor> Doctors { get; set; }
}
```

Next add an App.Config class to the project, and add to it the code from Listing 13-8, inside the ConnectionStrings section.

Listing 13-8. Connection String

```
<connectionStrings>
  <add name="Recipe3ConnectionString"
       connectionString="Data Source=.;
       Initial Catalog=EFRecipes;
       Integrated Security=True;
       MultipleActiveResultSets=True"
       providerName="System.Data.SqlClient" />
</connectionStrings>
```

To retrieve the doctors and the companies they work for without adding them to the context object, chain the AsNoTracking method to the query that fetches Doctors, appointments, and company information as we have done in Listing 13-9.

Listing 13-9. Doing a Simple Query Using the AsNoTracking Method

```
using (var context = new Recipe3Context())
{
    var company = new Company {Name = "Paola Heart Center"};
    var doc1 = new Doctor {Name = "Jill Mathers", Company = company};
    var doc2 = new Doctor {Name = "Robert Stevens", Company = company};
    var app1 = new Appointment
    {
        AppointmentDate = DateTime.Parse("3/18/2010"),
        Patient = "Karen Rodgers",
        Doctor = doc1
    };
    var app2 = new Appointment
    {
        AppointmentDate = DateTime.Parse("3/20/2010"),
        Patient = "Steven Cook",
        Doctor = doc2
    };
    context.Doctors.Add(doc1);
    context.Doctors.Add(doc2);
    context.Appointments.Add(app1);
```

```
        context.Appointments.Add(app2);
        context.Companies.Add(company);
        context.SaveChanges();
    }

using (var context = new Recipe3Context())
{
    Console.WriteLine("Entities tracked in context for Doctors...");

    // execute query using the AsNoTracking() method
    context.Doctors.Include("Company").AsNoTracking().ToList();

    Console.WriteLine("Number of entities loaded into context with AsNoTracking: {0}",
        context.ChangeTracker.Entries().Count());

    // execute query without the AsNoTracking() method
    context.Doctors.Include("Company").ToList();

    Console.WriteLine("Number of entities loaded into context without AsNoTracking: {0}",
        context.ChangeTracker.Entries().Count());

}
```

Following is the output of the code in Listing 13-9:

```
Entities tracked in context for Doctors...
Number of entities loaded into context with AsNoTracking: 0
Number of entities loaded into context without AsNoTracking: 3
```

How It Works

When chaining the AsNoTracking method to your query, the objects resulting from that query are not tracked in the context object. In our case, this includes the doctors and the companies the doctors work for because our query explicitly included these.

By default, the results of your queries are tracked in the context object. This makes updating and deleting objects effortless, but at the cost of some memory and CPU overhead. For applications that stream large numbers of objects, such as browsing products at an ecommerce website, using the AsNoTracking option can result in less resource overhead and better application performance.

As you are not caching the results of a query, each time you execute the query Entity Framework will need to materialize the query result. Normally, with change tracking enabled, Entity Framework will not need to re-materialize a query result if it is already cached in the context object.

When you include the AsNoTracking option (as we do in Listing 13-9), it only affects the current query for the given entity and any related entities included in the query. It does affect subsequent queries that do not include the AsNoTracking option, as demonstrated in Listing 13-9.

13-4. Efficiently Building a Search Query

Problem

You want to write a search query using LINQ so that it is translated to more efficient SQL. Additionally, you want to implement the Entity Framework Code-First approach.

Solution

Let's say that you have a model like the one shown in Figure 13-6.

Figure 13-6. *A simple model with a Reservation entity*

To start, this example leverages the Code-First approach for Entity Framework. In Listing 13-10, we create the entity class, Reservation.

Listing 13-10. The Reservation Entity Object

```
public class Reservation
{
    public int ReservationId { get; set; }
    public System.DateTime ResDate { get; set; }
    public string Name { get; set; }
}
```

Next, in Listing 13-11, we create the DbContext object, which is our gateway into Entity Framework functionality when leveraging the Code-First approach.

Listing 13-11. DbContext Object

```
public class Recipe5Context : DbContext
{
    public Recipe4Context()
        : base("Recipe4ConnectionString")
    {
        // disable Entity Framework Model Compatibility
        Database.SetInitializer<Recipe5Context>(null);
    }
```

```
protected override void OnModelCreating(DbModelBuilder modelBuilder)
{
    modelBuilder.Entity<Reservation>().ToTable("Chapter13.Reservation");
}

public DbSet<Reservation> Reservations { get; set; }
}
```

Next add an App.Config class to the project, and also add to it the code from Listing 13-12, under the ConnectionStrings section.

Listing 13-12. Connection String

```
<connectionStrings>
  <add name="Recipe4ConnectionString"
      connectionString="Data Source=.;
      Initial Catalog=EFRecipes;
      Integrated Security=True;
      MultipleActiveResultSets=True"
      providerName="System.Data.SqlClient" />
</connectionStrings>
```

You want to write a search query using LINQ to find reservations for a particular person, or reservations on a given date, or both. You might use the let keyword as we did in the *first* query in Listing 13-13 to make the LINQ expression fairly clean and easy to read. However, the let keyword is translated to more complex and often less efficient SQL. Instead of using the let keyword, consider explicitly creating two conditions in the where clause, as we did in the *second* query in Listing 13-13.

Listing 13-13. Using Both the let Keyword and Explicit Conditions in the Query

```
using (var context = new Recipe4Context())
{
    context.Reservations.Add(new Reservation
        {Name = "James Jordan", ResDate = DateTime.Parse("4/18/10")});
    context.Reservations.Add(new Reservation {Name = "Katie Marlowe",
        ResDate = DateTime.Parse("3/22/10")});
            context.Reservations.Add(new Reservation {Name = "Roger Smith",
        ResDate = DateTime.Parse("4/18/10")});
    context.Reservations.Add(new Reservation {Name = "James Jordan",
            ResDate = DateTime.Parse("5/12/10")});
            context.Reservations.Add(new Reservation {Name = "James Jordan",
                ResDate = DateTime.Parse("6/22/10")});
            context.SaveChanges();
        }

        using (var context = new Recipe4Context())
        {
            DateTime? searchDate = null;
            var searchName = "James Jordan";
```

```
        Console.WriteLine("More complex SQL...");
        var query2 = from reservation in context.Reservations
            let dateMatches = searchDate == null || reservation.ResDate == searchDate
            let nameMatches = searchName == string.Empty || reservation.Name.Contains(searchName)
            where dateMatches && nameMatches
            select reservation;
        foreach (var reservation in query2)
        {
            Console.WriteLine("Found reservation for {0} on {1}", reservation.Name,
                reservation.ResDate.ToShortDateString());
        }

        Console.WriteLine("Cleaner SQL...");
        var query1 = from reservation in context.Reservations
            where (searchDate == null || reservation.ResDate == searchDate)
                &&
                (searchName == string.Empty || reservation.Name.Contains(searchName))
            select reservation;
        foreach (var reservation in query1)
        {
            Console.WriteLine("Found reservation for {0} on {1}", reservation.Name,
                reservation.ResDate.ToShortDateString());
        }
    }
```

Following is the output of the code in Listing 13-13:

```
More complex SQL...
Found reservation for James Jordan on 4/18/2010
Found reservation for James Jordan on 5/12/2010
Found reservation for James Jordan on 6/22/2010
Cleaner SQL...
Found reservation for James Jordan on 4/18/2010
Found reservation for James Jordan on 5/12/2010
Found reservation for James Jordan on 6/22/2010
```

How It Works

Writing conditions inline, as we did in the *second* query in Listing 13-13, is not very good for readability or maintainability. Typically, we would use the let keyword to make the code cleaner and more readable. In some cases, however, this leads to more complex and often less efficient SQL code.

Let's take a look at the SQL generated by both approaches. Listing 13-14 shows the SQL generated for the *first* query. Notice that the where clause contains a case statement with quite a bit of cast'ing going on. If we had more parameters in our search query beyond just name and reservation date, the resulting SQL statement would get even more complicated.

Listing 13-14. SQL Generated When let Is Used in the LINQ Query

```
SELECT
[Extent1].[ReservationId] AS [ReservationId],
[Extent1].[ResDate] AS [ResDate],
[Extent1].[Name] AS [Name]
FROM [Chapter13].[Reservation] AS [Extent1]
WHERE (
  (CASE WHEN (@p__linq__0 IS NULL OR
         @p__linq__1 = CAST( [Extent1].[ResDate] AS datetime2))
       THEN cast(1 as bit)
       WHEN ( NOT (@p__linq__0 IS NULL OR
         @p__linq__1 = CAST( [Extent1].[ResDate] AS datetime2)))
       THEN cast(0 as bit) END) = 1) AND
  ((CASE WHEN ((@p__linq__2 = @p__linq__3) OR
         ([Extent1].[Name] LIKE @p__linq__4 ESCAPE N'~''))
       THEN cast(1 as bit)
       WHEN ( NOT ((@p__linq__2 = @p__linq__3) OR
       ([Extent1].[Name] LIKE @p__linq__4 ESCAPE N'~'')))
       THEN cast(0 as bit) END) = 1)
```

Listing 13-15 shows the SQL generated from the *second* query, where we created the conditions inline. This query is simpler and might execute more efficiently at runtime.

Listing 13-15. Cleaner, More Efficient SQL Generated When Not Using let in a LINQ Query

```
SELECT
[Extent1].[ReservationId] AS [ReservationId],
[Extent1].[ResDate] AS [ResDate],
[Extent1].[Name] AS [Name]
FROM [Chapter13].[Reservation] AS [Extent1]
WHERE (@p__linq__0 IS NULL OR
       @p__linq__1 = CAST( [Extent1].[ResDate] AS datetime2)) AND
      ((@p__linq__2 = @p__linq__3) OR
       ([Extent1].[Name] LIKE @p__linq__4 ESCAPE N'~''))
```

13-5. Making Change Tracking with POCO Faster
Problem

You are using POCO, and you want to improve the performance of change tracking while at the same time minimizing memory usage. Additionally, you want to implement the Entity Framework Code-First approach.

Solution

Suppose that you have a model with an account and related payments like the one shown in Figure 13-7.

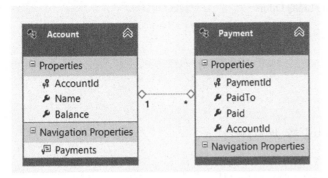

Figure 13-7. *A model with an Account entity and a related Payment*

To start, this example leverages the Code-First approach for Entity Framework. In Listing 13-16, we create two entity classes: Account and Payment. To achieve the best change-tracking performance, we need to allow Entity Framework to wrap our entity classes automatically with change-tracking proxy classes, which immediately notify the underlying change-tracking mechanism any time that the value of a property changes. With proxies, Entity Framework knows the state your entities at all times. When creating the proxy, notification events are added to the setter method of each property, which are processed by the Object State Manager. Entity Framework will automatically create a proxy class when two requirements are met: (1) all properties in an entity must be marked as *virtual*, and (2) any navigation property referencing a collection must be of type ICollection<T>. Meeting these requirements allows Entity Framework to override the class and add the necessary change-tracking plumbing.

Both of our Account and Payment entity classes meet these requirements, as seen in Listing 13-16.

Listing 13-16. Our Entity Classes with Properties Marked as virtual and the Navigation Properties Are of Type ICollection<T>

```csharp
public class Account
{
    public virtual int AccountId { get; set; }
    public virtual string Name { get; set; }
    public virtual decimal Balance { get; set; }
    public virtual ICollection<Payment> Payments { get; set; }
}

public class Payment
{
    public virtual int PaymentId { get; set; }
    public virtual string PaidTo { get; set; }
    public virtual decimal Paid { get; set; }
    public virtual int AccountId { get; set; }
}
```

Next, in Listing 13-17, we create the DbContext object, which is our gateway into Entity Framework functionality when leveraging the Code-First approach.

Listing 13-17. DbContext Object

```
public class Recipe5Context : DbContext
{
    public Recipe5Context()
        : base("Recipe5ConnectionString")
    {
        // Disable Entity Framework Model Compatibility
        Database.SetInitializer<Recipe6Context>(null);
    }

    protected override void OnModelCreating(DbModelBuilder modelBuilder)
    {
        modelBuilder.Entity<Account>().ToTable("Chapter13.Account");
        modelBuilder.Entity<Payment>().ToTable("Chapter13.Payment");
    }

    public DbSet<Account> Accounts { get; set; }
    public DbSet<Payment> Payments { get; set; }
}
```

Next add an App.Config class to the project, and add to it the code from Listing 13-18 under the ConnectionStrings section.

Listing 13-18. Connection String

```
<connectionStrings>
  <add name="Recipe5ConnectionString"
       connectionString="Data Source=.;
       Initial Catalog=EFRecipes;
       Integrated Security=True;
       MultipleActiveResultSets=True"
       providerName="System.Data.SqlClient" />
</connectionStrings>
```

The code in Listing 13-19 illustrates inserting, retrieving, and updating our model.

Listing 13-19. Inserting, Retrieving, and Updating Our Model

```
using (var context = new Recipe5Context())
{
    var watch = new Stopwatch();
    watch.Start();
    for (var i = 0; i < 5000; i++)
    {
        var account = new Account { Name = "Test" + i, Balance = 10M,
        Payments = new Collection<Payment> { new Payment {PaidTo = "Test" + (i + 1), Paid = 5M }},} ;
        context.Accounts.Add(account);
        Console.WriteLine("Adding Account {0}", i);
    }
    context.SaveChanges();
    watch.Stop();
    Console.WriteLine("Time to insert: {0} seconds", watch.Elapsed.TotalSeconds.ToString());
}
```

```
using (var context = new Recipe5Context())
{
    var watch = new Stopwatch();
    watch.Start();
    var accounts = context.Accounts.Include("Payments").ToList();
    watch.Stop();
    Console.WriteLine("Time to read: {0} seconds", watch.Elapsed.TotalSeconds.ToString());
    watch.Restart();
    foreach (var account in accounts)
    {
        account.Balance += 10M;
        account.Payments.First().Paid += 1M;
    }
    context.SaveChanges();
    watch.Stop();
    Console.WriteLine("Time to update: {0} seconds", watch.Elapsed.TotalSeconds.ToString());
}
```

How It Works

With later versions of Entity Framework, including version 6.0, we specificy *POCO classes* to represent entities. POCO is an abbreviation for a *Plain Old CLR Object*, which is a class that typically contains only states, or properties, that map to corresponding database columns. POCO classes have no dependencies beyond the .NET CLR base classes and, specifically, no dependency on Entity Framework.

Change tracking with POCO entity classes occurs using either snapshots or proxy classes. With the snapshot approach, Entity Framework takes a picture, so to speak, of the data values of an entity as it is loaded into the context object from a query or an Attach() operation. Upon a SaveChanges() operation, the original snapshot is compared to the current data values to determine the data values that have changed. Using this approach, Entity Framework maintains two copies of each object and compares them, generating the necessary corresponding SQL Update, Insert, and Delete statements. You might expect this approach to be very slow, but Entity Framework is very fast in finding the differences.

▪ **Note**   The Add() operation from the context object does not invoke a snapshot as the entity is new and there is no need to track changes to the individual values. Entity Framework marks the entity as added, and it will issue a SQL Insert statement upon a SaveChanges() operation.

The second approach, depicted in Listing 13-19, wraps the underlying entity POCO object with a proxy object that implements the IEntityWithChangeTracking interface. This proxy is responsible for notifying the Object State Manager of changes to values and relationships on the object. Entity Framework *automatically* creates these proxies for your POCO object when you mark all of the properties on your POCO class as *virtual* and mark all Navigation properties that return a collection as ICollection<T>. Proxies avoid the potentially complex object-by-object comparisons of the snapshot approach. It does, however, require some overhead to track each change as it occurs.

Although change-tracking proxies immediately notify the change tracker components about changes to the objects and avoid object comparisons, in practice, performance benefits are typically seen only when the model is quite complex and/or when few changes are made to a large number of objects. The model in Figure 13-7 is very simple, and every object is updated in the code in Listing 13-19. If you were to change the code to use snapshots, you would notice only a second or so saved for the updates when proxies are used.

■ Note Proxy classes can be troublesome in n-Tier scenarios where you need to serialize data to send to another physical tier, such as to a WCF or to a Web API client. See Recipe 9-7 for more detail.

13-6. Auto-Compiling LINQ Queries

Problem

You want to improve the performance of queries that are reused several times, and you would like to achieve this performance upgrade with no additional coding or configuration.

Solution

Let's say that you have a model like the one shown in Figure 13-8.

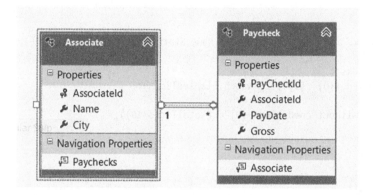

Figure 13-8. *A model with an Associate and its related Paycheck*

In this model, each Associate has zero or more paychecks. You have a LINQ query that is used repeatedly throughout your application, and you want to improve the performance of this query by compiling it just once and reusing the compiled version in subsequent executions.

When executing against a database, Entity Framework must *translate* your strongly typed LINQ query to a corresponding SQL query, based upon your database provider (SQL Server, Oracle, and so on). Beginning with version 5 of Entity Framework, each query translation is cached by default. This process is referred to as *auto-caching*. With each subsequent execution of a given LINQ query, the corresponding SQL query is retrieved directly from query plan cache, bypassing the translation step. For queries containing parameters, changing parameter values will still retrieve the same query. Interestingly, this query plan cache is shared among all instances of a context object instantiated with the application's AppDomain, meaning that, once cached, any context object in the AppDomain has access to it.

In Listing 13-10, we compare performance with caching enabled and then disabled. To illustrate the performance benefit, we've instrumented the code in Listing 13-10 to print the number of ticks for each of ten iterates taken for both the uncompiled and the compiled versions of the LINQ query. In this query, we can see that we get roughly a 2X performance boost. Most of this, of course, is due to the relatively high cost of compiling versus the low cost for actually performing this simple query.

Listing 13-20. Comparing the Performance of a Simple Compiled LINQ Query

```
private static void RunUncompiledQuery()
{
    using (var context = new EFRecipesEntities())
    {
        // Explicitly disable query plan caching
        var objectContext = ((IObjectContextAdapter) context).ObjectContext;
        var associateNoCache = objectContext.CreateObjectSet<Associate>();
        associateNoCache.EnablePlanCaching = false;

        var watch = new Stopwatch();
        long totalTicks = 0;

        // warm things up
        associateNoCache.Include(x => x.Paychecks).Where(a => a.Name.StartsWith("Karen")).ToList();

        // query gets compiled each time
        for (var i = 0; i < 10; i++)
        {
            watch.Restart();
            associateNoCache.Include(x => x.Paychecks).Where(a => a.Name.StartsWith("Karen")).ToList();
            watch.Stop();
            totalTicks += watch.ElapsedTicks;
            Console.WriteLine("Not Compiled #{0}: {1}", i, watch.ElapsedTicks);
        }
        Console.WriteLine("Average ticks without compiling: {0}", (totalTicks/10));
        Console.WriteLine("");
    }
}

private static void RunCompiledQuery()
{
    using (var context = new EFRecipesEntities())
    {
        var watch = new Stopwatch();
        long totalTicks = 0;

        // warm things up
        context.Associates.Include(x => x.Paychecks).Where(a => a.Name.StartsWith("Karen")).ToList();

        totalTicks = 0;
        for (var i = 0; i < 10; i++)
        {
            watch.Restart();
            context.Associates.Include(x => x.Paychecks).Where(a => a.Name.StartsWith("Karen")).ToList();
            watch.Stop();
            totalTicks += watch.ElapsedTicks;
            Console.WriteLine("Compiled #{0}: {1}", i, watch.ElapsedTicks);
        }
        Console.WriteLine("Average ticks with compiling: {0}", (totalTicks/10));
    }
}
```

Following is the output of the code in Listing 13-20:

```
Not Compiled #0: 10014
Not Compiled #1: 5004
Not Compiled #2: 5178
Not Compiled #3: 7624
Not Compiled #4: 4839
Not Compiled #5: 5017
Not Compiled #6: 4864
Not Compiled #7: 5090
Not Compiled #8: 4499
Not Compiled #9: 6942
Average ticks without compiling: 5907

Compiled #0: 3458
Compiled #1: 1524
Compiled #2: 1320
Compiled #3: 1283
Compiled #4: 1202
Compiled #5: 1145
Compiled #6: 1075
Compiled #7: 1104
Compiled #8: 1081
Compiled #9: 1084
Average ticks with compiling: 1427
```

How It Works

When you execute a LINQ query, Entity Framework builds an expression tree object for the query, which is then converted, or compiled, into an internal command tree. This internal command tree is passed to the database provider to be converted into the appropriate database commands (typically SQL). The cost of converting an expression tree can be relatively expensive depending on the complexity of the query and the underlying model. Models with deep inheritance or horizontal splitting introduce enough complexity in the conversion process that the compile time may become significant relative to the actual query execution time. However, in Version 5 of the Entity Framework, automatic query caching for LINQ queries was introduced. You can get an idea of the performance benefits of this feature by examining the results of Listing 13-20.

Additionally, as shown in Listing 13-20, you can disable the auto-compiling features by dropping down from the DbContext object into the underlying ObjectContext object, obtaining a reference to the entity object and setting its EnablePlanCaching property to false.

To track each compiled query, Entity Framework walks the nodes of the query expression tree and creates a hash, which becomes the key for that compiled query in the underlying query cache. For each subsequent call, Entity Framework will attempt to locate the hash key from the cache, eliminating the overhead cost of the query translation process. It's important to note that the cached query plan is independent of the context object, instead being tied to the AppDomain of the application, meaning that the cached query is available to all instances of a given Entity Framework context object.

Once the underlying query cache contains 800 or more query plans, a cache eviction process automatically kicks off. Each minute, a sweeping process removes entries based upon a LFRU (least frequently/recently used) algorithm, driven by hit count and age of the query.

Compiled queries are especially helpful in ASP.NET search page scenarios where parameter values may change, but the query is the same and can be reused on each page rendering. This works because a compiled query is *parameterized*, meaning that it can accept different parameter values.

13-7. Returning Partially Filled Entities

Problem

You have a property on an entity that is seldom read and updated. This property is expensive to read and update because of its size. To improve performance, you want to populate this property selectively.

Solution

Let's say that you have a model like the one shown in Figure 13-9.

Figure 13-9. *A model with a Resume entity with a Body property that contains the entire text of the applicant's resume*

We can simply avoid loading one or more properties on an entity by leveraging the SqlQuery() method from the context to execute a SQL statement. The code in Listing 13-21 illustrates this approach.

Listing 13-21. Returning Partially Filled Entities Using Both eSQL and ExecuteStoreQuery()

```
using (var context = new EFRecipesEntities())
{
    var r1 = new Resume
    {
        Title = "C# Developer",
        Name = "Sally Jones",
        Body = "...very long resume goes here..."
    };
    context.Resumes.Add(r1);
    context.SaveChanges();
}
```

```
using (var context = new EFRecipesEntities())
{
    // using SqlQuery()
    var result1 =
    context.Resumes.SqlQuery
        ("select ResumeId, Title, Name,'' Body from chapter13.Resume",
            "Resumes", MergeOption.AppendOnly).Single();
    Console.WriteLine("Resume body: {0}", result1.Body);

    var result2 =
    context.Database.SqlQuery<Resume>("select * from chapter13.Resume", "Resumes",
                    MergeOption.OverwriteChanges).Single();
    Console.WriteLine("Resume body: {0}", result2.Body);
}
```

Following is the output of the code in Listing 13-21:

```
Resume body:
Resume body: ...very long resume goes here...
```

How It Works

An approach for partially filling an entity is to use the SqlQuery() method that is exposed from the static Database object, which can be accessed from the DbContext object. Here we execute a SQL statement that fills all of the properties except for the Body property, which we initialize to the empty string. If needed, we can fill in the Body property from the database by setting the MergeOption to MergeOption.OverwriteChanges and requerying for the object for all of the properties. Be careful though, as the second query will overwrite any changes we've made to the object in memory. Keep in mind that this approach exposes the SQL query as string, which yields no compile-time checking or IntelliSense.

Recipe 13-8 shows a model-centric and perhaps cleaner approach to this problem.

13-8. Moving an Expensive Property to Another Entity
Problem

You want to move a property to another entity so that you can lazy load that entity. This is often helpful if the property is particularly expensive to load and rarely used.

Solution

As with the previous recipe, let's say that you have a model that looks like the one shown in Figure 13-10.

Figure 13-10. *A model with a Resume entity with a Body property that contains the entire text of the applicant's resume. In this recipe, we'll move the Body property to another entity*

We'll assume, as we did in the previous recipe, that the Body property for the Resume may contain a rather large representation of the applicant's resume. We want to move this property to another entity so that we can lazy load, only if we really want to read the resume.

To move the Body property to another entity, do the following:

1. Right-click the design surface, and select Add ➤ Entity. Name the new entity **ResumeDetail**, and uncheck the Create key property check box.

2. Move the Body property from the Resume entity to the ResumeDetail entity. You can use Cut/Paste to move the property.

3. Right-click the design surface, and select Add ➤ Association. Set the multiplicity to One on the Resume side and One on the ResumeDetail side. Check the Add foreign key properties box. (See Figure 13-11.)

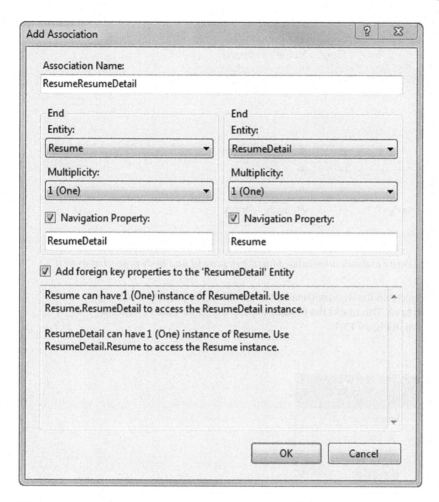

Figure 13-11. *Adding an association between Resume and ResumeDetail*

4. Change the name of the foreign key that was created by the association from ResumeResumeId to just **ResumeId**.

5. Select the ResumeDetail entity, and view the Mapping Details window. Map the entity to the Resume table. Map the Body property to the Body column. Map the ResumeId property to the ResumeId column. (See Figure 13-12.)

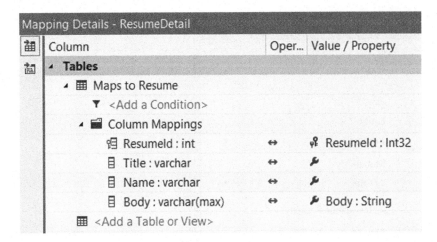

Figure 13-12. *Map the ResumeDetail entity to the Resume table. Map the ResumeId and Body properties as well*

6. Select the ResumeId property on the ResumeDetail entity and view the properties. Change the EntityKey property to true. This marks the ResumeId property as the entity's key. The completed model is shown in Figure 13-13.

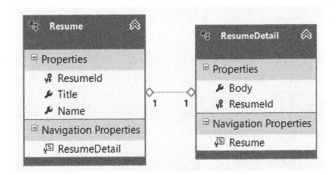

Figure 13-13. *The completed model with the Body property moved to the new ResumeDetail entity*

The code in Listing 13-22 demonstrates how to use the ResumeDetail entity.

Listing 13-22. *Using the ResumeDetail Entity to Lazy Load the Expensive Body Property*

```
using (var context = new EFRecipesEntities())
{
    var r1 = new Resume {Title = "C# Developer", Name = "Sally Jones"};
    r1.ResumeDetail = new ResumeDetail {Body = "...very long resume goes here..."};
    context.Resumes.Add(r1);
    context.SaveChanges();
}
```

```
using (var context = new EFRecipesEntities())
{
    var resume = context.Resumes.Single();
    Console.WriteLine("Title: {0}, Name: {1}", resume.Title, resume.Name);

    // note, the ResumeDetail is not loaded until we reference it
    Console.WriteLine("Body: {0}", resume.ResumeDetail.Body);
}
```

Following is the output of the code in Listing 13-22:

```
Title: C# Developer, Name: Sally Jones
Body: ...very long resume goes here...
```

How It Works

We avoided loading the expensive Body property on the Resume entity by moving the property to a new related entity. By splitting the underlying table across these two entities, we can exploit the default lazy loading of Entity Framework so that the Body property is loaded only when we reference it. This is a fairly clean approach to the problem, but it does introduce an additional entity into our model that we have to manage in our code.

■ **Note**   The following link shows how to move a property from one entity to another entity using the Code-First approach: http://msdn.microsoft.com/en-us/data/jj591617#2.8. This process is referred to as *Entity Splitting*, allowing the properties of an entity type to be spread across multiple tables.

13-9. Avoiding Include
Problem

You want to eagerly load a related collection without using Include(). Additionally, you want to implement the Entity Framework Code-First approach.

Solution

Let's say that you have a model like the one shown in Figure 13-14.

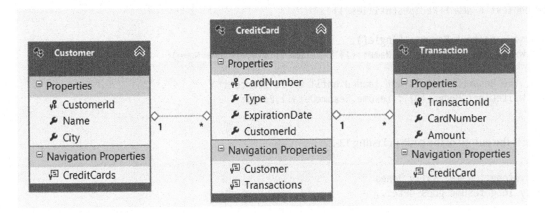

Figure 13-14. A model for a Customer, their CreditCards, and Transactions

To start, this example leverages the Code-First approach for Entity Framework. In Listing 13-23, we create the Customer, CreditCard, and Transaction entity classes.

Listing 13-23. The Reservation Entity Object

```
public class Customer
{
    public Customer()
    {
        CreditCards = new HashSet<CreditCard>();
    }

    public int CustomerId { get; set; }
    public string Name { get; set; }
    public string City { get; set; }

    public virtual ICollection<CreditCard> CreditCards { get; set; }
}

public class CreditCard
{
    public CreditCard()
    {
        Transactions = new HashSet<Transaction>();
    }

    public string CardNumber { get; set; }
    public string Type { get; set; }
    public System.DateTime ExpirationDate { get; set; }
    public int CustomerId { get; set; }

    public virtual Customer Customer { get; set; }
    public virtual ICollection<Transaction> Transactions { get; set; }
}
```

```
public class Transaction
{
    public int TransactionId { get; set; }
    public string CardNumber { get; set; }
    public decimal Amount { get; set; }

    public virtual CreditCard CreditCard { get; set; }
}
```

Next, in Listing 13-24, we create the DbContext object, which is our gateway into Entity Framework functionality when leveraging the Code-First approach.

Listing 13-24. DbContext Object

```
public class Recipe9Context : DbContext
{
    public Recipe9Context()
        : base("Recipe9ConnectionString")
    {
        // Disable Entity Framework Model Compatibility
        Database.SetInitializer<Recipe10Context>(null);
    }

    protected override void OnModelCreating(DbModelBuilder modelBuilder)
    {
        // explicilty specify primary key for CreditCard
        modelBuilder.Entity<CreditCard>().HasKey(x => x.CardNumber);

        modelBuilder.Entity<Customer>().ToTable("Chapter13.Customer");
        modelBuilder.Entity<CreditCard>().ToTable("Chapter13.CreditCard");
        modelBuilder.Entity<Transaction>().ToTable("Chapter13.Transaction");
    }

    public DbSet<CreditCard> CreditCards { get; set; }
    public DbSet<Customer> Customers { get; set; }
    public DbSet<Transaction> Transactions { get; set; }
}
```

Next add an App.Config class to the project, and add to it the code from Listing 13-25, under the ConnectionStrings section.

Listing 13-25. Connection String

```
<connectionStrings>
  <add name="Recipe9ConnectionString"
       connectionString="Data Source=.;
       Initial Catalog=EFRecipes;
       Integrated Security=True;
       MultipleActiveResultSets=True"
       providerName="System.Data.SqlClient" />
</connectionStrings>
```

To load all of the Customers in a given city together with their credit cards and transactions without using Include( ), explicitly load the entities and let Entity Framework fix up the associations, as shown in Listing 13-26.

Listing 13-26. Loading Related Entities without Using Include( )

```
using (var context = new Recipe9Context())
{
    var cust1 = new Customer { Name = "Robin Rosen", City = "Raytown" };
    var card1 = new CreditCard { CardNumber = "41949494338899",
                                    ExpirationDate = DateTime.Parse("12/2010"), Type = "Visa" };
    var trans1 = new Transaction { Amount = 29.95M };
    card1.Transactions.Add(trans1);
    cust1.CreditCards.Add(card1);
    var cust2 = new Customer { Name = "Bill Meyers", City = "Raytown" };
    var card2 = new CreditCard { CardNumber = "41238389484448",
                                    ExpirationDate = DateTime.Parse("12/2013"), Type = "Visa" };
    var trans2 = new Transaction { Amount = 83.39M };
    card2.Transactions.Add(trans2);
    cust2.CreditCards.Add(card2);
    context.Customers.Add(cust1);
    context.Customers.Add(cust2);
    context.SaveChanges();
}

using (var context = new Recipe9Context())
{
    var customers = context.Customers.Where(c => c.City == "Raytown");
    var creditCards = customers.SelectMany(c => c.CreditCards);
    var transactions = creditCards.SelectMany(cr => cr.Transactions);

    // execute queries, EF fixes up associations
    customers.ToList();
    creditCards.ToList();
    transactions.ToList();

    foreach (var customer in customers)
    {
        Console.WriteLine("Customer: {0} in {1}", customer.Name, customer.City);
        foreach (var creditCard in customer.CreditCards)
        {
            Console.WriteLine("\tCard: {0} expires on {1}",
                            creditCard.CardNumber, creditCard.ExpirationDate.ToShortDateString());
            foreach (var trans in creditCard.Transactions)
            {
                Console.WriteLine("\t\tTransaction: {0}", trans.Amount.ToString("C"));
            }
        }
    }
}
```

Following is the output of the code in Listing 13-26:

```
Customer: Robin Rosen in Raytown
        Card: 41949494338899 expires on 12/1/2010
                Transaction: $29.95
Customer: Bill Meyers in Raytown
        Card: 41238389484448 expires on 12/1/2013
                Transaction: $83.39
```

How It Works

The Include() method is a powerful and usually efficient way to eagerly load related entities. However, Include() does have some performance drawbacks. Although using Include() results in just one round trip to the database in place of the three shown in Listing 13-26, the single query is quite complex and, in some cases, may not perform as well as three much simpler queries. Additionally, the result set from this single, more complex query contains duplicate columns that increase the amount of data sent over the wire if the database server and the application are on separate machines. As a rule, the more Includes contained in your query, the higher the performance penalty.

On the flip side, not using an Include() method and iterating over a large number of Customers can generate an excessive number of small queries, resulting in a large performance hit as well. Chapter 5 discusses the trade-offs and alternate approaches in detail.

13-10. Generating Proxies Explicitly
Problem

You have POCO entities that use dynamic proxies. When you execute a query, you do not want to incur the cost of Entity Framework lazily creating the proxies.

Solution

Suppose that you have a model like the one shown in Figure 13-15.

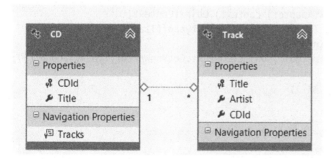

Figure 13-15. *A model for CDs and music titles*

The corresponding POCO classes are shown in Listing 13-27. Note how each property includes the virtual keyword and each reference to the Tracks property is of type ICollection. This will allow Entity Framework to create the tracking proxies dynamically. (See Recipe 13-5 for more information on tracking proxy objects.)

Listing 13-27. The POCO Classes Along with Our Object Context

```
public partial class CD
{
    public CD()
    {
        this.Tracks = new HashSet<Track>();
    }

    public int CDId { get; set; }
    public string Title { get; set; }

    public virtual ICollection<Track> Tracks { get; set; }
}

public partial class Track
{
    public string Title { get; set; }
    public string Artist { get; set; }
    public int CDId { get; set; }
}
```

To cause Entity Framework to generate the proxies before they are required (before an entity is loaded), we need to use the CreateProxyTypes() method on the object context, as illustrated in Listing 13-28.

Listing 13-28. Generating the tracking proxies before loading the entities

```
using (var context = new EFRecipesEntities())
{
        // to trigger proxy generation we need to drop-down into the underlying
        // ObjectContext object as DbContext does not expose the CreateProxyTypes() method

        var objectContext = ((IObjectContextAdapter) context).ObjectContext;
        objectContext.CreateProxyTypes(new Type[] { typeof(CD), typeof(Track) });
        var proxyTypes = ObjectContext.GetKnownProxyTypes();
        Console.WriteLine("{0} proxies generated!", ObjectContext.GetKnownProxyTypes().Count());

        var cds = context.CDs.Include("Tracks");
        foreach (var cd in cds)
        {
            Console.WriteLine("Album: {0}", cd.Title);
            foreach (var track in cd.Tracks)
            {
                Console.WriteLine("\t{0} by {1}", track.Title, track.Artist);
            }
        }
    }
```

Following is the output of the code in Listing 13-28:

```
2 proxies generated!
Album: Abbey Road
        Come Together by The Beatles
Album: Cowboy Town
        Cowgirls Don't Cry by Brooks & Dunn
Album: Long Black Train
        In My Dreams by Josh Turner
        Jacksonville by Josh Turner
```

How It Works

Dynamic proxies are created just before they are needed at runtime. This, of course, means that the overhead of creating the proxy is incurred on the first query. This lazy creation approach works well in most cases. However, you can generate the proxies before the entities are first loaded by calling the CreateProxyTypes() method.

The CreateProxyTypes() method takes an array of types and generates the corresponding tracking proxies. Once created, the proxies remain in the AppDomain for the life of the AppDomain. Notice that the lifetime of the proxy is tied to the AppDomain, not the object context. We could dispose of the object context and create another, and the proxies would not be disposed. You can retrieve the proxies in the AppDomain with the GetKnownProxyTypes() static method on the object context.

CHAPTER 14

Concurrency

Most applications that use sophisticated database management systems, such as Microsoft's SQL Server, are used by more than one person at a time. The concurrency concerns surrounding shared access to simple data files are often the motivating reason why developers turn to relational database systems to support their applications. Many, but not all, of the concurrency concerns evaporate when an application relies on a relational database for its data store. The concerns that remain usually involve detecting and controlling when an object state is different in memory than in the database. The recipes in this chapter provide an introduction to solving some of the problems typically faced by developers when it comes to detecting concurrency violations and controlling which copy of the object is ultimately persisted in the database.

14-1. Applying Optimistic Concurrency
Problem

You want to use optimistic concurrency with an entity in your model.

Solution

Let's suppose you have a model like the one shown in Figure 14-1.

Figure 14-1. *A Product entity describing products in your application*

The Product entity describes products in your application. You want to throw an exception if an intermediate update occurs between the time you retrieve a particular product entity and the time an update is performed in the database. To implement that behavior, do the following:

1. Add a column of type RowVersion to the table mapped to the Product entity.

2. Right-click the design surface, and select Update Model from Database. Update the model with the newly changed table. The updated model is shown in Figure 14-2.

Figure 14-2. *The updated model with the newly added TimeStamp property*

3. Right-click the TimeStamp property and select Properties. Change its Concurrency Mode property to Fixed.

The code in Listing 14-1 demonstrates that changing the underlying row in the table between the time the product entity is materialized and the time we update the table from changes in the product entity throws an exception.

Listing 14-1. Throwing an Exception If Optimistic Concurrency Is Violated

```
using (var context = new EF6RecipesContext())
{
    context.Products.Add(new Product
                        {
                            Name = "High Country Backpacking Tent",
                            UnitPrice = 199.95M
                        });

    context.SaveChanges();
}

using (var context = new EF6RecipesContext())
{
    // get the product
    var product = context.Products.SingleOrDefault();
    Console.WriteLine("{0} Unit Price: {1}", product.Name,
                    product.UnitPrice.ToString("C"));

    // update out of band
    context.Database.ExecuteSqlCommand(@"update chapter14.product set
            unitprice = 229.95 where productId = @p0", product.ProductId);
```

```
        // update the product via the model
        product.UnitPrice = 239.95M;
        Console.WriteLine("Changing {0}'s Unit Price to: {1}", product.Name,
                          product.UnitPrice.ToString("C"));

        try
        {
            context.SaveChanges();
        }
        catch (DbUpdateConcurrencyException ex)
        {
            Console.WriteLine("Concurrency Exception! {0}", ex.Message);
        }
        catch (Exception ex)
        {
            Console.WriteLine("Exception! {0}", ex.Message);
        }
}
```

The following is the output of the code in Listing 14-1:

```
High Country Backpacking Tent Unit Price: $199.95

Changing High Country Backpacking Tent's Unit Price to: $239.95

Concurrency Exception! Store update, insert, or delete statement affected an unexpected number
of rows (0). Entities may have been modified or deleted since entities were loaded. Refresh
ObjectStateManager entries.
```

How It Works

Optimistic concurrency is a low-contention concurrency strategy because rows are not locked when they are updated; rather it is up to the application to check for changes in row data before updating the row. The downside to optimistic concurrency is the potential for overwriting data if the application does not check for changes in the data before updating the database. Pessimistic concurrency, on the other hand, is a high-contention concurrency strategy because rows are locked during updates. The disadvantage of pessimistic concurrency is clearly the potential for degraded application performance caused by row locking, or even worse, deadlocks.

Optimistic concurrency is not enabled by default when tables are imported into a model. To enable optimistic concurrency, change the Concurrency Mode property of one of the entity's properties to Fixed. You do not have to use a TimeStamp property as we did in this recipe. You do need to choose a property that you know will be changed in every update to the underlying table. Typically, you would use a column whose value is generated by the database on each update. The TimeStamp column is a good candidate. If you choose another column, be sure to set the StoreGeneratedPattern property to Computed for the corresponding entity property. This will tell Entity Framework that the value is generated by the database. Entity Framework recognizes the TimeStamp data type as a Computed property.

In Listing 14-1, we inserted a new product into the database. We queried the model for the one product we inserted. Once we had the product, we updated the row out-of-band using the ExecuteSqlCommand() method to send a SQL update statement to the database changing the row. This out-of-band update simulates two users updating the same row simultaneously. On the database side, this update caused the UnitPrice to be changed to $229.95 and the TimeStamp column to be updated automatically by the database. After the out-of-band update, we changed the UnitPrice on the product in the database context to $239.95. At this point, the database context believes (incorrectly) that it has the most recent values for the product, including an update to the UnitPrice now set at $239.95. When we call SaveChanges(), Entity Framework generates an update statement with a where clause that includes both the ProductId and the TimeStamp values we have for the product. The value for this TimeStamp is the one retrieved when we read the product from the database before the out-of-band update. Because the out-of-band update caused the TimeStamp to change, the value for the TimeStamp column in the database is different from the value of the TimeStamp property on the product entity in the database context. The update statement will fail because no row is found in the table matching both the ProductId and the TimeStamp values. Entity Framework will respond by rolling back the entire transaction and throwing a DbUpdateConcurrencyException.

In responding to the exception, the code in Listing 14-1 printed a message and continued. This is probably not how you would handle a concurrency violation in a real application. One way to handle this exception is to refresh the entity with the current value of the concurrency column from the database. With the correct value for the concurrency column, a subsequent SaveChanges() will likely succeed. Of course, it might not for the same reason that it failed the first time, and you need to be prepared for this as well.

The DbUpdateConcurrencyException object has an Entries collection property, which contains a DbEntityEntry instance for each entity that fails to update. The DbEntityEntry class defines a Reload() method that will cause the entry to be updated with the values from the database (database wins), and all changes made to the entry in the database context are lost.

It is possible, however, to overwrite the entry's OriginalValues property such that SaveChanges() can be called on the database context without a concurrency violation, as shown in Listing 14-2.

Listing 14-2. Resolving a Concurrency Conflict in a Client Wins Scenario

```
bool saveChangesFailed;
do
{
    saveChangesFailed = false;
    try
    {
        context.SaveChanges();
    }
    catch (DbUpdateConcurrencyException ex)
    {
        saveChangesFailed = true;
        var entry = ex.Entries.Single();
        entry.OriginalValues.SetValues(entry.GetDatabaseValues());
    }
} while (saveChangesFailed);
```

In addition to the two aforementioned scenarios, it is possible to write custom code to update a conflicting entity with data from both the database and the client, or to allow user intervention to resolve data conflicts.

14-2. Managing Concurrency When Using Stored Procedures
Problem
You want to use optimistic concurrency when using stored procedures for the insert, update, and delete actions.

Solution
Let's suppose that we have a table like the one shown in Figure 14-3 and the entity shown in Listing 14-3, which is mapped to the table.

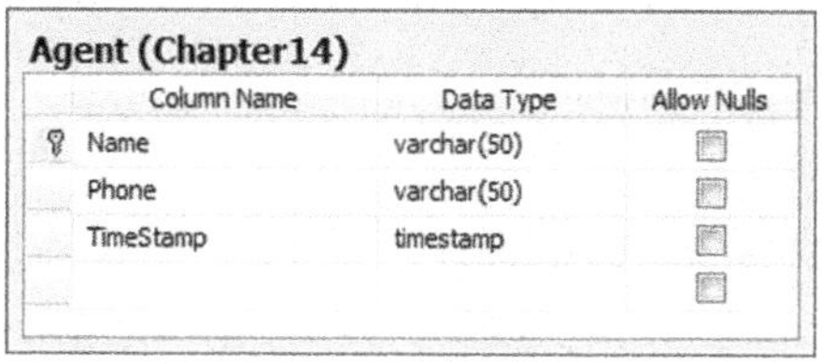

Figure 14-3. *The Agent table in our database*

Listing 14-3. The Agent Model

```
[Table("Agent", Schema = "Chapter14")]
public class Agent
{
    [Key]
    [MaxLength(50)]
    public string Name { get; set; }

    [Required]
    [MaxLength(50)]
    public string Phone { get; set; }

    [Timestamp]
    public byte[] TimeStamp { get; set; }
}
```

You want to use stored procedures to handle the insert, update, and delete actions for the model. These stored procedures need to be written so that they leverage the optimistic concurrency support provided in Entity Framework. Do the following to create the stored procedures and map them to actions:

1. Create the stored procedures in the database using the code in Listing 14-4.

Listing 14-4. Stored Procedures for the Insert, Update, and Delete actions

```
create procedure Chapter14.InsertAgent
(@Name varchar(50), @Phone varchar(50))
as
begin
  insert into Chapter14.Agent(Name, Phone)
  output inserted.TimeStamp
  values (@Name, @Phone)
end
go
create procedure Chapter14.UpdateAgent
(@Name varchar(50), @Phone varchar(50), @TimeStamp_Original TimeStamp, @RowsAffected int OUTPUT)
as
begin
  update Chapter14.Agent set Phone = @Phone where Name = @Name
  and TimeStamp = @TimeStamp_Original
  set @RowsAffected = @@ROWCOUNT
end
go
```

487

```
create procedure Chapter14.DeleteAgent
(@Name varchar(50), @TimeStamp_Original TimeStamp, @RowsAffected int OUTPUT)
as
begin
  delete Chapter14.Agent where Name = @Name and TimeStamp = @TimeStamp_Original
  set @RowsAffected = @@ROWCOUNT
end
```

2. Override the OnModelCreating method in your code-first DbContext class, and call Entity<Agent>().MapToStoredProcedures() to map the stored procedures to the insert, update, and delete actions on your agent model, as shown in Listing 14-5.

Listing 14-5. Overriding DbContext.OnModelCreating() to Map Stored Procedures to Insert, Update, and Delete Operations

```
protected override void OnModelCreating(DbModelBuilder modelBuilder)
{
base.OnModelCreating(modelBuilder);

modelBuilder
    .Entity<Agent>()
    .MapToStoredProcedures(agent =>
        {
            agent.Insert(i => i.HasName("Chapter14.InsertAgent"));
            agent.Update(u => u.HasName("Chapter14.UpdateAgent"));
            agent.Delete(d => d.HasName("Chapter14.DeleteAgent"));
        });

}
```

The code in Listing 14-6 demonstrates inserting and updating the database using the stored procedures. In the code, we update the phone numbers for both agents. For the first agent, we update the agent in the object context and save the changes. For the second agent, we do an out-of-band update before we update the phone using the object context. When we save the changes, Entity Framework throws an OptimisticConcurrencyException, indicating that the underlying database row was modified after the agent was materialized in the object context.

Listing 14-6. Demonstrating How Entity Framework and Our Insert and Update Stored Procedures Respond to a Concurrency Violation

```
using (var context = new EF6RecipesContext())
{
    context.Agents.Add(new Agent { Name = "Phillip Marlowe",
                                    Phone = "202 555-1212" });
    context.Agents.Add(new Agent { Name = "Janet Rooney",
                                    Phone = "913 876-5309" });
    context.SaveChanges();
}

using (var context = new EF6RecipesContext())
{
    // change the phone numbers
    var agent1 = context.Agents.Single(a => a.Name == "Janet Rooney");
```

```
        var agent2 = context.Agents.Single(a => a.Name == "Phillip Marlowe");
        agent1.Phone = "817 353-4458";
        context.SaveChanges();

        // update the other agent's number out-of-band
        context.Database.ExecuteSqlCommand(@"update Chapter14.agent
            set Phone = '817 294-6059' where name = 'Phillip Marlowe'");

        // now change it using the model
        agent2.Phone = "817 906-2212";
        try
        {
            context.SaveChanges();
        }
        catch (DbUpdateConcurrencyException ex)
        {
            Console.WriteLine("Exception caught updating phone number: {0}",
                              ex.Message);
        }
    }

using (var context = new EF6RecipesContext())
{
    Console.WriteLine("-- All Agents --");
    foreach (var agent in context.Agents)
    {
        Console.WriteLine("Agent: {0}, Phone: {1}", agent.Name, agent.Phone);
    }
}
```

The following is the output of the code in Listing 14-6. Notice that we caught the exception thrown during SaveChanges() and printed the exception message:

```
Exception caught updating phone number: Store update, insert, or delete statement

affected an unexpected number of rows (0). Entities may have been modified or deleted since entities
were loaded. Refresh ObjectStateManager entries.
-- All Agents --
Agent: Janet Rooney, Phone: 817 353-4458
Agent: Phillip Marlowe, Phone: 817 294-6059
```

How It Works

The key to leveraging the concurrency infrastructure in Entity Framework is in the implementation of the stored procedures (see Listing 14-4) and in how we mapped the input parameters and the result values. Let's look at each stored procedure.

The InsertAgent() procedure takes in the name and phone number for the agent and executes an insert statement. This results in the database computing a timestamp value that is inserted into the table along with the name and phone number. The select statement retrieves this newly generated timestamp. After the insert, the entity has the current values for the name and phone number and the newly generated timestamp. At that instant, the entity is in sync with the database.

With the UpdateAgent() procedure, Entity Framework automatically maps our Name and Phone properties to the stored procedure's parameters as long as the property names and parameter names match. However, we've named the timestamp parameter @TimeStamp_Original. This ensures that the original value for the TimeStamp property is sent to the database when we call the stored procedure. The where clause on the update statement includes the timestamp; if the timestamp value for the row in the database is different from the value in the entity, the update will fail. Because no rows are updated, Entity Framework responds by throwing a DbUpdateConcurrencyException. If the update succeeds, the new timestamp value is mapped to the TimeStamp property on the entity. At this point, the entity and row in the table are once again synchronized.

For the DeleteAgent() procedure, Entity Framework once again maps the Name and TimeStamp properties to the parameters of the procedure automatically. The where clause on the delete statement includes the primary key, Name, and the timestamp value; this ensures that the row is deleted if, and only if, no intermediate update of the row has occurred. If no row is deleted, Entity Framework will respond with a DbUpdateConcurrencyException.

Entity Framework relies on each of these stored procedures returning some indication of the number of rows affected by the operation. We've crafted each procedure to return this value either using a select statement that returns either one or zero rows, or the row count from the statement.

There are three ways, in order of precedence, that Entity Framework interprets the number of rows affected by a stored procedure: the return value from ExecuteNonQuery(), the number of rows returned, or an explicit output parameter (see Recipe 14-5).

The code in Listing 14-6 demonstrates that an intervening update, which we do out-of-band with the ExecuteSqlCommand() method, causes a concurrency violation when we update Phillip Marlowe's phone number.

14-3. Reading Uncommitted Data

Problem

Your application requires fast concurrent access with as little database overhead as possible, so you want to read uncommitted data using LINQ to entities.

Solution

Suppose you have an Employee entity like the one shown in Figure 14-4. You want to insert a new employee, but before the row is committed to the database, you want to read the uncommitted row into a different object context. To do this, create nested instances of the TransactionScope class and set the IsolationLevel of the innermost scope to ReadUncommitted, as shown in Listing 14-7. You will need to add a reference in your project to System.Transactions.

Figure 14-4. *An Employee entity*

Listing 14-7. Creating Nested TransactionScopes and Setting the IsolationLevel to ReadUncommitted

```
using (var context = new EF6RecipesContext())
{
    using (var scope1 = new TransactionScope())
    {
        // save, but don't commit
        var outerEmp = new Employee { Name = "Karen Stanfield" };
        Console.WriteLine("Outer employee: {0}", outerEmp.Name);
        context.Employees.Add(outerEmp);
        context.SaveChanges();

        // second transaction for read uncommitted
        using (var innerContext = new EF6RecipesContext())
        {
            using (var scope2 = new TransactionScope(
                TransactionScopeOption.RequiresNew,
                new TransactionOptions {
                    IsolationLevel = IsolationLevel.ReadUncommitted }))
            {
                var innerEmp = innerContext.Employees
                            .First(e => e.Name == "Karen Stanfield");
                Console.WriteLine("Inner employee: {0}", innerEmp.Name);
                scope1.Complete();
                scope2.Complete();
            }
        }
    }
}
```

The following is the output of the code in Listing 14-7:

```
Outer employee: Karen Stanfield
Inner employee: Karen Stanfield
```

How It Works

In SQL, one of the common ways of reading uncommitted data is to use the NOLOCK query hint. However, Entity Framework does not support the use of hints. In Listing 14-7, we used a TransactionScope with the IsolationLevel set to ReadUncommitted. This allowed us to read the uncommitted data from the outer TransactionScope. We did this in a fresh data context.

14-4. Implementing the "Last Record Wins" Strategy

Problem

You want to make sure that changes to an object succeed regardless of any intermediate changes to the database.

Solution

Suppose you have a model like the one shown in Figure 14-5.

Figure 14-5. *Our model with the ForumPost entity*

Our model represents posts by users of an Internet forum. Moderators of forums often want to review posts and possibly change or delete them. The changes a moderator makes need to take precedence over any changes made by the forum's users. In general, this can be implemented without much concern for concurrency, except when the user makes a change between the time the moderator retrieves the post and the when the moderator calls SaveChanges() to commit a change, such as a delete, to the database. In this case, we want the moderator's changes to overwrite the user's changes. We want the moderator to win.

To implement this, follow the pattern shown in Listing 14-8. Be sure to set the Concurrency Mode on the TimeStamp property to Fixed.

Listing 14-8. Implementing Last Record Wins

```
int postId = 0;
using (var context = new EF6RecipesContext())
{
    // post is created
    var post = new ForumPost { ForumUser = "FastEddie27", IsActive = false,
                Post = "The moderator is a great guy." };
    context.ForumPosts.Add(post);
    context.SaveChanges();
    postId = post.PostingId;
}

using (var context = new EF6RecipesContext())
{
    // moderator gets post to review
    var post = context.ForumPosts.First(p => p.PostingId  == postId);
    Console.WriteLine("Post by {0}: {1}", post.ForumUser, post.Post);
```

```
    // poster changes post out-of-band
    Context.Database.ExecuteSqlCommand(@"update chapter14.forumpost
            set post='The moderator''s mom dresses him funny.'
            where postingId = @p0", new object[] { postId.ToString() });
    Console.WriteLine("Fast Eddie changes the post");

    // moderator doesn't trust Fast Eddie
    if (string.Compare(post.ForumUser, "FastEddie27") == 0)
        post.IsActive = false;
    else
        post.IsActive = true;

    try
    {
        // refresh any changes to the TimeStamp
        var postEntry = context.Entry(post);
        postEntry.OriginalValues.SetValues(postEntry.GetDatabaseValues());
        context.SaveChanges();
        Console.WriteLine("No concurrency exception.");
    }
    catch (DbUpdateConcurrencyException exFirst)
    {
        try
        {
            // try one more time.
            var postEntry = context.Entry(post);
            postEntry.OriginalValues.SetValues(postEntry.GetDatabaseValues());
            context.SaveChanges();
        }
        catch (DbUpdateConcurrencyException exSecond)
        {
            // we tried twice...do something else
        }
    }
}
```

The following is the output of the code in Listing 14-8:

```
Post by FastEddie27: The moderator is a great guy.
Fast Eddie changes the post
No concurrency exception.
```

How It Works

The TimeStamp property is marked for concurrency because its ConcurrencyMode is set to Fixed. As part of the update statement, the value of the TimeStamp property is checked against the value in the database. If they differ, Entity Framework will throw a DbUpdateConcurrencyException. We've seen this behavior in the previous recipes in this chapter. What's different here is that we want the change from the client, in this case the moderator, to overwrite the newer row in the database. We do this by repeating a particular strategy; however, even using this strategy, it's possible that we will not be able to update our data successfully.

493

The strategy we use in Listing 14-8 is to obtain the DbEntityEntry that is tracking changes to our ForumPost object and then refresh the OriginalValues property with the values currently in the data store. Armed with the latest TimeStamp property, our call to SaveChanges() should succeed. There is a chance, especially in a highly concurrent environment, that some intervening update could occur to change the row before our update hits the database. If this occurs, Entity Framework will throw a DbUpdateConcurrencyException. If that should occur, we try to repeat our DbEntityEntry refresh in the catch block and call SaveChanges() again.

Even with these two approaches in place, it is still possible for an intervening update to occur between the refresh and the time the update is executed on the database.

14-5. Getting Affected Rows from a Stored Procedure
Problem

You want to return the number of rows affected by a stored procedure through an output parameter.

Solution

Entity Framework uses the number of rows affected by an operation to determine whether the operation succeeded or the operation failed because of a concurrency violation. When using stored procedures (see Recipe 14-2), one of the ways to communicate the number of rows affected by an operation is to return this value as an output parameter of the stored procedure.

Let's suppose you have a model like the one shown in Figure 14-6.

Figure 14-6. *Our model with the Account entity*

To return the number of rows affected by the stored procedures mapped to the insert, update, and delete actions, do the following:

1. Create the stored procedures in the database using the code in Listing 14-9.

Listing 14-9. The Stored Procedures for the Insert, Update, and Delete Actions

```
create procedure [Chapter14].[UpdateAccount]
(@AccountNumber varchar(50), @Name varchar(50), @Balance decimal, @TimeStamp TimeStamp,
 @RowsAffected int output)
as
begin
  update Chapter14.Account
  output inserted.TimeStamp
  set Name = @Name, Balance = @Balance
```

```
  where AccountNumber = @AccountNumber and TimeStamp = @TimeStamp
  set @RowsAffected = @@ROWCOUNT
end


go


create procedure [Chapter14].[InsertAccount]
(@AccountNumber varchar(50), @Name varchar(50), @Balance decimal,
 @RowsAffected int output)
as
begin
  insert into Chapter14.Account (AccountNumber, Name, Balance)
  output inserted.TimeStamp
  values (@AccountNumber, @Name, @Balance)
  set @RowsAffected = @@ROWCOUNT
end


go


create procedure [Chapter14].[DeleteAccount]
(@AccountNumber varchar(50), @TimeStamp TimeStamp,
@RowsAffected int output)
as
begin
  delete Chapter14.Account where AccountNumber = @AccountNumber and
        TimeStamp = @TimeStamp
  set @RowsAffected = @@ROWCOUNT
end
```

2. Right-click the design surface, and select Update Model from Database. Select the stored procedures you created in Step 1. Click Finish. This will import the stored procedures into the model.

3. View the Mapping Details window for the Account entity. Click the Map Entity to Functions button on the left side of the tool window. Map the insert, update, and delete actions to the stored procedures, as shown in Figure 14-7. Make sure that you map the Result column to the TimeStamp property for both the insert and update actions. For the update action, check the Use Original Value box for the procedure's TimeStamp parameter. For each procedure, check the Rows Affected Parameter boxes, as shown in Figure 14-7.

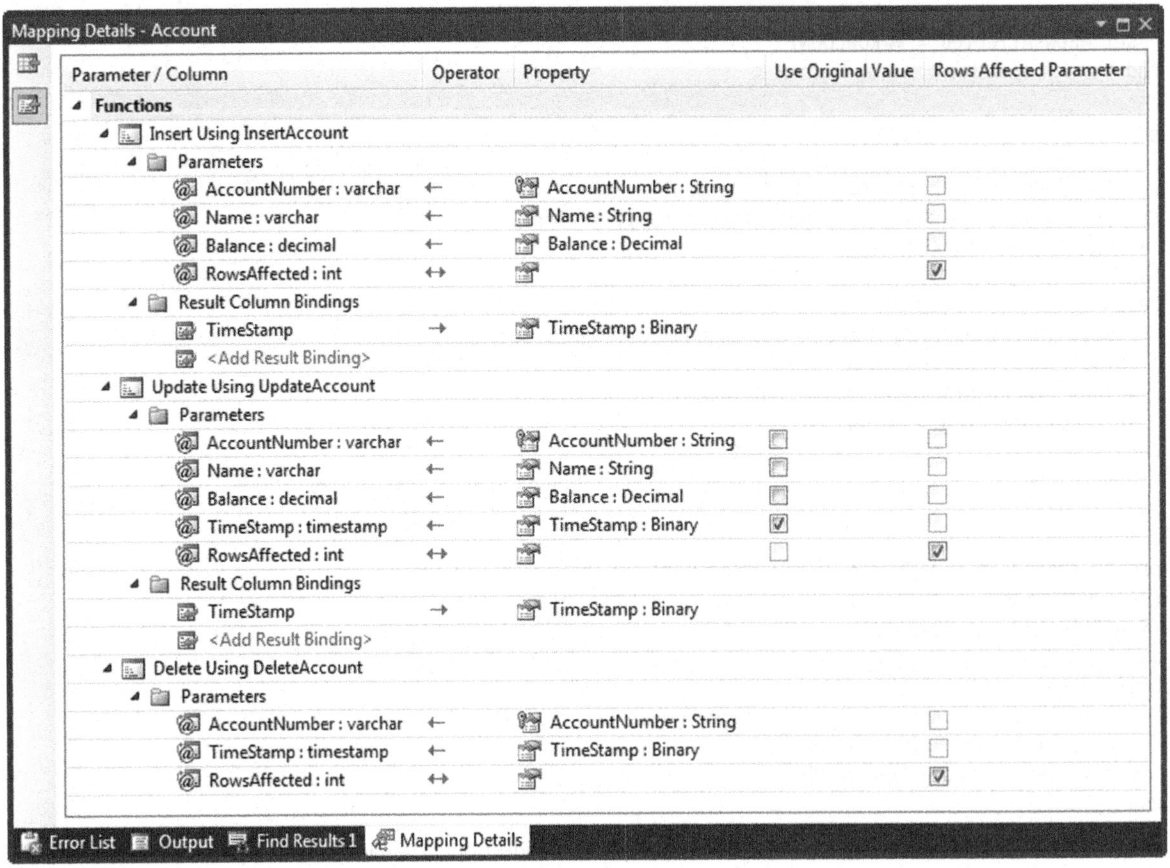

Figure 14-7. *When mapping the stored procedures to the insert, update, and delete actions, make sure that you check the Rows Affected Parameter check boxes and Use Original Value check box as shown*

When we call the SaveChanges() method in Listing 14-10 to update, insert, or delete, these actions are performed by the stored procedures in Listing 14-9 because of the mappings shown in Figure 14-7. Both the insert and update procedures return the updated TimeStamp value. This value is used by Entity Framework to enforce optimistic concurrency.

Listing 14-10. *Demonstrating the stored procedures mapped to the insert, update, and delete actions*

```
using (var context = new EF6RecipesContext())
{
    context.Accounts.Add(new Account { AccountNumber = "8675309",
                            Balance = 100M, Name = "Robin Rosen"});
    context.Accounts.Add(new Account { AccountNumber = "8535937",
                            Balance = 25M, Name = "Steven Bishop"});
    context.SaveChanges();
}
```

```
using (var context = new EF6RecipesContext())
{
    // get the account
    var account = context.Accounts.First(a => a.AccountNumber == "8675309");
    Console.WriteLine("Account for {0}", account.Name);
    Console.WriteLine("\tPrevious Balance: {0}", account.Balance.ToString("C"));

    // some other process updates the balance
    Console.WriteLine("[Rogue process updates balance!]");
    context.Database.ExecuteSqlCommand(@"update chapter14.account set balance = 1000
                        where accountnumber = '8675309'");

    // update the account balance
    account.Balance = 10M;

    try
    {
        Console.WriteLine("\tNew Balance: {0}", account.Balance.ToString("C"));
        context.SaveChanges();
    }
    catch (DbUpdateConcurrencyException ex)
    {
        Console.WriteLine("Exception: {0}", ex.Message);
    }
}
```

The following is the output of the code in Listing 14-10:

```
Account for Robin Rosen
        Previous Balance: $100.00
[Rogue process updates balance!]
        New Balance: $10.00
Exception: Store update, insert, or delete statement affected an unexpected number of rows (0).
Entities may have been modified or deleted since entities were loaded. Refresh ObjectStateManager
entries.
```

How It Works

The code in Listing 14-10 demonstrates using the stored procedures we've mapped to the insert, update, and delete actions. In the code, we purposely introduce an intervening update between the retrieval of an account object and saving the account object to the database. This rogue update causes the TimeStamp value to be changed in the database after we've materialized the object in the DbContext. This concurrency violation is detected by Entity Framework because the number of rows affected by the UpdateAccount() procedure is zero.

The mappings shown in Figure 14-7 tell Entity Framework how to keep the TimeStamp property correctly synchronized with the database and how to be informed of the number of rows affected by the insert, update, or delete actions. The Result Column for the insert and the update actions is mapped to the TimeStamp property on the entity. For the update action, we need to make sure that Entity Framework uses the original value from the entity when it constructs the statement invoking the UpdateAccount() procedure. These two settings keep the TimeStamp property synchronized with the database. Because our stored procedures return the number of rows affected by their respective updates in an output parameter, we need to check the Rows Affected Parameter box for this parameter for each of the action mappings.

14-6. Optimistic Concurrency with Table Per Type Inheritance

Problem

You want to use optimistic concurrency in a model that uses Table per Type inheritance.

Solution

Let's suppose you have the tables shown in Figure 14-8, and you want to model these tables using Table per Type inheritance and use optimistic concurrency to ensure that updates are persisted correctly. To create the model supporting optimistic concurrency, do the following:

1. Add a TimeStamp column to the Person table.

2. Create a new class that inherits from DbContext in your project.

3. Create new POCO entities for Person, Instructor, and Student, as shown in Listing 14-11. The Person entity should be abstract because we do not want to create a person entity directly, while both the Instructor and Student entities will inherit from the Person entity.

4. Add an auto-property of type DbSet<Person> to the DbContext subclass.

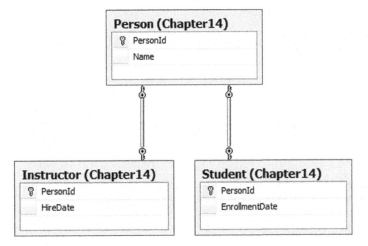

Figure 14-8. *A database diagram with our Person table and the related Instructor and Student tables*

Listing 14-11. Entity Classes Reflecting Our Table per Type Inheritance Model with the TimeStamp Property Added to the Person Class

```
[Table("Person", Schema = "Chapter14")]
public abstract class Person
{
    [Key]
    public int PersonId { get; set; }

    public string Name { get; set; }

    [Timestamp]
    public byte[] TimeStamp { get; set; }
}
```

```
[Table("Student", Schema = "Chapter14")]
public class Student : Person
{
    public DateTime? EnrollmentDate { get; set; }
}

[Table("Instructor", Schema = "Chapter14")]
public class Instructor : Person
{
    public DateTime? HireDate { get; set; }
}
```

The code in Listing 14-12 demonstrates what happens in the model when an out-of-band update happens.

Listing 14-12. Testing the Model by Applying a Rogue Update

```
using (var context = new EF6RecipesContext())
{
    var student = new Student { Name = "Joan Williams",
                                 EnrollmentDate = DateTime.Parse("1/12/2010") };
    var instructor = new Instructor { Name = "Rodger Keller",
                                 HireDate = DateTime.Parse("7/14/1992") };
    context.People.Add(student);
    context.People.Add(instructor);
    context.SaveChanges();
}

using (var context = new EF6RecipesContext())
{
    // find the student and update the enrollment date
    var student = context.People.OfType<Student>()
                    .First(s => s.Name == "Joan Williams");
    Console.WriteLine("Updating {0}'s enrollment date", student.Name);

    // out-of-band update occurs
    Console.WriteLine("[Apply rogue update]");
    context.Database.ExecuteSqlCommand(@"update chapter14.person set name = 'Joan Smith'
        where personId =
        (select personId from chapter14.person where name = 'Joan Williams')");

    // change the enrollment date
    student.EnrollmentDate = DateTime.Parse("5/2/2010");
    try
    {
        context.SaveChanges();
    }
    catch (DbUpdateConcurrencyException ex)
    {
        Console.WriteLine("Exception: {0}", ex.Message);
    }
}
```

The following is the output of the code in Listing 14-12:

```
Updating Joan Williams's enrollment date
[Apply rogue update]
Exception: Store update, insert, or delete statement affected an unexpected number of rows (0).
Entities may have been modified or deleted since entities were loaded. Refresh ObjectStateManager
entries.
```

How It Works

In Listing 14-12, the code retrieves a student entity. An intervening update occurs to the Person table before the code updates the EnrollmentDate property on the entity and calls SaveChanges(). Entity Framework detects the concurrency violation when updating the tables in the database because the value in the TimeStamp column in the Person table does not match the TimeStamp value in the student entity. Entity Framework applies concurrency at the entity level. Before the Student table is updated, the Person table is updated with a meaningless or dummy update and the new TimeStamp value is obtained. This can be seen in the trace in Listing 14-13. If this update fails to affect any rows, Entity Framework knows that the underlying table was changed since the last read. This would cause Entity Framework to throw an OptimisticConcurrencyException.

Listing 14-13. Entity Framework Updates the TimeStamp in the Base Table Prior to Performing the Update in the Derived Table

```
exec sp_executesql N'declare @p int
update [Chapter14].[Person]
output [Inserted].[TimeStamp]
set @p = 0
where (([PersonId] = @0) and ([TimeStamp] = @1))
select [TimeStamp]
from [Chapter14].[Person]
where @@ROWCOUNT > 0 and
[PersonId] = @0',N'@0 int,@1 binary(8)',@0=10,@1=0x0000000000007D19
```

Note that, if the rogue update occurred on the Student table in the database, the TimeStamp column in the Person table would not have been changed and Entity Framework would not have detected a concurrency violation. This is an important point to remember. The concurrency detection illustrated here extends just to rogue updates to the base entity.

14-7. Generating a Timestamp Column with Model First

Problem

You want to use Model First, and you want an entity to have a TimeStamp property for use in optimistic concurrency.

Solution

To use Model First and create an entity with a TimeStamp property, do the following:

1. Find the T4 Template that is used to generate the DDL for Model First. This file is located in Program Files\Microsoft Visual Studio 10.0\Common7\IDE\Extensions\Microsoft\ Entity Framework Tools\DBGen\SSDLToSQL10.tt. Copy this file, and rename this copy to SSDLToSQL10Recipe7.tt. Place the copy in the same folder as the original.

2. Replace the line that starts with [<#=Id(prop.Name)#>] with the code in Listing 14-14. We'll use this modified T4 Template to generate the DDL for our database.

Listing 14-14. Replace the Line in the T4 Template with This Line

```
[<#=Id(prop.Name)#>]
<#if (string.Compare(prop.Name,"TimeStamp",true) == 0)
{#>TIMESTAMP<#} else { #><#=prop.ToStoreType()#><#} #>
<#=WriteIdentity(prop, targetVersion)#> <#=WriteNullable(prop.Nullable)#>
<#=(p < entitySet.ElementType.Properties.Count - 1) ? "," : ""#>
```

3. Add a new ADO.NET Entity Data Model to your project. Start with an Empty Model.

4. Right-click the design surface, and select Add ➤ Entity. Name this new entity PhonePlan. Change the Key Property name to PhonePlanId. Click OK.

5. Add Scalar properties for Minutes, Cost, and TimeStamp. Change the type for the Minutes property to Int32. Change the type for the Cost property to Decimal.

6. Change the type of the TimeStamp property to Binary. Change its StoreGeneratedPattern to Computed. Change the Concurrency Mode to Fixed.

7. Right-click the design surface, and view the Properties. Change the DDL Generation Template to SSDLToSQL10Recipe7.tt. This is the template that you modified in step 2. Change the Database Schema Name to Chapter14.

8. Right-click the design surface, and click Generate Database from Model. Select the connection and click Next. The generated DDL is shown in the dialog box. Listing 14-15 shows an extract from the generated DDL that creates the PhonePlan table. Click Finish to complete the generation.

Listing 14-15. The DDL that creates the PhonePlan table

```
-- Creating table 'PhonePlans'
CREATE TABLE [Chapter14].[PhonePlans] (
[PhonePlanId] int  IDENTITY(1,1) NOT NULL,
[Minutes] int   NOT NULL,
[Cost] decimal(18,0)   NOT NULL,
[TimeStamp] TIMESTAMP   NOT NULL
);
GO
```

How It Works

The TimeStamp data type is not a portable type. Not all database vendors support it. It is unlikely that this type will be supported at the conceptual layer in future versions of Entity Framework. However, future versions will likely improve the user experience in selecting or modifying the appropriate T4 template that will generate the DDL.

Index

■ D

■ E

■ F

■ G

Get the eBook for only $10!

Now you can take the weightless companion with you anywhere, anytime. Your purchase of this book entitles you to 3 electronic versions for only $10.

This Apress title will prove so indispensible that you'll want to carry it with you everywhere, which is why we are offering the eBook in 3 formats for only $10 if you have already purchased the print book.

Convenient and fully searchable, the PDF version enables you to easily find and copy code—or perform examples by quickly toggling between instructions and applications. The MOBI format is ideal for your Kindle, while the ePUB can be utilized on a variety of mobile devices.

Go to www.apress.com/promo/tendollars to purchase your companion eBook.

Lightning Source UK Ltd.
Milton Keynes UK

9 781430 257882